Bloom's Modern Critical Views

Bloom's Modern Critical Views

Alexander
  Solzhenitsyn
Sophocles
John Steinbeck
Tom Stoppard
Jonathan Swift
Amy Tan
Alfred, Lord Tennyson
Henry David Thoreau
J.R.R. Tolkien
Leo Tolstoy

Ivan Turgenev
Mark Twain
John Updike
Kurt Vonnegut
Derek Walcott
Alice Walker
Robert Penn Warren
Eudora Welty
Edith Wharton
Walt Whitman
Oscar Wilde

Tennessee Williams
Thomas Wolfe
Tom Wolfe
Virginia Woolf
William Wordsworth
Jay Wright
Richard Wright
William Butler Yeats
Emile Zola

Bloom's Modern Critical Views

JANE AUSTEN

Edited and with an introduction by
Harold Bloom
Sterling Professor of the Humanities
Yale University

CHELSEA HOUSE
PUBLISHERS
A Haights Cross Communications Company

Philadelphia

Printed and bound in the United States of America.

10 9 8 7 6 5 4 3 2 1

Library of Congress Cataloging-in-Publication Data
Jane Austen / edited and with an introduction by Harold Bloom.
     p. cm. -- (Bloom's modern critical views)
Includes bibliographical references and index.
   ISBN: 0-7910-7656-3
 1. Austen, Jane, 1775–1817--Criticism and interpretation.
2. Women and literature--England--History--19th century. I.
Bloom, Harold. II. Title. III. Series.
  PR4037.J28 2003
  823'.7--dc21

                      2003 14156

Chelsea House Publishers
1974 Sproul Road, Suite 400
Broomall, PA 19008-0914

http://www.chelseahouse.com

Contributing Editor: Pamela Loos

Cover designed by Terry Mallon

Cover photo: Bettman/CORBIS

Layout by EJB Publishing Services

Contents

Editor's Note

My Introduction traces in Jane Austen's four masterpieces—*Pride and Prejudice*, *Mansfield Park*, *Emma*, and *Persuasion*—the heritage of the Protestant Female Will, in imaginative descent from Samuel Richardson's *Clarissa*.

Ruth apRoberts defends the aesthetic eminence of Austen's *Sense and Sensibility*, while the magisterial critic Martin Price intricately balances manners and morals in Austen.

Our pioneer Feminist critics, Sandra M. Gilbert and Susan Gubar, analyze Austen's earlier writings as instances of her subversion of some conventional expectations perhaps harbored towards a woman writer.

Ian Watt, remarkable chronicler of the rise of the novel as a genre, outlines Austen's modes of comic aggression, after which Ann Molan, defining "persuasion" in Austen's *Persuasion*, sees it as an implicit kind of self-reliance.

The late Tony Tanner, keen scholar of the novel, grants to *Pride and Prejudice* Austen's intricate balance between energy and order, while John Bayley, an authority upon characterization, shows us the marvelous interplay between Emma's intelligence and the banality she knows she must cheerfully sustain.

Roger Gard returns us to Emma's romance "in a not very romantic world," after which Stuart M. Tave, masterly always upon Austen, charmingly presents *Pride and Prejudice* as Elizabeth's education of Darcy into the comic mode, rather as Rosalind educates Orlando in Shakespeare's *As You Like It*.

Mansfield Park, to Jo Alyson Parker, subtly interweaves Austen's traditionalism and her sly subversion of patriarchal values, while John

Wiltshire explores aspects of Austen's relationship both to Shakespeare and to Dr. Samuel Johnson, greatest of Shakespearean critics.

In this volume's concluding essay, Laura Dabundo sensitively isolates the Wordsworthian element in what might be termed Austen's "poetics of silence."

HAROLD BLOOM

Introduction

I

The oddest yet by no means inapt analogy to Jane Austen's art of representation is Shakespeare's—oddest, because she is so careful of limits, as classical as Ben Jonson in that regard, and Shakespeare transcends all limits. Austen's humor, her mode of rhetorical irony, is not particularly Shakespearean, and yet her precision and accuracy of representation is. Like Shakespeare, she gives us figures, major and minor, utterly consistent each in her or his own mode of speech and being, and utterly different from one another. Her heroines have firm selves, each molded with an individuality that continues to suggest Austen's reserve of power, her potential for creating an endless diversity. To recur to the metaphor of oddness, the highly deliberate limitation of social scale in Austen seems a paradoxical theater of mind in which so fecund a humanity could be fostered. Irony, the concern of most critics of Austen, seems more than a trope in her work, seems indeed to be the condition of her language, yet hardly accounts for the effect of moral and spiritual power that she so constantly conveys, however implicitly or obliquely.

Ian Watt, in his permanently useful *The Rise of the Novel*, portrays Austen as Fanny Burney's direct heir in the difficult art of combining the rival modes of Samuel Richardson and Henry Fielding. Like Burney, Austen is thus seen as following the Richardson of *Sir Charles Grandison*, in a "minute presentation of daily life," while emulating Fielding in "adopting a more detached attitude to her narrative material, and in evaluating it from a comic and objective point of view." Watt goes further when he points out that Austen tells her stories in a discreet variant of Fielding's manner "as a confessed author," though her ironical juxtapositions are made to appear not

A portion of this introduction originally appeared in *The Western Canon*. © 1994 by Harold Bloom.

those of "an intrusive author but rather of some august and impersonal spirit of social and psychological understanding."

And yet, as Watt knows, Austen truly is the daughter of Richardson, and not of Fielding, just as she is the ancestor of George Eliot and Henry James, rather than of Dickens and Thackeray. Her inwardness is an ironic revision of Richardson's extraordinary conversion of English Protestant sensibility into the figure of Clarissa Harlowe, and her own moral and spiritual concerns fuse in the crucial need of her heroines to sustain their individual integrities, a need so intense that it compels them to fall into those errors about life that are necessary for life (to adopt a Nietzschean formulation). In this too they follow, though in a comic register, the pattern of their tragic precursor, the magnificent but sublimely flawed Clarissa Harlowe.

Richardson's *Clarissa*, perhaps still the longest novel in the language, seems to me also still the greatest, despite the achievements of Austen, Dickens, George Eliot, Henry James, and Joyce. Austen's Elizabeth Bennet and Emma Woodhouse, Eliot's Dorothea Brooke and Gwendolen Harleth, James's Isabel Archer and Milly Theale—though all these are Clarissa Harlowe's direct descendants, they are not proportioned to her more sublime scale. David Copperfield and Leopold Bloom have her completeness; indeed Joyce's Bloom may be the most complete representation of a human being in all of literature. But they belong to the secular age; Clarissa Harlowe is poised upon the threshold that leads from the Protestant religion to a purely secular sainthood.

C.S. Lewis, who read Milton as though that fiercest of Protestant temperaments had been an orthodox Anglican, also seems to have read Jane Austen by listening for her echoings of the New Testament. Quite explicitly, Lewis named Austen as the daughter of Dr. Samuel Johnson, greatest of literary critics, and rigorous Christian moralist:

> I feel ... sure that she is the daughter of Dr. Johnson: she inherits
> his commonsense, his morality, even much of his style.

The Johnson of *Rasselas* and of *The Rambler*, surely the essential Johnson, is something of a classical ironist, but we do not read Johnson for his ironies, or for his dramatic representations of fictive selves. Rather, we read him as we read Koheleth; he writes wisdom literature. That Jane Austen is a wise writer is indisputable, but we do not read *Pride and Prejudice* as though it were Ecclesiastes. Doubtless, Austen's religious ideas were as profound as Samuel Richardson's were shallow, but *Emma* and *Clarissa* are Protestant novels without being in any way religious. What is most original about the representation of Clarissa Harlowe is the magnificent intensity of her slowly described dying, which goes on for about the last third of Richardson's vast novel, in a Puritan ritual that celebrates the preternatural strength of her will. For that is Richardson's sublime concern: the self-reliant apotheosis of the Protestant will. What is tragedy in *Clarissa* becomes serious or moral comedy in *Pride and Prejudice* and *Emma*, and something just the other side of comedy in *Mansfield Park* and *Persuasion*.

II

Rereading *Pride and Prejudice* gives one a sense of Proustian ballet beautifully working itself through in the novel's formal centerpiece, the deferred but progressive mutual enlightenment of Elizabeth and Darcy in regard to the other's true nature. "Proper pride" is what they learn to recognize in one another; propriety scarcely needs definition in that phrase, but precisely what is the pride that allows amiability to flourish? Whatever it is in Darcy, to what extent is it an art of the will in Elizabeth Bennet? Consider the superb scene of Darcy's first and failed marriage proposal:

> While settling this point, she was suddenly roused by the sound of the doorbell, and her spirits were a little fluttered by the idea of its being Colonel Fitzwilliam himself, who had once before called late in the evening, and might now come to inquire particularly after her. But this idea was soon banished, and her spirits were very differently affected, when, to her utter amazement, she saw Mr. Darcy walk into the room. In an hurried manner he immediately began an inquiry after her health, imputing his visit to a wish of hearing that she were better. She answered him with cold civility. He sat down for a few moments, and then getting up, walked about the room. Elizabeth was surprised, but said not a word. After a silence of several minutes, he came towards her in an agitated manner, and thus began:
> "In vain have I struggled. It will not do. My feelings will not be repressed. You must allow me to tell you how ardently I admire and love you."
> Elizabeth's astonishment was beyond expression. She stared, coloured, doubted, and was silent. This he considered sufficient encouragement; and the avowal of all that he felt, and had long felt for her, immediately followed. He spoke well; but there were

feelings besides those of the heart to be detailed, and he was not more eloquent on the subject of tenderness than of pride. His sense of her inferiority—of its being a degradation—of the family obstacles which judgment had always opposed to inclination, were dwelt on with a warmth which seemed due to the consequence he was wounding, but was very unlikely to recommend his suit.

In spite of her deeply-rooted dislike, she could not be insensible to the compliment of such a man's affection, and though her intentions did not vary for an instant, she was at first sorry for the pain he was to receive; till, roused to resentment by his subsequent language, she lost all compassion in anger. She tried, however, to compose herself to answer him with patience, when he should have done. He concluded with representing to her the strength of that attachment which, in spite of all his endeavours, he had found impossible to conquer; and with expressing his hope that it would now be rewarded by her acceptance of his hand. As he said this, she could easily see that he had no doubt of a favourable answer. He *spoke* of apprehension and anxiety, but his countenance expressed real security. Such a circumstance could only exasperate farther, and, when he ceased, the colour rose into her cheeks, and she said:

"In such cases as this, it is, I believe, the established mode to express a sense of obligation for the sentiments avowed, however unequally they may be returned. It is natural that obligation should be felt, and if I could *feel* gratitude, I would now thank you. But I cannot—I have never desired your good opinion, and you have certainly bestowed it most unwillingly. I am sorry to have occasioned pain to anyone. It has been most unconsciously done, however, and I hope will be of short duration. The feelings which, you tell me, have long prevented the acknowledgment of your regard, can have little difficulty in overcoming it after this explanation."

Mr. Darcy, who was leaning against the mantelpiece with his eyes fixed on her face, seemed to catch her words with no less resentment than surprise. His complexion became pale with anger, and the disturbance of his mind was visible in every feature. He was struggling for the appearance of composure, and would not open his lips till he believed himself to have attained it. The pause was to Elizabeth's feelings dreadful. At length, in a voice of forced calmness, he said:

"And this is all the reply which I am to have the honour of expecting! I might, perhaps, wish to be informed why, with so little *endeavour* at civility, I am thus rejected. But it is of small importance."

Stuart M. Tave believes that both Darcy and Elizabeth become so changed by one another that their "happiness is deserved by a process of mortification begun early and ended late," mortification here being the wounding of pride. Tave's learning and insight are impressive, but I favor the judgment that Elizabeth and Darcy scarcely change, and learn rather that they complement each other's not wholly illegitimate pride. They come to see that their wills are naturally allied, since they have no differences upon the will. The will to what? Their will, Austen's, is neither the will to live nor the will to power. They wish to be esteemed precisely where they estimate value to be high, and neither can afford to make a fundamental error, which is both the anxiety and the comedy of the first proposal scene. Why after all does Darcy allow himself to be eloquent on the subject of his pride, to the extraordinary extent of conveying "with a warmth" what Austen grimly names as "his sense of her inferiority"?

As readers, we have learned already that Elizabeth is inferior to no one, whoever he is. Indeed, I sense as the novel closes (though nearly all Austen critics, and doubtless Austen herself, would disagree with me) that Darcy is her inferior, amiable and properly prideful as he is. I do not mean by this that Elizabeth is a clearer representation of Austenian values than Darcy ever could be; that is made finely obvious by Austen, and her critics have developed her ironic apprehension, which is that Elizabeth incarnates the standard of measurement in her cosmos. There is also a transcendent strength to Elizabeth's will that raises her above that cosmos, in a mode that returns us to Clarissa Harlowe's transcendence of her society, of Lovelace, and even of everything in herself that is not the will to a self-esteem that has also made an accurate estimate of every other will to pride it ever has encountered.

I am suggesting that Ralph Waldo Emerson (who to me is sacred) was mistaken when he rejected Austen as a "sterile" upholder of social conformities and social ironies, as an author who could not celebrate the soul's freedom from societal conventions. Austen's ultimate irony is that Elizabeth Bennet is inwardly so free that convention performs for her the ideal function it cannot perform for us: it liberates her will without tending to stifle her high individuality. But we ought to be wary of even the most distinguished of Austen's moral celebrants, Lionel Trilling, who in effect defended her against Emerson by seeing *Pride and Prejudice* as a triumph "of morality as style." If Emerson wanted to see a touch more Margaret Fuller in Elizabeth Bennet (sublimely ghastly notion!), Trilling wanted to forget the Emersonian law of Compensation, which is that nothing is got for nothing:

> The relation of Elizabeth Bennet to Darcy is real, is intense, but it expresses itself as a conflict and reconciliation of styles: a formal rhetoric, traditional and rigorous, must find a way to accomodate a female vivacity, which in turn must recognize the principled demands of the strict male syntax. The high moral import of the novel lies in the fact that the union of styles is accomplished without injury to either lover.

Yes and no, I would say. Yes, because the wills of both lovers work by similar dialectics, but also no, because Elizabeth's will is more intense and purer, and inevitably must be dimmed by her dwindling into a wife, even though Darcy may well be the best man that society could offer to her. Her pride has playfulness in it, a touch even of the Quixotic. Uncannily, she is both her father's daughter and Samuel Richardson's daughter as well. Her wit is Mr. Bennet's, refined and elaborated, but her will, and her pride in her will, returns us to Clarissa's Puritan passion to maintain the power of the self to confer esteem, and to accept esteem only in response to its bestowal.

III

John Locke argues against personifying the will: persons can be free, but not the will, since the will cannot be constrained, except externally. While one sleeps, if someone moved one into another room and locked the door, and there one found a friend one wished to see, still one could not say that one was free thus to see whom one wished. And yet Locke implies that the process of association does work as though the will were internally constrained. Association, in Locke's sense, is a blind substitution for reasoning, yet is within a reasoning process, though also imbued with affect. The mind, in association, is carried unwillingly from one thought to another, by accident as it were. Each thought appears, and carries along with it a crowd of unwanted guests, inhabitants of a room where the thought would rather be alone. Association, on this view, is what the will most needs to be defended against.

Fanny Price, in *Mansfield Park*, might be considered a co-descendant, together with Locke's association-menaced will, of the English Protestant emphasis upon the will's autonomy. Fanny, another precursor of the Virginia Woolf of *A Room of One's Own*, was shrewdly described by Lionel Trilling as "overtly virtuous and consciously virtuous," and therefore almost impossible to like, though Trilling (like Austen) liked Fanny very much. C. S. Lewis, though an orthodox moralist, thought Fanny insipid: "But into Fanny, Jane Austen, to counterbalance her apparent insignificance, has put really nothing except rectitude of mind; neither passion, nor physical courage, nor wit, nor resource." Nothing, I would say, except the Protestant will, resisting the powers of association and asserting its very own persistence, its own sincere intensity, and its own isolate sanctions. Trilling secularized these as "the sanctions of principle" and saw *Mansfield Park* as a novel that "discovers in principle the path to the wholeness of the self which is peace." That is movingly said, but secularization, in literature, is always a failed trope, since the distinction between sacred and secular is not actually a literary but rather a societal or political distinction. *Mansfield Park* is not less Protestant than *Paradise Lost*, even though Austen, *as a writer*, was as much a sect of one as John Milton was.

Fanny Price, like the Lockean will, fights against accident, against the crowding out of life by associations that are pragmatically insincere not because they are random, but because they are irrelevant, since whatever is not the will's own is irrelevant to it. If Fanny herself is an irony it is as Austen's allegory of her own defense against influences, human and literary, whether in her family circle or in the literary family of Fanny Burney, Fielding, and Richardson. Stuart Tave shrewdly remarks that: "*Mansfield Park* is a novel in which many characters are engaged in trying to establish influence over the minds and lives of others, often in a contest or struggle for control." Fanny, as a will struggling only to be itself, becomes at last the spiritual center of Mansfield Park precisely because she has never sought power over any other will. It is the lesson of the Protestant will, whether in Locke or Austen, Richardson or George Eliot, that the refusal to seek power over other wills is what opens the inward eye of vision. Such a lesson, which we seek in Wordsworth and in Ruskin, is offered more subtly (though less sublimely) by Austen. Fanny, Austen's truest surrogate, has a vision of what Mansfield Park is and ought to be, which means a vision also of what Sir Thomas Bertram is or ought to be. Her vision is necessarily moral, but could as truly be called spiritual, or even aesthetic.

Perhaps that is why Fanny is not only redeemed but can redeem others. The quietest and most mundane of visionaries, she remains also one of the firmest: her dedication is to the future of Mansfield Park as the idea of order it once seemed to her. Jane Austen may not be a Romantic in the high

Shellyan mode, but Fanny Price has profound affinities with Wordsworth, so that it is no accident that *Mansfield Park* is exactly contemporary with *The Excursion*. Wordsworthian continuity, the strength that carries the past alive into the present, is the program of renovation that Fanny's pure will brings to Mansfield Park, and it is a program more Romantic than Augustan, so that Fanny's will begins to shade into the Wordsworthian account of the imagination. Fanny's exile to Portsmouth is so painful to her not for reasons turning upon social distinctions, but for causes related to the quiet that Wordsworth located in the bliss of solitude, or Virginia Woolf in a room of one's own:

> Such was the home which was to put Mansfield out of her head, and teach her to think of her cousin Edmund with moderated feelings. On the contrary, she could think of nothing but Mansfield, its beloved inmates, its happy ways. Everything where she now was was in full contrast to it. The elegance, propriety, regularity, harmony, and perhaps, above all, the peace and tranquillity of Mansfield, were brought to her remembrance every hour of the day, by the prevalence of everything opposite to them *here*.
>
> The living in incessant noise was, to a frame and temper delicate and nervous like Fanny's, an evil which no super-added elegance or harmony could have entirely atoned for. It was the greatest misery of all. At Mansfield, no sounds of contention, no raised voice, no abrupt bursts, no tread of violence, was ever heard; all proceeded in a regular course of cheerful orderliness; everybody had their due importance; everybody's feelings were consulted. If tenderness could be ever supposed wanting, good sense and good breeding supplied its place; and as to the little irritations, sometimes introduced by Aunt Norris, they were short, they were trifling, they were as a drop of water to the ocean, compared with the ceaseless tumult of her present abode. Here, everybody was noisy, every voice was loud (excepting, perhaps, her mother's, which resembled the soft monotony of Lady Bertram's, only worn into fretfulness). Whatever was wanted was halloo'd for, and the servants halloo'd out their excuses from the kitchen. The doors were in constant banging, the stairs were never at rest, nothing was done without a clatter, nobody sat still, and nobody could command attention when they spoke.

In a review of the two houses, as they appeared to her before the end of a week, Fanny was tempted to apply to them Dr. Johnson's celebrated judgment as to matrimony and celibacy, and say, that though Mansfield Park might have some pains, Portsmouth could have no pleasures.

The citation of Dr. Johnson's aphorism, though placed here with superb wit, transcends irony. Austen rather seeks to confirm, however implicitly, Johnson's powerful warning, in *The Rambler*, number 4, against the overwhelming realism of Fielding and Smollett (though their popular prevalence is merely hinted):

But if the power of example is so great, as to take possession of the memory by a kind of violence, and produce effects almost without the intervention of the will, care ought to be taken, that, when the choice is unrestrained, the best examples only should be exhibited; and that which is likely to operate so strongly, should not be mischievous or uncertain in its effects.

Fanny Price, rather more than Jane Austen perhaps, really does favor a Johnsonian aesthetic, in life as in literature. Portsmouth belongs to representation as practiced by Smollett, belongs to the cosmos of *Roderick Random*. Fanny, in willing to get back to Mansfield Park, and to get Mansfield Park back to itself, is willing herself also to renovate the world of her creator, the vision of Jane Austen that is *Mansfield Park*.

IV

Sir Walter Scott, reviewing *Emma* in 1815, rather strangely compared Jane Austen to the masters of the Flemish school of painting, presumably because of her precision in representing her characters. The strangeness results from Scott's not seeing how English Austen was, though the Scots perspective may have entered into his estimate. To me, as an American critic, *Emma* seems the most English of English novels, and beyond question one of the very best. More than *Pride and Prejudice*, it is Austen's masterpiece, the largest triumph of her vigorous art. Her least accurate prophecy as to the fate of her fictions concerned *Emma*, whose heroine, she thought, "no one but myself will much like."

Aside from much else, Emma is immensely likable, because she is so extraordinarily imaginative, dangerous and misguided as her imagination frequently must appear to others and finally to herself. On the scale of being, Emma constitutes an answer to the immemorial questions of the Sublime: More? Equal to? Or less than? Like Clarissa Harlowe before her, and the strongest heroines of George Eliot and Henry James after her, Emma Woodhouse has a heroic will, and like them she risks identifying her will with her imagination. Socially considered, such identification is catastrophic, since the Protestant will has a tendency to bestow a ranking upon other selves, and such ranking may turn out to be a personal phantasmagoria. G. Armour Craig rather finely remarked that: "society in *Emma* is not a ladder. It is a web of imputations that link feelings and conduct." Yet Emma herself, expansionist rather than reductionist in temperament, imputes more fiercely and freely than the web can sustain, and she threatens always, until she is enlightened, to dissolve the societal links, in and for others, that might allow some stability between feelings and conduct.

Armour Craig usefully added that: "*Emma* does not justify its heroine nor does it deride her." Rather it treats her with ironic love (not loving irony). Emma Woodhouse is dear to Jane Austen, because her errors are profoundly imaginative, and rise from the will's passion for autonomy of vision. The splendid Jane Fairfax is easier to admire, but I cannot agree with Wayne Booth's awarding the honors to her over Emma, though I admire the subtle balance of his formulation:

> Jane is superior to Emma in most respects except the stroke of good fortune that made Emma the heroine of the book. In matters of taste and ability, of head and of heart, she is Emma's superior.

Taste, ability, head, and heart are a formidable fourfold; the imagination and the will, working together, are an even more formidable twofold, and clearly may have their energies diverted to error and to mischief. Jane Fairfax is certainly more *amiable* even than Emma Woodhouse, but she is considerably less interesting. It is Emma who is meant to charm us, and who does charm us. Austen is not writing a tragedy of the will, like *Paradise Lost*, but a great comedy of the will, and her heroine must incarnate the full potential of the will, however misused for a time. Having rather too much her own way is certainly one of Emma's powers, and she does have a disposition to think a little too well of herself. When Austen says that these were "the real evils indeed of Emma's situation," we read "evils" as lightly as the author will let us, which is lightly enough.

Can we account for the qualities in Emma Woodhouse that make her worthy of comparison with George Eliot's Gwendolen Harleth and Henry James's Isabel Archer? The pure comedy of her context seems world enough for her; she evidently is not the heiress of all the ages. We are persuaded, by Austen's superb craft, that marriage to Mr. Knightley will more than suffice to fulfill totally the now perfectly amiable Emma. Or are we? It is James's genius to suggest that while Osmond's "beautiful mind" was a prison of the spirit for Isabel, no proper husband could exist anyway, since neither Touchett nor Goodwood is exactly a true match for her. Do we, presumably against Austen's promptings, not find Mr. Knightley something of a confinement also, benign and wise though he be?

I suspect that the heroine of the Protestant will, from Richardson's Clarissa Harlowe through to Virginia Woolf's Clarissa Dalloway, can never find fit match because wills do not marry. The allegory or tragic irony of this dilemma is written large in Clarissa, since Lovelace, in strength of will and splendor of being, actually would have been the true husband for Clarissa (as he well knows) had he not been a moral squalor. His death-cry ("Let this expiate!") expiates nothing, and helps establish the long tradition of the Anglo-American novel in which the heroines of the will are fated to suffer either overt calamities or else happy unions with such good if unexciting men as Mr. Knightley or Will Ladislaw in *Middlemarch*. When George Eliot is reduced to having the fascinating Gwendolen Harleth fall hopelessly in love with the prince of prigs, Daniel Deronda, we sigh and resign ourselves to the sorrows of fictive overdetermination. Lovelace or Daniel Deronda? I myself do not know a high-spirited woman who would not prefer the first, though not for a husband!

Emma is replete with grand comic epiphanies, of which my favorite comes in volume 3, chapter 11, when Emma receives the grave shock of Harriet's disclosure that Mr. Knightley is the object of Harriet's hopeful affections:

> When Harriet had closed her evidence, she appealed to her dear Miss Woodhouse, to say whether she had not good ground for hope.
>
> "I never should have presumed to think of it at first," said she, "but for you. You told me to observe him carefully, and let his behavior be the rule of mine—and so I have. But now I seem to feel that I may deserve him; and that if he does choose me, it will not be any thing so very wonderful."
>
> The bitter feelings occasioned by this speech, the many bitter feelings, made the utmost exertion necessary on Emma's side to enable her to say in reply,

"Harriet, I will only venture to declare, that Mr. Knightley is the last man in the world, who would intentionally give any woman the idea of his feeling for her more than he really does."

Harriet seemed ready to worship her friend for a sentence so satisfactory; and Emma was only saved from raptures and fondness, which at the moment would have been dreadful penance, by the sound of her father's footsteps. He was coming through the hall. Harriet was too much agitated to encounter him. "She could not compose herself—Mr. Woodhouse would be alarmed—she had better go;"—with most ready encouragement from her friend, therefore, she passed off through another door—and the moment she was gone, this was the spontaneous burst of Emma's feelings: "Oh God! that I had never seen her!"

The rest of the day, the following night, were hardly enough for her thoughts.—She was bewildered amidst the confusion of all that had rushed on her within the last few hours. Every moment had brought a fresh surprise; and every surprise must be matter of humiliation to her.—How to understand it all! How to understand the deceptions she had been thus practising on herself, and living under!—The blunders, the blindness of her own head and heart!—she sat still, she walked about, she tried her own room, she tried the shrubbery—in every place, every posture, she perceived that she had acted most weakly; that she had been imposed on by others in a most mortifying degree; that she had been imposing on herself in a degree yet more mortifying; that she was wretched, and should probably find this day but the beginning of wretchedness.

The acute aesthetic pleasure of this turns on the counterpoint between Emma's spontaneous cry: "Oh God! that I had never seen her!" and the exquisite comic touch of: "She sat still, she walked about, she tried her own room, she tried the shrubbery—in every place, every posture, she perceived that she had acted most weakly." The acute humiliation of the will could not be better conveyed than by "she tried the shrubbery" and "every posture." Endlessly imaginative, Emma must now be compelled to endure the mortification of reducing herself to the postures and places of those driven into corners by the collapse of visions that have been exposed as delusions. Jane Austen, who seems to have identified herself with Emma, wisely chose to make this moment of ironic reversal a temporary purgatory, rather than an infernal discomfiture.

V

"Persuasion" is a word derived from the Latin for "advising" or "urging," for recommending that it is good to perform or not perform a particular action. The word goes back to a root meaning "sweet" or "pleasant," so that the good of performance or nonperformance has a tang of taste rather than of moral judgment about it. Jane Austen chose it as the title for her last completed novel. As a title, it recalls *Sense and Sensibility* or *Pride and Prejudice* rather than *Emma* or *Mansfield Park*. We are given not the name of a person or house and estate, but of an abstraction, a single one in this case. The title's primary reference is to the persuasion of its heroine, Anne Elliot, at the age of nineteen, by her godmother, Lady Russell, not to marry Captain Frederick Wentworth, a young naval officer. This was, as it turns out, very bad advice, and, after eight years, it is mended by Anne and Captain Wentworth. As with all of Austen's ironic comedies, matters end happily for the heroine. And yet each time I finish a rereading of this perfect novel, I feel very sad.

This does not appear to be my personal vagary; when I ask my friends and students about their experience of the book, they frequently mention a sadness which they also associate with *Persuasion*, more even than with *Mansfield Park*. Anne Elliot, a quietly eloquent being, is a self-reliant character, in no way forlorn, and her sense of self never falters. It is not *her* sadness we feel as we conclude the book: it is the novel's somberness that impresses us. The sadness enriches what I would call the novel's canonical persuasiveness, its way of showing us its extraordinary aesthetic distinction.

Persuasion is among novels what Anne Elliot is among novelistic characters—a strong but subdued outrider. The book and the character are not colorful or vivacious; Elizabeth Bennett of *Pride and Prejudice* and Emma Woodhouse of *Emma* have a verve to them that initially seems lacking in Anne Elliot, which may be what Austen meant when she said that Anne was "almost too good for me." Anne is really almost too subtle for us, though not for Wentworth, who has something of an occult wavelength to her. Juliet McMaster notes "the kind of oblique communication that constantly goes on between Anne Elliot and Captain Wentworth, where, though they seldom speak to each other, each constantly understands the full import of the other's speech better than their interlocutors do."

That kind of communication in *Persuasion* depends upon deep "affection," a word that Austen values over "love." "Affection" between woman and man, in Austen, is the more profound and lasting emotion. I think it is not too much to say that Anne Elliot, though subdued, is the creation for whom Austen herself must have felt the most affection, because she lavished her own gifts upon Anne. Henry James insisted that the novelist must be a sensibility upon which absolutely nothing is lost; by that test (clearly a limited one) only Austen, George Eliot, and James himself, among all those writing in English, would join Stendhal, Flaubert, and Tolstoy in a rather restricted pantheon. Anne Elliot may well be the one character in all of prose fiction upon whom nothing is lost, though she is in no danger of turning into a novelist. The most accurate estimate of Anne Elliot that I have seen is by Stuart Tave:

> Nobody hears Anne, nobody sees her, but it is she who is ever at the center. It is through her ears, eyes, and mind that we are made to care for what is happening. If nobody is much aware of her, she is very much aware of everyone else and she perceives what is happening to them when they are ignorant of themselves ... she reads Wentworth's mind, with the coming troubles he is causing for others and himself, before those consequences bring the information to him.

The aesthetic dangers attendant upon such a paragon are palpable: how does a novelist make such a character persuasive? Poldy, in Joyce's *Ulysses*, is overwhelmingly persuasive because he is so complete a person, which was the largest of Joyce's intentions. Austen's ironic mode does not sanction the representation of completeness: we do not accompany her characters to the bedroom, the kitchen, the privy. What Austen parodies in *Sense and Sensibility* she raises to an apotheosis in *Persuasion*: the sublimity of a particular, inwardly isolated sensibility. Anne Elliot is hardly the only figure in Austen who has an understanding heart. Her difference is in her almost preternatural acuteness of perception of others and of the self, which are surely the qualities that most distinguish Austen as a novelist. Anne Elliot is to Austen's work what Rosalind of *As You Like It* is to Shakespeare's: the character who almost reaches the mastery of perspective that can be available only to the novelist or playwright, lest all dramatic quality be lost from the novel or play. C.L. Barber memorably emphasized this limitation:

> The dramatist tends to show us one thing at a time, and to realize that one thing, in its moment, to the full; his characters go to extremes, comical as well as serious; and no character, not even a Rosalind, is in a position to see all around the play and so be completely poised, for if this were so the play would cease to be dramatic.

I like to turn Barber's point in the other direction: more even than Hamlet or Falstaff, or than Elizabeth Bennet, or than Fanny Price in *Mansfield Park*, Rosalind and Anne Elliot are almost completely poised, nearly able to see all around the play and the novel. Their poise cannot transcend perspectivizing completely, but Rosalind's wit and Anne's sensibility, both balanced and free of either excessive aggressivity or defensiveness, enable them to share more of their creators' poise than we ever come to do.

Austen never loses dramatic intensity; we share Anne's anxiety concerning Wentworth's renewed intentions until the novel's conclusion. But we rely upon Anne as we should rely upon Rosalind; critics would see the rancidity of Touchstone as clearly as they see the vanity of Jacques if they placed more confidence in Rosalind's reactions to everyone else in the play, as well as to herself. Anne Elliot's reactions have the same winning authority; we must try to give the weight to her words that is not extended by the other persons in the novel, except for Wentworth.

Stuart Tave's point, like Barber's, is accurate even when turned in the other direction; Austen's irony is very Shakespearean. Even the reader must fall into the initial error of undervaluing Anne Elliot. The wit of Elizabeth Bennet or of Rosalind is easier to appreciate than Anne Elliot's accurate sensibility. The secret of her character combines Austenian irony with a Wordsworthian sense of deferred hope. Austen has a good measure of Shakespeare's unmatched ability to give us persons, both major and minor, who are each utterly consistent in her or his separate mode of speech, and yet completely different from one another. Anne Elliot is the last of Austen's heroines of what I think we must call the Protestant will, but in her the will is modified, perhaps perfected, by its descendant, the Romantic sympathetic imagination, of which Wordsworth, as we have seen, was the prophet. That is perhaps what helps to make Anne so complex and sensitive a character.

Jane Austen's earlier heroines, of whom Elizabeth Bennet is the exemplar, manifested the Protestant will as direct descendants of Samuel Richardson's Clarissa Harlowe, with Dr. Samuel Johnson hovering nearby as moral authority. Marxist criticism inevitably views the Protestant will, even in its literary manifestations, as a mercantile matter, and it has become fashionable to talk about the socioeconomic realities that Jane Austen excludes, such as the West Indian slavery that is part of the ultimate basis for the financial security most of her characters enjoy. But all achieved literary works are founded upon exclusions, and no one has demonstrated that increased consciousness of the relation between culture and imperialism is of the slightest benefit whatsoever in learning to read *Mansfield Park*. *Persuasion* ends with a tribute to the British navy, in which Wentworth has an honored place. Doubtless Wentworth at sea, ordering the latest batch of disciplinary floggings, is not as pleasant as Wentworth on land, gently appreciating the joys of affection with Anne Elliot. But once again, Austen's is a great art founded upon exclusions, and the sordid realities of British sea power are no more relevant to *Persuasion* than West Indian bondage is to *Mansfield Park*. Austen was, however, immensely interested in the pragmatic and secular consequences of the Protestant will, and they seem to me a crucial element in helping us appreciate the heroines of her novels.

Austen's Shakespearean inwardness, culminating in Anne Elliot, revises the moral intensities of Clarissa Harlowe's secularized Protestant martyrdom, her slow dying after being raped by Lovelace. What removes Clarissa's will to live is her stronger will to maintain the integrity of her being. To yield to the repentant Lovelace by marrying him would compromise the essence of her being, the exaltation of her violated will. What is tragedy in Clarissa is converted by Austen into ironic comedy, but the will's drive to maintain itself scarcely alters in this conversion. In *Persuasion* the emphasis is on a willed exchange of esteems, where both the woman and the man estimate the value of the other to be high. Obviously outward considerations of wealth, property, and social standing are crucial elements here, but so are the inward considerations of common sense, amiability, culture, wit, and affection. In a way (it pains me to say this, as I am a fierce Emersonian) Ralph Waldo Emerson anticipated the current Marxist critique of Austen when he denounced her as a mere conformist who would not allow her heroines to achieve the soul's true freedom from societal conventions. But that was to mistake Jane Austen, who understood that the function of convention was to liberate the will, even if convention's tendency was to stifle individuality, without which the will was inconsequential.

Austen's major heroines—Elizabeth, Emma, Fanny, and Anne—possess such inward freedom that their individualities cannot be repressed. Austen's art as a novelist is not to worry much about the socioeconomic genesis of that inner freedom, though the anxiety level does rise in *Mansfield Park* and *Persuasion*. In Austen, irony becomes the instrument for invention, which Dr. Johnson defined as the essence of poetry. A conception of inward freedom that centers upon a refusal to accept esteem except from one upon whom one has conferred esteem, is a conception of the highest degree of irony. The supreme comic scene in all of Austen must be Elizabeth's rejection of Darcy's first marriage proposal, where the ironies of the dialectic of will and esteem become very nearly outrageous. That high comedy, which continued in *Emma*, is somewhat chastened in *Mansfield Park*, and then becomes something else, unmistakable but difficult to name, in *Persuasion*, where Austen has become so conscious a master that she seems to have changed the nature of willing, as though it, too, could be persuaded to become a rarer, more disinterested act of the self.

No one has suggested that Jane Austen becomes a High Romantic in *Persuasion*; her poet remained William Cowper, not Wordsworth, and her favorite prose writer was always Dr. Johnson. But her severe distrust of imagination and of "romantic love," so prevalent in the earlier novels, is not a factor in *Persuasion*. Anne and Wentworth maintain their affection for each other throughout eight years of hopeless separation, and each has the power of imagination to conceive of a triumphant reconciliation. This is the material for a romance, not for an ironical novel. The ironies of *Persuasion* are frequently pungent, but they are almost never directed at Anne Elliot and only rarely at Captain Wentworth. There is a difficult relation between Austen's repression of her characteristic irony about her protagonists and a certain previously unheard plangency that hovers throughout *Persuasion*. Despite Anne's faith in herself she is very vulnerable to the anxiety, which she never allows herself to express, of an unlived life, in which the potential loss transcends yet includes sexual unfulfillment. I can recall only one critic, the Australian Ann Molan, who emphasizes what Austen strongly implies, that "Anne ... is a passionate woman. And against her will, her heart keeps asserting its demand for fulfillment." Since Anne had refused Wentworth her esteem eight years before, she feels a necessity to withhold her will, and thus becomes the first Austen heroine whose will and imagination are antithetical.

Although Austen's overt affinities remained with the Aristocratic Age, her authenticity as a writer impelled her, in *Persuasion*, a long way toward the burgeoning Democratic Age, or Romanticism, as we used to call it. There is no civil war within Anne Elliot's psyche, or within Austen's; but there is the emergent sadness of a schism in the self, with memory taking the side of imagination in an alliance against the will. The almost Wordsworthian power of memory in both Anne and Wentworth has been noted by Gene Ruoff. Since Austen was anything but an accidental novelist, we might ask why she chose to found *Persuasion* upon a mutual nostalgia. After all, the rejected Wentworth is even less inclined to will a renewed affection than Anne is, and yet the fusion of memory and imagination triumphs over his will also. Was this a relaxation of the will in Jane Austen herself? Since she returns to her earlier mode in *Sanditon*, her unfinished novel begun after *Persuasion* was completed, it may be that the story of Anne Elliot was an excursion or indulgence for the novelist. The parallels between Wordsworth and *Persuasion* are limited but real. High Romantic novels in England, whether of the Byronic kind like *Jane Eyre* and *Wuthering Heights* or of a Wordsworthian sort like *Adam Bede*, are a distinctly later development. The ethos of the Austen heroine does not change in *Persuasion*, but she is certainly a more problematic being, tinged with a new sadness concerning life's limits. It may be that the elegant pathos *Persuasion* sometimes courts has a connection to Jane Austen's own ill health, her intimations of her early death.

Stuart Tave, comparing Wordsworth and Austen, shrewdly noted that both were "poets of marriage" and both also possessed "a sense of duty understood and deeply felt by those who see the integrity and peace of their own lives as essentially bound to the lives of others and see the lives of all in a more than merely social order." Expanding Tave's insight, Susan Morgan pointed to the particular affinity between Austen's *Emma* and Wordsworth's great "Ode: Intimations of Immortality from Recollections of Earliest Childhood." The growth of the individual consciousness, involving both gain and loss for Wordsworth but only gain for Austen, is the shared subject. Emma's consciousness certainly does develop, and she undergoes a quasi-Wordsworthian transformation from the pleasures of near solipsism to the more difficult pleasures of sympathy for others. Anne Elliot, far more mature from the beginning, scarcely needs to grow in consciousness. Her long-lamented rejection of Wentworth insulates her against the destructiveness of hope, which we have seen to be the frightening emphasis of the earlier Wordsworth, particularly in the story of poor Margaret. Instead of hope, there is a complex of emotions, expressed by Austen with her customary skill:

> How eloquent could Anne Elliot have been,—how eloquent, at least, were her wishes on the side of early warm attachment, and a cheerful confidence in futurity, against that over-anxious caution which seems to insult exertion and distrust Providence!— She had been forced into prudence in her youth, she learned romance as she grew older—the natural sequel of an unnatural beginning.

Here learning romance is wholly retrospective; Anne no longer regards it as being available to her. And indeed Wentworth returns, still resentful after eight years, and reflects that Anne's power with him is gone forever. The qualities of decision and confidence that make him a superb naval commander are precisely what he condemns her for lacking. With almost too meticulous a craft, Austen traces his gradual retreat from this position, as the power of memory increases its dominance over him and as he learns that his jilted sense of her as being unable to act is quite mistaken. It is a beautiful irony that he needs to undergo a process of self-persuasion while Anne waits, without even knowing that she is waiting or that there is anything that could rekindle her hope. The comedy of this is gently sad, as the reader waits also, reflecting upon how large a part contingency plays in the matter.

While the pre-Socratics and Freud agree that there are no accidents, Austen thinks differently. Character is fate for her also, but fate, once activated, tends to evade character in so overdetermined a social context as Austen's world. In rereading *Persuasion*, though I remember the happy conclusion, I nevertheless feel anxiety as Wentworth and Anne circle away from each other in spite of themselves. The reader is not totally persuaded of a satisfactory interview until Anne reads Wentworth's quite agonized letter to her:

> "I can listen no longer in silence. I must speak to you by such means as are within my reach. You pierce my soul. I am half agony, half hope. Tell me not that I am too late, that such precious feelings are gone for ever. I offer myself to you again with a heart more your own, than when you almost broke it eight years and a half ago. Dare not say that man forgets sooner than woman, that his love has an earlier death. I have loved none but you. Unjust I may have been, weak and resentful I have been, but never inconstant. You alone have brought me to Bath. For you alone I think and plan.—Have you not seen this? Can you fail to have understood my wishes?—I had not waited even these ten days, could I have read your feelings, as I think you must have penetrated mine. I can hardly write. I am every instant hearing something which overpowers me. You sink your voice, but I can distinguish the tones of that voice, when they would be lost on others.—Too good, too excellent creature! You do us justice indeed. You do believe that there is true attachment and constancy among men. Believe it to be most fervent, most undeviating in
>
> F. W.

> "I must go, uncertain of my fate; but I shall return hither, or follow your party, as soon as possible. A word, a look will be enough to decide whether I enter your father's house this evening or never."

I cannot imagine such a letter in *Pride and Prejudice*, or even in *Emma* or *Mansfield Park*. The perceptive reader might have realized how passionate

Anne was, almost from the start of the novel, but until this there was no indication of equal passion in Wentworth. His letter, as befits a naval commander, is badly written and not exactly Austenian, but it is all the more effective thereby. We come to realize that we have believed in him until now only because Anne's love for him provokes our interest. Austen wisely has declined to make him interesting enough on his own. Yet part of the book's effect is to persuade the reader of the reader's own powers of discernment and self-persuasion; Anne Elliot is almost too good for the reader, as she is for Austen herself, but the attentive reader gains the confidence to perceive Anne as she should be perceived. The subtlest element in this subtlest of novels is the call upon the reader's own power of memory to match the persistence and intensity of the yearning that Anne Elliot is too stoical to express directly.

The yearning hovers throughout the book, coloring Anne's perceptions and our own. Our sense of Anne's existence becomes identified with our own consciousness of lost love, however fictive or idealized that may be. There is an improbability in the successful renewal of a relationship devastated eight years before which ought to work against the texture of this most "realistic" of Austen's novels, but she is very careful to see that it does not. Like the author, the reader becomes persuaded to wish for Anne what she still wishes for herself. Ann Molan has the fine observation that Austen "is most satisfied with Anne when Anne is most dissatisfied with herself." The reader is carried along with Austen, and gradually Anne is also persuaded and catches up with the reader, allowing her yearning a fuller expression.

Dr. Johnson, in *The Rambler* 29, on "The folly of anticipating misfortunes," warned against anxious expectations of any kind, whether fearful or hopeful:

> because the objects both of fear and hope are yet uncertain, so we ought not to trust the representations of one more than the other, because they are both equally fallacious; as hope enlarges happiness, fear aggravates calamity. It is generally allowed, that no man ever found the happiness of possession proportionate to that expectation which incited his desire, and invigorated his pursuit; nor has any man found the evils of life so formidable in reality, as they were described to him by his own imagination.

This is one of a series of Johnsonian pronouncements against the dangerous prevalence of the imagination, some of which his disciple Austen had certainly read. If you excluded such representations, on the great critic's advice, then Wordsworth could not have written at all, and Austen could not have written *Persuasion*. Yet it was a very strange book for her to write, this master of the highest art of exclusion that we have known in the Western novel. Any novel by Jane Austen could be called an achieved ellipsis, with everything omitted that could disturb her ironic though happy conclusions. *Persuasion* remains the least popular of her four canonical novels because it is the strangest, but all her work is increasingly strange as we approach the end of the Democratic Age that her contemporary Wordsworth did so much to inaugurate in literature. Poised as she is at the final border of the Aristocratic Age, she shares with Wordsworth an art dependent upon a split between a waning Protestant will and a newly active sympathetic imagination, with memory assigned the labor of healing the divide. If the argument of my book has any validity, Austen will survive even the bad days ahead of us, because the strangeness of originality and of an individual vision are our lasting needs, which only literature can gratify in the Theocratic Age that slouches toward us.

RUTH apROBERTS

Sense and Sensibility,
or *Growing Up Dichotomous*

*S*ense *and Sensibility* has traditionally been considered, along with
Northanger Abbey, a kind of early prentice work, and in spite of the delight it
occasions and the light it spreads, "unsuccessful." I want to insist on its
success, its importance within the Austen canon, and its importance in
general. I want to suggest some connections with the poets, and show
Austen, in this book particularly, performing some perennially important
activities, such as testing abstractions against realities, laughing, and coping
with the dissociation of sensibility. Even such a perceptive critic as A. Walton
Litz has recently found the abstract tags of the title "obstacles to the
maturing artist,"—"the author is caught in the web of a language which tends
to describe 'types,' not individuals."[1] I suggest, rather, that the novel has a
sound base in that dichotomous abstraction of the title. *Sense and Sensibility*,
Pride and Prejudice, Persuasion—"It is not for nothing," says Gilbert Ryle,
"that these titles are composed of abstract nouns. *Sense and Sensibility* really
is about the relations between Sense and Sensibility or, as we might put it,
between Head and Heart, Thought and Feeling, Judgement and Emotion."[2]
This novel is, then, a part of what might be the oldest tradition of the verbal
animal. Being in itself is altogether too hard to think about as the "blooming,
buzzing confusion" which (in William James's phrase) it probably is, and in
our linguistic fictions we posit aspects of it in order to deal with it: Anima and

From *Nineteenth-Century Fiction* 30, no. 3 (December 1975). © 1975 by the Regents of the
University of California.

Corpus, Soul and Body, Mind and Body, Head and Heart. Most often there is something left over, the very self, which when it speaks poems we are in our linguistic desperation reduced to calling the *persona*, which is—of all things—a mask, the real self being so unthinkable.

Sometimes our linguistic fictions are abstractions, like thought and feeling. Sometimes they are clearly metaphor, Head and Heart, for instance, a physiological metaphor for things felt to be separable processes of being. Probably the physical head has no more proprietary claim to "thinking" than the heart has to "feeling." Sometimes they are obscurely metaphor, *anima* being at bottom the invisible but felt breath or wind, and *corpus* being the material, kickable substance. We know finally that these things are not absolute entities, but they are indispensable to thinking. As Bentham said of the fictions of language in general, they are "impossible but indispensable."[3] For it is only by their means that we are able to say a great deal about the way things are; they open areas of discourse otherwise inaccessible.

The Emperor Hadrian could address his soul, his *anima*, in a five-line poem that has kept its force over the long space of time since the second century:

> Animula vagula blandula
> hospes comesque corporis
> quae nunc abibis in loca
> pallidula rigida nudula
> nec ut soles dabis jocos.

The diminutives manage to objectify the tenderness felt for the soul, so vulnerable, fragile, tenuous, and errant we sense it to be. *Hospes*, yes: both host and guest of the body but more than either, as in the hospitality relationship that in the Near East is preeminent and sacred in its rights and obligations; *comes*, yes: that is the good working relationship, a comradeship. The soul threatened by the severed relationship must feel its future forlorn indeed, stark, bare, desolate. The emperor, however, marvels that his soul might lose what is apparently for him its most characteristic and essential function, the making of jokes! the most astoundingly mysterious aspect of consciousness, that recoil upon itself which is wit and laughter. One reason the poem is an enduring challenge to translators is the way it ends surprisingly, on the mystery of laughter in very humble terms. The Latin *dabis jocos* is just about as low as English "crack jokes." Among the translators of Jane Austen's time, the young Byron felt he had to reverse the order of the ending:

Ah! gentle, fleeting, wav'ring sprite,
Friend and associate of this clay!
   To what unknown regions borne,
Wilt thou now wing thy distant flight?
No more with wonted humour gay,
   But pallid, cheerless, and forlorn.[4]

But let us note above all that the use of the body–soul dichotomy made this important and subtle statement of Hadrian's possible, and keeps it functional. Man must always have used such concepts as soon as he used language. This particular body–soul concept is the one that under the impulse of Christianity gives birth to a whole series of texts such as those many medieval debates of the Body and Soul, to keep to dichotomies; or, moving to pluralities, the dramas of the virtues and vices. Always the self is there, listening and observing and learning, both stage and audience for the debate or for the morality play. These old art forms worked well, we might surmise, because they are so obviously metaphorical. No one believes the soul can really talk to the body.

Personification of aspects of personality opens whole new worlds of theology too; and as Christianity exploited the body–soul dichotomy, the dichotomy tended to harden into doctrine, and ultimately the soul came to be considered literally the immortal part. The immortal soul, if we retain the sense of it as fictive, may be thought of as a useful fiction in the line of Hans Vaihinger's theory of fictions, and the Als-Ob, the As-If. Our actions may be the better or more successful if we act as if the soul was an immortal part which will take the consequences of our behavior. It can be argued that when the metaphor hardens into doctrine it becomes less useful. To "believe" that the soul is a literally immortal separable entity may make a closing off of the mind instead of an opening into new phases of discourse. We can become anxious about "belief," and malfunction can occur. Matthew Arnold deplored this literalism of belief, and called it the "prison of Puritanism";[5] in his diagnosis it lay at the root of the Victorian malaise. Something similar may be responsible for what T.S. Eliot deplored as the "dissociation of sensibility."

As literalism was developing in the late eighteenth century, along with the evangelical movement, the most current philosophical dichotomy was the intellect–emotion one, preeminently the Sense and Sensibility of Jane Austen. The philosophical background has been well explored in Descartes, Locke, Hume, Berkeley, and Shaftesbury; the literary cult of sensibility—in Sterne, MacKenzie, and the poets—is a well-known chapter in the history of

English literature; and the linguistic background reveals itself in an hour or so with the *Oxford English Dictionary*, or most conveniently and delightfully in C.S. Lewis's essay on "Sense (with Sentence, Sensibility and Sensible)."[6] From the cluster of words growing out of the Latin *sentio* matrix, develops a set of words with widely divergent uses, from something like *logos* or "meaning," in *sentence*, to the Austen pair of sense–reason, and sensibility–responsiveness. Lewis quotes Dr. Johnson on the relevance of this last meaning to art: "the ambition of superior sensibility and superior eloquence dispose the lovers of arts to receive rapture at one time and communicate it at another"; and Cowper on its relevance to moral sympathy: "Grant, Kind heav'n, to me, Sweet Sensibility." And he takes the Dashwood girls of course as the *locus classicus* of the two uses. It is "a semantic situation," he says, which can hardly last, the two meanings being so divergent; and the "half-punning antithesis" of the Austen title preserves the unstable moment. Her terms are certainly used as mutually exclusive categories for experience, nicely caught in the title of the French translation of 1815: *Raison et sensibilité, où les deux manières d'aimer*.

Certainly the title sets the novel in the long and august line of fictive dichotomies from the old body–soul one, through such little allegories as Tennyson's "The Two Voices," and the Victorian commonplace of conscience as the "still small voice" of God within us (developed rather oddly out of the Elijah story), holding its adversary the beast-in-man in check; and the great nineteenth-century debate of Heart and Head, perhaps most nobly done by Dostoyevsky; surviving in the twentieth century in the mind–body myth, which Ryle has been at pains to expose as fictive in his famous *Concept of Mind*.[7] We are liable to error if we "believe" in the dualism. But meantime, all these dichotomies are, however "impossible," quite "indispensable." The danger is to forget the fictiveness, for once the terms become current, they reinforce themselves as concepts and are more and more liable to harden into things "believed in" as reality.

Jane Austen in *Sense and Sensibility* starts with a fictive dichotomy but warns us against it from the beginning. In the first description of the two girls, Elinor, though obviously representing sense, has feelings that are strong, and Marianne, though obviously representing sensibility, has a distinguished intellect. It is not a case where the author finds she must modify her theme in the course of the novel; she knows what she is about from the first. This is not going to be a morality play, nor a set of Jonsonian humors, nor a simplistic cautionary tale. But with the title in front of us, we are certainly at first invited to test the characters on its polarity. Austen is too often connected only with novelists, and we might have the courage to connect her with the poets, her contemporaries. Blake, characteristically forthright, asserts: "To generalize is to be an idiot." Austen, too, refuses us the generalization. Blake also asserts, forthright again: "Without contraries is no progression." I propose that Austen takes her contraries or antitheses not as ends, but as means, to a kind of progression or education. I think the antitheses characteristic of the Enlightenment are a kind of product or conclusion. But Austen's antitheses are not so much enlightened epigrammatic conclusions, but phases of process. Take from *Sense and Sensibility* a typical series of antitheses: Elinor and Marianne

> had too much sense to be desirable companions to the former [Lady Middleton]; and by the latter [the Steeles] they were considered with a jealous eye, as intruding on *their* ground, and sharing the kindness which they wanted to monopolize. Though nothing could be more polite than Lady Middleton's behaviour to Elinor and Marianne, she did not really like them at all. Because they neither flattered herself nor her children, she could not believe them good-natured; and because they were fond of reading, she fancied them satirical.... Their presence was a restraint both on her and on Lucy. It checked the idleness of one, and the business of the other. Lady Middleton was ashamed of doing nothing before them, and the flattery which Lucy was proud to think of and administer at other times, she feared they would despise her for offering.[8]

This play of antitheses, diagrammed by "the former" and "the latter," "because" and "because," "the one" and "the other," "ashamed" and "feared," is a means toward discovery by contrasts. All these oppositions are temporarily useful structures, to be dropped in series and replaced by others.

One of Jane Austen's Victorian critics, Richard Simpson, had a keen perception of this antithesis as method. In general, he understood that in "growth through contradictions we see the highest exercise of the critical faculty." He notes that Austen rejects the simple black and white view, sees the good in the evil, and the evil even in the good, and all this is perceived in action.

> It is her thorough consciousness that man is a social being, and that apart from society there is not even the individual.... She contemplates virtues not as fixed quantities, or as definable qualities, but as continual struggles and conquests, as progressive

states of mind, *advancing by repulsing their contraries* [my italics]....
A character ... unfolded itself to her ... as ... a composite force,
which could only exhibit what it was by exhibiting what it did.[9]

Simpson goes on to relate this aspect of her art to Cowper, and we remember
that of all her books it is this one where Cowper is most involved. According
to Cowper, "By ceaseless action all that is subsists." "He that attends to his
interior self, / That has a heart and keeps it; has a mind / That hungers, and
supplies it; and who seeks / A social, not a dissipated life, / Has business."[10]
This novel is a Cowperian exercise, where it is initially proposed that we test
all by the bipolar gauge of Sense–Sensibility or mind–heart, and yet we are
warned from the first against taking this gauge as absolute. We find that not
only must the heart be "kept"—protected, guided, disciplined—but also the
mind must be "supplied"—fed, exercised, and developed. And the test is not
the initial bipolar one finally, but something else that measures the
adjustment or integration of mind–heart. The test is a social business, and
social business is the determination of morality. Everyone is tested first on
the Sense–Sensibility gauge, and events prove that gauge grossly inadequate.
The John Dashwoods, early on in the splendid second chapter, where they
cut down the inheritance of the girls all for their own good, make a fine
demonstration of how sense or prudence can be the most egregious
selfishness. Mrs. Jennings is wonderfully deficient in both sense and
sensibility, and yet comes out very high on that other gauge. The evaluation
of each character is adjusted and changed as the novel proceeds. The events
are a series of multidimensional tests that demonstrate the fallacy of the
premise. It even recalls Bertrand Russell's fable of the barber. In town A, you
remember, you can divide all the men into two classes, those that shave
themselves and those that are shaved by the barber. The categories seem
perfectly unexceptionable. But events bring us in contact with Mr. Jones, the
barber himself. And what do we do with *him*? Our categorization is revealed
as inadequate.

   This slight-seeming little novel bears the weight of much analysis, and
is looking increasingly important in the Austen canon. Historically, it
appears to use and to criticize the abstract intellection of the Enlightenment,
and at the same time anticipates the novelistic realism of the nineteenth
century. Austen would have us beat our dichotomies into pluralities, as more
closely adapted to what will be felt to be the variety of reality, the relativistic
view of life. When she departs from simple antithesis into the triplet, I think
she moves significantly closer to relativism. When Marianne sings at the
Middleton's party, there are three significant reactions:

> Sir John was loud in his admiration at the end of every song, and
> as loud in his conversation with the others while every song
> lasted. Lady Middleton frequently called him to order, wondered
> how any one's attention could be diverted from music for a
> moment, and asked Marianne to sing a particular song which
> Marianne had just finished. Colonel Brandon alone, of all the
> party, heard her without being in raptures. He paid her only the
> compliment of attention. (35)

There are two kinds of false rapture here, and one nonrapture. Elements one
and two are clearly anti-Marianne; element three, or Brandon, is antirapture
but pro-Marianne and so breaks out of the categories, thereby moving
forward and anticipating how Marianne's simplicities will be modified.

Other events yield more complicated results. When the John
Dashwoods, unaccustomed as they are to giving anything away, do give a
dinner, there appeared "no poverty of any kind, except of conversation."
"When the ladies withdrew to the drawing-room after dinner, this poverty
was particularly evident," for the only topic was the comparative heights of
two little boys.

> Had both the children been there, the affair might have been
> determined too easily by measuring them at once; but as Harry
> only was present, it was all conjectural assertion on both sides,
> and every body had a right to be equally positive in their opinion,
> and to repeat it over and over again as often as they liked.
> The parties stood thus:
> The two mothers, though each really convinced that her own
> son was the tallest, politely decided in favour of the other.
> The two grandmothers, with not less partiality, but more
> sincerity, were equally earnest in support of their own
> descendant.
> Lucy, who was hardly less anxious to please one parent than
> the other, thought the boys were both remarkably tall for their
> age, and could not conceive that there could be the smallest
> difference in the world between them; and Miss Steele, with yet
> greater address gave it, as fast as she could, in favour of each.
> Elinor, having once delivered her opinion on William's side,
> by which she offended Mrs. Ferrars and Fanny still more, did not
> see the necessity of enforcing it by any farther assertion; and
> Marianne, when called on for hers, offended them all, by

declaring that she had no opinion to give, as she had never thought about it. (233–34)

We have here four pairs of reactions, balanced against each other and within themselves in remarkable and hilarious symmetry. We all use contrasting pairs as a way of thinking, with parallelisms in our sentences or poems, in the analogies of metaphor, and in the doublings of allegory. Behind this activity we may see the outline of a mathematical structure. The Bourbaki school have described the mathematical method par excellence as the reduction of data to isomorphisms; and the structuralists take this to be the model of all human activity. An analogous principle has emerged out of Boolean algebra into a method for machines that is a binary—or isomorphological—system. All data may be programmed by this system, and one proceeds from data so obtained into new series of isomorphs and new results. The work of Kurt Gödel sustains the principle that no systems or results are final and complete—one moves on.[11] I propose that Jane Austen's series of eight reactions to the conversational poverty situation are dealt with by isomorphs. First we have four relations balanced by four nonrelations. Then the first four are reduced to a pair of mothers, and a pair of grandmothers, in balance. Then the two mothers are discovered to balance each other precisely, indistinguishable in their partiality, their smug confidence and their hypocrisy. The two grandmothers are equally indistinguishable, both grown old in partiality and both even impatient with hypocrisy. The second set of four balances the first in some ways. Mothers:grandmothers = Steeles:Dashwoods in respect of closeness of interest and degrees of honesty. The two Steeles, however, differentiate themselves one from the other with the most ingenious and exquisite nicety, but the differences are pretense and we recognize the sisters as beautifully indistinguishable in corruption. Elinor and Marianne we know well enough to recognize their common ground in this exigency: both would be appalled at the intellectual desperation, and partly bored, partly "satirically" amused, since both are basically honest women. Similarities granted, the delicate distinctions can now appear in relief. Elinor, ever the more dutiful in social obligations, makes a compromise, satisfies her honesty by a single statement of opinion, being willing to offend one faction to a degree. Marianne, uncompromisingly honest, is willing to offend them all. In this testing event, we have discovered through the use of isomorphs a certain rich discrepancy which enables us to move on to a new level of discourse. Marianne's sensibility emerges as an unwillingness to sense the feelings of others and hence a reversal into lack of sensibility. Her feelings, initially authentic, through being fostered have taken on something histrionic which is inauthentic and which closes to her that empathy we owe to the people we encounter. Against the thoughtlessness of Marianne is set the extended social consciousness of Elinor.

On the same evening, when the gentlemen join the ladies, John Dashwood goes so far in generosity as to bring attention to Elinor's painting on a pair of screens. Again the members of the party are tested and the results recorded in sharp almost tabular form, revealing kinds and degrees of insolence and philistinism, till it is too much for Marianne. She cannot bear to have Elinor's art slighted, and she rudely snatches the screens from Fanny, "to admire them herself as they ought to be admired." It is an adorable action. Her love breaks the pattern of politeness, and we progress to a yet more advanced level of complication. The whole account of the evening is— I hope my analysis does not altogether disguise the fact—very funny. If the structuralists would find in mathematical isomorphisizing a model for distinctively human activity, and if one feels with Hadrian that it is the essence of the distinctively human *anima* to make jokes, one might suspect there is a connection. It is true that by means of our isomorphs we discover and define discrepancies, which can make us laugh. To judge by the geometrical games Hadrian played in designing the Pantheon, he had thought a good deal about mathematics as well as his soul, and maybe he had an intimation of isomorphs. At any rate the funniness of the Austen novels is immeasurably important in the way it spreads back out over us in waves of benign awareness. Its working is absolutely unfathomable. Man, says Foucault, amounts to "a simple pleat in consciousness,"[12] and that might be a description of *homo sapiens, homo ludens,* or even, particularly, *homo jocans.*

Some of the scenes that open out new perspectives are grimmer in humor than the one of the Dashwoods' dinner party. The most difficult test for Elinor occurs when we know that Willoughby has betrayed Marianne, and we know that Elinor is in similar distress: Lucy Steele has told her under pledge of secrecy that she, Lucy, is engaged to Elinor's beloved Edward. Lucy calls on Mrs. Jennings, Marianne is suffering upstairs; Mrs. Jennings is called out, and Elinor is left alone with Lucy. This is bad enough, with Lucy's insufferable arrogance, but Elinor's torture is compounded when Edward himself is announced. "The very circumstance, in its unpleasantest form, which they would each have been most anxious to avoid, had fallen on them—They were not only all three together, but were together without the relief of any other person" (241). Edward is virtually paralyzed, Lucy is sly and smirkingly quiet, and so Elinor must labor under the weight not only of her broken heart but of all the social duty. She is obliged to volunteer all the information about her mother's health, their coming to town, &c. which Edward ought to have inquired about, but never did.

Her exertions did not stop here; for she soon afterwards felt herself so heroically disposed as to determine, under pretence of fetching Marianne, to leave the others by themselves: and she really did it, and that in the handsomest manner, for she loitered away several minutes on the landing-place, with the most high-minded fortitude. (241–42)

It is some small comfort to us all that we may suspect her nobility to be a little tempered with sadism: just let Edward face this charming fiancée of his! just let Lucy try to find words for the impossible situation! But when Elinor returns with Marianne, Marianne in her naïveté says everything that might increase the pain for Elinor. And Marianne thinks she herself is the martyr! There is a mathematical kind of thoroughness in the way Austen wrings each aspect of irony from the dialogue here.

The anguish of the testing is a learning process and it is not just Marianne who learns. We ourselves see that Mrs. Dashwood and Marianne have adopted the fashionable new cult of sensibility out of motives which in themselves are hardly culpable: lively intelligence and sensitivity to life and art. But the more they indulge themselves in the histrionics of sensibility, the more Elinor, aware of the danger, is obliged to appear priggish in reaction. The grave danger to personality becomes obvious in Marianne's case. She has become vulnerable. Her severe physical illness symbolizes the moral danger; her physical resistance has been lowered by sensibility as has her psychic resistance, and she is nearly lost in more ways than one. If the heroine of *Northanger Abbey* suffers from "factual gullibility" in Ryle's terms,[13] Marianne can be said to be a victim of "cultural gullibility." The dichotomy of *Sense and Sensibility* is thus proved invalid, even dangerous, and we discard it for other gauges that seem to sort better with behavioral actualities. Yet because the dichotomy had seemed valid initially, we might be the more prepared now to take our new gauges and standards as provisional. Learning is a dialectical process and does not stop.

Learning is also a function of humanity. Innateness is not enough. We remember that when Elinor reproves Marianne for visiting Willoughby's house alone with him, Marianne retorts in Rousseauistic terms: "if there had been any real impropriety in what I did, I should have been sensible of it at the time, for we always know when we are acting wrong" (68). But events contradict her, and it is part of the pattern of this book that the Rousseauistic natural man is consistently put down. Children do not come off well in *Sense and Sensibility*. It is foolish to classify Jane Austen as a child-hater, for we know perfectly well that she was an excellent aunt and a great instigator of laughter and joy. But there was no nonsense, one can be sure, about "Thou best philosopher." The young John Dashwood runs no danger of being idealized; he

> gained on the affections of his uncle, by such attractions as are by no means unusual in children of two or three years old; an imperfect articulation, an earnest desire of having his own way, many cunning tricks, and a great deal of noise. (4)

The Middleton children are quite unable to assert any innate goodness in the ambiance of stupidity and indulgence that their mother makes for them. They are utter spoiled brats, of very limited usefulness.

> On every formal visit a child ought to be of the party, by way of provision for discourse. In the present case it took up ten minutes to determine whether the boy were most like his father or mother, and in what particular he resembled either, for of course every body differed, and every body was astonished at the opinion of the others. (31)

And then, as we have seen, there is the John Dashwood party when the two boys' heights afford the only straw of interest for desperate conversationalists. One imagines Elinor's and Marianne's distaste for those spoiled monsters; the Steeles, however, exploit the sentimental idealization of the young for their own interests. They "doat," they say, on children, quite indiscriminately whenever the mother may be flattered thereby; they are in raptures over behavior that should get a swift smack. This is a society that in reality sacrifices children. Margaret, the younger sister of Elinor and Marianne, would certainly never be so spoiled by her mother, but is at thirteen quite naturally bound to be trying, and makes herself a party to the worst of Mrs. Jennings's vulgar teasing. "As she had already imbibed a good deal of Marianne's romance, without having much of her sense" (7), the prognosis is not good. Since Austen also tells us she is "a good-humoured well-disposed girl" we gather the material is good enough. The emphasis is on the telling value of upbringing.

Ryle observes that Austen's "ethical vocabulary and idioms are quite strongly laced with aesthetic terms";[14] and I think *Sense and Sensibility* is of all her novels the one most concerned with art, language, and their relationship to morality.[15] The superiority of Marianne and Elinor and their mother consists in good part in their cultivation. Barton Cottage is full of books and music, and the inhabitants habitually read poetry aloud, and paint, and collect prints. The idle Philistines, the Middletons, Steeles, etc., are quite astonished to find the Barton Dashwoods so frequently "employed." Edward's unfortunate entanglement with Lucy really came about from idleness. His mother denies him an active profession, he is not entered at Oxford till he is nineteen, and shy and self-deprecating as he is, he is vulnerable to Lucy. Man is language in a sense that Austen intimates here; this is a study of cliché in behavior as well as in language. Lucy Steele is retrograde on both counts.[16] The values of cultivation and of virtue go for the most part hand in hand, though even here Austen refuses us the easy generalization: Mrs. Jennings is the walking exception, the vulgarian who is full of generosity. Whoever it was who said the exceptions to moral rules are about as frequent proportionately as the exceptions to grammatical rules, would find corroboration in the sort of life-grammar that Austen codifies for us.[17] But to grant exceptions is not to insist any the less on the value of the rules. Grammar is simply hard.

Some time ago, Mark Schorer professed "our surest way of knowing the values out of which a novel comes lies in the examination of style, more particularly of metaphor," and he found in Austen a high proportion of terms of commerce, property, credit, interest, account, tax, insurance, and so on. Schorer did not apply this to mean that Austen's values were entirely material; he had far too fine a sense of them for that. But he accommodated his theory by asserting the "tension" between material and moral.[18] Surely the moral interest is at the center. And the "surest way" of knowing her values is not to discover how she gives herself away by her metaphors but to observe what the novel is "about" in Ryle's plain sense. Metaphors are a means to an end. Our overriding business is to determine the virtuous life, and because that is difficult we turn to metaphor. And we find the terms of our metaphor in those interests that are all too familiar in our fallen state: commerce, property, credit, etc. So the moralist makes particular use of our frailty: "Lay up for yourselves treasures in heaven"; the figure is taken from banking. We must know where to put our "money." Similarly the parable of the talents is a figure taken from investment; and we had better be able to give a good accounting.

If the good artist is to be a good investment advisor, she will not allow us our easy generalities. From the first, Austen refused to let us take sense–sensibility as an absolute good–evil polarity, and, as her theme and variations act themselves out in the events, the odd thing is that sensibility rejoins virtue. The fashionable new lifestyle had its origin in the love of virtue: it was the eighteenth-century moralists who invented it. It becomes, however, excessively fashionable and its virtuous pretensions prove hollow, or even treacherous. We return to the principle, then, chastened and educated, to recognize that the fount of decency is the ability to feel, first for ourselves, and then, with good hope, for others. Austen's contemporary, Keats, asserts "the holiness of the heart's affections." "I have felt ...," says Wordsworth, and that is his authority. Mill discovers the prime importance of a "due balance among the faculties" and turns to Wordsworth for the necessary "culture of the feelings." There is a pattern of peripeteia in the movement of *Sense and Sensibility* that acts on various levels. In the main action, which is "the extraordinary fate" of Marianne Dashwood, "born to discover the falsehood of her own opinions, and to counteract, by her conduct, her most favourite maxims," the once despised Colonel Brandon becomes her beloved husband; she "could never love by halves; and her whole heart became, in time, as much devoted to her husband, as it had once been to Willoughby" (378–79). Her capacity for passion is finally exercised, but in a way that was hardly to be expected. Austen is alert to a score of such peripeteias, major and minor: Mrs. Ferrars, Elinor observes after the reversals of the roles of Robert and Edward, "has actually been bribing one son with a thousand a-year, to do the very deed which she disinherited the other for intending to do" (366). Little do we know, indeed, what reversals time will bring. There is a model for this in linguistic processes: out of the cluster of words from Latin *sentio* came the branching family of *sense* and *sensibility* to produce in time for Jane Austen a doublet that paradoxically represents something like opposites, and then moves back to converge into the *sentio–sensi* matrix: "I have felt...." In a similarly peripatetic movement our heuristic fictions lead us back to the unity of being. Sensibility is, at least for a time, reassociated.

Notes

1. A. Walton Litz, *Jane Austen: A Study of Her Artistic Development* (New York: Oxford Univ. Press, 1965), pp. 77–78.

2. Gilbert Ryle, "Jane Austen and the Moralists," in *Critical Essays on Jane Austen*, ed. B. C. Southam (London: Routledge and Kegan Paul, 1968), pp. 106–7.

3. *Bentham's Theory of Fictions*, ed. C. K. Ogden (Paterson, N.J.: Littlefield, Adams, 1959). See "Linguistic Fictions," p. 15.

4. The poem is generally printed among Byron's Juvenilia. Latin text (except punctuation) from *Minor Latin Poets*, ed. J. W. Duff and A. M. Duff, Loeb Classical Library (Cambridge, Mass.: Harvard Univ. Press; London: Heinemann, 1985), p. 444.

5. The idea of the "prison" as literalism is perhaps best developed in "The True Greatness of the Old Testament," in *Literature and Dogma*, Vol. VI of *The Complete Prose Works of Matthew Arnold*, ed. R. H. Super (Ann Arbor: Univ. of Michigan Press, 1968), p. 390.

6. *Studies in Words* (Cambridge: Cambridge Univ. Press, 1960), ch. 6.

7. *The Concept of Mind* (New York: Barnes and Noble, 1949). See also "The Physical Basis of Mind," A Symposium with Lord Samuel and A. J. Ayer; *The Physical Basis of Mind*, ed. Peter Laslett (London: Blackwell, 1950), pp. 75–79, rpt. in *Body, Mind and Death*, ed. Antony Flew (New York: Macmillan, 1964), pp. 245–64.

8. *Sense and Sensibility*, pp. 246–47. All quotations and page references are from Vol. I of *The Novels of Jane Austen*, ed. R. W. Chapman, 3rd ed. (London: Oxford Univ. Press, 1933).

9. "Jane Austen," *North British Review*, 52 (1870), 129–52.

10. Cowper, quoted by Simpson, pp. 137, 140.

11. For an accessible survey of structuralist mathematics, see Jean Piaget, *Le Structuralisme* (Paris: Presses Universitaires de France, 1974), esp. ch. 2. For some suggestions of relevance to literary theory, see my "Waiting for Gödel," in *Language, Logic, and Genre*, ed. Wallace Martin (Lewisburg, Pa.: Bucknell Univ. Press, 1974), pp. 28–43.

12. Quoted in Piaget, p. 45.

13. Ryle, "Jane Austen," p. 114.

14. Ibid., p. 117.

15. For an excellent study of this matter see Donald D. Stone, "Sense and Semantics in Jane Austen," *NCF*, 25 (1970), 31–50.

16. See K. C. Phillipps, "Lucy Steele's English," *English Studies*, Anglo-American Supplement, 50 (1969), lx–lxi.

17. C.S. Lewis in his fine essay on Jane Austen uses the phrase "grammar of conduct." See "A Note on Jane Austen," in *Jane Austen: A Collection of Critical Essays*, ed. Ian Watt (Englewood Cliffs, N.J.: Prentice-Hall, 1963), p. 33.

18. "Fiction and the 'Analogical Matrix,'" in *The World We Imagine: Selected Essays by Mark Schorer* (New York: Farrar, Straus and Giroux, 1968), pp. 24–28.

MARTIN PRICE

Manners,
Morals, and Jane Austen

Let us imagine a picture story in schematic pictures, and thus more like
the narrative in a language than a series of realistic pictures.... Let us
remember too that we don't have to translate such pictures into realistic
ones in order to "understand" them, any more than we ever translate
photographs or film pictures into coloured pictures, although black-and-
white men or plants in reality would strike us as unspeakably strange and
frightful.[1]

Jane Austen's novels present a world more schematic than we are
accustomed to find in more recent fiction. The schematism arises in part
from her "vocabulary of discrimination,"[2] those abstract words which classify
actions in moral terms. Wittgenstein's remarks recall the adaptability of our
responses, the readiness of our minds to discover how a literary work conveys
its meanings and to make insensible adjustments to the forms its signs may
take. Black-and-white photography can make discriminations and tonal
gradations that cannot be achieved by color, just as, in another case, an
engraving can define a structure through line that a painting renders with
less precision or emphasis in its fuller range of effects. Translation into a new
medium or language sharpens our awareness of certain elements and of the
functions they serve. Our initial question is to ask what Jane Austen's mode
of fiction is designed to reveal.

From *Nineteenth-Century Fiction* 30, no. 3 (December 1975). © 1975 by the Regents of the
University of California.

Let us consider a passage in which Elinor and Marianne Dashwood accompany Lady Middleton to a party in London:

> They arrived in due time at the place of destination, and as soon as the string of carriages before them would allow, alighted, ascended the stairs, heard their names announced from one landing-place to another in an audible voice, and entered a room splendidly lit up, quite full of company, and insufferably hot. When they had paid their tribute of politeness by curtesying to the lady of the house, they were permitted to mingle in the crowd, and take their share of the heat and inconvenience, to which their arrival must necessarily add.[3]

Much that might be shown is not. (One may think of the ball Emma Bovary attends at Vaubyessard or the Moscow ball at which Kitty loses Vronsky to Anna Karénina.) We trace the rituals of entry with the Dashwood sisters, reaching the goal only to find it acutely oppressive. At this point the irony becomes firmer and the diction more abstract ("their tribute of politeness") as they observe the required forms, and are "permitted" to participate in the mutual affliction that such a party too easily becomes. The pattern of the experience, not least the ironic pattern of the final clause, takes the place of particular detail.

Another ball is that held at the Crown in *Emma*:

> The ball proceeded pleasantly. The anxious cares, the incessant attentions of Mrs. Weston, were not thrown away. Every body seemed happy; and the praise of being a delightful ball, which is seldom bestowed till after a ball has ceased to be, was repeatedly given in the very beginning of the existence of this. Of very important, very recordable events, it was not more productive than such meetings usually are. (326)

One can say of either scene that Jane Austen presents it for recognition rather than seeks to imagine it anew. It is meant to recall a world we know or at least know about, and there is little effort to catch its sensory qualities or evoke it pictorially. What Jane Austen stresses in the first case is the tissue of ceremony and protocol that shrouds an unpleasant reality. In the second, a scene of comparative informality where all the guests are known to each other, we see the social machine run smoothly and comfortably.

In a world of recognition, people are defined less by isolated features than by their total address. We see characters in Jane Austen's novels as we see many people in life, recognizing them as familiar but hardly able to enumerate their features. We may recognize a friend at a distance by stance or gait, by the way he enters traffic or passes others on the street. The process of recognition is composed of a series of small perceptions which, if their combination is right, bring along a familiar total form. In some cases, a very small number of perceptions (or, for the novelist, specifications) will serve. Jane Austen's introduction of characters tends to stress qualities that are not directly visible but will shape and account for the behavior that follows.

> The Musgroves, like their houses, were in a state of alteration, perhaps of improvement. The father and mother were in the old English style, and the young people in the new. Mr. and Mrs. Musgrove were a very good sort of people; friendly and hospitable, not much educated, and not at all elegant. Their children had more modern minds and manners. There was a numerous family; but the only two grown up, excepting Charles, were Henrietta and Louisa, young ladies of nineteen and twenty, who had brought from a school at Exeter all the usual stock of accomplishments, and were now, like thousands of other young ladies, living to be fashionable, happy, and merry. Their dress had every advantage, their faces were rather pretty, their spirits extremely good, their manners unembarrassed and pleasant; they were of consequence at home, and favourites abroad. (*Persuasion*, 40–41)

Here Jane Austen provides us with representative members of a social class, its two generations exhibiting change without conflict. The Musgroves looking forward towards modernity as warmly as Sir Walter Elliot retraces his lineage in his favorite book. The Musgroves are at once representative, even undistinguishable from most others of their age and class; yet happy, assured, comfortable in their world, all that Anne Elliot is not. In the sentences that follow, we have an explicit report of Anne's thoughts, but here too the author imposes her own ironic presence:

> Anne always contemplated them as some of the happiest creatures of her acquaintance; but still, saved as we all are by some comfortable feeling of superiority from wishing for the possibility of exchange, she would not have given up her own

more elegant and cultivated mind for all their enjoyments; and envied them nothing but that seemingly perfect good understanding and agreement together, that good-humoured mutual affection, of which she had known so little herself with either of her sisters. (41)

We can be sure that the narrative voice supplies the characterization of Anne's mind, serving up, so to speak, the reasons for the superiority that Anne probably thinks she feels as mere difference.

There is another interesting case of the introduction of minor characters, in this case Dr. Grant, the clergyman who succeeds Mr. Norris in the living at Mansfield in *Mansfield Park*. We first learn of his identity through Tom Bertram, whose gambling debts force Sir Thomas to dispose of the church living he had meant to hold for his younger son, Edmund. Tom rather cheaply consoles himself that "the future incumbent, whoever he might be, would, in all probability, die very soon." Dr. Grant, he is at first troubled to learn, is a "hearty man of forty-five"; but Tom can surmount hard fact with hopefulness: "But 'no, he was a short-neck'd, apoplectic sort of fellow, and, plied well with good things, would soon pop off'" (24). When the Grants arrive, they are seen through the eager observation of Mrs. Norris:

> The Grants showing a disposition to be friendly and sociable, gave great satisfaction in the main among their new acquaintance. They had their faults, and Mrs. Norris soon found them out. The Dr. was very fond of eating, and would have a good dinner every day; and Mrs. Grant, instead of contriving to gratify him at little expense, gave her cook as high wages as they did at Mansfield Park, and was scarcely ever seen in her offices. Mrs. Norris could not speak with any temper of such grievances, nor of the quantity of butter and eggs that were regularly consumed in the house. (31)

The Grants enter unobtrusively, becoming more vivid in the imagination of the foreground characters than in our direct awareness of them. They acquire greater importance with the coming of the Crawfords, but they have already gained by then a certain stability in our minds through indirectly presented details.

Their departure from the novel, too, is incidental to the careers of the major characters. The Grants move to London where they provide a home for Mary Crawford. Dr. Grant, by indulging in "three great institutionary dinners in one week" (469), brings on the apoplectic death Tom Bertram has so easily prophesied. Dr. Grant's death, moreover, releases the Mansfield living "just after" Edmund and Fanny have "been married long enough to begin to want an increase of income, and feel their distance from the paternal abode an inconvenience" (473). It is apt that the Grants, who are seen as background figures, more deeply recessed than the principals, should participate as well in the neat interlocking of parts that creates the comic ending.

We have so far considered a world given us for recognition but an action that is ingeniously directed towards a comic ending. Clearly two kinds of recognition are involved; in the first case familiar customs, scenes, and institutions; in the second, familiar literary stereotypes and structures. We are never in serious doubt, as we read Jane Austen's novels, that they will take a comic form and find a bright resolution. There are countless indications of this as we read. They come from the narrative control, its brisk judgments and ironic asides, and the cool tone which in almost every case keeps us from that self-forgetful immersion in a scene that a literature of sentiment demands. There is only a small distance between a narrative voice that orders events pointedly, describing them in terms which are full of implicit judgment, and a voice that, becoming self-conscious, calls attention to the artifice of the whole narrative process. Even in so slight an effect as we see in the passage on the Grants, the whole game is cheerfully exposed: "Mrs. Norris could not speak with any temper of such grievances." Mrs. Norris is incapable of recognizing how she converts the Grants' ample consumption into an occasion for the exercise of her own aggressive self-righteousness. The splendor of "grievances" lies in its groundlessness and its consequent display of the energy with which Mrs. Norris's converting imagination shapes her world. Because the term "grievances" makes the conversion for Mrs. Norris, and without her consciousness, it calls our attention to a narrator who can so precisely fix the absurdity of obsession.

The comic frame of these novels allows us to pursue such irony with pleasure, to scrutinize the world they present with enough freedom to observe its incongruities as well as its implicit purposiveness. It is in manners that Jane Austen's world exhibits greatest density, for manners are concrete, complex orderings, both personal and institutional. They are a language of gestures, for words too become gestures when they are used to sustain rapport; most of our social ties are established in "speech acts" or "performative utterances." Such a language may become a self-sufficient system: polite questions that expect no answers, the small reciprocal duties of host and guest, or elder and younger; the protocol and management of deference. Such a code provides a way of formalizing conduct and of distancing feeling; we do not feel the less for giving that feeling an accepted form, which allows us to control its expression in shared rituals.

There is a striking instance of this control in *Emma*. All the company at Hartfield have been invited to spend an evening with the Westons at Randalls. John Knightley is outraged at the imposition:

> "here are we ... setting forward voluntarily, without excuse, in defiance of the voice of nature, which tells man, in every thing given to his view or his feelings, to stay at home himself, and keep all under shelter that he can;—here are we setting forward to spend five dull hours in another man's house, with nothing to say or to hear that was not said and heard yesterday, and may not be said and heard again tomorrow." (113)

In contrast we have the effusive Mr. Elton:

> "This is quite the season indeed for friendly meetings. At Christmas every body invites their friends about them, and people think little of even the worst weather. I was snowed up at a friend's house once for a week. Nothing could be pleasanter. I went for only one night, and could not get away till that very day se'nnight." (115)

We may shudder in behalf of Mr. Elton's friend and equally in behalf of John Knightley's hosts. But in fact both men must adjust to the social scene.

> Some change of countenance was necessary for each gentleman as they walked into Mrs. Weston's drawing-room;—Mr. Elton must compose his joyous looks, and Mr. John Knightley disperse his ill-humour. Mr. Elton must smile less, and Mr. John Knightley more, to fit them for the place.—Emma only might be as nature prompted, and shew herself just as happy as she was. To her, it was real enjoyment to be with the Westons. (117)

One could perhaps speak of John Knightley's initial regard for this society as "unregulated hatred," which undergoes regulation as he enters the drawing-room. His charges are undoubtedly accurate, and they are the kind of charge that Jane Austen often brings into her account of such occasions—"nothing to say or hear that was not said and heard yesterday, and may not be said and heard again tomorrow." Yet the standard of conversation upon such occasions need not be so demanding; clearly the warmth of having "friends about them" (in Mr. Elton's words) is sufficient for most, and the conversation of friends may be an occasion, above all, for recognition and reaffirmation, for pleasures that are only incidentally registered in the words spoken. "The happiest conversation," Dr. Johnson once remarked, "is that of which nothing is distinctly remembered but a general effect of pleasing impression"; and elsewhere he spoke of it as "a calm quiet interchange of sentiments."[4]

While manners may be a self-sufficient code, more a game than a system of signifiers, still at their most important they imply feelings and beliefs, moral attitudes which stand as their ultimate meaning and warrant. Both passion and principle are stable. When they change, the change is slow and massive. When they are in conflict, the conflict is sharp and convulsive. In the middle range, that of manners, change is frequent, less momentous, and less costly; we call it accommodation. To the extent that manners allow us to negotiate our claims with others, they become a system of behavior that restrains force and turns aggression into wit or some other gamelike form of combat.

So at least we may say of manners in the ideal sense. But Jane Austen's concern is not simply with good manners but with manners of all kinds, boorish, insolent, graceful, rigid, pompous, or easy. I would cite Lionel Trilling's well-known definition of manners as "a culture's hum and buzz of implication.... the whole evanescent context in which its explicit statements are made. It is that part of a culture which is made up of half-uttered or unuttered or unutterable expressions of value. They are hinted at by small actions, sometimes by the arts of dress or decoration, sometimes by tone, gesture, emphasis, or rhythm, sometimes by the words that are used with a special frequency or a special meaning."[5] Manners have, therefore, considerable suppleness and ambiguity. We may see in them a comic incongruity, a failure of behavior to realize intention, or a deliberate use of the conventions of courtesy to express cold distaste or angry resentment. We may find a conflict between the code of a society and the code of moral principle; and manners may become a code of socially acceptable immorality. The possibilities are, in fact, endless. Surely a central issue is the one that David Lodge has stated with admirable clarity:

> In brief, Jane Austen creates a world in which the social values which govern behaviour at Mansfield Park are highly prized ... but only when they are informed by some moral order of value which transcends the social....

A code of behaviour which demands such a delicate adjustment of social and moral values is by no means easy to live up to. It demands a constant state of watchfulness and self-awareness on the part of the individual, who must not only reconcile the two scales of value in personal decisions but, in the field of human relations, must contend with the fact that an attractive or unexceptionable social exterior can be deceptive.

Lodge provides us with two codes, one of terms that establish "an order of social or secular value" (e.g., agreeable, correct, fit, harmony, peace, regularity) and another of terms that suggest "a more moral or spiritual order of value" (e.g., conscience, duty, evil, principle, vice). The former code tends to assert "the submission of the individual to the group," the latter "the possibility of the individual having to go against the group." The two codes overlap; they are not "unambiguously distinguished or opposed," and they require, therefore, unremitting exercise of judgment.[6]

All of this is valuable, but one might wish to add another dimension to the scheme. There are times when personal feelings are sacrificed to both the moral and the social orders, when the moral order can itself become a refuge from self-awareness. To live entirely by principle, as Mrs. Norris persuades herself she does, or as Fanny Price in a quite different way would like to do, may be almost as destructive as to remain oblivious of a moral order. What seems most important to Jane Austen is a mind that has range and stretch, an unconstricted consciousness that can make significant choices. This is not to suggest that Jane Austen's characters must engage in vice to know its import, nor is it to deny that Fanny Price, even when she is all but imprisoned in fears of doing wrong, earns our sympathy. The most original and influential of recent critics of Jane Austen is Lionel Trilling, and he is never sharper than in his discussion of the "chief offence" of *Mansfield Park* for the modern reader:

> This lies ... in the affront it offers to an essential disposition of the modern mind, a settled and cherished habit of perception and judgement—our commitment to the dialectical mode of apprehending reality is outraged by the militant categorical certitude with which *Mansfield Park* discriminates between right and wrong. This disconcerts and discomfits us. It induces in us a species of anxiety. As how should it not? A work of art, notable for its complexity, devotes its energies, which we cannot doubt are of a very brilliant kind, to doing exactly the opposite of what we have learned to believe art ideally does and what we most love

it for doing, which is to confirm the dialectical mode and mitigate the constraints of the categorical. *Mansfield Park* ruthlessly rejects the dialectical mode and seeks to impose the categorical constraints the more firmly upon us.[7]

There is often a moment, recognized only in retrospect, when a great "offence" becomes a new orthodoxy. We may have reached a moment when moral rigor has a renewed attraction, even a romantic appeal; and it is not to question the praise *Mansfield Park* has been given to see it as a telling symbol of what we miss. The leech-gatherer of Wordsworth's poem appears on the moor just when the poet's delight has turned to despair, and the aged pedestrian has a meaning for the poet he hardly has for himself: "Such a figure, in such a place, a pious self-respecting, miserably infirm ... Old Man telling such a tale!"[8]

If we are to disencumber Jane Austen of the role of moralist, we must distinguish between moral assertion and moral imagination. Let me present an instance from *Sense and Sensibility*. Mrs. Ferrars, who is an imperious and vain mother, fond of her least worthy children, disinherits her son Edward when he announces his intention to marry Lucy Steele. But Lucy breaks the engagement in order to marry the new heir, his brother Robert, and frees Edward in turn to marry Elinor Dashwood, whom he genuinely loves. Edward turns to his mother for forgiveness:

> After a proper resistance on the part of Mrs. Ferrars, just so violent and so steady as to preserve her from that reproach which she always seemed fearful of incurring, the reproach of being too amiable, Edward was admitted to her presence, and pronounced to be again her son.
>
> Her family had of late been exceedingly fluctuating. For many years of her life she had had two sons; but the crime and annihilation of Edward a few weeks ago, had robbed her of one; the similar annihilation of Robert had left her for a fortnight without any; and now, by the resuscitation of Edward, she had one again.
>
> In spite of his being allowed once more to live, however, he did not feel the continuance of his existence secure, till he had revealed his present engagement; for the publication of that circumstance, he feared, might give a sudden turn to his constitution, and carry him off as rapidly as before. (373)

In the first of these sentences we see a mock-rationale such as alone can explain Mrs. Ferrars's behavior in any terms but willfulness. In the second paragraph, the irrational vigor of that will is caught in the fluctuating fortunes of her family, as members in turn suffer "annihilation" and "resuscitation." And finally this fiction of her godlike power to crush and restore is assumed with literal mock-solemnity. The comic energy expands in the course of the passage: Mrs. Ferrars's fantasies are recognized as her reality, as well they may be, since her will is matched by her power; and the narrative quietly accepts her vision, by a method that is akin to *erlebte Rede*.[9]

Clearly Jane Austen means us to see the tyranny and failure of love, but these are too obvious to demand our full attention; they are the substratum upon which the fantastic edifice of will is erected, and the elaboration of that edifice commands our wonder. Or to change the metaphor, we can see the singular tenacity with which character is sustained, the formidable genius of the passions to find pretexts and saving illusions or, somehow, at any rate, to generate an idiom of respectability. We can see this even more in the brilliant second chapter of the novel, where John and Fanny Dashwood collaborate in casuistry. They pare away his obligations to his sisters ("related to him only by half blood, which she considered as no relationship at all"). They magnify the value of what they might surrender ("How could he answer it to himself to rob his child, and his only child too, of so large a sum?"). They reduce the claims of others upon them ("They will be much more able to give *you* something"). And at last they cultivate resentment to dissolve any obligation to fulfill his father's request ("Your father thought only of *them*"). The projected settlement of three thousand pounds contracts at last to officious advice and (perhaps) an occasional small gift. What is dazzling is not the selfishness of the Dashwoods, formidable as that is, but the brilliant efficiency and ease of their self-justification.

It is here that one sees Jane Austen's moral imagination shaping comic invention, as it so often had in Henry Fielding before her. For the progressive contraction of the Dashwoods' spirit is caught with that splendid assurance of movement we can see in Lady Booby's resolution to call back Joseph Andrews once she has dismissed him. The movement defeats all scruple, and in the case of the Dashwoods it overthrows each scruple with a show of splendid moral righteousness as well.

It is by such deftness that one can best identify comic movement. It eludes scruple just as it eludes physical obstacles; the comic decision has much in common with the comic chase in films; there is the same miraculous evasion of every blocking force, whether the strictures of reason or the traffic ahead. In the comic hero such movement becomes the deft avoidance of threatening intrigues, of blocking elders, of false rigidities and narrow conventions. In such fools as the Dashwoods or Mrs. Ferrars, the deftness lies not in their consciousness but in their passion; and what it eludes is not a false restriction but the censorship of decency. So of Lucy Steele, the author writes that her intrigue and its success "may be held forth as a most encouraging instance of what an earnest, an unceasing attention to self-interest, however its progress may be apparently obstructed, will do in securing every advantage of fortune, with no other sacrifice than that of time and conscience" (376).

It may, of course, be said that Jane Austen uses her comic celebration of ingenious villainy as a way of insisting all the more, through ironic understatement, upon its evil. The hard egoism that makes these characters imperturbable provides a striking contrast to the vulnerability and pathos that both Elinor and Marianne at times exhibit. The moral insight which the irony evokes and reinforces lives deep in the conception of the novel and informs all its parts; yet the insight is not what the novel seeks to create but rather that upon which it draws. Such comic characters as the John Dashwoods may be morally discredited, but they survive admirably. The novel rests not upon their satiric exposure but their comic performance.

There is an element of pathos in a comic bore like Miss Bates in *Emma*. Her compulsive talking only awakens us to the narrow life that finds its fulfillment in this kind of release. We need not keep in focus the emptiness that finds vicarious existence in gossip or the ardor for attachment that intensifies and distends each minute detail of commonplace encounters. In short, our sense of all that displaced feeling that floods into silly words does not overweigh the impression of their silliness, nor does our sense of motive distract our attention from the resourcefulness of the motive power, the alacrity with which all experience is translated into an obsessive idiom. We retain enough comic detachment for the most part to regard Miss Bates with amusement, and it is significant that our own surprise at her modest expression of pain after Emma's insult marks a shift in our awareness of Miss Bates somewhat as, through Knightley's comments, it marks an epoch in Emma's "developement of self" (409).

For those who are themselves self-absorbed, such bores as Miss Bates may become very irksome. The attention they fail to give makes the attention they demand all the more troubling. Screened from others by their volubility, needing only the pretext of an audience, they yield little of what one feels is owed one, and for one with claims so large as Emma's, they represent a peculiar affront. So that we find Emma chafing under the strain, while Knightley is sufficiently his own man to be detached and liberal: he can endure the nonsense, see the pathos and warmth, and recollect above all the duties of consideration.

Miss Bates is a special case of the bores and fools we find throughout Jane Austen's novels. Some are aggressively sociable, like Sir John Middleton, others archly prying like his mother-in-law, Mrs. Jennings; some pretentious and alternately servile or smug like Collins, some oppressively rude and patronizing like Augusta Elton. The one trait they all share is deficiency of awareness, indifference to others' feelings or privacy, obtuseness about their own motives. They tend to be great talkers, talking not so much for victory, like Dr. Johnson, as for survival; they retain their stable existence, their life of untroubled repetition, by blocking off reality with talk.

The comic limitations remain in those characters who are at once more plausible and treacherous. They seem, at first, to be of the very spirit of comedy themselves, for they are dedicated to play. And they help to remind us that Jane Austen's novels have themselves provided the materials of a game for those readers who are sometimes called Janeites. Games have every charm until they are used to displace broader awareness and deeper feelings. It is this quality we see in such figures as Frank Churchill or the Crawfords. Frank has "smooth, plausible manners," but he wins Mr. Knightley's criticism, even before he arrives, for his failure to visit his father. Knightley's words are like the more peremptory moral assertions that Jane Austen herself adopts at times. Of Tom Bertram she writes, at the close of *Mansfield Park*, "He became what he ought to be, useful to his father, steady and quiet, and not living merely for himself" (462). So in *Emma*, she writes of Mrs. Weston: "She was happy, she knew she was happy, and knew she ought to be happy" (304). Knightley speaks in similar vein about Frank Churchill:

> "There is one thing, Emma, which a man can always do, if he chuses, and that is, his duty; not by manoeuvring and finessing, but by vigour and resolution. It is Frank Churchill's duty to pay this attention to his father. He knows it to be so, by his promises and messages; but if he wished to do it, it might be done." (146)

Frank Churchill is essentially a young man who cannot resist "manoeuvring and finessing." His love of games comes out in his readiness to foster Emma's unpleasant conjectures about Jane. Frank knows the truth and cannot reveal it; but he gains enormous pleasure from helping Emma to imagine scandal that permits her the comfort of superiority to Jane. Frank in turn can enjoy his superiority to Emma: he is playing a game of his own in which she participates unknowingly and to her ultimate shame. Even if we credit his belief that Emma has guessed the truth, the game he thinks he is playing with Emma and the game she, in her ignorance, thinks she is playing with him (the complication is deliberate) are both of them little less shameful than the actual ones, and we see their culmination at Box Hill. In fact, Knightley sees in Frank's professed belief a further sign of his disingenuousness:

> "Always deceived in fact by his own wishes, and regardless of little besides his own convenience.—Fancying you to have fathomed his secret. Natural enough!—his own mind full of intrigue, that he should suspect it in others.—Mystery; Finesse— how they pervert the understanding! My Emma, does not every thing serve to prove more and more the beauty of truth and sincerity in all our dealings with each other?"   (445–46)

Emma, in her recovery, recognizes Frank's motives as her own: "I am sure it was a source of high entertainment to you, to feel that you were taking us all in.... I think there is a little likeness between us." But what most distinguishes Frank from Emma is his reluctance to give up the game. As he dwells lovingly upon his memories of others' deception, Jane says "in a conscious, low, but steady voice, 'How you can bear such recollections, is astonishing to me!— They will sometimes obtrude—but how you can court them!'" (478, 480).

Frank Churchill's games strike us as immature; they are games of exclusion and superiority. Henry Crawford's games are a more radical part of his nature, and far more painful in their consequences. As he is first introduced in *Mansfield Park* we learn of his light-hearted intention to make the Bertram sisters like him. "He did not want them to die of love; but with sense and temper which ought to have made him judge and feel better, he allowed himself great latitude on such points" (45). The Bertram sisters are "an amusement to his sated mind," but one feels that the satiation is as much with himself as with pleasures. Henry's love of role-playing seems a search, for distraction, from a self he indulges but hardly respects. The accounts that William gives of naval service fire Henry's fancy: the "glory of heroism, of usefulness, of exertion, of endurance, made his own habits of selfish indulgence appear in shameful contrast" (236). And later with Edmund he imagines himself a clergyman preaching, only to recognize shrewdly enough his need to exercise power over an audience and to coerce an eager response. But it is significant that Henry reveals his unsteadiness and does so with no cynical pleasure. Fanny, once he has planned to win her heart, awakens in him a deeper purpose.

Henry has "moral taste enough" to respond to her sensibility and her capacity for feeling. His decision to make her his wife is in some sense what Shaftesbury saw in the awakening of taste, the beginning of an ascent from the aesthetic to the moral, from gallantry to a love of the Good.[10] These are somewhat ample terms to bring to this text, but it seems clear that Henry Crawford would wish to be saved from a self that wearies him and to find a new order of life in marriage to Fanny. He had, we are told with severe irony, "too much sense not to feel the worth of good principles in a wife, though he was too little accustomed to serious reflection to know them by their proper name"; and so, in his praise of her firmness of character, he unknowingly "expressed what was inspired by the knowledge of her being well principled and religious" (294). There is considerable subtlety in this identification of an attraction that Henry Crawford feels but cannot recognize. His relapse is a failure not of consciousness but of will: "the temptation of immediate pleasure was too strong for a mind unused to make any sacrifice to right" (467). Henry acts as he does with no love for Maria, and "without the smallest inconstancy of mind" towards Fanny, the one woman "whom he had rationally, as well as passionately loved" (468, 469).

Henry Crawford's relapse is more interesting and moving than his sister's self-betrayal. Throughout the novel, Mary carries herself with great style, if not always with delicacy. She accepts her own outrageousness disarmingly: "Selfishness must always be forgiven you know, because there is no hope of a cure," or, "Nothing ever fatigues me, but doing what I do not like." In a world of hypocrisy and inhibition, this seems fresh and natural, except of course that it also seems calculated to gain its end. She is insincere only in assuming that sincerity alone—and it is often courageous—will acquit her. Her sincerity loses its spontaneity as we hear it too often, and it vanishes altogether in the painful exposure of that last "saucy playful smile," which seems held by the text as in a frozen film sequence, its futility turning to grimace.

There is a troubling moment at the close of *Mansfield Park*. Edmund has seen Mary's limitations and avowedly rejected her, but Fanny can see that the choice is not yet a firm resolve. At that moment, as if to administer a dose of truth that will cure or kill, Fanny tells him that the prospect of his brother's death and of his own inheritance may have restored him to eligibility in Mary's eyes (459). It is a cruel revelation but perhaps a necessary one. Edmund is seldom seen without irony during the later part of the book, and it is appropriate that by demanding Fanny as a confidante of his grief, he find himself in love with her. "She was of course only too good for him; but as nobody minds having what is too good for them, he was very steadily earnest in pursuit of the blessing" (471). As for Fanny herself, she "must have been a happy creature in spite of all that she felt or thought she felt, for the distress of those around her" (461).

The larger irony that informs all of Jane Austen's comic art is a sense of human limitation. This is not a cynical vision; it may be affectionate enough, even a tribute to those feelings we value warmly. In *Sense and Sensibility* Elinor and Edward wait impatiently for the parsonage to be refurbished in time for their marriage: "after experiencing, as usual, a thousand disappointments and delays, from the unaccountable dilatoriness of the workmen, Elinor, as usual, broke through the first positive resolution of not marrying till every thing was ready" (374). The use of "as usual" catches the typicality both of their situation and of Elinor's decision. That they sense their situation as unique is equally clear; they are understandably self-absorbed and impatient with workmen who seem, through some strange indifference, "unaccountably" dilatory. There is gentle amusement with the irrationality, so little typical of Elinor but so generally typical of brides. One is reminded of Gibbon's account of his parents' marriage: "Such is the beginning of a love tale at Babylon or at Putney," or even more of his account of his own coming to an awareness of love: "it less properly belongs to the memoirs of an individual than to the natural history of the species."

Jane Austen constantly insists upon the limitations of our feelings. Does Henry Tilney love Catherine Morland? Yes, but the narrator "must confess that his affection originated in nothing better than gratitude; or, in other words, that a persuasion of her partiality for him had been the only cause of giving her a serious thought. It is a new circumstance in romance ... and dreadfully derogatory of an heroine's dignity" (243). Is Willoughby a rake? No, he genuinely loves Marianne. "But that he was for ever inconsolable, that he fled from society, or contracted an habitual gloom of temper, or died of a broken heart, must not be depended on—for he did neither. He lived to exert, and frequently to enjoy himself" (379). So, too, Henry Crawford might well have won Fanny Price's love, for "her influence over him had already given him some influence over her" (467). And Colonel Brandon wins all of Marianne's love in time, for Marianne "could never love by halves" (379). The endings of the novels insist upon the capacity for self-repair and recovery; they provide the consolation of the finite for those who are easily deluded. Mrs. Grant's words to Mary Crawford on marriage are apt:

> "You see the evil, but you do not see the consolation. There will
> be little rubs and disappointments every where, and we are all apt

to expect too much; but then, if one scheme of happiness fails, human nature turns to another; if the first calculation is wrong, we make a second better; we find comfort somewhere." (46)

"I purposely abstain from dates," we read at the close of *Mansfield* Park, "that every one may be at liberty to fix their own, aware that the cure of unconquerable passions, and the transfer of unchanging attachments, must vary much as to time in different people.—I only intreat every body to believe that exactly at the time when it was quite natural that it should be so, and not a week earlier, Edmund did cease to care about Miss Crawford, and became as anxious to marry Fanny, as Fanny herself could desire" (470).

This pleasure in human absurdity gives us, in Charles Lamb's words, "all that neutral ground of character, which stood between vice and virtue; or which in fact was indifferent to neither, where neither properly was called in question; that happy breathing place from the burthen of a perpetual moral questioning"; it allows us to "take an airing beyond the diocese of the strict conscience."[11] It is one thing to see men and women as fallible, another to insist that they are corrigible. If nature can be trusted to correct what men cannot, if man is never quite so good or so evil as he intends or imagines, we are freed of the stringency of the moral passions, which, as Lionel Trilling has remarked, can be "even more willful and imperious and impatient than the self-seeking passions." Our moral judgments are at once necessary and dangerous; they exercise our deepest passions, but they terminate our free awareness. The commitment they require brings an end to exploration and openness. In that sense, among others, the moral passions are "not only liberating, but also restrictive," and "moral realism," as opposed to passions, is "the perception of the dangers of the moral life itself."[12] It is the sense of the problematic that we must preserve, a sense of the difficulty of such judgments, of their cost and of the dubious gratification they often provide.

The comic sense is compatible with moral imagination if not moral passion; its awareness of limitation need not provide a surrender of all judgment, and in fact the idea of limitation is itself a judgment. Yet it is also a recognition that the moral passions cannot trespass beyond certain limits. The effort to sustain moral consciousness at the same level of intensity in all our experience becomes a form of destructive anxiety. We may sense the consequences of the imperceptible choice and insist upon the fact of choice; yet we cannot always be bringing scruple and moral anxiety to each gesture of our lives or even, easier though it may prove, of the lives of others. There is at last a residual innocence we must grant to experience, a power to absorb us, to awaken curiosity, to claim our attention and affections with simple immediacy. We can see this best in the detached and free observation a busy mind like Emma's can achieve on the village street:

> Harriet, tempted by every thing and swayed by half a word, was always very long at a purchase; and while she was still hanging over muslins and changing her mind, Emma went to the door for amusement.—Much could not be hoped from the traffic of even the busiest part of Highbury;—Mr. Perry walking hastily by, Mr. William Cox letting himself in at the office door, Mr. Cole's carriage horses returning from exercise, or a stray letter-boy on an obstinate mule, were the liveliest objects she could presume to expect; and when her eyes fell only on the butcher with his tray, a tidy old woman travelling homewards from shop with her full basket, two curs quarrelling over a dirty bone, and a string of dawdling children round the baker's little bow-window eyeing the gingerbread, she knew she had no reason to complain, and was amused enough; quite enough still to stand at the door. A mind lively and at ease, can do with seeing nothing, and can see nothing that does not answer. (233)

It is not often, however, that we find Emma's mind both "lively" and "at ease." Its liveliness is usually a form of "eagerness" or self-assertion, such as we find in different ways in Marianne Dashwood or in Mary Crawford, to whom Edmund Bertram would grant the "rights of a lively mind." This "eagerness" betrays impatience with the limits of the actual: it may take the form of a wishful shaping of reality with self-gratifying fantasy or (in the case of Mary) more deliberate cultivation of outrageous assertions as much for their effect as for their partial truth. Those who are fully "at ease" may achieve something of what Wordsworth celebrated as a "wise passiveness," that is, an openness to experience that restrains the shaping will and allows oneself to be confronted by whatever is unpredictably there. We may see this receptiveness as opposed to both the moral passions and the self-seeking passions, for in both we find a closing of the mind to the variety of experience, an assumption of superiority, whether in the name of principle or in the name of wit. Marianne's impatience with the vulgarity of Mrs. Jennings, Mary Crawford's impatience with the dull conventionalities of the pious, and Emma's impatience with Miss Bates have this much in common.

Once Emma has been reproached by Mr. Knightley for being so "unfeeling" and "insolent" in her wit, she begins to be freed of the force of self-seeking passions and to undergo a true "developement of self." By the time she is ready to receive Knightley's proposal, she has achieved something like the receptiveness Wordsworth celebrated: "Never had the exquisite sight, smell, sensation of nature, tranquil, warm, and brilliant after a storm, been more attractive to her. She longed for the serenity they might gradually introduce" (424). Not the least significant word in that passage is "gradually." We think of Anne Elliot's walk to Winthrop: "where the ploughs at work, and the fresh-made path spoke the farmer, counteracting the sweets of poetical despondence, and meaning to have spring again" (85).

Notes

1. Ludwig Wittgenstein, *Zettel*, ed. G. E. M. Anscombe and G. H. von Wright (Berkeley: Univ. of California Press, 1970), para. 241–42.

2. The phrase is from David Lodge, *Language of Fiction* (New York: Columbia Univ. Press, 1966), p. 99. See also Norman Page, *The Language of Jane Austen* (Oxford: Blackwell, 1972).

3. *Sense and Sensibility*, p. 175. References to the novels, hereafter placed in the text, are to *The Novels of Jane Austen*, ed. R. W. Chapman, 3rd ed. (London: Oxford Univ. Press, 1932–34).

4. *Boswell's Life of Johnson*, ed. G. B. Hill, rev. L. F. Powell, 6 vols. (Oxford: Clarendon Press, 1934–50), IV, 50; II, 359. Cf. *Northanger Abbey*: "Though in all probability not an observation was made, nor an expression used by either which had not been made and used some thousands of times before, under that roof, in every Bath season, yet the merit of their being spoken with simplicity and truth, and without personal conceit, might be something uncommon" (p. 72).

5. "Manners, Morals, and the Novel," in *The Liberal Imagination* (New York: Viking, 1950), pp. 206–7.

6. Lodge, pp. 101–4.

7. *Sincerity and Authenticity* (Cambridge, Mass.: Harvard Univ. Press, 1972), p. 79.

8. Wordsworth to Sara Hutchinson, 14 June 1802, *The Early Letters of William and Dorothy Wordsworth*, ed. Ernest de Selincourt (New York: Oxford Univ. Press, 1935), p. 306.

9. On Jane Austen's use of *erlebte Rede* or "free indirect discourse," see Norman Page, pp. 123 ff.

10. On Jane Austen and Shaftesbury, see Gilbert Ryle, "Jane Austen and the Moralists," in *Critical Essays on Jane Austen*, ed. B. C. Southam (London: Routledge and Kegan Paul, 1968), pp. 106–22. I have dealt with aesthetic and moral taste in Shaftesbury in *To the Palace of Wisdom* (New York: Doubleday, 1964), ch. 3.

11. "On the Artificial Comedy of the Last Century," *The Works of Charles and Mary Lamb*, ed. E. V. Lucas (London: Methuen, 1903), II, 142.

12. "Manners, Morals, and the Novel," in *The Liberal Imagination*, pp. 219–22; and see also the essay in that volume on Henry James's *The Princess Casamassima*, pp. 58–92. I trust it will be clear throughout that I am not taking issue with Lionel Trilling's own discussion of Jane Austen but with critics of less subtle and dialectical mind who have given her work high seriousness of the wrong kind.

SANDRA M. GILBERT AND SUSAN GUBAR

Shut Up in Prose: Gender and Genre in Austen's Juvenilia

"Run mad as often as you chose; but do not faint—"
—Sophia to Laura, *Love and Freindship*

They shut me up in Prose—
As when a little Girl
They put me in the Closet—
Because they liked me "still"—

—Emily Dickinson

Can you be more confusing by laughing. Do say yes. We
are extra. We have the reasonableness of a woman and
we say we do not like a room. We wish we were married.
—Gertrude Stein

She is twelve years old and already her story is written in
the heavens. She will discover it day after day without
ever making it; she is curious but frightened when she
contemplates this life, every stage of which is foreseen
and toward which every day moves irresistibly.
—Simone de Beauvoir

Not a few of Jane Austen's personal acquaintans might have echoed Sir
Samuel Egerton Brydges, who noticed that "she was fair and handsome,
slight and elegant, but with cheeks a little too full," while "never suspect[ing]

she was an authoress."[1] For this novelist whose personal obscurity was more complete than that of any other famous writer was always quick to insist either on complete anonymity or on the propriety of her limited craft, her delight in delineating just "3 or 4 Families in a Country Village."[2] With her self-deprecatory remarks about her inability to join "strong manly, spirited sketches, full of Variety and Glow" with her "little bit (two Inches wide) of Ivory,"[3] Jane Austen perpetuated the belief among her friends that her art was just an accomplishment "by a lady," if anything "rather too light and bright and sparkling."[4] In this respect she resembled one of her favorite contemporaries, Mary Brunton, who would rather have "glid[ed] through the world unknown" than been "suspected of literary airs—to be shunned, as literary women are, by the more pretending of their own sex, and abhorred, as literary women are, by the more pretending of the other!—my dear, I would sooner exhibit as a ropedancer."[5]

Yet, decorous though they might first seem, Austen's self-effacing anonymity and her modest description of her miniaturist art also imply a criticism, even a rejection, of the world at large. For, as Gaston Bachelard explains, the miniature "allows us to be world conscious at slight risk."[6] While the creators of satirically conceived diminutive landscapes seem to see everything as small because they are themselves so grand, Austen's analogy for her art—her "little bit (two Inches wide) of Ivory"—suggests a fragility that reminds us of the risk and instability outside the fictional space. Besides seeing her art metaphorically, as her critics would too, in relation to female arts severely devalued until quite recently[7] (for painting on ivory was traditionally a "ladylike" occupation), Austen attempted through self-imposed novelistic limitations to define a secure place, even as she seemed to admit the impossibility of actually inhabiting such a small space with any degree of comfort. And always, for Austen, it is women—because they are too vulnerable in the world at large—who must acquiesce in their own confinement, no matter how stifling it may be.

But it is precisely to the limits of her art that Austen's most vocal critics have always responded, with both praise and blame. The tone is set by the curiously backhanded compliments of Sir Walter Scott, who compares her novels to "cornfields and cottages and meadows," as opposed to "highly adorned grounds" or "the rugged sublimities of a mountain landscape." The pleasure of such fiction is, he explains, such that "the youthful wanderer may return from his promenade to the ordinary business of life, without any chance of having his head turned by the recollection of the scene through which he has been wandering."[8] In other words, the novels are so unassuming that they can be easily forgotten. Mundane (like cornfields) and small (like cottages) and tame (like meadows), they wear the "commonplace face" Charlotte Brontë found in *Pride and Prejudice*, a novel Brontë scornfully describes as "a carefully fenced, highly cultivated garden, with neat borders and delicate flowers; but no glance of a bright, vivid physiognomy, no open country, no fresh air, no blue hill, no bonny beck."[9]

Spatial images of boundary and enclosure seem to proliferate whenever we find writers coming to terms with Jane Austen, as if they were displaying their own anxieties about what she represents. Edward Fitzgerald's comment—"She is capital as far as she goes: but she never goes out of the Parlour"—is a classic in this respect, as is Elizabeth Barrett Browning's breezy characterization of the novels as "perfect as far as they go—that's certain. Only they don't go far, I think."[10] It is hardly surprising that Emerson is "at a loss to understand why people hold Miss Austen's novels at so high a rate," horrified as he is by what he considers the trivializing domesticity and diminution of her fiction:

> ... vulgar in tone, sterile in artistic invention, imprisoned in the wretched conventions of English society, without genius, wit, or knowledge of the world. Never was life so pinched and narrow. The one problem in the mind of the writer in both the stories I have read, *Persuasion*, and *Pride and Prejudice*, is marriageableness. All that interests in any character introduced is still this one, Has he or (she) the money to marry with, and conditions, conforming? 'Tis "the nympholepsy of a fond despair," say, rather, of an English boarding-house. Suicide is more respectable.[11]

But the conventionally masculine judgment of Austen's triviality is probably best illustrated by Mark Twain, who cannot even bring himself to spell her name correctly in a letter to Howells, her staunchest American defender: Poe's "prose," he notes, "is unreadable—like Jane Austin's," adding that there is one difference: "I could read his prose on salary, but not Jane's. Jane is entirely impossible. It seems a great pity that they allowed her to die a natural death."[12] Certainly D.H. Lawrence expresses similar hostility for the lady writer in his attack on Austen as "this old maid" who "typifies 'personality' instead of character, the sharp knowing in apartness instead of knowing in togetherness, and she is, to my feeling, thoroughly unpleasant, English in the bad, mean, snobbish sense of the word."[13]

Repeatedly, in other words, Austen was placed in the double bind she would so convincingly dramatize in her novels, for when not rejected as artificial and convention-bound, she was condemned as natural and therefore a writer almost in spite of herself. Imagining her as "the brown thrush who tells his story from the garden bough," Henry James describes Austen's "light felicity," her "extraordinary grace," as a sign of "her unconsciousness":

> ... as if ... she sometimes, over her work basket, her tapestry flowers, in the spare, cool drawing-room of other days, feel a-musing, lapsed too metaphorically, as one may say, into wool gathering, and her dropped stitches, of these pardonable, of these precious moments, were afterwards picked up as little touches of human truth, little glimpses of steady vision, little master-strokes of imagination.[14]

A stereotypical "lady" author, Austen is here diminished into a small personage whose domestic productions result in artistic creation not through the exacting craft by which the male author weaves the intricate figures in his own carpets, but through fortuitous forgetfulness on the part of the lady (who drops her stitches unthinkingly) and through the presumably male critical establishment that picks them up afterwards to view them as charming miniatures of imaginative activity. The entire passage radiates James's anxiety at his own indebtedness to this "little" female precursor who, to his embarrassment, taught him so much of this presumably masterful art. Indeed, in a story that examines Austen's curious effect on men and her usefulness in male culture, Rudyard Kipling has one of his more pugnacious characters insist that Jane Austen "did leave lawful issue in the shape o' one son; an' 'is name was 'Enery James."[15]

In "The Janeites" Kipling presents several veterans from World War I listening to a shell-shocked ex-Garrison Artillery man, Humberstall, recount his experiences on the Somme Front, where he had unexpectedly discovered a secret unit of Austen fans who call themselves the Society of the Janeites. Despite the seeming discrepancy between Austen's decorously "feminine" parlor and the violent, "masculine" war, the officers analyze the significance of their restricting ranks and roles much as Austen analyzes the meaning of her characters' limiting social positions. Not only does Humberstall discover that Austen's characters are "only just like people you'd run across any day," he also knows that "They're all on the make, in a quiet way, in Jane." He is not surprised, therefore, when the whole company is blown to pieces by one man's addlepated adherence to a code: as his naming of the guns after Austen's "heavies" demonstrates, the ego that creates all the problems for her characters is the same ego that shoots Kipling's guns. Paradoxically, moreover, the firings of "General Tilney" and "The Lady Catherine de

Bugg" also seem to point our attention to the explosive anger behind the decorous surfaces of Austen's novels, although the men in the trenches find in the Austen guns the symbol of what they think they are fighting for.

Using Austen the same way American servicemen might have exploited pin-up girls, the Society of Janeites transforms their heroine into a nostalgic symbol of order, culture, England, in an apocalyptic world where all the old gods have failed or disappeared. But Austen is adapted when adopted for use by masculine society, and she functions to perpetuate the male bonding and violence she would herself have deplored. Clearly Kipling is involved in ridiculing the formation of religious sects or cults, specifically the historical Janeites who sanctified Austen into the apotheosis of propriety and elegance, of what Ann Douglas has called in a somewhat different context the "feminization" of culture. But Kipling implies that so-called feminization is a male-dominated process inflicted upon women. And in this respect he illustrates how Austen has herself become a victim of the fictionalizing process we will see her acknowledging as women's basic problem in her own fiction.

Not only a parody of what male culture has made of the cult of Jane, however, "The Janeites" is also a tribute to Austen, who justifies her deification as the patron saint of the officers by furnishing Humberstall with what turns out to be a password that literally saves his life by getting him a place on a hospital train. By pronouncing the name "Miss Bates," Humberstall miraculously survives circumstances as inauspicious as those endured by Miss Bates herself, a spinster in Emma whose physical, economic, and social confinement is only mitigated by her good humor. Certainly Humberstall's special fondness for Persuasion—which celebrates Captain Harville's "ingenious contrivances and nice arrangements ... to turn the actual space to the best possible account"[16]—is not unrelated to his appreciation of Austen herself: "There's no one to touch Jane when you're in a tight place." From Austen, then, Humberstall and his companions have gained not only an analysis of social conventions that helps make sense of their own constricted lives, but also an example of how to inhabit a small space with grace and intelligence.

It is eminently appropriate that the Army Janeites try to survive by making the best of a bad situation, accepting their tight place and digging in behind the camouflage-screens they have constructed around their trenches. While their position is finally given away, their attitude is worthy of the writer who concerns herself almost exclusively with characters inhabiting the common sitting room. Critical disparagement of the triviality of this place is related to values that find war or business somehow qualitatively more "real" or "significant" than, for example, the politics of the family.[17] But critics who patronize or castigate Austen for her acceptance of limits and boundaries are overlooking a subversive strain in even her earliest stories: Austen's courageous "grace under pressure" is not only a refuge from a dangerous reality, it is also a comment on it, as W. H. Auden implied:

> You could not shock her more than she shocks me;
>   Beside her Joyce seems innocent as grass.
> It makes me most uncomfortable to see
>   An English spinster of the middle class
>   Describe the amorous effects of "brass,"
> Reveal so frankly and with such sobriety
> The economic basis of society.[18]

Although she has become a symbol of culture, it is shocking how persistently Austen demonstrates her discomfort with her cultural inheritance, specifically her dissatisfaction with the tight place assigned women in patriarchy and her analysis of the economics of sexual exploitation. At the same time, however, she knows from the beginning of her career that there is no other place for her but a tight one, and her parodic strategy is itself a testimony to her struggle with inadequate but inescapable structures. If, like Scott and Brontë, Emerson and James, we continue to see her world as narrow or trivial, perhaps we can learn from Humberstall that "there's no one to touch Jane when you're in a tight place." Since this tight place is both literary and social, we will begin with the parodic juvenilia and then consider "the amorous effects of 'brass'" in *Northanger Abbey* to trace how and why Austen is centrally concerned with the impossibility of women escaping the conventions and categories that, in every sense, belittle them.

Jane Austen has always been famous for fireside scenes in which several characters comfortably and quietly discuss options so seemingly trivial that it is astonishing when they are transformed into important ethical dilemmas. There is always a feeling, too, that we owe to her narrator's art the significance with which such scenes are invested: she seemed to know about the burdens of banality and the resulting pressure to subject even the smallest gestures to close analysis. A family in *Love and Freindship* (1790) sit by the fireplace in their "cot" when they hear a knock on the door:

> My Father started—"What noise is that," (said he.) "It sounds like a loud rapping at the door"—(replied my Mother.) "it does indeed." (cried I.) "I am of your opinion; (said my Father) it

certainly does appear to proceed from some uncommon violence exerted against our unoffending door." "Yes (exclaimed I) I cannot help thinking it must be somebody who knocks for admittance."

"That is another point (replied he;) we must not pretend to determine on what motive the person may knock—tho' that someone *does* rap at the door, I am partly convinced."[19]

Clearly this discursive speculation on the knocking at the door ridicules the propensity of sentimental novelists to record even the most exasperatingly trivial events, but it simultaneously demonstrates the common female ennui at having to maintain polite conversation while waiting for a prince to come. In other words, such juvenilia is important not only because in this early work Austen ridicules the false literary conventions that debase expression, thereby dangerously falsifying expectations, especially for female readers, but also because she reveals here her awareness that such conventions have inalterably shaped women's lives. For Jane Austen's parody of extravagant literary conventions turns on the culture that makes women continually vulnerable to such fantasies.

Laura of *Love and Freindship* is understandably frustrated by the banal confinement of the fireside scene: "Alas," she laments, "how am I to avoid those evils I shall never be exposed to?" Because she is allowed to pursue those evils with indecorous abandon, *Love and Freindship* is a good place to begin to understand attitudes more fully dramatized there than elsewhere in Austen's fiction. With a singular lack of the "infallible discretion"[20] for which it would later become famous, Austen's adolescent fiction includes a larger "slice of life" than we might at first expect: thievery and drunkenness, matricide and patricide, adultery and madness are common subjects. Moreover, the parodic melodrama of this fiction unfolds through hectic geographical maneuverings, particularly through female escapes and escapades quite unlike those that appear in the mature novels.

Laura, for instance, elopes with a stranger upon whom, she immediately decides, the happiness or misery of her future life depends. From her humble cottage in the vale of Uske, she travels to visit Edward's aunt in Middlesex, but she must leave immediately after Edward boasts to his father of his pride in provoking that parent's displeasure by marrying without his consent. Running off in Edward's father's carriage, the happy couple meet up with Sophia and Augustus at "M," but they are forced to remove themselves quickly when Augustus is arrested for having "gracefully purloined" his father's money. Alone in the world, after taking turns fainting on the sofa, the two girls set out for London but end up in Scotland, where they successfully encourage a young female relative to elope to Gretna Green. Thrown out in punishment for this bad advice, Laura and Sophia meet up with their dying husbands, naturally in a phaeton crash. Sophia is fittingly taken off by a galloping consumption, while Laura proceeds by a stagecoach in which she is reunited with her husband's long-lost family who have been traveling back and forth from Sterling to Edinburgh for reasons that are far too complicated and ridiculous to relate here.

Of course her contrivance of such a zany picaresque does not contradict Austen's later insistence on the limits of her artistic province, since the point of her parody is precisely to illustrate the dangerous delusiveness of fiction which seriously presents heroines like Laura (and stories like *Love and Freindship*) as models of reality. While ridiculing ludicrous literary conventions, Austen also implies that romantic stories create absurd misconceptions. Such novelistic clichés as love at first sight, the primacy of passion over all other emotions and/or duties, the chivalric exploits of the hero, the vulnerable sensitivity of the heroine, the lovers' proclaimed indifference to financial considerations, and the cruel crudity of parents are all shown to be at best improbable; at worst they are shown to provide manipulative roles and hypocritical jargon which mask materialistic and libidinal egoism.

Living lives regulated by the rules provided by popular fiction, these characters prove only how very bankrupt that fiction is. For while Laura and Sophia proclaim their delicate feelings, tender sentiments, and refined sensibilities, they are in fact having a delightful time gratifying their desires at the expense of everyone else's. Austen's critique of the ethical effects of such literature is matched by her insistence on its basic falsity: adventure, intrigue, crime, passion, and death arrive with such intensity, in such abundance, and with such rapidity that they lose all reality. Surely they are just the hectic daydreams of an imagination infected by too many Emmelines and Emilias.[21] The extensive itinerary of a heroine like Laura is the most dramatic clue that her story is mere wish-fulfillment, one especially attractive to women who live at home confined to the domestic sphere, as do such heroines of Austen's nonparodic juvenilia as Emma Watson of *The Watsons* and Catharine of the early fiction "Catharine."

Significantly, however, Emma Watson and Catharine are both avid readers of romance, just as Austen herself was clearly one of those young women whose imagination had, in fact, been inalterably affected by all the escapist literature provided them, then as now. Not the least of the curious effects of *Love and Freindship* results from the contradiction between the narrator's insistent ridicule of her heroines and their liveliness, their general willingness to get on with it and catch the next coach. Laura and Sophia are really quite attractive in their exuberant assertiveness, their exploration and exploitation of the world, their curiously honest expression of their needs, their rebellious rejection of their fathers' advice, their demands for autonomy, their sense of the significance and drama of their lives and adventures, their gullible delight in playing out the plots they have admired. The girls' rebellion against familial restraints seems to have so fascinated Austen that she reiterates it almost obsessively in *Love and Freindship*, and again in a hilarious letter when she takes on the persona of an anonymous female correspondent who cheerfully explains, "I murdered my Father at a very early period of my Life, I have since murdered my Mother, and I am now going to murder my Sister."[22] The matricides and patricides make such characters seem much more exuberantly alive than their sensible, slow-witted, dying parents. It is this covert counterpoint that makes suspicious the overt "moral" of *Love and Freindship*, suggesting that though Austen appears to be operating in a repressive tradition, many of her generic moral signals are merely convenient camouflage.

At first glance, Sophia and Laura seem related to a common type in eighteenth-century literature. Like Biddy Tipkins of Steele's *The Tender Husband*, Coleman's *Polly Honeycombe*, and Lydia Languish of Sheridan's *The Rivals*, for instance, these girls are filled with outlandish fancies derived from their readings in the circulating library. Illustrating the dangers of feminine lawlessness and the necessity of female submission, female quixotes of eighteenth-century fiction typically exemplify the evils of romantic fiction and female assertion. The abundance of such heroines in her juvenilia would seem to place Austen in precisely the tradition Ellen Moers has recently explored, that of the educating heroine who preaches the necessity of dutiful restraint to female readers, cautioning them especially against the snares of romance. But Austen did not admire the prototypical Madame do Genlis; she was "disgusted" with her brand of didacticism[23] and with the evangelic fervor of novelists who considered themselves primarily moralists.[24]

Far from modeling herself on conservative conduct writers like Hannah Moore or Dr. Gregory or Mrs. Chapone,[25] Austen repeatedly demonstrates her alienation from the aggressively patriarchal tradition that constitutes her Augustan inheritance, as well as her agreement with Mary Wollstonecraft that these authors helped "render women more artificial, weak characters, than they would otherwise have been."[26] A writer who could parody *An Essay on Man* to read "*Ride where you may*, Be Candid where you can" [italics ours] is not about to vindicate the ways of God to man.[27]

Nor is she about to justify the ways of Pope to women. One suspects that Austen, like Marianne Dashwood, appreciates Pope no more than is proper.[28] Even Dr. Johnson, whom she obviously does value, has his oracular rhetorical style parodied, first in the empty abstractions and antitheses that abound in the juvenilia,[29] and later in the mouth of *Pride and Prejudice*'s Mary Bennet, a girl who prides herself on pompous platitudes. Finally, Austen attacks *The Spectator* repeatedly, at least in part for its condescension toward female readers. The Regency, as well as her own private perspective as a woman, inalterably separates Austen from the Augustan context in which she is so frequently placed. Like her most mature heroine, Anne Elliot of *Persuasion*, she sometimes advised young readers to reflect on the wisdom of essayists who sought to "rouse and fortify the mind by the highest precepts, and the strongest examples, of moral and religious endurance," but she too is "eloquent on a point in which her own conduct would ill bear examination" (*P*, I, chap. 11).

If Austen rejects the romantic traditions of her culture in a parody like *Love and Freindship*, she does so not by way of the attack on feminine flightiness so common in conduct literature, or, at least, she uses this motif to mask a somewhat different point. *Love and Freindship* is the first hint of the depth of her alienation from her culture, especially as that culture defined and circumscribed women. Far from being the usual appeal for female sobriety and submission to domestic restraints so common in anti-romantic eighteenth-century literature, *Love and Freindship* attacks a society that trivializes female assertion by channeling it into the most ridiculous and unproductive forms of behavior. With nothing to do in the world, Sophia and Laura become addicts of feeling. Like all the other heroines of Austen's parodic juvenilia, they make an identity out of passivity, as if foreshadowing the bored girls described by Simone de Beauvoir, who "give themselves up to gloomy and romantic daydreams"

> Neglected, "misunderstood," they seek consolation in narcissistic fancies: they view themselves as romantic heroines of fiction, with self-admiration and self-pity. Quite naturally they become coquettish and stagy, these defects becoming more conspicuous at puberty. Their malaise shows itself in impatience, tantrums, tears; they enjoy crying—a taste that many women retain in later years—largely because they like to play the part of victims.... Little girls sometimes watch themselves cry in a mirror, to double the pleasure.[30]

Sophia and Laura do make a cult of passivity, fainting and languishing dramatically on sofas, defining their virtues and beauty in terms of their physical weakness and their susceptibility to overwhelming passions.

In this way, and more overtly by constantly scrutinizing their own physical perfections, they dramatize de Beauvoir's point that women, in typical victim fashion, become narcissistic out of their fear of facing reality. And because they pride themselves not only on their frailty but also on those very "accomplishments" that insure it, their narcissism is inextricably linked to masochism, for they have been successfully socialized into believing that their subordinate status in society is precisely the fulfillment they crave. Austen is very clear on the reasons for their obsessive fancies: Sophia and Laura are the victims of what Karen Horney has recently identified as the "overvaluation of love" and in this respect, according to Austen, they typify their sex.[31] Encouraged to know and care only about the love of men, Laura and Sophia are compulsive and indiscriminate in satisfying their insatiable need for being loved, while they are themselves incapable of authentic feeling. They would and do go to any lengths to "catch" men, but they must feign ignorance, modesty, and indifference to amatory passion. Austen shows how popular romantic fiction contributes to the traditional notion that women have no other legitimate aim but to love men and how this assumption is at the root of "female" narcissism, masochism, and deceit. She could hardly have set out to create a more heretical challenge to societal definitions of the feminine.

Furthermore, *Love and Freindship* displays Austen's concern with the rhetorical effect of fiction, not in terms of the moral issues raised by Dr. Johnson in his influential essay "On Fiction," but in terms of the psychological destruction such extravagant role models and illusory plots can wreak. De Beauvoir writes of "stagy" girls who "view themselves as romantic heroines of fiction"; and at least one of the reasons Laura and Sophia seem so grotesque is that they are living out predetermined plots: as readers who have accepted, even embraced, their status as characters, they epitomize the ways in which women have been tempted to forfeit interiority and the freedom of self-definition for literary roles. For if, as we might infer from Kipling, Austen herself was destined to become a sanctified symbol, her characters are no less circumscribed by fictional stereotypes and plots that seem to transform them into manic puppets. Like Anne Elliot, who explains that she will "not allow books to prove anything" because "men have had every advantage of us in telling their own story," Austen retains her suspicions about the effect of literary images of both sexes, and she repeatedly resorts to parodic strategies to discredit such images, deconstructing, for example, Richardson's influential ideas of heroism and heroinism.

Refusing to appreciate such angelic paragons as Clarissa or Pamela, Austen criticizes the morally pernicious equation of female virtue with passivity, or masculinity with aggression. From *Lady Susan* to *Sanditon*, she rejects stories in which women simply defend their virtue against male sexual advances. Most of her heroines resemble Charlotte Heywood, who picks up a copy of *Camilla* only to put it down again because "She had not *Camilla's* Youth, & had no intention of having her Distress."[32] Similarly, Austen criticizes the Richardsonian rake by implying that sentimental fiction legitimizes the role of the seducer-rapist, thereby encouraging men to act out their most predatory impulses. Sir Edward of *Sanditon* is only the last of the false suitors who models himself on Lovelace, his life's primary objective being seduction. For Austen, the libertine is a relative of the Byronic hero, and she is quite sure that his dangerous attractions are best defused through ridicule: "I have read the *Corsair*, mended my petticoat, & have nothing else to do," she writes in a letter that probably best illustrates the technique.[33] Because she realizes that writers like Richardson and Byron have truthfully represented the power struggle between the sexes, however, she does seek a way of telling their story without perpetuating it. In each of her novels, a seduced-and-abandoned plot is embedded in the form of an interpolated tale told to the heroine as a monitory image of her own more problematic story.

For all her ladylike discretion, then, Austen is rigorous in her revolt against the conventions she inherited. But she expresses her dissent under the cover of parodic strategies that had been legitimized by the most conservative writers of her time and that therefore were then (and remain now) radically ambiguous. Informing her recurrent use of parody is her belief that the inherited literary structures which are not directly degrading to her sex are patently irrelevant. Therefore, when she begins *Sense and Sensibility* with a retelling of *King Lear*, her reversals imply that male traditions need to be evaluated and reinterpreted from a female perspective: instead of the evil daughter castrating the old king by whittling away at his retinue of knights ("what need one?"), Austen represents the male heir and his wife persuading themselves to cheat their already unjustly deprived sisters of a rightful share of the patrimony ("Altogether, they will leave five hundred a-year amongst them, and what on earth can four women wait for more than that?" [*SS*, I, chap. 2]). When Maria Bertram echoes the caged bird of Sterne's *A Sentimental Journey*, complaining that the locked gates of her future husband's grounds are too confining—"I cannot get out, as the starling said"[34]—she reflects on the dangers of the romantic celebration of personal liberty and self-expression for women who will be severely punished if they insist on getting out.

Whether here, or in her parodies of Fanny Burney and Sir Samuel Egerton Brydges in *Pride and Prejudice*, Austen dramatizes how damaging it has been for women to inhabit a culture created by and for men, confirming perhaps more than any of her sisterly successors the truth of Mary Ellmann's contention that

> for women writers, as for Negro, what others have said bears
> down on whatever they can say themselves. Both are like people
> looking for their own bodies under razed buildings, having to
> clear away debris. In their every effort to formulate a new point
> of view, one feels the refutation of previous points of view—a
> weight which must impede spontaneity.[35]

Austen demystifies the literature she has read neither because she believes it misrepresents reality, as Mary Lascelles argues, nor out of obsessive fear of emotional contact, as Marvin Mudrick claims, nor because she is writing Tory propaganda against the Jacobins, as Marilyn Butler speculates,[36] but because she seeks to illustrate how such fictions are the alien creations of writers who contribute to the enfeebling of women.

But though Ellmann's image is generally helpful for an understanding of the female artist, in Austen's case it is a simplification. Austen's culture is not a destroyed rubble around her corpse. On the contrary, it is a healthy and powerful architecture which she must learn to inhabit. Far from looking under razed buildings or (even more radically) razing buildings herself, Austen admits the limits and discomforts of the paternal roof, but learns to live beneath it. As we have seen, however, she begins by laughing at its construction, pointing out exactly how much of that construction actually depends on the subjugation of women. If she wishes to be an architect herself, however, she needs to make use of the only available building materials—the language and genres, conventions and stereotypes at her disposal. She does not reject these, she reinvents them. For one thing, she has herself admired and enjoyed the literature of such sister novelists as Maria Edgeworth, Mrs. Radcliffe, Charlotte Lennox, Mary Brunton, and Fanny Burney. For another, as we have seen, regardless of how damaging they have been, the conventions of romantic fiction have been internalized by the women of her culture and so they do describe the psychology of growing up female. Finally, these are the only available stories she has. Austen makes a virtue of her own confinement, as her heroines will do also.

By exploiting the very conventions she exposes as inadequate, she demonstrates the power of patriarchy as well as the ambivalence and confinement of the female writer. She also discovers an effective subterfuge for a severe critique of her culture. For even as she dramatizes her own alienation from a society she cannot evade or transcend, she subverts the conventions of popular fiction to describe the lonely vulnerability of girls whose lives, if more mundane, are just as thwarted as those they read about so obsessively. For all their hilarious exaggeration, then, the incidents and characters of the juvenilia reappear in the later novels, where they portray the bewilderment of heroines whose guides are as inadequate as the author's in her search for a way of telling their story.

Just as Laura languishes in the Vale of Uske at the beginning of *Love and Freindship*, for example, the later heroines are confined to homes noteworthy for their suffocating atmosphere. The heroine of "Catharine" is limited to the company of an aunt who fears that all contact with society will engage the girl's heart imprudently. Living in her aunt's inexorably ordered house, Catharine has nothing to do but retreat to a romantically constructed bower, a place of adolescent illusions. Boredom is also a major affliction for Catherine Morland and Charlotte Heywood, who are involved in the drudgery of educating younger siblings in secluded areas offering few potential friends, as it is for the seemingly more privileged Emma, who suffers from intellectual loneliness, as well as the blazing fires, closed windows, and locked doors of her father's house. The Dashwood sisters move into a cottage with parlors too small for parties, and Fanny Price only manages to remove herself from her suffocatingly cramped home in Portsmouth to the little white attic which all the other occupants of Mansfield Park have outgrown. When the parental house is not downright uncomfortable because of its inadequate space, it is still a place with no privacy. Thus the only person able to retreat from the relentlessly trivial bustle at the Bennets is the father, who has his own library. Furthermore, as Nina Auerbach has shown, all the girls inhabit houses that are never endowed with the physical concreteness and comfort that specificity supplies.[37] The absence of details suggests how empty and unreal such family life feels, and a character like Anne Elliot, for example, faces the sterile elegance of her father's estate confined and confused by one of the few details the reader is provided, the mirrors in her father's private dressing room.

One reason why the adventures of the later heroines seem to supply such small relief to girls "doomed to waste [their] Days of Youth and Beauty in a humble Cottage in the Vale" is that most, like Laura, can only wait for an unpredictable and unreliable knock on the door. What characterizes the excursions of all these heroines is their total dependency on the whim of wealthier family or friends. None has the power to produce her own itinerary and none knows until the very last moment whether or not she will be taken on a trip upon which her happiness often depends. All the heroines of Austen's fiction very much want to experience the wider world outside their parents' province; each, though, must wait until lucky enough to be asked to accompany a chaperone who frequently only mars the pleasure of the adventure. Although in her earliest writing Austen ridicules the rapidity and improbability of coincidence in second-rate fiction, not a few of her own plots save the heroines from stagnation by means of the overtly literary device of an introduction to an older person who is so pleased with the heroine that "at parting she declares her sole *ambition* was to have her accompany them the next morning to Bath, whither they were going for some weeks."[38]

It is probably for this reason that, from the juvenilia to the posthumously published fragments, there is a recurrent interest in the horse and carriage. It is not surprising in the juvenilia to find a young woman marrying a man she loathes because he has promised her a new chaise, with a silver border and a saddle horse, in return for her not expecting to go to any public place for three years.[39] Indeed, not a few of the heroines recall the plight of two characters in the juvenilia who go on a walking tour through Wales with only one pony, ridden by their mother: not only do their sketches suffer, being "not such exact resemblances as might be wished, from their being taken as [they] ran along," so do their feet as they find themselves hopping home from Hereford.[40] Still, they are delighted with their excursion, and their passion for travel reminds us of the runaways who abound in Austen's novels, young women whose imaginations are tainted by romantic notions which fuel their excessive materialism or sexuality, and who would do anything with anyone in order to escape their families: Eliza Brandon, Julia and Maria Bertram, Lydia Bennet, Lucy Steele, and Georgianna Darcy are all "prepared for matrimony by an hatred of home, restraint, and tranquillity" (*MP*, II, chap. 3). Provided with only the naive clichés of sentimental literature, they insist on acting out those very plots Austen would—but therefore cannot—exorcise from her own fiction.

But hopping home from Hereford also recalls Marianne Dashwood who, like Fanny Price, is vitally concerned with her want of a horse: this pleasure and exercise is not at these girls' disposal primarily because of its expense and impropriety. Emma Woodhouse is subjected to the unwelcome proposals of Mr. Elton because she cannot avoid a ride in his carriage, and Jane Bennet becomes seriously ill at a time when her parents' horses cannot be spared. Similarly, Catherine Morland and Mrs. Parker are both victimized by male escorts whose recklessness hazards their health, if not their lives. It is no small testimony of her regard for their reciprocal partnership that Anne Elliot sees the lively and mutually self-regulating style of the Crofts' driving of their one-horse chaise as a good representation of their marriage. Coaches, barouche-landaus, and curricles are the crucial factors that will determine who goes where with whom on the expeditions to places like Northanger, Pemberly, Donwell Abbey, Southerton, and Lyme.

Every trivial social occasion, each of the many visits and calls endured if not enjoyed by the heroines, reminds us that women are dependent on fathers or brothers for even this most limited form of movement, when they are not indebted to wealthy widows who censure and criticize officiously.[41] Not possessing or controlling the means of transportation, each heroine is defined as different from the poorest men of her neighborhood, all of whom can convey themselves wherever they want or need to go. Indeed, what distinguishes the heroines from their brothers is invariably their lack of liberty: while Austen describes how younger brothers are as financially circumscribed as their sisters, for instance in their choosing of a mate, she always insists that the caste of gender takes precedence over the dictates of class; as poor a dependent as William Price is far more mobile than both his indigent sisters and his wealthy female cousins. For Austen, the domestic confinement of women is not a metaphor so much as a literal fact of life, enforced by all those elaborate rules of etiquette governing even the trivial morning calls that affect the females of each of the novels. The fact that "he is to purvey, and she to smile"[42] is what must have enraged and repelled readers like Brontë and Barrett Browning. As Anne Elliot explains, "We live at home, quiet, confined and our feelings prey upon us" (*P*, II, chap. 11).

According to popular moralists of Austen's day, what would be needed for a satisfied life in such uncongenial circumstances would be "inner resources." Yet these are what most of the young women in her novels lack, precisely because of the inadequate upbringing with which they have been provided by absent or ineffectual mothers. In fact, though Austen's juvenilia often ridicules fiction that portrays the heroine as an orphan or foundling or neglected stepdaughter, the mature novelist does not herself supply her female protagonists with very different family situations. In *A Vindication of the Rights of Woman* Mary Wollstonecraft explained that "woman ... a slave in every situation to prejudice, seldom exerts enlightened maternal affection; for she either neglects her children, or spoils them by improper indulgences."[43] Austen would agree, although she focuses specifically on mothers who fail in their nurturing of daughters. Emma Woodhouse, Emma

Watson, Catharine, and Anne Elliot are literally motherless, as are such minor characters as Clara Brereton, Jane Fairfax, the Steele sisters, Miss Tilney, Georgianna Darcy, the Miss Bingleys, Mary Crawford, and Harriet Smith. But those girls who have living mothers are nonetheless neglected or overindulged by the absence of enlightened maternal affection.

Fanny Price "might scruple to make use of the words, but she must and did feel that her mother was a partial, ill-judging parent, a dawdle, a slattern, who neither taught nor restrained her children, whose house was the scene of mismanagement and discomfort ... who had no talent, no conversation, no affection toward herself" (*MP*, III, chap. 8). Mrs. Price, however, is not much different from Mrs. Dashwood and Mrs. Bennet, who are as immature and silly as their youngest daughters, and who are therefore unable to guide young women into maturity. Women like Lady Bertram, Mrs. Musgrove, and Mrs. Bates are a burden on their children because their ignorance, indolence, and folly, resulting as they do in neglect, seem no better than the smothering love of those women whose officiousness spoils by improper indulgence. Fanny Dashwood and Lady Middleton of *Sense and Sensibility*, for example, are cruelly indifferent to the needs of all but their children, who are therefore transformed by such inauspicious attention into noisy, bothersome monsters. Lady Catherine de Bourgh proves conclusively that authoritative management of a daughter's life cannot be identified with nurturing love: coldly administering all aspects of her daughter's growth, overbearing Lady Catherine produces a girl who "was pale and sickly; her features, though not plain, were insignificant; and she spoke very little, except in a low voice."[44]

Because they are literally or figuratively motherless, the daughters in Austen's fiction are easily persuaded that they must look to men for security. Although their mothers' example proves how debilitating marriage can be, they seek husbands in order to escape from home. What feminists have recently called matrophobia—fear of becoming one's mother[45]—supplies one more motive to flee the parental house, as does the financial necessity of competing for male protection which their mothers really cannot supply. The parodic portrait in "Jack and Alice" of the competition between drunken Alice Johnson and the accomplished tailor's daughter, Lucy, for the incomparable Charles Adams (who was "so dazzling a Beauty that none but Eagles could look him in the Face") is thus not so different from the rivalry Emma Woodhouse feels toward Harriet Smith or Jane Fairfax over Mr. Knightley. And it is hardly surprising when in the juvenilia Austen pushes this fierce female rivalry to its fitting conclusion, describing how poor Lucy falls a victim to the envy of a female companion "who jealous of her superiour charms took her by poison from an admiring World at the age of seventeen."[46]

Austen ridicules the easy violence that embellishes melodrama even as she explores hostility between young women who feel they have no alternative but to compete on the marriage market. Like Charlotte Lucas, many an Austen heroine, "without thinking highly either of men or of matrimony," considers marriage "the only honourable provision for well-educated young women of small fortune, their pleasantest preservation from want" (*PP*, I, chap. 22). And so, at the beginning of *The Watsons*, one sister has to warn another about a third that, "There is nothing she would not do to get married.... Do not trust her with any secrets of your own, take warning by me, do not trust her." Because such females would rather marry a man they dislike than teach school or enter the governess "slave-trade,"[47] they fight ferociously for the few eligible men who do seem attractive. The rivalries between Miss Bingley and Miss Bennet, between Miss Dashwood and Miss Steele, between Julia and Maria Bertram for Henry Crawford, between the Musgrove sisters for Captain Wentworth are only the most obvious examples of fierce female competition where female anger is deflected from powerful male to powerless female targets.

Throughout the juvenilia, most hilariously in "Frederic and Elfrida," Austen ridicules the idea, promulgated by romantic fiction, that the only events worth recording are marriage proposals, marriage ceremonies, engagements made or broken, preparations for dances where lovers are expected, amatory disappointments, and elopements. But her own fiction is essentially limited to just such topics. The implication is clear: marriage is crucial because it is the only accessible form of self-definition for girls in her society. Indeed, Austen's silence on all other subjects becomes itself a kind of statement, for the absences in her fiction prove how deficient are the lives of girls and women, even as they testify to her own deprivation as a woman writer. Yet Austen actually uses her self-proclaimed and celebrated acceptance of the limits of her art to mask a subversive critique of the forms of self-expression available to her both as an artist and as a woman, for her ridicule of inane literary structures helps her articulate her alienation from equally inadequate societal strictures.

Austen was indisputably fascinated by double-talk, by conversations that imply the opposite of what they intend, narrative statements that can only confuse, and descriptions that are linguistically sound, but indecipherable or tautological. We can see her concern for such matters in "Jack and Alice," where dictatorial Lady Williams is adamant in giving her friend unintelligible advice about a proposed trip to Bath:

> "What say you to accompanying these Ladies: I shall be miserable without you—t'will be a most pleasant tour to you—I hope you'll go; if you do I am sure t'will be the Death of me— pray be persuaded."[48]

Almost as if she were taking on the persona of Mrs. Slipslop or Mrs. Malaprop (that wonderful "queen of the dictionary") or Tabitha Bramble, Austen engages here in the same kind of playful nonsense that occurs in the narrator's introduction to the story of "Frederic and Elfrida" ("The Uncle of Elfrida was the Father of Frederic; in other words, they were first cousins by the Father's side") or in "Lesley Castle" ("We are handsome, my dear Charlotte, very handsome and the greatest of our Perfections is, that, we are entirely insensible of them ourselves"). Characteristically, in Austen's juvenilia one girl explains, "if a book is well written, I always find it too short," and discovers that her friend agrees: "So do I, only I get tired of it before it is finished."[49] What is so wonderful about these sentences is the "ladylike" way in which they quietly subvert the conventions of language, while managing to sound perfectly acceptable, even grammatically elegant and decorous.

With its insistent evocation of two generic frameworks, the *Bildungsroman* and the burlesque, *Northanger Abbey* (1818) supplies one reason for Austen's fascination with coding, concealing, or just plain not saying what she means, because this apparently amusing and inoffensive novel finally expresses an indictment of patriarchy that could hardly be considered proper or even permissible in Austen's day. Indeed, when this early work was published posthumously—because its author could not find a publisher who would print it during her lifetime—it was the harsh portrayal of the patriarch that most disturbed reviewers.[50] Since we have already seen that Austen tends to enact her own ambivalent relationship to her literary predecessors as she describes her heroines' vulnerability in masculine society, it is hardly surprising to find that she describes Catherine Morland's initiation into the fashionable life of Bath, balls, and marriage settlements by trying to come to terms with the complex and ambiguous relationship between women and the novel.

Northanger Abbey begins with a sentence that resonates as the novel progresses: "No one who had ever seen Catherine Morland in her infancy, would have supposed her born to be an heroine." And certainly what we see of the young Catherine is her unromantic physical exuberance and health. We are told, moreover, that she was "fond of all boys' plays, and greatly preferred cricket not merely to dolls, but to the more heroic enjoyments of infancy, nursing a dormouse, feeding a canary-bird, or watering a rose-bush" (I, chap. 1). Inattentive to books, uninterested in music or drawing, she was "noisy and wild, hated confinement and cleanliness, and loved nothing so well in the world as rolling down the green slope at the back of the house" (I, chap. 1). But at fifteen Catherine began to curl her hair and read, and "from fifteen to seventeen she was in training for a heroine" (I, chap. 1). Indeed her actual "training for a heroine" is documented in the rest of the novel, although, as we shall see, it is hard to imagine a more uncongenial or unnatural course of instruction for her or for any other spirited girl.

Puzzled, confused, anxious to please, and above else innocent and curious, Catherine wonders as she wanders up and down the two traditional settings for female initiation, the dance hall at Bath and the passageways of a gothic abbey. But Austen keeps on reminding us that Catherine is typical because she is not born to be a heroine: burdened with parents who were "not in the least addicted to locking up ... daughters", Catherine could "not write sonnets" and had "no notion of drawing" (I, chap. 1). There is "not one lord" in her neighborhood—"not even a baronet" (I, chap. 2)—and on her journey to Bath, "neither robbers nor tempests befriend" her (I, chap. 2). When she enters the Upper Rooms in Bath, "not one" gentleman starts with wonder on beholding her, "no whisper of eager inquiry ran round the room, nor was she once called a divinity by anybody" (I, chap. 2). Her room at the Abbey is "by no means unreasonably large, and contained neither tapestry nor velvets" (II, chap. 6). Austen dramatizes all the ways in which Catherine is unable to live up to the rather unbelievable accomplishments of Charlotte Smith's and Mrs. Radcliffe's popular paragons. Heroines, it seems, are not born like people, but manufactured like monsters, and also like monsters they seem fated to self-destruct. Thus *Northanger Abbey* describes exactly how a girl in search of her life story finds herself entrapped in a series of monstrous fictions which deprive her of primacy.

To begin with, we see this fictionalizing process most clearly in the first section at Bath. Sitting in the crowded, noisy Upper Rooms, awaiting a suitable partner, Catherine is uncomfortably situated between Mrs. Thorpe, who talks only of her children, and Mrs. Allen, who is a monomaniac on the subject of gowns, hats, muslins, and ribbons. Fit representatives not only of fashionable life but also of the state of female maturity in an aristocratic and patriarchal society, they are a constant source of irritation to Catherine, who is happy to be liberated from their ridiculous refrains by Isabella and John

Thorpe. Yet if Mrs. Allen and Mrs. Thorpe are grotesque, the young Thorpes are equally absurd, for in them we see what it means to be a fashionable young lady or gentleman. Isabella is a heroine with a vengeance: flirting and feigning, she is a sister of the earlier Sophia and Laura who runs after men with a single-minded determination not even barely disguised by her protestations of sisterly affection for Catherine. Contorted "with smiles of most exquisite misery, and the laughing eye of utter despondency" (I, chap. 9), Isabella is continually acting out a script that makes her ridiculous. At the same time, her brother, as trapped in the stereotypes of masculinity as she is in femininity, continually contradicts himself, even while he constantly boasts about his skill as a hunter, his great gig, his incomparable drinking capacity, and the boldness of his riding. Not only, then, do the Thorpes represent a nightmarish version of what it means to see oneself as a hero or heroine, they also make Catherine's life miserable by preying on her gullibility and vulnerability.

What both the Thorpes do is lie to her and about her until she is entrapped in a series of coercive fictions of their making. Catherine becomes the pawn in Isabella's plot, specifically the self-consciously dramatic romance with James Morland in which Catherine is supposed to play the role of sisterly intimate to a swooning, blushing Isabella: Isabella continually gives Catherine clues that she ought to be soliciting her friend's confessions of love or eliciting her anxieties about separating from her lover, clues which Catherine never follows because she never quite catches their meaning. Similarly, John Thorpe constructs a series of fictions in which Catherine is first the object of his own amorous designs and then a wealthy heiress whom General Tilney can further fictionalize. Catherine becomes extremely uncomfortable as he manipulates all these stories about her, and only her ignorance serves to save her from the humiliating realization that her invitation to Northanger depends on General Tilney's illusive image of her.

When Henry Tilney points out to Catherine that "man has the advantage of choice, woman only the power of refusal" (I, chap. 10), he echoes a truth articulated (in a far more tragic circumstance) by Clarissa, who would give up choice if she could but preserve "the liberty of *refusal*, which belongs to my Sex."[51] But in Austen's parodic text, Henry makes a point that is as much about fiction as it is about marriage and dancing, his purported subjects: Catherine is as confined by the clichéd stories of the other characters as Austen is by her need to reject inherited stories of what it means to be a heroine. Unlike her author, however, Catherine "cannot speak well enough to be unintelligible" (II, cap. 1), so she lapses into silence when the Thorpes' version of reality contradicts her own, for instance when Isabella seats herself near a door that commands a good view of everybody entering because "it is so out of the way" (II, chap. 3), or when, in spite of John Thorpe's warnings about the violence of his horses, his carriage proceeds at a safe speed. Repeatedly, she does not understand "how to reconcile two such very different accounts of the same thing" (I, chap. 9). Enmeshed in the Thorpes' misinterpretations, Catherine can only feebly deflect Isabella's assertion that her rejection of John Thorpe represents the cooling of her first feelings: "You are describing what never happened" (II, chap. 3). While Catherine only sporadically and confusedly glimpses the discrepancies between Isabella's stated hatred of men and her continual coquetry, or John Thorpe's assertion that he saw the Tilneys driving up the Lansdown Road and her own discovery of them walking down the street, Austen is clearly quite conscious of the lies which John and his sister use to falsify Catherine's sense of reality, just as she is aware of the source of these lies in the popular fiction of her day.

Yet, despite her distaste for the falsity of fictional conventions, Austen insists quite early in the novel that she will not reject the practitioners of her own art: "I will not adopt that ungenerous and impolitic custom so common with novel-writers, of degrading by their contemptuous censure the very performances, to the number of which they are themselves adding" (I, chap. 5). In an extraordinary attack on critics of the novel, Austen makes it quite clear that she realizes male anthologists of Goldsmith, Milton, Pope, Prior, Addison, Steele, and Sterne are customarily praised ahead of the female creators of works like *Cecelia*, *Camilla*, or *Belinda*, although the work of such men is neither original nor literary. Indeed, as if to substantiate her feeling that prejudice against the novel is widespread, she shows how even an addicted reader of romances (who has been forced, like so many girls, to substitute novel reading for a formal education) needs to express disdain for the genre. In the important expedition to Beechen Cliff, we find Catherine claiming to despise the form. Novels, she says, are "not clever enough" for Henry Tilney because "gentlemen read better books" (I, chap. 14). But her censure is really, of course, a form of self-deprecation.

The novel is a status-deprived genre, Austen implies, because it is closely associated with a status-deprived gender. Catherine considers novels an inferior kind of literature precisely because they had already become the province of women writers and of a rapidly expanding female audience. Again and again we see the kind of miseducation novels confer on Catherine, teaching her to talk in inflated and stilted clichés, training her to expect impossibly villainous or virtuous behavior from people whose motives are more complex than she suspects, blinding her to the mundane selfishness of her contemporaries. Yet Austen declares that novel writers have been an "injured body," and she explicitly sets out to defend this species of composition that has been so unfairly decried out of "pride, ignorance, or fashion" (I, chap. 5).

Her passionate defense of the novel is not as out of place as it might first seem, for if *Northanger Abbey* is a parody of novelistic clichés, it also resembles the rest of the juvenilia in its tendency to rely on these very conventions for its own shape. Austen is writing a romance as conventional in its ways as those she criticizes: Catherine Morland's most endearing quality is her inexperience, and her adventures result from the Allens' gratuitous decision to take her as a companion on their trip to Bath, where she is actually introduced to Henry Tilney by the Master of Ceremonies, and where a lucky mistake causes his father to invite her to visit, appropriately enough, his gothic mansion. Like so many of Pamela's daughters, Catherine marries the man of her dreams and is thereby elevated to his rank. In other words, she succeeds in doing what Isabella is so mercilessly punished for wanting to do, making a good match. Finally, in true heroine style, Catherine rejects the false suitor for the true one[52] and is rescued for felicity by an ending no less aggressively engineered than that of most sentimental novels.

As if justifying both her spirited defense of sister novelists and the romantic shape of her heroine's story, Austen has Catherine admit a fierce animosity for the sober pages of history. Catherine tells Henry Tilney and his sister that history "tells [her] nothing that does not either vex or weary [her]. The quarrels of popes and kings, with wars or pestilences, in every page; *the men all so good for nothing, and hardly any women at all*—it is very tiresome" [italics ours] (I, chap. 14). She is severely criticized for this view; but she is, after all, correct, for the knowledge conferred by historians does seem irrelevant to the private lives of most women. Furthermore, Austen had already explored this fact in her only attempt at history, a parody of Goldsmith's *History of England*, written in her youth and signed as the work of "a partial, prejudiced, and ignorant Historian."[53] What is conveyed in this early joke is precisely Catherine's sense of the irrationality, cruelty, and irrelevance of history, as well as the partisan spleen of most so-called objective historians. Until she can place herself, and two friends, in the company of Mary Queen of Scots, historical events seem as absurdly distant from Austen's common concerns as they do to Charlotte Brontë in *Shirley*, George Eliot in *Middlemarch*, or Virginia Woolf in *The Years*, writers who self-consciously display the ways in which history and historical narration only indirectly affect women because they deal with public events never experienced at first hand in the privatized lives of women.

Even quite late in Austen's career, when she was approached to write a history of the august House of Cobourg, she refused to take historical "reality" seriously, declaring that she could no more write a historical romance than an epic poem, "and if it were indispensable for me to keep it up and never relax into laughing at myself or other people, I am sure I should be hung before I had finished the first chapter."[54] While in this letter she could defend her "pictures of domestic life in country villages" with a sure sense of her own province as a writer, Austen's sympathy and identification with Catherine Morland's ignorance is evident elsewhere in her protestation that certain topics are entirely unknown to her. She cannot portray a clergyman sketched by a correspondent because

> Such a man's conversation must at times be on subjects of science and philosophy, of which I know nothing; or at least be occasionally abundant in quotations and allusions which a woman who, like me, knows only her own mother tongue, and has read very little in that, would be totally without the power of giving. A classical education, or at any rate a very extensive acquaintance with English literature, ancient and modern, appears to me quite indispensable for the person who would do justice to your clergyman; and I think I may boast myself to be, with all possible vanity, the most unlearned and uninformed female who ever dared to be an authoress.[55]

Like Fanny Burney, who refused Dr. Johnson's offer of Latin lessons because she could not "devote so much time to acquire something I shall always dread to have known,"[56] Austen seems to have felt the need to maintain a degree of ladylike ignorance.

Yet not only does Austen write about women's miseducation, not only does she feel herself to be a victim of it; in *Northanger Abbey* she angrily attacks their culturally conditioned ignorance, for she is clearly infuriated that "A woman especially, if she have the misfortunate of knowing anything, should conceal it as well as she can" (I, chap. 14). Though "imbecility in females is a great enhancement of their personal charms," Austen sarcastically admits that some men are "too reasonable and too well informed themselves to desire any thing more in woman than ignorance" (I, chap. 14). When at Beechen Cliff Henry Tilney moves from the subject of the natural landscape to a discussion of politics, the narrator, like Catherine, keeps still. Etiquette, it seems, would forbid such discussions (for character and author alike), even if ignorance did not make them impossible. At the same time, however, both Catherine and Austen realize that history and politics, which have been completely beyond the reach of women's experience, are far from sanctified by such a divorce. "What in the midst of that mighty drama [of history] are girls and their blind visions?" Austen might have asked, as George Eliot would in *Daniel Deronda*. And she might have answered similarly that in these "delicate vessels is borne onward through the ages the treasures of human affection."[57] Ignoring the political and economic activity of men throughout history, Austen implies that history may very well be a uniform drama of masculine posturing that is no less a fiction (and a potentially pernicious one) than gothic romance. She suggests, too, that this fiction of history is finally a matter of indifference to women, who never participate in it and who are almost completely absent from its pages. Austen thus anticipates a question Virginia Woolf would angrily pose in *Three Guineas*: "what does 'patriotism' mean to [the educated man's sister]? Has she the same reasons for being proud of England, for loving England, for defending England?"[58] For, like Woolf, Austen asserts that women see male-dominated history from the disillusioned and disaffected perspective of the outsider.

At the same time, the issue of women's reasons for "being proud of England, for loving England, for defending England" is crucial to the revision of gothic fiction we find in *Northanger Abbey*. Rather than rejecting the gothic conventions she burlesques, Austen is very clearly criticizing female gothic in order to reinvest it with authority. As A. Walton Litz has demonstrated, Austen disapproves of Mrs. Radcliffe's exotic locales because such settings imply a discrepancy between the heroine's danger and the reader's security.[59] Austen's heroine is defined as a reader, and in her narrative she blunders on more significant, if less melodramatic, truths, as potentially destructive as any in Mrs. Radcliffe's fiction. Catherine discovers in the old-fashioned black cabinet something just as awful as a lost manuscript detailing a nun's story. Could Austen be pointing at the real threat to women's happiness when she describes her heroine finding *a laundry list*? Moreover, while Catherine reveals her own naive delusions when she expects to find Mrs. Tilney shut up and receiving from her husband's pitiless hands "a nightly supply of coarse food" (II, chap. 8), she does discover that "in suspecting General Tilney of either murdering or shutting up his wife, she had scarcely sinned against his character, or magnified his cruelty" (II, chap. 15).

Using the conventions of gothic even as she transforms them into a subversive critique of patriarchy, Austen shows her heroine penetrating to the secret of the Abbey, the hidden truth of the ancestral mansion, to learn the complete and arbitrary power of the owner of the house, the father, the General. In a book not unfittingly pronounced *North/anger*, Austen rewrites the gothic not because she disagrees with her sister novelists about the confinement of women, but because she believes women have been imprisoned more effectively by miseducation than by walls and more by financial dependency, which is the authentic ancestral curse, than by any verbal oath or warning. Austen's gothic novel is set in England because— even while it ridicules and repudiates patriarchal politics (or perhaps *because* it does so)—it is, as Robert Hopkins has shown, the most political of Jane Austen's novels. Hopkins's analysis of the political allusions in *Northanger Abbey* reveals not only the mercenary General's "callous lack of concern for the commonweal," but also his role "as an inquisitor surveying possibly seditious pamphlets." This means that Henry Tilney's eulogy of an England where gothic atrocities can presumably never occur because "every man is surrounded by a neighborhood of voluntary spies" (II, chap. 9) refers ironically to the political paranoia and repression of the General, whose role as a modern inquisitor reflects Austen's sense of "the nightmarish political world of the 1790s and very early 1800s."[60] The writers of romance, Austen implies, were not so much wrong as simplistic in their descriptions of female vulnerability. In spite of her professed or actual ignorance, then, Austen brilliantly relocates the villain of the exotic, faraway gothic locale here, now, in England.

It is significant, then, that General Tilney drives Catherine from his house without sufficient funds, without an escort for the seventy-mile journey, because she has no fortune of her own. Ellen Moers may exaggerate in her claim that "money and its making were characteristically female rather than male subjects in English fiction,"[61] but Austen does characteristically explore the specific ways in which patriarchal control of women depends on women being denied the right to earn or even inherit their own money. From *Sense and Sensibility*, where a male heir deprives his sisters of their home, to *Pride and Prejudice*, where the male entail threatens the Bennet girls with marriages of convenience, from *Emma*, where Jane Fairfax must become a governess if she cannot engage herself to a wealthy husband, to *Persuasion*, where the widowed Mrs. Smith struggles ineffectually against poverty, Austen reminds her readers that the laws and customs of England may, as Henry Tilney glowingly announces, insure against wife-murder (II, chap. 10), but they do not offer much more than this minimal security for a wife not beloved, or a woman not a wife: as Austen explains in a letter to her favorite niece, "single women have a dreadful propensity for being poor."[62] Thus, in all her novels Austen examines the female powerlessness that underlies monetary pressure to marry, the injustice of inheritance laws, the ignorance of women denied formal education, the psychological vulnerability of the heiress or widow, the exploited dependency of the spinster, the boredom of the lady provided with no vocation. And the powerlessness implicit in all these situations is also a part of the secret behind the graceful and even elegant surfaces of English society that Catherine manages to penetrate. Like Austen's other heroines, she comes to realize that most women resemble her friend Eleanor Tilney, who is only "a nominal mistress of [the house]"; her "real power is nothing" (II, chap. 13).

Catherine's realization that the family, as represented by the Tilneys, is a bankrupt and coercive institution matches the discoveries of many of Austen's other heroines. Specifically, her realization that General Tilney controls the household despite his lack of honor and feeling matches Elizabeth Bennet's recognition that her father's withdrawal into his library is destructive and selfish, or Emma Woodhouse's recognition that her valetudinarian father has strengthened her egotism out of *his* selfish need for her undivided attention. More than the discoveries of the others, though, Catherine's realization of General Tilney's greed and coercion resembles Fanny Price's recognition that the head of the Bertram family is not only fallible and inflexible in his judgment but mercenary in his motives. In a sense, then, all of Austen's later heroines resemble Catherine Morland in their discovery of the failure of the father, the emptiness of the patriarchal hierarchy, and, as Mary Burgan has shown, the inadequacy of the family as the basic psychological and economic unit of society.[63]

Significantly, all these fathers who control the finances of the house are in their various ways incapable of sustaining their children. Mr. Woodhouse quite literally tries to starve his family and guests, while Sir Walter Elliot is too cheap to provide dinners for his daughters, and Sir Thomas Bertram is so concerned with the elegance of his repast that his children only seek to escape his well-stocked table. As an exacting gourmet, General Tilney looks upon a "tolerably large eating-room as one of the necessities of life" (II, chap. 6), but his own appetite is not a little alarming, and the meals over which he presides are invariably a testimony to his childrens' and his guest's deprivation. Continually oppressed at the General's table with his incessant attentions, "perverse as it seemed, [Catherine] doubted whether she might not have felt less, had she been less attended to" [II, chap. 5]. What continues to mystify her about the General is "why he should say one thing so positively, and mean another all the while" (II, chap. 11). In fact, Austen redefines the gothic in yet another way in *Northanger Abbey* by showing that Catherine Morland is trapped, not inside the General's Abbey, but inside his fiction, a tale in which she figures as an heiress and thus a suitable bride for his second son. Moreover, though it may be less obvious, Catherine is also trapped by the interpretations of the General's children.

Even before Beechen Cliff Elinor Tilney is "not at home" to Catherine, who then sees her leaving the house with her father (I, chap. 12). And on Beechen Cliff, Catherine finds that her own language is not understood. While all the critics seem to side with Henry Tilney's "corrections" of her "mistakes," it is clear from Catherine's defense of herself that her language quite accurately reflects her own perspective. She uses the word *torment*, for example, in place of *instruct* because she knows what Henry Tilney has never experienced

> "You think me foolish to call instruction a torment, but if you had been as much used as myself to hear poor little children first learning their letters and then learning to spell, if you had ever seen how stupid they can be for a whole morning together, and how tired my poor mother is at the end of it, as I am in the habit of seeing almost every day of my life at home, you would allow that to *torment* and to *instruct* might sometimes be used as synonymous words." [I, chap. 14]

Immediately following this linguistic debate, Catherine watches the Tilneys' "viewing the country with the eyes of persons accustomed to drawing," and hears them talking "in phrases which conveyed scarcely any idea to her" (I, chap. 14). She is convinced moreover that "the little which she could understand ... appeared to contradict the very few notions she had entertained on the matter before." Surely instruction which causes her to doubt the evidence of her own eyes and understanding is a kind of torment. And she is further victimized by the process of depersonalization begun in Bath when she wholeheartedly adopts Henry's view and even entertains the belief "that Henry Tilney could never be wrong" (I, chap. 14).

While the Tilneys are certainly neither as hypocritical nor as coercive as the Thorpes, they do contribute to Catherine's confused anxiety over the validity of her own interpretations. Whenever Henry talks with her, he mockingly treats her like a "heroine," thereby surrounding her with clichéd language and clichéd plots. When they meet at a dance in Bath, he claims to worry about the poor figure he will make in her journal, and while his ridicule is no doubt meant for the sentimental novels in which every girl covers reams of paper with the most mundane details of her less than heroic life, such ridicule gratuitously misinterprets (and confuses) Catherine. At

Northanger, when she confides to Henry that his sister has taught her how to love a hyacinth, he responds with approbation: "a taste for flowers is always desirable in your sex, as a means of getting you out of doors, and tempting you to more frequent exercise than you would otherwise take!" This, although we know that Catherine has always been happy outdoors; she is left quietly to protest that "Mamma says I am never within" (II, chap. 7). Furthermore, as Katrin Ristkok Burlin has noticed, it is Henry who provides Catherine with the plot that really threatens to overwhelm her in the Abbey.[64] While General Tilney resembles the fathers of Austen's mature fiction in his attempts to watch and control his children as an author would "his" characters—witness the narcissistic Sir Walter and the witty Mr. Bennet—it is Henry Tilney who teaches Catherine at Beechen Cliff to view nature aesthetically, and it is he, as his father's son, who authors the gothic story that entraps Catherine in the sliding panels, ancient tapestries, gloomy passageways, funereal beds, and haunted halls of Northanger.

Of course, though Austen's portrait of the artist as a young man stresses the dangers of literary manipulation, Henry's miniature gothic *is* clearly a burlesque, and no one except the gullible Catherine would ever be taken in for a minute. Indeed, many critics are uncomfortable with this aspect of the novel, finding that it splits here into two parts. But the two sections are not differentiated so much by the realism of the Bath section and the burlesque of the Abbey scenes as by a crucial shift in Catherine, who seems at the Abbey finally to fall into literacy, to be confined in prose. The girl who originally preferred cricket, baseball, and horseback riding to books becomes fascinated with Henry Tilney's plot because it is the culminating step in her training to become a heroine, which has progressed from her early perusal of Gray and Pope to her shutting herself up in Bath with Isabella to read novels and her purchasing a new writing desk which she takes with her in the chaise to Northanger. Indeed, what seems to attract Catherine to Henry Tilney is his lively literariness, for he is very closely associated with books. He has read "hundreds and hundreds" of novels (I, chap. 14), all of which furnish him with misogynistic stereotypes for her. This man whose room at Northanger is littered with books, guns, and greatcoats is a specialist in "young ladies' ways."

"Everybody allows that the talent of writing agreeable letters is peculiarly female," Henry explains, and that female style is faultless except for "a general deficiency in subject, a total inattention to stops, and a very frequent ignorance of grammar" (I, chap. 3). Proving himself a man, he says, "no less by the generosity of my soul, than the clearness of my head" (I, chap. 14), Henry has "no patience with such of my sex as disdain to let themselves sometimes down to the comprehension of yours." He feels, moreover, that "perhaps the abilities of women are neither sound nor acute—neither vigorous nor keen. Perhaps they want observation, discernment, judgment, fire, genius and wit" (I, chap. 14). For all his charming vivacity, then, Henry Tilney's misogyny is closely identified with his literary authority so that, when his tale of Northanger sounds "just like a book" to Catherine (II, chap. 5), she is bound to be shut up inside this "horrid" novel by finally acquiescing to her status as a character.

Yet Catherine is one of the first examples we have of a character who gets away from her author, since her imagination runs away with the plot and role Henry has supplied her. Significantly, the story that Catherine enacts involves her in a series of terrifying, gothic adventures. Shaking and sweating through a succession of sleepless nights, she becomes obsessed with broken handles on chests that suggest "premature violence" to her, and "strange ciphers" that promise to disclose "hidden secrets" (II, chap. 6). Searching for clues to some impending evil or doom, she finds herself terrified when a cabinet will not open, only to discover in the morning that she had locked it herself; and, worse, she becomes convinced of Mrs. Tilney's confinement and finds herself weeping before the monument to the dead woman's memory. The monument notwithstanding, however, she is unconvinced of Mrs. Tilney's decease because she knows that a waxen figure might have been introduced and substituted in the family vault. Indeed, when she does not find a lost manuscript to document the General's iniquity, Catherine is only further assured that this villain has too much wit to leave clues that would lead to his detection.

Most simply, of course, this section of *Northanger Abbey* testifies to the delusions created when girls internalize the ridiculous expectations and standards of gothic fiction. But the anxiety Catherine experiences just at the point when she has truly come like a heroine to the home of the man of her dreams seems also to express feelings of confusion that are more than understandable if we remember how constantly she has been beset with alien visions of herself and with incomprehensible and contradictory standards for behavior. Since heroines are not born but made, the making of a heroine seems to imply an unnatural acquiescence in all these incomprehensible fictions: in Austen seems to be implying that the girl who becomes a heroine will become ill, if not mad. Here is the natural consequence of a young lady's sentimental education in preening, reading, shopping, and dreaming. Already, in Bath, caught between the contradictory claims of friends and relatives, Catherine meditates "by turns, on broken promises and broken arches, phaetons and false hangings, Tilneys and trap-doors" (I, chap. 11), as if she inhabits Pope's mad Cave of Spleen. Later, however, wandering through the Abbey at night, Catherine could be said to be searching finally for her own true story, seeking to unearth the past fate of a lost female who will somehow unlock the secret of her own future. Aspiring to become the next Mrs. Tilney, Catherine is understandably obsessed with the figure of the last Mrs. Tilney, and if we take her fantasy seriously, in spite of the heavy parodic tone here, we can see why, for Mrs. Tilney is an image of herself. Feeling confined and constrained in the General's house, but not understanding why, Catherine projects her own feelings of victimization into her imaginings of the General's wife, whose mild countenance is fitted to a frame in death, as presumably in life, and whose painting finds no more favor in the Abbey than her person did. Like Mary Elizabeth Coleridge in "The Other Side of a Mirror," Catherine confronts the image of this imprisoned, silenced woman only to realize "I am she!" Significantly, this story of the female prisoner is Catherine's only independent fiction, and it is a story that she must immediately renounce as a "voluntary, self-created delusion" (II, chap. 10) which can earn only her self-hatred.

If General Tilney is a monster of manipulation, then, Catherine Morland, as George Levine has shown, is also "an incipient monster," not very different from the monsters that haunt Austen's contemporary, Mary Shelley.[65] But Catherine's monstrosity is not just, as Levine claims, the result of social climbing at odds with the limits imposed by the social and moral order; it is also the result of her search for a story of her own. Imaginative and sensitive, Catherine genuinely believes that she can become the heroine of her own life story, that she can author herself, and thereby define and control reality. But, like Mary Shelley's monster, she must finally come to terms with herself as a creature of someone else's making, a character trapped inside an uncongenial plot. In fact, like Mary Shelley's monster, Catherine cannot make sense of the signs of her culture, and her frustration is at least partially reflected in her fiction of the starving, suffering Mrs. Tilney. That she sees herself liberating this female prisoner is thus only part of her delusion, because Catherine is destined to fall not just from what Ellen Moers calls "heroism" but even from authorship and authority: she is fated to be taught the indelicacy of her own attempt at fiction-making. Searching to understand the literary problems that persistently tease her, seeking to find the hidden origin of her own discomfort, we shall see that Catherine is motivated by a curiosity that links her not only to Mary Shelley's monster, but also to such rebellious, dissatisfied inquirers as Catherine Earnshaw, Jane Eyre, and Dorothea Brooke.

Mystified first by the Thorpes, then by the Tilneys, Catherine Morland is understandably filled with a sense of her own otherness, and the story of the imprisoned wife fully reveals both her anger and her self-pity. But her gravest loss of power comes when she is fully "awakened" and "the visions of romance were over" (II, chap. 10). Forced to renounce her story-telling, Catherine matures when "the anxieties of common life began soon to succeed to the alarms of romance" (II, chap. 10). First, her double, Isabella, who has been "all for ambition" (II, chap. 10), must be completely punished and revealed in all her monstrous aspiration. Henry Tilney is joking when he exclaims that Catherine must feel "that in losing Isabella, you lose half yourself" (II, chap. 10); but he is at least partially correct, since Isabella represents the distillation of Catherine's ambition to author herself as a heroine. For this reason, the conversations about Isabella's want of fortune and the difficulty this places in the way of her marrying Captain Tilney raise Catherine's alarms about herself because, as Catherine admits, "she was as insignificant, and perhaps as portionless, as Isabella" (II, chap. 11).

Isabella's last verbal attempt to revise reality is extremely unsuccessful; its inconsistencies and artificialities strike even Catherine as false. "Ashamed of Isabella, and ashamed of having ever loved her" (II, chap. 12), Catherine therefore begins to awaken to the anxieties of common life, and her own fall follows close upon Isabella's. Driven from the General's house, she now experiences agitations "mournfully superior in reality and substance" to her earlier imaginings (II, chap. 13). Catherine had been convinced by Henry of the "absurdity of her curiosity and her fears," but now she discovers that he erred not only in his sense of Isabella's story ("you little thought of its ending so" [II, chap. 10]), but also in his sense of hers. Not the least of Catherine's agitations must involve the realization that she has submitted to Henry's estimate that her fears of the General were "only" imaginary, when all along she had been right.

This is why *Northanger Abbey* is, finally, a gothic story as frightening as any told by Mrs. Radcliffe, for the evil it describes is the horror described by writers as dissimilar as Charlotte Perkins Gilman, Phyllis Chesler, and Sylvia Plath, the terror and self-loathing that results when a woman is made to disregard her personal sense of danger, to accept as real what contradicts her perception of her own situation. More dramatic, if not more debilitating, examples can be cited to illustrate Catherine's confusion when she realizes she has replaced her own interiority or authenticity with Henry's inadequate judgments. For the process of being brainwashed that almost fatally confuses Catherine has always painfully humiliated women subjected to a maddening process that Florence Rush, in an allusion to the famous Ingrid Bergman movie about a woman so driven insane, has recently called "gaslighting."[66]

While "a heroine returning, at the close of her career, to her native village, in all the triumph of recovered reputation" would be "a delight" for writer and reader alike, Austen admits, "I bring my heroine to her home in solitude and disgrace" (II, chap. 14). Catherine has nothing else to do but "to be silent and alone" (II, chap. 14). Having relinquished her attempt to gain a story or even a point of view, she composes a letter to Elinor that will not pain her if Henry should chance to read it. Like so many heroines, from Snow White to Kate Brown, who stands waiting for the kettle to boil at the beginning of *Summer Before the Dark*, Catherine is left with nothing to do but wait:

> She could neither sit still, not employ herself for ten minutes together, walking round the garden and orchard again and again, as if nothing but motion was voluntary; and it seemed as if she could even walk about the house rather than remain fixed for any time in the parlour. [II, chap. 15]

Her mother gives her a book of moral essays entitled *The Mirror*, which is what must now supplant the romances, for it tells stories appropriate to her "silence and sadness" (II, chap. 15). From this glass coffin she is rescued by the prince whose "affection originated in nothing better than gratitude" for her partiality toward him (II, chap. 15).

In spite of Henry's faults and the inevitable coercion of his authority over her, his parsonage will of course be a more pleasant dwelling than either the General's Abbey or the parental cot. Within its well-proportioned rooms, the girl who so enjoyed rolling down green slopes can at least gain a glimpse through the windows of luxuriant green meadows; in other words, Catherine's future home holds out the promise that women can find comfortable spaces to inhabit in their society. Austen even removes Elinor Tilney from "the evils of such a home as Northanger" (II, chap. 16), if only by marrying her to the gentleman whose servant left behind the laundry list. Yet the happy ending is the result of neither woman's education since, Austen implies, each continues to find the secret of the Abbey perplexing. We shall see that in this respect Catherine's fate foreshadows that of the later heroines, most of whom are also "saved" when they relinquish their subjectivity through the manipulations of a narrator who calls attention to her own exertions and thereby makes us wonder whether the lives of women not so benevolently protected would have turned out quite so well.

At the same time, even if the marriage of the past Mrs. Tilney makes us wonder about the future Mrs. Tilney's prospects for happiness, Austen has successfully balanced her own artistic commitment to an inherited literary structure that idealizes feminine submission against her rebellious imaginative sympathies. With a heavy reliance on characters who are readers, all of Austen's early parodies point us, then, to the important subject of female imagination in her mature novels. But it is in *Northanger Abbey* that this novelist most forcefully indicates her consciousness of what Harold Bloom might call her "belatedness," a belatedness inextricably related to her definition of herself as female and therefore secondary. Just as Catherine Morland remains a reader, Austen presents herself as a "mere" interpreter and critic of prior fictions, and thereby quite modestly demonstrates her willingness to inhabit a house of fiction not of her own making.

NOTES

Epigraphs: Jane Austen, *Love and Freindship in The Works of Jane Austen*, ed. R. W. Chapman, vol. 6 (London: Oxford University Press, 1954), p. 102; *Poems*, J. 613; "Have They Attacked Mary. He Giggled. (A Political Caricature)," in *Selected Writings of Gertrude Stein*, ed. Carl Van Vechten (New York: Vintage, 1962), p. 533; *The Second Sex*, p. 279.

1. *The Autobiography, Times, Opinions and Contemporaries of Sir Egerton Bridges* (London, 1834), vol. 2, chap. 3, p. 41, quoted by Frank Bradbrook, *Jane Austen and Her Predecessors* (Cambridge: Cambridge University Press, 1967), p. 401.

2. To Ann Austen, 9 September 1814, *Jane Austen's Letters to Her Sisters Cassandra and Others*, ed. R. W. Chapman (2d ed. London: Oxford University Press, 1952), p. 401.

3. To J. Edward Austen, 16 December 1816, *Austen's Letters*, pp. 468–69.

4. To Cassandra Austen, 4 February 1813, *Austen's Letters*, p. 299.

5. Quoted by Anne Katharine Elwood, *Memoirs of the Literary Ladies of England* (London, 1843), 2:216.

6. Gaston Bachelard, *The Poetics of Space*, p. 161.

7. Only recently have such traditionally "feminine" arts of women as drawn threadwork, crochet, lace-making, embroidery, and china-painting been rescued from devaluation by the artists working with Judy Chicago in her "Dinner Party Project." See the interview with Chicago in *Chrysalis* 4 (1977): 89–101.

8. Walter Scott, unsigned review of *Emma* in *Quarterly Review* (March 1816), reprinted in *Jane Austen: The Critical Heritage*, ed. B. C. Southam (New York: Barnes & Noble, 1968), p. 68.

9. Charlotte Brontë to G.H. Lewes, 1 January 1848, reprinted in *Critical Heritage*, p. 126.

10. The remark by Fitzgerald is quoted by John Halperin in his fine analysis "Jane Austen's Nineteenth-Century Critics," in *Jane Austen: Bicentenary Essays*, ed.

John Halperin (Cambridge: Cambridge University Press, 1975), p. 23 and footnoted there to the *Letters of Edward Fitzgerald*, vol. 2 (London, 1894), p. 131. Elizabeth Barrett Browning's remark is found in a letter to Ruskin, 5 November 1855, *Letters of Elizabeth Barrett Browning*, 2: 217.

11. *Journals of Ralph Waldo Emerson: 1856–1863*, ed. E. W. Emerson and W. E. Forbes (Boston: Houghton Mifflin, 1913), 9:336–37.

12. Mark Twain to William Dean Howells, January 18, 1909, reprinted in *The Portable Mark Twain*, ed. Bernard DeVoto (New York: Viking, 1946), p. 785.

13. D.H. Lawrence, "A Propos of Lady Chatterley's Lover," in *Sex, Literature and Censorship*, ed. Harry T. Moore (New York: Twayne Publishers, 1953), p. 119. This remark resembles the comment of Kingsley Amis, who claims that Austen's "judgment and her moral sense were corrupted," in *What Became of Jane Austen? and Other Questions* (London: Jonathan Cape, 1970), p. 17.

14. Henry James, "The Lesson of Balzac," *The Future of the Novel: Essays on the Art of Fiction*, ed. Leon Edel (New York: Vintage, 1956), pp. 100–01.

15. Rudyard Kipling, "The Janeites," *The Writings in Prose and Verse of Rudyard Kipling* (New York: Scribner's, 1926, vol. 31, pp. 159–91.

16. Jane Austen, *Persuasion*, ed. R. W. Chapman (New York: Norton, 1958), vol. I, chap. 11. Volume and chapter numbers will appear parenthetically in the text. Readers with texts where the chapters are consecutively numbered can convert their chap. 13 to Chapman's vol. II, chap. 1.

17. Donald Greene asks whether there is "not a good deal of machismo—our old friend 'male chauvinism'—built into the critical values that would downgrade Jane Austen's novels" in an interesting essay, "The Myth of Limitation" in *Jane Austen Today*, ed. Joel Weinscheimer (Athens, Ga.: University of Georgia Press, 1975), p. 168.

18. W.H. Auden, "Letter to Lord Byron," *Collected Longer Poems* (New York: Random House, 1969), p. 41.

19. Jane Austen, *Love and Freindship* in *Minor Works, The Works of Jane Austen*, ed. R. W. Chapman (London: Oxford University Press, 1954), vol. VI, p. 79. Subsequent quotations of the minor works are taken from this volume.

20. Virginia Woolf, "Jane Austen," *The Common Reader* (New York: Harcourt, Brace and World, 1925), p. 140.

21. Mary Lascelles, *Jane Austen and Her Art* (Oxford: Clarendon Press, 1939), p. 60.

22. "A Letter from a Young lady, whose feelings being too strong for her Judgement led her into the commission of Errors which her Heart disapproved," *Minor Works*, p. 175.

23. To Cassandra Austen, 7 January 1807, *Austen's Letters*, p. 48.

24. To Cassandra Austen, 24 January 1809, *Austen's Letters*, p. 256.

25. Frank Bradbrook, *Jane Austen and Her Predecessors*, pp. 24–27.

26. Mary Wollstonecraft, *A Vindication of the Rights of Woman*, ed. Carol H. Poston (New York: Norton, 1975), p. 22. Also see Lloyd W. Brown, "Jane Austen and the Feminist Tradition," *Nineteenth-Century Fiction* 28 (1973): 321–38.

27. "A Collection of Letters: Letter the Second," *Minor Works*, p. 154.

28. *Sense and Sensibility*, in *The Novels of Jane Austen*, ed. R. W. Chapman (London: Oxford University Press, 1943), vol. I, chap. 10. Subsequent references to volume and chapter will appear parenthetically in the text. Readers using editions where chapters are consecutively numbered can key into Chapman's system by converting chapters 23 to 36 into vol. II chapters 1–14 and chapters 37–50 into vol. III, chapters 1–14.

29. A. Walton Litz, *Jane Austen: A Study of Her Artistic Development* (New York: Oxford University Press, 1965), p. 50.

30. De Beauvoir, *The Second Sex*, p. 277.

31. Karen Horney, "The Overvaluation of Love," *Female Psychology* (New York: Norton, 1967), pp. 182–213.

32. *Sanditon*, in *Minor Works*, p. 390, chap. 6. Subsequent references to chapter numbers appear parenthetically in the text.

33. To Cassandra Austen, 5 March 1814, *Austen's Letters*, p. 379.

34. Jane Austen, *Mansfield Park* in *The Novels of Jane Austen*, ed. R. W. Chapman (London: Oxford University Press, 1923), vol. I, chap. 10. Subsequent references to chapter and volume will appear parenthetically in the text. Chapman's vol. I includes chapters 1–18; II, chapters 1–13, and III, chapters 1–17.

35. Mary Ellmann, *Thinking About Women* (New York: Harcourt Brace Jovanovich, 1968), p. 199.

36. Lascelles, *Jane Austen and Her Art*; Mudrick, *Jane Austen: Irony as Defense and Discovery* (Berkeley: University of California Press, 1968); Butler, *Jane Austen and the War of Ideas* (Oxford: Clarendon Press, 1975).

37. Nina Auerbach, "Austen and Alcott on Matrimony," *Novel* 10, no. 1 (Fall 1976): 6–26.

38. Jane Austen, "Jack and Alice," *Minor Works*, p. 24.

39. "The Three Sisters: A Novel," *Minor Works*, p. 66.

40. "A Tour Though Wales—in a Letter from a Young Lady," *Minor Works*, p. 177.

41. "Letter the Third From a Young Lady in distressed Circumstances to her friend," *Minor Works*, pp. 156–60.

42. Jane Austen, *Northanger Abbey* in *The Works of Jane Austen*, ed. R. W. Chapman (London: Oxford University Press, 1943), vol. I, chap. 10. Subsequent references to volume and chapter will appear parenthetically in the text. Chapman's edition divides the novel into two volumes, the first ending with chapter 15.

43. Mary Wollstonecraft, *A Vindication*, p. 151.

44. Jane Austen, *Pride and Prejudice* in *The Works of Jane Austen*, ed. R. W. Chapman (London: Oxford University Press, 1940), vol. II, chap. 6. Subsequent references to volume and chapter will appear parenthetically in the text. Volume I includes chapters 1 to 34; volume II, chapters 1 to 19; volume III, chapters 1 to 19.

45. Adrienne Rich, *Of Woman Born* (New York: Norton, 1976), p. 235; Lynn Sukenick, "Feeling and Reason in Doris Lessing's Fiction," *Contemporary Literature* 14 (Fall 1974): 519; Judith Kegan Gardiner, "A Wake for Mothers: The Maternal Deathbed in Women's Fiction," *Feminist Studies* 4 (June 1978): 146–65.

46. "Jack and Alice," p. 13 and p. 28.

47. Jane Austen, *Emma* in *The Works of Jane Austen*, ed. R. W. Chapman (London: Oxford University Press, 1933), vol. II, chap. 17. Subsequent references to volume and chapter will appear parenthetically in the text. Volume I includes chapters 1 to 18: II, chapters 1 to 18: III, chapters 1 to 19.

48. "Jack and Alice," *Minor Works*, p. 21.

49. "Frederic and Elfrida," *Minor Works*, p. 4; "Lesley Castle," p. 111, and "Catharine," p. 199.

50. See the objections to the villainy of the General voiced by Maria Edgeworth and by the *British Critic*, in *British Heritage*, p. 17.

51. Samuel Richardson, *Clarissa* (New York: Everyman, 1962), 1:226–27.

52. Darrel Mansell, *The Works of Jane Austen* (New York: Barnes and Noble, 1973), discusses the false suitor in all of Austen's novels, and Jean Kennard discusses the two-suitor convention in nineteenth-century fiction in *Victims of Convention* (Hamden, Conn.: Archon Books, 1978).

53. "The History of England," *Minor Works*, pp. 139–50.

54. To James Stanier Clarke, 1 April 1816, *Austen's Letters*, pp. 452–53.

55. To James Stanier Clarke, 11 Dec. 1815, *Austen's Letters*, p. 443.

56. Quoted in an extremely useful essay by Irene Tayler and Gina Luria, "Gender and Genre: Women in British Romantic Literature," in *What Manner of Woman: Essays on English and American Life and Literature*, ed. Marlene Springer (New York: New York University Press, 1977), p. 102.

57. George Eliot, *Daniel Deronda* (Baltimore: Penguin, 1967), p. 160.

58. Virginia Woolf, *Three Guineas* (New York: Harcourt Brace and World, 1966), p. 9.

59. Litz, *Jane Austen*, p. 64.

60. Robert Hopkins, "General Tilney and the Affairs of State: The Political Gothic of Northanger Abbey," *Philological Quarterly*, forthcoming. Alistair M. Duckworth also explains how Henry Tilney's ironical reconstruction of his sister's irrational fears of a riot is actually a description of the Gordon Riots of 1780; thus the passage ironically illustrates how well founded Elinor's fears are. See *The Improvement of the Estate* (Baltimore: Johns Hopkins University Press, 1971), p. 96.

61. Ellen Moers, *Literary Women*, p. 67.

62. In this letter to Fanny Knight, Austen goes on to admit the obvious, that this "is one very strong argument in favour of Matrimony," 13 March 1817, *Austen's Letters*, p. 483.

63. Mary Burgan, "Mr. Bennet and the Failures of Fatherhood in Jane Austen's Novels," *Journal of English and German Philology* (Fall 1975): 536–52.

64. Katrin Ristkok Burlin, "'The Pen of the Contriver': The Four Fictions of *Northanger Abbey*," in Halperin, *Bicentenary Essays*, pp. 89–111.

65. George Levine, "Translating the Monstrous: *Northanger Abbey*," *Nineteenth-Century Fiction* (December 1975): 335–50; also see Donald Greene, "Jane Austen's Monsters," in *Bicentenary Essays*, pp. 272–78.

66. Florence Rush, "The Freudian Cover-Up: The Sexual Abuse of Children," *Chrysalis* 1 (1977): 31–45. Rush describes how young girls are made to feel responsible for parental abuse, much as rape victims have been made to feel guilty for the crimes perpetrated against them.

IAN WATT

Jane Austen and the Traditions of Comic Aggression: Sense and Sensibility*

I'm very sorry that I have not been able to work out a topic that is suitable for this happy occasion. Instead, I have had to fall back onto a theme from a work in progress. I've long been intending to develop some things that were omitted from *The Rise of the Novel* to make it shorter and clearer in structure. It is to be called *Gothic and Comic: Two Variations on the Realistic Tradition*. As regards the comic tradition, one of the central arguments is that when Jane Austen began to write there was no established narrative tradition that would serve her turn. More specifically, earlier writers of English comic novels, such as Fielding, Smollett, and Fanny Burney, had in different ways adopted the polar opposition between good and bad characters which is typical of stage comedy from the Greeks on. Through the finer and more detailed psychological calibration of her narrative, Jane Austen made the hero and heroine psychologically complex, and therefore capable of internal and external development. By this means the traditional conflict of "good" and "bad" characters in comedy was internalised as a conflict within and between the "good" characters; and this enabled Jane Austen to discover the answer to Horatio Bottomley's prayer—"I pray that the bad be made good, and the good nice, and the nice, interesting."

The prayer is very rarely answered—alas!—either in life or in art; but one can surely say about Elizabeth Bennet and Emma Woodhouse that they

From *Persuasions* no. 3 (December 16, 1981). © 1981 by Ian Watt.

are not only good and nice, but interesting. They are made interesting because they are idiosyncratic mixtures of character traits, mixtures by no means limited to the good and unexceptionable qualities. For the purposes of comedy there remained a further task—the protagonists had to take over many of the aggressive functions which stage comedy has traditionally allotted to other actors—to the witty helpers, blocking characters, and villains. It is this, I think, that constitutes Jane Austen's greatest originality as an artist; and I would add that this literary originality is based on her psychological and moral realism, which gave the aggressive impulses a role which went far beyond the thought of her time, and, in some ways, of ours.

I will first illustrate the general idea by looking at *Emma* and *Pride and Prejudice*; and then I will consider *Sense and Sensibility* as an early stage in Jane Austen's development of the treatment of aggression.

Jane Austen's novels contain three main types of comic aggression, and all of them involve the "good" characters as well as the others. The first category—which I will call the social—is concerned with how people have different ways of hitting back at the restraints which social life exacts.

Most of the social gatherings described by Jane Austen provide illustrations. In the first social occasion in *Emma*, for instance, the party at the Westons' is dominated by the dialectic of constraint and hostility, and it thus serves as symbolic prelude to the novel's climactic scene on Box Hill. On the one hand, there are the positive, outgoing feelings, however strained, which are directed towards congeniality and sociability, and are expressed through compliments, jesting, and amiability; on the other hand, there are the contrary negative impulses of resentment at whatever threatens or inhibits the individual's status, habits, or convictions.

Every topic of conversation, we notice, evokes some note of hostility. For instance, Isabella Knightley's maternal zeal leads her to an odiously gratuitous pretence of benevolence in connections with Mrs. Churchill: "What a blessing that she never had any children! Poor little creatures, how unhappy she would have made them!" Then Mr. John Knightley comes in to give an alarmist account of the snow, "Concluding with these words to Mr. Woodhouse: 'This will prove a spirited beginning of your winter engagements, sir. Something new for your coachman and horses to be making their way through a storm of snow.'"

Others try to comfort poor Mr. Woodhouse, but his tormentor is "pursuing his triumph rather unfeelingly," and continues sardonically: "I admired your resolution very much, sir ... in venturing out in such weather, for of course you saw there would be snow very soon. Every body must have seen the snow coming on. I admired your spirit; and I dare say we shall get home very well. Another hour or two's snow can hardly make the road impassable; and we are two carriages; if *one* is blown over in the bleak part of the common field there will be the other at hand...."

John Knightley's gleeful malice towards poor Mr. Woodhouse's timidity is authorised by his ideology; he is unkind only in the pursuit of a higher truth. The truth is the pointless folly of social life in general, and it has as its primary axiom that dinner-parties are "in defiance of the law of nature"—an axiom which strikes a death blow at two of the cardinal values of comedy—laughter and feasting.

Here, as in most of the social gatherings in *Emma*, harmony only prevails when the group is happily engaged in the malicious criticism of third parties. The most intransigent and socially-destructive manifestation of aggression occurs when some challenge arises to the imperative need of the individual ego to maintain its own image of itself in the face of the outside world. This need produces the cruellest deliberate act in *Emma*, when Mr. Elton refuses to dance with Harriet Smith at the ball in the Crown; his pride has been offended, and seeks revenge. In Jane Austen, however, unconscious cruelty is much commoner, and most often arises from a mere refusal or inability to understand other people. Mr. Woodhouse, for instance, is genuinely kind in his way; but, lacking the controls of intelligence or awareness, his phobias often lead him into the milder forms of cruelty, invective and lying. Thus his tyrannical valetudinarianism leads him to disappoint Mrs. Bates's eager anticipation of a "delicate fricassée of sweetbread and asparagus," on the grounds that the latter were not "quite boiled enough"; the same phobia emerges in a more rancorous verbal form when the arrival of gruel in his family circle becomes the occasion for "pretty severe Philippics upon the many houses where it was never met with tolerable."

It would certainly be wrong, I must observe, to infer that Jane Austen condemns all social forms of aggression. For one thing, it is manifested by every character in *Emma* about whom we can make a judgment, except for two, and they are the exceptions which prove the rule: I mean Mrs. Bates and Harriet Smith—good people no doubt, but intellectually null, with one of them—Harriet—not yet arrived at maturity, and the other—Mrs. Bates— long past it.

I come now to the other two kinds of comic aggression—the interpersonal and the internal—as they are manifested in *Pride and Prejudice*. The personal relations between Elizabeth and Darcy are dominated by the aggressive elements in their characters; these alone replace the roles of the villains, the blocking characters, and the mistaken identities in traditional comedy. This replacement depends on two narrative techniques: first, the aggressive impulses at play in the comic arena are psychologised in the "courtship" of the protagonists; and they are also psychologised as conflicts inside the egos of both the lovers.

These conflicts in the personalities of Elizabeth and Darcy provide the mechanism of the main plot. At first the aggressive aspects of their characters block their separation even before they are actually acquaintances. Darcy's pride leads him to reject Bingley's suggestion that he dance with her—"She is tolerable; but not handsome enough to tempt *me*; and I am in no humour at present to give consequence to young ladies who are slighted by other men." Elizabeth overhears him, and her offended pride, exacerbated by Meryton gossip and Wickham's lies, insulates her from Darcy's rapidly changing feelings. The whole of their relationship is thus presented as an adaptation and recombination of one of the most standard modes of comic aggression, invective, to the purposes of psychological and moral realism. Elizabeth and Darcy begin by insulting the other to third parties; later their acquaintance develops almost exclusively through bouts of contemptuous raillery which are as close to the verbal combats of Greek comedy as the manners of Regency England allowed.

The reason for the tradition of invective in comedy is presumably that it offers a symbolic release from the constraints on which civilisation depends; as Freud put it, "The man who first flung a word of abuse at his enemy instead of a spear was the founder of civilisation." But in the kind of novel which Jane Austen wrote the invective and the wit-combats cannot be treated as they usually are in stage comedy, in Aristophanes, for example; they cannot merely stop, and be succeeded by a quick change to feasting, song, dance, and marriage. For in *Pride and Prejudice* the substance of the debate between the two lovers is very real—it expresses the deepest divisions in the way the protagonists see the world and experience the circumstances of their place in it. Jane Austen's moral solution to these divisions is exactly what the solution, if any, would be in real life: the pains of self-education— the realisaton of the errors, the delusions, and the prejudices of the self. In narrative terms Jane Austen brings the pattern of invective to a climax by a dual psychological transformation: interpersonal aggression is internalised in both hero and heroine.

In Darcy's case we do not see the process of self-punishment at work; but we can surmise that nothing else would lead him to propose marriage to Elizabeth. Then her insulting rejection apparently causes Darcy to take his self-punishment much further and he writes his abject explanatory letter. Now it is Elizabeth's turn. At first reading she is sure that "it was all pride and insolence," as regards Jane, while as regards Wickham, "she wished to discredit it entirely." Elizabeth then protests "that she would never look in (the letter) again," and we are already expecting the quick change of mind which the comic reversal requires. It soon comes: "in half a minute the letter was unfolded again." Elizabeth faces "the mortifying perusal of all that related to Wickham." From this second perusal there slowly emerges the deep personal humiliation of having to recognize how completely she has been taken in by this handsome scoundrel. From this traditional comic discovery of having been deceived, Elizabeth's negative emotions, which had previously all been directed outwards against Darcy, rapidly now alter their course and are directed inwards in a self-discovery of unflinching psychological rigour:

> "How despicably have I acted!" she cried.—"I who have prided myself on my discernment!—I, who have valued myself on my abilities! who have often disdained the generous candour of my sister, and gratified my vanity, in useless or blameable distrust— How humiliating is this discovery!—Yet, how just a humiliation!—Had I been in love, I could not have been more wretchedly blind. But vanity, not love, has been my folly.— Pleased with the preference of one, and offended by the neglect of the other, on the very beginning of our acquaintance, I have courted prepossession and ignorance, and driven reason away, where either were concerned. Till this moment, I never knew myself."

Now Elizabeth must come to terms with the fact that in many matters she shares with Darcy the same moral impulses, of which the most basic is to face the truth, even when it is deeply mortifying to the self. As a result Elizabeth joins Darcy in emerging from her deepest humiliation with a salutary increment of self-knowledge: they both undergo a parallel process of education through mortification.

Sense and Sensibility offers many examples of social, interpersonal, and internalised aggression. At the same time *Sense and Sensibility* is also, as one would expect from an earlier work, much closer than *Pride and Prejudice* or *Emma* to the classical tradition of comedy, and to Fanny Burney. The characters in *Sense and Sensibility*, for instance, tend to be more simply good or bad; the plot develops almost entirely through external events rather than inward changes in the protagonists; and although at the end Marianne and Edward Ferrars blame themselves for their past actions, they do so in spoken apologies to Elinor, and so there is no real analogy to the mortification scenes of Elizabeth or Emma.

First, social aggression. In *Sense and Sensibility* the battlefields of civility are littered with casualties. The most openly hostile characters are those who are wholly concerned with improving their financial and social condition; the way that John and Fanny Dashwood treat Mrs. Dashwood, Elinor, and Marianne is as gratuitous and persistently malicious as the behaviour of any stage villain. Having forced her husband to betray his promise, and his father's last wishes, Fanny Dashwood persuades herself—and John—that it is they who have been wronged; in the last tortuous extravagances of aggressive projection, John and Fanny even come to the persuasion that Elinor is as falsely designing as they are, and that she is trying to ensnare Fanny's brother, Edward Ferrars, in marriage. So, we observe, Fanny's observations of Edward's affectionate manner to Elinor give rise to her rudest outburst: "it was enough ... to make her uneasy; and at the same time, (which was still more common), to make her uncivil. She took the first opportunity of affronting her mother-in-law on the occasion, talking to her so expressively of her brother's great expectations, of Mrs. Ferrars' resolution that both her sons should marry well, and of the danger attending any young woman who attempted to *draw him in*; that Mrs. Dashwood could neither pretend to be unconscious, nor endeavour to be calm."

Jane Austen pursues her theme remorselessly; and we see manipulative aggression becoming compulsive in the best stage traditions of the miser's monomania. The parallel hostility of Lucy to Elinor is expressed in false pretences of friendship which make it merely a polite variation on the same theme of ruthless social competitiveness. For example, when she meets the Dashwood sisters in London, Lucy gushes: "'I should have been quite disappointed if I had not found you here *still*,' said she repeatedly, with a strong emphasis on the word. 'But I always thought I *should*. I was almost sure you would not leave London yet awhile, though you *told* me, you know, at Barton, that you should not stay above a *month*. But I thought, at the time, that you would most likely change your mind when it came to the point. It would have been such a great pity to have went away before your brother and sister came. And now to be sure you will be in no hurry to be gone. I am amazingly glad you did not keep to *your word*.'" Lucy's attempts at poisoned badinage are as unsatisfactory as her grammar; a fatal garrulity betrays her intentions long before she has finished, and thus reveals her unwitting violation of the first law of sarcasm—a rapidity that leaves no time for a riposte, let alone a yawn.

Lucy Steele, like John and Fanny Dashwood and Mrs. Ferrars, is a one-dimensional comic villain; she evokes unremitting dislike from the reader and the narrator alike. The other main group in the cast of *Sense and Sensibility* are also one-trait comic characters whose function is to be the butt of the narrator's running joke. Whenever they appear, we are asked to join in mocking Sir John Middleton's smothering hospitality, his wife's bored egocentricity, Mrs. Jenkins' misguided preoccupation with matchmaking, Mr. Palmer's boorish rudeness, and Mrs. Palmer's silly laugh.

Mr. Palmer cannot be denied the honour of being the ancestor of John Knightley; he never says anything that is *not* aggressive, and utterly refuses the slightest concessions to social civility. At Barton Park he draws even that most minimal of conversational counters, the weather, into his aggressive symbolic system: "'How horrid all this is!' said he. 'Such weather makes every thing and every body disgusting. Dullness is as much produced within doors as without, by rain. It makes one detest all one's acquaintance. What the devil does Sir John mean by not having a billiard room in his house? How few people know what comfort is! Sir John is as stupid as the weather!'" Elinor, astonished at Mrs. Palmer's forbearance at her husband's rudeness, observes him closely, and decides that he is not "so genuinely and unaffectedly ill-natured or ill-bred as he wished to appear ... It was the desire of appearing superior to other people."

The nearest parallel in *Sense and Sensibility* to the wit combats of Darcy and Elizabeth are—I suppose—the dialogues between Elinor and Marianne. There are, of course, many important differences: for one thing, the fairly strict dichotomy in the novel between good and bad characters means that Elinor and Marianne are often the victims of unprovoked social aggression from the rest of the world, so that the reader usually sympathises with them against all the unfair, unjust, and hostile circumstances in which they find themselves; secondly, Elinor comes to us as a person having, unlike Marianne, nothing to learn, so that there is a built-in asymmetry in the relations between the two sisters; and thirdly, their dialogue does not lead to change or permanent understanding. *Sense and Sensibility* was originally entitled "Elinor and Marianne"; and this would have been appropriate in a way that "Elizabeth and Darcy" would not have been, because although Elinor and Marianne have some of both qualities they function as symbolic and permanent opposites as far as their relationships to each other are concerned.

Marianne never has a hostile thought which she forces herself to repress; she openly attacks Edward for his reserve, speaks very rudely to Mrs. Ferrars in defense of Elinor, and is openly indignant at John Dashwood's account of Mrs. Ferrars's disinheriting Edward. In each case, Marianne's anger is justified, but Elinor's obtrusively different behavior brings into question her openness in expressing it.

Whenever Elinor's criticism has ethical foundations and she believes that speaking may be useful or is morally obligatory, she gives her view openly and earnestly. Thus Elinor cautions Mrs. Jenkins against her gossiping about Marianne and Willoughby: "you are doing a very unkind thing"; and she upbraids Miss Steele for listening at a keyhole and reporting what she has overheard. Under other conditions, and if her target is sufficiently dense, Elinor voices her opinion ironically; for example, when John Dashwood complains to her about his financial difficulties, we are told that Elinor, recalling how much cash he has withheld from her family, at first "could only smile." But when John presses his demand for her sympathy, saying "'You may guess, after all these expenses, how very far we must be from being rich, and how acceptable Mrs. Ferrars' kindness is,'" Elinor responds with adroitly ironical duplicity: "'Certainly,' said Elinor; 'and assisted by her liberality, I hope you may yet live to be in easy circumstances.'" She has read the barometer of complacent self-importance correctly, and her sarcasm goes right over John's head: "'Another year or two may do much towards it,' he gravely replied."

However, when John goes on to tell Elinor of his having pulled down all the walnut trees on the Dashwoods' beloved old property, Elinor in the best tradition of Mrs. Radcliffe's Emily de St. Aubert and Goethe's Werther, is really angry: but, we note, "Elinor kept her concern and her censure to herself; and was very thankful that Marianne was not present, to share the provocation." There is the same reserve when she watches the hopelessly duped Mrs. Ferrars being kind to Lucy Steele: "while (Elinor) smiled at a graciousness so misapplied, she could not but reflect on the mean-spirited folly from which it sprung, nor observe the studied attentions with which the Miss Steeles courted its continuance, without thoroughly despising them all four." As Robyn Housley has observed, "Elinor at her angriest is Elinor at her most silent"; Elinor knows that in her circumstances discretion is the best weapon which sense supplies for the defence of sensibility.

Compared to her behavior in public, Elinor's responses to her sister are much less reserved. From the beginning Elinor teases Marianne about the imprudence and danger of her excessive sensibility. Thus Elinor attempts to caution Marianne against her fast-growing friendship with Willoughby: "'You know what he thinks of Cowper and Scott, you are certain of his estimating their beauties as he ought, and you have received every assurance of his admiring Pope no more than is proper. But how is your acquaintance to be long supported, under such extraordinary dispatch of every subject for discourse? You will soon have exhausted each favourite topic. Another meeting will suffice to explain his sentiments on picturesque beauty, and second marriages, and then you can have nothing farther to ask'—." Marianne rejects the warning and counter-attacks by asserting her superior sensitivity: "But I see what you mean ... I have erred against every commonplace notion of decorum; I have been open and sincere where I ought to have been reserved, spiritless, dull, and deceitful:—had I talked only of the weather and the roads, and had I spoken only once in ten minutes, this reproach would have been spared."

Later, when Marianne has received Willoughby's letter, Elinor's advice becomes passionately serious: "'Exert yourself, dear Marianne, if you would not kill yourself and all who love you. Think of your mother; think of her misery while you suffer; for her sake you must exert yourself.'" Marianne remains blind to Elinor's efforts and responds with self-indulgent insult: "'I cannot, I cannot,' cried Marianne; 'leave me, leave me, if I distress you; leave me, hate me, forget me! but do not torture me so. Oh! how easy for those who have no sorrow of their own to talk of exertion!'"

Marianne's willful ignorance would remain invincible but for a combination of further accidents—the discovery of Edward's engagement to Lucy Steele, and Marianne's recovery. On both of these occasions, Marianne certainly voices bitter self-accusation, and her words certainly sound like attempts at self-mortification. But her change of heart surely lacks inwardness and depth.

> "Oh! Elinor," she cried, "you have made me hate myself for ever.—How barbarous have I been to you!—you, who have been my only comfort, who have borne with me in all my misery, who have seemed to be only suffering for me!—Is this my gratitude!—Is this the only return I can make you? Because your merit cries out upon myself, I have been trying to do it away."

The ensuing commentary suggests that the narrator, at least, is not wholly persuaded that Marianne's remorse may not be yet another form of high emotional self-indulgence:

> In such a frame of mind as she was now in, Elinor had no difficulty in obtaining from her whatever promise she required; and at her request, Marianne engaged never to speak of the affair to any one with the least appearance of bitterness:—to meet Lucy without betraying the smallest increase of dislike to her;—and

even to see Edward himself, if chance should bring them together, without any diminution of her usual cordiality.—These were great concessions;—but where Marianne felt that she had injured, no reparation could be too much for her to make.

The listing of Marianne's promises builds up to a climax that is surely one of tolerant irony; and it suggests that there is still a residue of self-dramatising emotionalism in Marianne: her prime need is still to make herself interesting to herself. Of course, we don't really know if we are dealing with a reliable narrator or not, or what she is reliable about. Is it a prediction, coming out of authorial foreknowledge of the future, that Marianne will never change her ways? Or is it just the persistently ironic tone that everyone except Elinor evokes from the narrator? We do not know, and so, although we are not persuaded that Marianne undergoes the mortification of internal aggression, as we are with Elizabeth and Emma, neither are we persuaded that we know how we should see her.

At this point, having tried, in the small hours of the night, to bring my argument to some sort of a conclusion, and having failed, I fell asleep. Happily, for the narrator of *Sense and Sensibility* appeared and claimed the right to speak in her own defence. When I woke up, however, I was unfortunately unable to recall her exact words, except for the first sentence:

I see what you would be at, Mr. Watt,—and, yes, I suppose I am in my own way what you call modern—disgusting word! I first thought about this two generations ago when a copy of *Abinger Harvest* arrived in Heaven. I noticed that E. M. Forster wrote about T. S. Eliot's "The Love Song of J. Alfred Prufrock": "The author was irritated by tea-parties, and not afraid to say so...." It set me thinking: "What's so new about that? And why should people be afraid to say so? But I suppose we are, and I was." Perhaps that's why my family tried to cover up the role of aggression in my novels when they put up that memorial brass to me in Winchester Cathedral, in 1872, that ends with the quotation from Proverbs (XXX, xxiv): "... in her tongue is the law of kindness." Surely they should have noticed from my novels, if they looked nowhere else, that the law of kindness is a very complicated one to obey especially if you also try to obey the law of truth. I think I did that battle rather well in Emma.

Of course it was more difficult, in my day, at least, for a woman: they were supposed to be all kindness, and truth was left to the men, like the right to anger. Men were entitled to have what the psychologists called "pugnacity," as long as most of it was whipped out of them at school; but women weren't supposed to have any, or at least not to show it. It wasn't easy for me when I started writing because I knew I wasn't like that at all. In *Northanger Abbey* I gave the "wrong" side of myself, the one that did not always think nice thoughts, to a man, Henry Tilney: and I'm afraid that later on I did the same thing a good deal in the other novels. In a way I wish Emerson's "Self-Reliance" had been written then, at least the beginning, when he says: "In every work of genius we recognise our own rejected thoughts."

I started trying to do more with my "own rejected thoughts" in *Sense and Sensibility*, but I was timid: I hid behind Elinor, and let her hide behind me. of course, we had a lot of fun together—when we collaborated, for instance, when, after one of Robert Ferrars' interminable vapid pomposities we wrote: "Elinor agreed to it all, for she did not think he deserved the compliment of rational opposition." I do believe that it's no good pretending that society isn't just what we see it is; and I don't think my novels make aggression any commoner or more brutal than it is in ordinary life. That's why I thought that the article by D. W. Harding—"Regulated Hatred: An Aspect of the Work of Jane Austen"—is unfair. He understands my writing very well, I think, and gives me one good clue about why people have been admiring my novels more and more over the years. But why does he use the word "hatred"? That denies the normality of most of the aggressive feelings and actions which I show in my novels because I observe them in the real world. Does Mr. Harding really think that it would be dangerous to eat the Donwell Abbey strawberries out of fear that Mrs. Elton might have poison hidden away in "all her apparatus of happiness"? Of course, in your century as in mine, the passions take a much less extreme form than those which animated the wars of Troy. But isn't there still, expressed in different manners, the same flux and reflux of aggressive motives as once inspired Homer, and as still animate the crowd when they laugh to see Punch and Judy trying to knock each other's brains out??

It is surely misunderstanding of kindness to think it should blind us to society's lack of it. Shouldn't we attack those who pretend to ignore that lack? Surely that's what comedy is for? After all, when intelligent, sensitive and principled people meet, what better thing is there for them to do than share their assurance that they are seeing the same world. Isn't it bracing to face together our recognition of irremediable truths? And what better use can there be of our wit and experience than to write novels which make people who understand them laugh in liberated complicity at all the foolish and dangerous manifestations of aggression that are there in the world and in ourselves?

But I've talked too long. You seem quite gentleman-like, so I'm sure you'll keep this talk as secret as Elinor kept Lucy Steele's about her engagement to Edward Ferrars. Oh, no, thank you, don't get up, I can see myself to the door. In fact, I don't use doors any more. I'm much freer than I was in the old days.

NOTE

* Since this address was prepared in haste, and for a very particular occasion and audience, Ian Watt wishes it to be considered not as a "publication" but merely as a printed souvenir for the members of the Jane Austen Society of North America.

ANN MOLAN

Persuasion in Persuasion

*P*ersuasion is generally regarded as a rather different novel from what we might have expected from Jane Austen's earlier achievements, and the obvious question is whether it is a new departure or a petering out. As many critics have noticed, there are technical imperfections that Jane Austen might well have removed had she lived—rather like the change she did make to the resolution so that it no longer looked like a favour to her heroine from the hand of fate. But if there are some grounds for some critics' reservations about the novel, there are none for supposing it a lesser achievement than Jane Austen's earlier work. Clearly, it is different; but it is also, I think, a real development.

It is important to notice how different it is in style and attitude from the earlier work, for the more or less familiar social setting and encounters tend to obscure this. Unlike other heroines', Anne Elliot's circumstances demand that she *release* her imagination, her fancy, from a reality which is fully recognized as only too intractable. Where earlier novels had portrayed many kinds of vanity, this explores the possible vanity of human wishes. In *Persuasion* there is a kind of seriousness and searchingness that can contemplate, far more steadily than in any of the earlier novels, the impotence of human yearnings to fashion or find their fulfilment, for this is a real possibility with Anne. The scope and terms of the novel are indicated

From *The Critical Review* no. 24 (1982). © 1982 by Ann Molan.

in an early remark about Anne: "How eloquent could Anne Elliot have been,—how eloquent, at least, were her wishes ..." (Penguin ed., p. 58). We are to discover that the eloquence of wishes, of fancy, and the insistence of them, is not a matter of the rhetoric of will, or of day-dreaming or of romantic self-delusion, but of persuasion.

The title of the novel actually focuses most of its central interests. In any human situation, what one confronts and what one brings to the encounter, the possibilities within and without the self, what one is persuaded of and what one is persuaded by, weave an intricate knot of compulsions and restraints. This, I would argue, is at the centre of *Persuasion*; and much of the novel's energy comes from the way the various strands of the knot join, resist and determine each other. Anne's case does not represent the rival claims of feeling and of prudential caution, or even of autonomous decision and persuadability. Such oppositions collapse upon examination, for persuadability is as much a factor in Anne's eventual happiness as it was in her earlier loss of Wentworth. In other words, Jane Austen penetrates the intrinsic doubleness of persuasion, its ability to destroy and fashion, its ineradicable presence in all human dealings, and the riskiness of deciding one's lot by something uncertifiable. Where there is some margin for doubt or personally attributed meaning, persuasion becomes important and correspondingly risky—as we see in Anne's earlier "persuasion" that marrying Wentworth would have disastrous consequences, and (later in the book) in her "persuasion" that she could reawaken his love. All "persuasions" and all persuading are seen to issue from the need to sustain something as well as the need to venture something; and this applies to the pleas of feelings as well as the pleas of reason, or of cold, hard facts. And if there is a self-preserving necessity in Anne's persuading herself of a real value in the places where she is obliged to spend her time, yet the exertion this requires from a spirit not limply pliable indicates a hope, a demand on life, that will later persuade her rather differently.

The tone of *Persuasion* has a seriousness born of the steady contemplation of the way things can go awry or go nowhere at all. Anne Elliot is very much alone in her world, more than most of the other Austen heroines; but there are ways of being alone, and ways of coping with it, which are set against hers quite early in the novel and ensure that our sympathies are neither sentimental nor undiscriminating. Elizabeth uses her long-nursed resentment about William Elliot to "fill the vacancies" of her life (p. 40), for instance; Mary's response to having "not seen a creature the whole morning" (p. 64) is one of manipulative hypochondria. By contrast, Anne has more substantial inner resources, which helps make us see that the seriousness of her predicament is correspondingly deeper.

Unlike Jane Austen's other heroines', Anne's life is closing down, its horizons becoming narrow and unexpandable. She has done with the world, the world has done with her, and if only she can reconcile her heart to it, her task seems to be to acquit herself well as a useful second-rank member of the community. This is far from the case with the other heroines. We enter upon their lives at the point where their scope is broadest because so much is potential, when the constrictions of belonging to one family are being shed before the constrictions of entering another one have been adopted. Nor is this simply a matter of Anne being older than they. Age is important but not in some automatic way, for it matters more what Anne's life has meant for her to that age, and the fact that her opportunities for happiness seem to have been used up and come to nothing. Yet what matters even more are the feelings and capacities for feeling that age has brought with it. Emma is in a position to be "vexed" (and her age is part of that); Anne, on first seeing Wentworth, to have "a revival of former pain". The difference between "pain" and "vexation" signals a lot here. On Wentworth's appearance in Bath, Anne is overcome by "agitation, pain, pleasure, a something between delight and misery" (p. 185). Even such mixed feelings as these are a welcome relief from incidents of unalloyed suffering, as when Anne finds herself uncontrollably but quietly weeping in the midst of a joyous gathering, because Wentworth is engaged with someone else. Words of a different tone and cadence from "vexation" are necessary to render the disturbances that come to Anne's heart and mind.

As Jane Austen presents her, Anne is not the victim of a rigidly limiting social world. Anne has cast away her own happiness, allowing herself to be persuaded to choose a course that actually limits her to her own family—a family that hardly amounts to a home. She has not been hard done by or duped. It is important that Anne's father did not forbid the marriage to Wentworth, and that she was not absolutely obliged to obey Lady Russell's advice. To import the Cinderella theme (as D. W. Harding does, with some qualifications, in his introduction to the Penguin edition) obscures Anne's agency in her life, which we need to appreciate if we are to take her story seriously. Jane Austen gives due weight to all the tangled factors restraining and enticing Anne, so that we are by no means persuaded to any simple verdict about her early decision, such as that of Frederick Wentworth or Lady Russell. The very ordinariness of her case is part of its complexity: it was no whirlwind, fairy-tale romance of star-crossed lovers, but rather, "he had nothing to do, and she had hardly any body to love" (p. 55). The lovers exist in a world which they didn't create, but in which they must live. What should Anne have done, then? As we are made to see it, there is no minimizing the extreme difficulty and hazard of her deciding to marry Wentworth. She is very young, and her feelings are untested. We remember Anne's own mother (and Fanny Price's mother plunged into penury), and the unhappiness that a mistake of this kind inflicted on them. And we need not doubt that Sir Walter would be as good as his word in cutting her off. The cost of accepting and complying with the demands of her social world, and the cost of repudiating them, are both given their full weight. For Anne, the latter course would mean breaking every connection she has, and rejecting the advice of the one sensible person around, Lady Russell. If Jane Austen had made her heroine just a year or two older, it might have made our judgment easier, not because of the legal age of independence, but because we are more content for an adult woman to take her chances in that kind of risk than we are for someone on the threshold like Anne. In these ways, our own venturing and withholding of judgment on the issue are a bit similar to Anne's own.

Of course, we are never in any doubt that Anne made a disastrous mistake, and we cannot be satisfied to adopt the hindsight answer to the "right and wrong" of it that Anne finally gives to Wentworth. But it makes a big difference how we understand Anne's refusal: whether we see it as the timid yielding of someone whose feelings are weak enough to be easily diverted, or as the action of someone whose unusual maturity can admit many points of view apart from her own, but whose inexperience prevents her seeing through them. If we adopt the former view, then it becomes too easy thenceforth to see Anne as a willing door-mat for all and sundry, a self-effacing, spineless convenience who didn't have enough courage to grasp her own life when it was handed to her on a plate. However, as the incident and situation are elaborated by Jane Austen, this view comes to seem unwarrantable. So while we are far from taking Lady Russell's part, we are not entirely of Wentworth's persuasion about the matter either. His own case might look like a compelling argument for trust in one's deepest impulses: "His genius and ardour had seemed to foresee and to command his prosperous path" (p. 58), but with no less genius and ardour, Anne's path is impeded by more factors than Wentworth understands. Wentworth should not have assumed that her situation was the same as his; indeed as we look back on the whole episode, we cannot help seeing that his response was less mature and self-possessed than hers, closer to being "captiously irritable" (p. 226), even if we might not want to go that far. But certainly we cannot see Anne's refusal of Wentworth at the age of nineteen as a denial of her capacity to live according to her heart. If it were, her life and her story would be much simpler.

In its early chapters, then, the novel creates a world not reducible to terms of simple alternatives, especially simple moral alternatives. Indeed, the notion that the novel and the reader can easily fix on or derive any "system" of values seems to ignore most about Jane Austen's enterprise. The novel is not of that expository temper at all; it is much more interested in (and questioning of) the process by which Anne's happiness is secured than in attempts to make the outcome "signify" some moral generalization.

Jane Austen's viewpoint clearly overlaps with her heroine's, of course, but they are not identical: Anne is not "as right as her author", as is often thought. To take this view is to leave too much out of account, especially the way the prose so often works to place Anne's version of things. However, it is true that Anne is quite without illusions, either about her own decisive life's choice or about the capacities for life in the people around her, whether at Kellynch, Uppercross or Bath. She is as quick to sense something fishy about Mr Elliot's appearing when there was "nothing to gain" (p. 153), for example, as she is to understand the nature of Mary's malady. People are always avowing the opposite of what they really want, thinly masking self-interest with a veneer of social forms, and material considerations are forever determining the most important human affairs. None of this escapes Anne's eye. Yet Anne's balance is not upset by the extent of duplicity and caprice she sees around her. Her vision is not clouded by bitterness or cynical resignation, although there are seductions for her in both modes of distancing. And of course this clarity and astringent judgment are even more characteristic of Jane Austen herself. "Mr Shepherd laughed, as he knew we must" (p. 47); "A lady, without a family, was the very best preserver of furniture" (p. 51); "His two other children were of very inferior value" (p. 37). The presence of this acerbic note in the novel, especially directed against the people who foil things, is perfectly gauged to correspond with the seriousness of the losses incurred for someone like Anne. This is not to say that Jane Austen's characteristic irony is absent or sour. The way characters like the Musgroves persuade themselves into their own attitudes, for example, is as amusing as the way they persuade themselves of others' attitudes.

Yet for Anne, as distinct from Jane Austen, merely to comment on and expose her world is not sufficient. She must make her own place in it as well. She has to exert all her energies to achieve a resignation to the emptiness her life holds out to her, to live in the world without expectations, and to make do with incentives to action and gratifications which leave her heart in abeyance: "... she had the satisfaction of knowing herself extremely useful there" (p. 137). To live this way, just about all the vital centres of her life must be shut down. The continual chafing abrasion of having her heart awakened in that world is something from which she must protect herself. The re-appearance of Wentworth is to disturb that calm, however, and Anne's fevered apprehension of his arrival shows her to be quite riveted by the prospect, even though "soon she began to wish that she could feel secure even for a week" (p. 79). She is thankful that no one knows or would care about her former alliance to Wentworth, and we can only be thankful too. After Mary's first meeting with Wentworth, we have sufficient evidence to confirm the novel's intimations about this:

> "... Henrietta asked him what he thought of you, when they went away; and he said, 'You were so altered he should not have known you again.'"
>
> Mary had no feelings to make her respect her sister's in a common way; but she was perfectly unsuspicious of being inflicting any particular wound. (p. 85)

As it is, what Anne has to suffer from Mary's coarse vanity is bad enough, but we know there are several who would not scruple to "inflict a peculiar wound" had they known the whole story. The novel does not see it as a perverse trifling with her best interests when Anne concludes about her removal to the same village as Wentworth that "this was against her" (p. 115).

Jane Austen gives full weight to such conclusions drawn by Anne, but she also maintains an ironic perspective on her. And here it is important that we notice how much the title of the novel gathers into itself, for the book is interested in the various modes and motives of *self*-persuasion—more, indeed, than in persuasion by others; and it is still more interested in what people are persuaded of and therefore what they will find to be persuaded by, and in the moral qualities involved in this to-and-fro process. Anne is certainly subjected to this kind of scrutiny, since persuasion is and has been one of the most obvious determinants of her life. But the way Jane Austen scrutinizes her, along with the other characters, involves a very delicate kind of irony and wit.

On the walk to Winthrop, Louisa Musgrove extorts from Wentworth an avowal which many readers have taken to be the novel's "position" on persuadability: "My first wish for all, whom I am interested in, is that they should be firm" (p. 110). As we soon see, however, Louisa's subsequent self-persuasion that she can win Wentworth by displays of "firmness" is precisely what leads her to reject his counter-persuasions to watch her step on the

Cobb. The apparently simple, straightforward distinction between "persuasion" and "firmness" dissolves; in fact, the two episodes involving Louisa and Wentworth undercut any such notion, since involved in both episodes are contrary directions and levels of persuasion. Anne, we notice, has no such notion. What she sees in the incident on the Cobb is what she also mentally insists on against Wentworth: that, although she cannot articulate fully the complexities we see develop in her own life, "She thought it could scarcely escape him to feel, that a persuadable temper might sometimes be as much in favour of happiness, as a very resolute character" (p. 136). After all, reality is a great persuader—as Anne knows all too well and as Louisa, impelled by the romantic urgings of her heart, and with her sights set only on securing Wentworth—discovers.

But, of course, questions about what "reality" is to a person, and how much it *can* persuade him, and what it can persuade him of, all arise at the very beginning of the novel, with Sir Walter Elliot. His vanity, his obsession with the Baronetage, and his repulsive attitude to his wife's death are very much to the point: "Precisely such had the paragraph originally stood from the printer's hands; but Sir Walter had *improved* it ... by *inserting most accurately* the day of the month on which he had lost his wife" (p. 35; my italics). In Sir Walter's eyes, the more room one takes up in the Baronetage, the more firmly established one is as a person; births and deaths are equally grist to the mill of Sir Walter's lofty self-esteem, equally a source of satisfaction and diversion. Unlike Louisa, he is very attentive to facts; but it is an attentiveness that is chillingly falsifying just because it is negligent of the *human* facts. His meticulous addition to the record of his wife's death blandly ignores and erases any record of her existence as a wife. Can we say that the reality of the past is unaffected by such persuasion about it, especially as it is preserved in the present and guides action in the future? Against Sir Walter's we are clearly invited to put Anne's sense of and relation to her past: "With all these circumstances, recollections and feelings, she could not hear that Captain Wentworth's sister was likely to live at Kellynch, without a revival of former pain" (p. 58); or "... it was highly incumbent on her to clothe her imagination, her memory, and all her ideas in as much of Uppercross as possible" (p. 70). These life-lines to human meanings (which often feel, to Anne, like millstones around her neck) spell out just what Sir Walter lacks—recollections, feelings, imagination, memory and ideas; and it is precisely these, we notice, that make the persuasiveness of *her* "reality" at once so powerful to her and so painful.

Nevertheless, the novel does not present the mere capacity to feel, to remember, to imagine, and to be persuaded accordingly, as a moral ideal, for the novel insists on the crucial difficulty: "How quick come the reasons for approving what we like!" (p. 46). This wry comment from the author is prompted by the plans to let Kellynch and remove the Elliots to Bath; but the same point is revealed again and again: the subtle but crucial difference between the legitimate claims of personal exigence, and the universal tendency to rationalize one's preference by selective attention, self-delusion and evasion of the claims of others. Lady Russell on the desirability of moving to Bath is only one example of the process. So is the humourous episode, later on, when Charles and Mary Musgrove are dealing with their invitation to meet Captain Wentworth and the rival claims of their sick child: once again personal preference gradually turns into moral obligation through manoeuvring facts and other people.

And yet even on this process the novel is anything but simple-minded, for it shows the process as also an every-day, tacitly understood and mutually employed means of coming to an arrangement. The meeting of the owners and the tenants of Kellynch is a case in point: "This meeting of the two parties proved highly satisfactory, and decided the whole business at once. Each lady was previously well disposed for an agreement, and saw nothing, therefore, but good manners in the other" (p. 60). The amusement here goes with the recognition, the acceptance, of this rather questionable process of pre-disposing oneself and others as a necessary way of expediting important social transactions. There are many instances of this in the novel, and in none of them is anyone deliberately setting out to pull the wool over people's eyes. Rather, each of the characters is of some inner persuasion about grades of value—a persuasion that has a degree of wilfulness in it, and a certain dispositional, abiding quality, a characteristic leaning towards something. Because of this each finds himself being persuaded about certain possibilities in the world as though these things were pressed upon him for recognition. The sentence about the letting of Kellynch leaps in lightning sequence from the ladies' interests, to what they saw, conjoined by that very telling "therefore". This highlights the potential danger as well as the humour in the readiness with which people construct reality according to purely private specifications. "Persuasion", it seems, has a lot to do with how one channels, amplifies and distorts the truth—often through recounting versions of it, but always with the object of reconciling or aligning the conscious self and the rest of the world. The process is often tacit or unavowed, but of course is always likely to run up against resistance from somewhere or other.

It is no coincidence, I think, that hard on the heels of the letting of Kellynch and that telling "therefore", Anne undertakes her own self-persuasion about the prospects of going to Bath: "It would be most right, and most wise, and, therefore, must involve least suffering, to go with the others" (p. 61). Of course, Anne's reconciling of self and world here is in the reverse direction to other reconcilings we have witnessed or are soon to witness. She is trying to shape her deeper feelings and dispositions so as to conform with an apparently fixed external arrangement of things; and she is also attributing to that arrangement a weight of propriety and moral sanction to "justify" her accepting what, in reality, she cannot influence. The attempt is more futile than in some way reprehensible. The spare, tough word "suffering" is not overbalanced by the meagre suitability of the plan as Anne is invoking it, a suitability that looks all the more meagre for its having to be iterated so strongly as "*most* right, and *most* wise". This is a good example of how complex Jane Austen's attitudes are. She appreciates how little Anne is a person to leap to moralizing self-negation, and yet how much Anne's position makes the adoption of such self-protective measures necessary to her. The effort of control evinced in the rhythm of the first half of the sentence makes clear that this self-repression goes against the grain with Anne, just as it testifies to the unbudging resistance of that self which has the capacity to suffer. The bald statement of her "persuasion" here—that feelings order themselves (to some degree; it is only the "*least* suffering") according to external conveniences—ironically highlights the incongruity of placing the two kinds of consideration on the same plane. Indeed, the sentence works—to refine this irony by placing the logic Anne tries to impose on these: considerations against the real lack of logic we see in them (for how much logic is there in "therefore" here?). What we are made to realize is that the "persuasion" that accords this minor, relative role to feelings, is not right and unwise. Rather than being dissolved, the connection reverses itself. Anne cannot afford to see this.

This little example is more significant than it looks at first sight and not only because it is one of the earliest indications of Anne's rigorous, sober clarity in assessing the possibilities of life in her world, and her refusal to indulge in personal fantasies of thwarted or renewable prospects with a Prince Charming. This very unblinkering, we find, can tip over into another kind of blindness. If, as is often noted, Anne can see clearly in all directions, then an exception must be made for her vision of herself. It is true, of course, that what one sees does not delimit what is there, nor does it entirely and automatically determine what one experiences. In this case it is anything but reprehensible that Anne should often try to impose a certain vision on herself and over and over again, set about to "teach herself" or "persuade herself". And yet always present at these moments is a contrary impulsion or invitation within her to lend herself to promptings that well up in her rather than to those that are borne in upon her. The course of the novel traces Anne's response to the challenge of admitting her own persuasion.

The most ineradicable persuasion Anne has she can admit because it seems to her a purely academic point now. It is simply this: that she would have been able to weather all sorts of trials had her heart asserted its attachment to Wentworth, and that "she should yet have been a happier woman in maintaining the engagement, than she had been in the sacrifice of it" (p. 58). Yet by this point (Ch. 4) the novel has already suggested that the process of persuasion (especially self-persuasion) can actively narrow or expand one's world, not be a more passive matter of merely ignoring or recognizing it. So we may well start to wonder if this persuasion of Anne's is as academic as she supposes. As the novel unfolds, it becomes a testing of her on every detail of it—not now in the maintaining of a formal engagement, but in the maintaining of an engagement of her hopes. Her persuasion has to resist all the trials she could have anticipated, and more, since it now takes on the quality of a certain kind of faith or attestation. Clearly, that faith is very different from a naive trust that if one believes in something hard enough, then it will come true. What the novel presents in her, and tests, is the quality of her moral being; for, as I have been trying to suggest, the novel constantly insists that this depends in part on what a person expects from the world, and this influences in turn what the person partly creates, partly finds in his "persuasions" about the world and himself.

The continued engagement of Anne's hopes is signalled very early in the novel by a deduction she attempts to toss off: "She had only navy lists and newspapers for her authority, but she could not doubt his being rich;—and, in favour of his constancy, she had no reason to believe him married" (p. 58). The novel immediately takes up the crucial point about the "eloquence" of Anne's wishes, tying the essentially prospective nature of wishes (however they are cast) to the apparently finalized past. This "eloquence" already marks Anne off from anyone else in the novel; and for that to be the dominant quality of the story one tells oneself, of the way one rehearses things and hence acknowledges their reality, bespeaks a certain moral character akin to fidelity. It is finally her "eloquence" with Captain Harville about precisely the point of her firmest persuasion, evincing a deep adherence to what she is saying, that opens the way for Wentworth's return to Anne.

We realize quite early on that Anne's heart has always belonged to Wentworth, and realize moreover what an ardent and passionate attachment it is during the discussion on the letting of Kellynch, when it requires great effort before she can "harden her nerves sufficiently" (p. 58) to endure conversation about anything connected with him. Harden her nerves she might, harden her heart she cannot. In contrast to the world she has to live in, which is either shallow or heartless, Anne is a woman of very deep feeling: indeed, although it is uncommon to say so, a passionate woman. And against her will, her heart keeps asserting its demand for fulfilment. No one in the novel has any kinship with her in this capacity for deep and faithful feeling. Part of Jane Austen's exploration of different kinds of persuasion and persuadability is the juxtaposition of Anne's capacity with the incapacity of others. At one extreme there is Louisa Musgrove and Mary, with their self-indulgence and sentimentality; at the other is the rigid barrenness of Elizabeth's propriety, not admitting feeling at all. Anne is sharply distinguished from all these. Her lively, sensitive heart repeatedly dislodges her composure. Whenever her deepest emotions are touched into life, her only recourse is escape to solitude, for her world certainly allows her no way her feelings and needs can be expressed. To Anne herself, these moments of disruption are a repeated reminder of what cannot be repressed. To us, they are evidence of the resurgence and tenacity of hope in a life that seemes to have no warrant for it. But of course the unacknowledged, involuntary reflexes of feeling to which she is subject early in the book hardly establish a solid and compelling "persuasion" about her life. The moral seriousness of the novel demands a more active assent and venturing by Anne for any happiness to be secured.

Jane Austen's sense of Anne's life and its prospects is a very delicately flexible one, and because of this she earns the right, at a certain point, to become uncompromising in her demands for and of her heroine. The first prospect author and heroine broach may seem to unite their voices in the plan to negotiate it: "With the prospect of spending at least two months at Uppercross, it was highly incumbent on her to clothe her imagination, her memory, and all her ideas in as much of Uppercross as possible" (p. 70). Yet if we attend to the metaphor, it will strike us as very odd indeed: the notion of these lively human faculties being "clothed", rather than spinning the fabric of life, is as ill-fitting as Uppercross is to Anne's capacities. Jane Austen is well aware of the incongruity, of course; the metaphor places Anne's proposal to clothe and tailor the yearnings of her heart in "house-keeping, neighbours, dress; dancing, and music" (p. 69) as insufficient to all it is trying to deal with; yet the metaphor also registers Jane Austen's sober sense of why it was "highly incumbent" on Anne to try. Still, the stress falls on the sluggishness of Anne's ruminations, and her over-willed compliance with what is borne in on her, which undermine what she is trying to believe: that "she must now submit to feel that another lesson, in the art of knowing our own nothingness beyond our own circle, was become necessary for her" (p.

69). There is certainly some truth to reality in this "lesson", but it cannot wholly persuade her because it denies the reality—the verve and "eloquence"—of her deepest wishes and desires. Jane Austen is fully aware of both elements of Anne's "reality"—which is a major reason why the novel avoids both sentimental wish-fulfilment and callousness. The sense of the intransigence of desire must not be compromised or weakened by any toning down of all it has to contend with.

One way of acknowledging but coping with the "nothingness" Anne's world holds out to her is for her to sink her energies into serving the needs of those round about. Jane Austen gives this impulse its due credit: "To be claimed as a good, though in an improper style, is at least better than being rejected as no good at all" (p. 61), although even here there is a hint of the self-pity into which it so easily slides and from which Anne barely retrieves herself a short time later: "as for herself, she was left with as many sensations of comfort, as were, perhaps, ever likely to be hers. She knew herself to be of the first utility to the child ..." (p. 83). In fact, to plead the promotion of others' welfare can be the most dangerous persuasion of all, because it seems to be so morally unimpeachable. Its value is brought under scrutiny very early, especially in regard to Anne's rejection of Wentworth:

> But it was not a merely selfish caution, under which she acted, in putting an end to it. Had she not imagined herself consulting his good, even more than her own, she could hardly have given him up.—The belief of being prudent, and self-denying principally for his advantage, was her chief consolation, under the misery of a parting—a final parting ... (p. 56)

As the novel sees it, Anne's belief in self-abnegation and self-sacrifice is anything but despicable; but it is also seen to be at best a consoling distraction, and at worst an active destroyer of the chance to bestow herself where the gift can be most creative. Even Anne is led to place this persuasion against a persuasion of her value and legitimate needs as a woman, though this is not a matter of conscious debate but of catching herself expecting rather more from life than merely being useful to others—as, for example, in her pain at Wentworth's reaction to the foiling of his plan that she should nurse Louisa after the accident: "but his evident surprise and vexation ... made but a mortifying reception of Anne; or must at least convince her that she was valued only as she could be useful to Louisa" (p. 135).

Anne's deeper self protests against her life being so cut back, and the spirit of the novel contains an even stronger protest. The thrust of the novel, like that of Anne's own life, is towards a belief in some possible fuller and deeper fulfilment. There is a vital trenchancy in the writing—in its urgings, admonitions and injunctions, its distancing from Anne's attempts to cut back her expectations, or to moralize her way out of her feelings, or to take refuge in self-pity and self-censure. In this way a demand is made that Anne persuade herself of such a possibility of fulfilment and then act on the persuasion. Thus Jane Austen delights in any evidence of Anne's resurgent spirits. She is delicately amused, in a tender yet uncompromising way, at the extent to which Anne's reviving hopes are troublesome to her—rejoicing because they are the only avenue to renewed life and vigour for Anne, yet taking the pain and agitation seriously. Jane Austen's irony towards Anne has the same sober gentleness. On Mrs Croft's tantalizing conversation about one or other of her brothers, Anne leaps to the assumption that Frederick is in question until tipped off by the mention of marriage:

> She could now answer as she ought.... She immediately felt how reasonable it was, that Mrs Croft should be thinking and speaking of Edward, and not of Frederick; and with shame at her own forgetfulness, applied himself to the knowledge of their former neighbour's present state, with proper interest. (p. 75)

The contrast between the involuntary veering of Anne's thoughts and the reasoning she imposes on them produces a very characteristic kind of smile in the writing.

It is also characteristic of Jane Austen's attitude towards her heroine that she is most satisfied with Anne when Anne is most dissatisfied with herself. After the first meeting with Wentworth, Anne attempts to deal with her response: "Soon, however, she began to reason with herself, and try to be feeling less" (p. 85). The attempt to slump into a fact that won't be ignored: "Alas! with all her reasonings, she found, that to retentive feelings eight years may be little more than nothing." The control of tone is masterly here, for while maintaining the sense this has for Anne, Jane Austen conveys something on her own account altogether different, for that "Alas!" has a buoyancy that makes it sound like anything but commiseration. She is amused at Anne's "reasonings", knowing that her less rational wisdom of heart will assert itself and supplant her more guarded appraisals: "Now, how were his sentiments to be read? Was this like wishing to avoid her? And the next moment she was hating herself for the folly which asked the question" (p. 85). Yet clearly, Jane Austen is also loving her for the wisdom which asked the question, which she well knows to be a very foolish sort of wisdom indeed. The puny fortifications of Anne's "utmost wisdom" against the onslaught of what she hopes for from Wentworth are not in the least ridiculed by Jane Austen, or blown away by a puff of romantic fervour. They are presented as both poignantly naive and only too well apprised of the consequences she can expect if they are abandoned. Infused in all Jane Austen's irony about Anne is a deep care for her pain, as, in this section, there is no overlooking or dismissing of the "peculiar wound" inflicted on Anne or of the "silent, deep mortification" which is all she is left with from the upsurge of her need. On this occasion Anne's pang of misery is caused by Wentworth's thinking her "altered beyond his knowledge". The irony of his saying that, when she is centrally unaltered in her need of him, has a touch of bitterness on Anne's behalf because it sees how powerful is his kind of knowledge and how ineffectual is hers. Anne attempts to talk herself out of her feelings again: "Yet she soon began to rejoice that she had heard [his words]. They were of sobering tendency; they allayed agitation; they composed, and consequently must make her happier" (p. 86). The very uncomposed rhythm and logic of these reflections, and the clear sense and feeling of Anne's pain, prevent any comfortable superiority to her evasion. On another level, it is as difficult for us to demand that Anne abandon this safeguarding refuge as it is for Anne to venture beyond it.

And this, I think, is partly Jane Austen's point about the value of such "persuasions" as Anne's. Because Anne loves Wentworth the way she does (and he has his reality in the book through her loving him), she cannot help herself venturing her hopes again and again. By the time she discovers him to be in Bath, she has fully embraced her real persuasion of her life's true home. She no longer tries to subject her feelings to a false persuasion of self-abnegation or denial, but respects their unmanageability. On the discovery that Wentworth's attachment to Louisa has been dissolved, "She had some feelings which she was ashamed to investigate. They were too much like joy, senseless joy" (p. 178). She has now learned that her feelings and hopes are not to be sacrificed and cannot be sacrificed, no matter how perilous the course of action they oblige her to follow. Jane Austen remains very clear-eyed about this. Against Anne's developments, she places Benwick, for whom such a respect and cherishing of feeling plunges into self-indulgence as he complacently hugs his grief, feeding off it and risking nothing. But Jane Austen underlines Anne's realism in other ways. By the time Anne catches a glimpse of Wentworth out of the shop window, for example, she is so firmly reconciled to the direction her life is taking, that she is able to laugh at her own paltry and token gestures to divert it:

> She now felt a great inclination to go to the outer door; she
> wanted to see if it rained. Why was she to suspect herself of
> another motive? Captain Wentworth must be out of sight. She
> left her seat, she would go, one half of her should not be always
> so much wiser than the other half, or always suspecting the other
> of being worse than it was. She would see if it rained. (p. 185)

Anne's self-teasing and irony here are as lively as Jane Austen's; and she is
aware too, that the questions of where suspicion and trust should lie, where
wisdom and folly are apportioned—in venturing or in restraining herself?—
have been answered long ago, counter to the apparent direction of these
rhetorical denials. Anne's ability to have a joke on herself is one of the
strongest clues to the vigour of her orientation. If Anne "learned romance as
she grew older", it certainly has nothing of the melting mood about it.

The attitude of readiness for fulfilment that Jane Austen develops in
Anne has none of the manipulative calculation with which other characters
set about securing what they want. The novel is too subtle to see this as a
simple opposition, however, of self-assertion versus deference or doormat
behaviour. The kinds of assertion open to and pursued by all the characters
in the novel vary enormously, but there is very little unabashed declaration
of need to those from whom they hope to gain. Anne chooses instead to
expose her self and its needs, with all the risks that involves. Thus at the
concert in Bath, she finally steels herself against the coldness of her father
and sister, against her own misgivings and uncertainty about the state of
Wentworth's heart, and makes a deliberate approach to him, offers an
invitation to change the terms of their relationship. In this situation Anne
decisively fulfils her potentiality to answer to the world with whole-hearted,
self-venturing vigour, at the same time abandoning those defences against
hurt which have supported her for so long.

This is the point of greatest vulnerability for Anne. However,
Wentworth recognizes and responds to her venturing, making it for her the
moment of supreme self-establishing. As we discover, he has been
undergoing a testing of his own heart's orientation. So how does this happy
ending sit with the rest of the novel? Is it merely a fairy-tale ending, which
ignores the moral complexity elaborated so far?

This is an obvious question, especially if we grasp the seriousness of the
story up to the ending, but not altogether a simple one to answer. If we find
the ending somehow insufficient, as I think we do, it is not because we want
to protest that such stories do not have happy endings, that it would have
been in some way more honest or unflinching for Jane Austen to have left

Anne's prospects barren, thereby affirming that desires and needs such as hers do not have much chance of affecting the world. But on the other hand, we are not inclined to say that the novel only makes sense if Anne and Wentworth are re-united. In fact, on this point the novel seems to take the least indulgent, the least absolute and tendentious course, by insisting that such endings *can* happen (but not often), and can efface some (but not all) of the pain and injury that has gone before. The price exacted by those eight long years can never be fully restored. No, the ending is unsatisfactory not because Jane Austen chose the wrong one out of several possible outcomes, but because it suggests that Anne's venturing is morally justified only by its consequences. But how valid a principle is this applied to Anne's case? Just as there was no external reason, or promise, or calculation of likely consequences, sufficient to prompt Anne's self-persuasion, so we do not judge her self-persuasion "good or bad only as the event decides" (p. 248). For the force of the novel's thinking about persuasion does not hinge on any such general principle of judgment, any more than the value of Anne's morally self-creating actions depends on what those actions can secure. Although Jane Austen does not get it quite clearly into focus, the fact is that her subtle, dramatic, evaluative sense of Anne cannot be reduced to any such general moral principle or calculation. The course of the novel has been making this clear in its delicate shaping of demands on and within Anne, always through the power of its dramatization rather than through any crude assertions. A case in point is the novel's clear recognition, in the way it elaborates and juxtaposes different episodes, that self-sacrifice, however appealing psychologically, may not be of much moral value. Many critics lament that Jane Austen has not explained how we should judge whether persuasion and persuadability are good or bad. Yet if there is anything unsatisfactory about the ending, it is precisely that it seems to offer, or at least suggest, just such an explanation. For what the novel embodies in the fortunes of Anne Elliot is a different kind of insight: that the life that cannot be repressed has only the assurance of its own pulse to rely upon, a pulse that cannot be reduced to "reasonable" calculations or expectations, or to pious principles, or to self-exaltation. To accept this pulse—an acceptance that is the heart of any persuasion—is both a kind of victory and a kind of surrender. When all is said and done and achieved, *Persuasion* is about Anne Elliot's belief *in* her self rather than her belief *that* her self can win through. The kind of moral intelligence required for this venture is as honest, courageous and fine as Jane Austen has created in any character—or shown in any of her own writing.

TONY TANNER

Knowledge and Opinion:
Pride and Prejudice

Why do you like Miss Austen so very much? I am puzzled on that
point.... I had not seen *Pride and Prejudice* till I read that sentence of
yours, and then I got the book. And what did I find? An accurate
daguerreotyped portrait of a commonplace face; a carefully fenced,
highly cultivated garden, with neat borders and delicate flowers; but no
glance of a bright, vivid physiognomy, no open country, no fresh air, no
blue hill, no bonny beck. I should hardly like to live with her ladies and
gentlemen, in their elegant but confined houses.

Thus Charlotte Brontë expressed her dissatisfaction with one of the most
enduringly popular of all English novels, in a letter to G.H. Lewes written in
1848. I shall return to the terms of her criticism later, and the significance of
their connotations, but the directness of her negative response prompts us to
reconsider the reasons for the lasting appeal of the novel and what relevance,
if any, it can still have for people living in very different social conditions. I
want to suggest various approaches to the novel, which may help to clarify its
achievement in terms of its own time and also suggest why the form of that
achievement could become distasteful to a Romantic such as Charlotte
Brontë. I also hope that by showing the different ways we may look at the
novel, its abiding relevance for all of us may become more readily
apprehensible.

From *Jane Austen*. © 1986 by Tony Tanner.

It is indeed possible to call its relevance to the society of the time into question, for, during a decade in which Napoleon was effectively engaging, if not transforming, Europe, Jane Austen composed a novel in which the most important events are the fact that a man changes his manners and a young lady changes her mind. Soldiers do appear, but in the marginal role of offering distractions to young girls, which in one case goes as far as to produce an elopement. However, we should be careful here in case we adduce this fact to demonstrate Jane Austen's ignorance of—or indifference to—contemporary history. She makes it clear that the soldiers are the militia—and her readers would have recognised them as part of the body of men specifically raised for the defence of England in the event of an invasion from France (which was distinctly feared at the time). However, since the invasion never came, the men in the militia had plenty of leisure and could be a disruptive presence in the community—as Mr Wickham (a militia officer) is. It is Darcy who pays his debts and buys him a commission in the socially more prestigious regular army. Here again, as Christopher Kent has noted in '"Real Solemn History" and Social History' (in *Jane Austen in a Social Context*), Jane Austen makes another telling contemporary point-for those who can read 'acutely' enough:

> Even as a regular soldier, Wickham is not sent abroad, but to Newcastle in the turbulently industrial North. This recalls another point: that the army was not simply for use against foreign enemies. In the almost complete absence of effective police forces in England the army was central to the maintenance of order at home.

Jane Austen must have known about the troubles in the industrial North just as she would surely have known about the naval mutinies of 1797 (thought to be Jacobin-inspired), given that she had brothers in the navy. So contemporary history *does* touch the periphery of this novel (it is more in evidence in her subsequent work). Nevertheless it is true to say that, although history is discernible out of the corner of the eye (it is contemporary history which brings about the arrival of the disrupter figure, Wickham—who is more of a danger to the community than the French, or mutinous sailors, or agitating workers), the overall impression given by the book is of a small section of society locked in an almost—*almost*—timeless, ahistorical present in which very little will or can, or even should, change. (It will be very different by the time we get to *Persuasion*.)

For the most part the people are as fixed and repetitive as the linked routines and established social rituals which dominate their lives. Money is a potential (never an actual) problem, and courtship has its own personal dramas; but everything tends towards the achieving of satisfactory marriages—which is exactly how such a society secures its own continuity and minimises the possibility of anything approaching violent change. In such a world a change of mind—an act by which consciousness demonstrates some independence from the patterns of thought which have predetermined its readings of things—can indeed come to seem a fairly momentous event, an internal modification matched in this novel by an external modification in an individual's behaviour. Let me put it this way. For the first two parts of the book Mr Darcy and Elizabeth Bennet believe that they are taking part in an action which, if turned into a fiction, should be called *Dignify and Perception*. They have to learn to see that their novel is more properly called *Pride and Prejudice*. For Jane Austen's book is, most importantly, about prejudging and rejudging. It is a drama of recognition—re-cognition, that act by which the mind can look again at a thing and if necessary make revisions and amendments until it sees the thing as it really is. As such it is thematically related to the dramas of recognition which constitute the great tradition of Western tragedy—*Oedipus Rex*, *King Lear*, *Phèdre*—albeit the drama has now shifted to the comic mode, as is fitting in a book which is not about the finality of the individual death but the ongoingness of social life.

I am not forgetting the immense charm of Elizabeth Bennet which has so much to do with the appeal of the book: 'I must confess that I think her as delightful a creature as ever appeared in print, and how I shall be able to tolerate those who do not like *her* at least I do not know ...', wrote Jane Austen in a letter; and indeed her combination of energy and intelligence, her gay resilience in a society tending always towards dull conformity, would make her a worthy heroine in a Stendhal novel, which cannot be said for many English heroines. But at this point I want to suggest that a very important part of the book is how it touches on, indeed dramatises, some aspects of the whole problem of knowledge. Eighteenth-century philosophers had, of course, addressed themselves to what Locke called 'the discerning faculties of a man' with unusual analytic rigour, considering not only the question of what we know, but also the more reflexive matter of *how* we know what we know, and the limits set on knowledge by the very processes and instruments of cognition. John Locke asserted at the start of his *Essay Concerning Human Understanding* that it was 'worth while to search out the bounds between opinion and knowledge; and examine by what measures, in things whereof we have no certain knowledge, we ought to regulate our assent and moderate our persuasion'. And he added, in a *caveat* which is important for understanding much eighteenth-century literature, 'Our business here is not to know all things, but those which concern our conduct.' Locke pointed out how, because of 'settled habit', often 'we take that for the perception of our sensation which is an idea formed by our judgement'. This fairly accurately sums up Elizabeth's earlier reactions to Darcy. She identifies her sensory perceptions as judgements, or treats impressions as insights. In her violent condemnation of Darcy and the instant credence she gives to Wickham, no matter how understandable the former and excusable the latter, Elizabeth is guilty of 'Wrong Assent, or Error', as Locke entitled one of his chapters. In it he gives some of the causes of man's falling into error, and they include 'Received hypotheses', 'Predominant passions or inclinations' and 'Authority'. These are forces and influences with which every individual consciousness has to contend if it is to make the lonely struggle towards true vision, as Elizabeth's consciousness does; and the fact that whole groups and societies can live in the grip of 'Wrong Assent, or Error', often with intolerably unjust and cruel results, only helps to ensure the continuing relevance of this happy tale of a girl who learned to change her mind.

The first title Jane Austen chose for the work which was finally called *Pride and Prejudice* was *First Impressions*, and I think this provides an important clue to a central concern of the final version. We cannot know how prominently 'first impressions' figured in the first version, since it is lost. There has, needless to say, been a great deal of scholarship devoted to the putative evolution of the novel, and I shall here quote from Brian Southam's *Jane Austen's Literary Manuscripts*, since his research in this area is well in advance of my own. He suggests that the book may have started out as another of Jane Austen's early burlesques, though adding that little remains in the final form to indicate such an origin.

> The object of the burlesque is hinted at in the title, for the phrase 'first impressions' comes directly from the terminology of sentimental literature, and Jane Austen would certainly have met it in *Sir Charles Grandison*, where its connotations are briefly defined. She would have known a more recent usage in *The Mysteries of Udolpho* (1794), where the heroine is told that by resisting first impressions she will 'acquire that steady dignity of mind, that can alone counter-balance the passions'. Here, as commonly in popular fiction, 'first impressions' exhibit the strength and truth of the heart's immediate and intuitive response, usually love at first sight. Jane Austen had already

attacked this concept of feeling in 'Love and Freindship', and in *Sense and Sensibility* it is a deeply-founded trait of Marianne's temperament.... There is a striking reversal of this concept in *Pride and Prejudice*, yet in circumstances altogether unsentimental.

He is referring to Elizabeth's 'first impressions' of Darcy's house, Pemberley, which are, as it were, accurate and authenticated by the book. She is also right, we might add, in her first impressions of such figures as Mr Collins and Lady Catherine de Bourgh. But she is wrong in her first impressions of Wickham; and her first impressions of Darcy, though to a large extent warranted by the evidence of his deportment and tone, are an inadequate basis for the rigid judgement which she then erects upon them.

Mr Southam suggests that 'the original title may have been discarded following the publication of a *First Impressions* by Mrs Holford in 1801', and he repeats R. W. Chapman's original observation that the new title almost certainly came from the closing pages of Fanny Burney's *Cecilia*. This book also concerns a very proud young man, Mortimer Delvile, who cannot bring himself to give up his family name, which is the rather perverse condition on which alone Cecilia may inherit a fortune from her uncle. The relationship between this book and Jane Austen's novel has also been explored by other critics and it will suffice here to quote from the wise Dr Lyster's speech near the end of the book:

> 'The whole of his unfortunate business', said Dr Lyster, 'has been the result of PRIDE AND PREJUDICE. Your uncle, the Dean, began it, by his arbitrary will, as if an ordinance of his own could arrest the course of nature! ... Your father, Mr Mortimer, continued it with the same self-partiality, preferring the wretched gratification of tickling his ear with a favourite sound, to the solid happiness of his son with a rich and deserving wife. Yet this, however, remember: if to PRIDE AND PREJUDICE you owe your miseries, so wonderfully is good and evil balanced, that to PRIDE AND PREJUDICE you will also owe their termination.'

But, while conceding that the phrase 'first impressions' may be more than a glancing blow aimed at the conventions of the sentimental novel, I want to suggest a further possible implication in Jane Austen's original title. Without for a moment suggesting that she read as much contemporary philosophy as she did fiction (though with so intelligent a woman it is scarcely impossible), I think it is worth pointing out that 'impressions' is one of the key words in David Hume's philosophy, and the one to which he gives pre-eminence as the source of our knowledge. Thus from the beginning of the *Treatise of Human Nature*:

> All the perceptions of the human mind resolve themselves into two distinct kinds, which I shall call IMPRESSIONS and IDEAS. The difference betwixt these consists in the degrees of force and liveliness, with which they strike upon the mind, and make their way into our thought or consciousness. Those perceptions, which enter with most force and violence, we may name *impressions*; and under this name I comprehend all our sensations, passions and emotions, as they make their first appearance in the soul. By *ideas* I mean the faint image of these in thinking and reasoning.... There is another division of our perceptions, which it will be convenient to observe, and which extends itself both to our impressions and ideas. This division is into SIMPLE and COMPLEX.... I observe that many of our complex ideas never had impressions, that corresponded to them, and that many of our complex impressions never are exactly copied in ideas. I can imagine to myself such a city as the *New Jerusalem*, whose pavement is gold and walls are rubies, tho' I never saw any such. I have seen *Paris*; but shall I affirm that I can form such an idea of that city, as will perfectly represent all its streets and houses in their real and just proportions?

Elizabeth has a lively mind—her liveliness is indeed one of the qualities which wins Darcy to her—and her impressions are comparably lively, since the quality of the registering consciousness necessarily affects the intensity of the registered impressions. Similarly she is capable both of complex impressions and of complex ideas—more of this later. Her problem, in Hume's terms, is that her complex ideas are not always firmly based on her complex impressions obtained from the scenes before her. Here we notice that eighteenth-century suspicion of imagination to which Jane Austen partially subscribed, since it was likely to make you believe ideas not based on impressions—to confuse the New Jerusalem and Paris. (In rebelling against eighteenth-century philosophy and psychology, Blake was to assert the primacy of the faculty which could envision the New Jerusalem and elevate it over the mere perception of Paris.)

If, says Hume, we wish to understand our ideas, we must go back to our impressions: 'By what invention can we throw light upon these ideas, and render them altogether precise and determinate to our intellectual view? Produce the impressions or original sentiments, from which the ideas are copied.' That is from *An Enquiry Concerning Human Understanding*. In the *Enquiry Concerning the Principles of Morals* he also stresses that

> the senses alone are not implicitly to be depended on; but that we must correct their evidence by reason, and by considerations, derived from the nature of the medium, the distance of the object, and the disposition of the organ, in order to render them, within their sphere, the proper *criteria* of truth and falsehood.

And 'a false relish may frequently be corrected by argument and reflection'. Impressions beget inclinations, and those inclinations may then come under the consideration of reason. But reason, being cool and disengaged, is not a motive to action, and directs only the impulse received from appetite or inclination, by showing us the means of attaining happiness or avoiding misery. One further quotation:

> In every situation or incident, there are many particular and seemingly minute circumstances, which the man of greatest talent is, at first, apt to overlook, though on them the justness of his conclusions, and consequently the prudence of his conduct, entirely depend.... The truth is, an unexperienced reasoner could be no reasoner at all, were he absolutely unexperienced.

Without experience, no reason; without impressions, no experience. This suggests the particular importance of 'first impressions', because, although they may well need subsequent correction, amplification, supplementation, and so on, they constitute the beginning of experience. All the above quotations from Hume seem to me to apply very aptly to *Pride and Prejudice* and I do not think this aptness needs spelling out. For Jane Austen, as for Hume, the individual needs to be *both* an experiencer *and* a reasoner: the former without the latter is error-prone, the latter without the former is useless if not impossible (as exemplified by Mary Bennet's sententious comments; she is *all* 'cool and disengaged' reason, and thus no reasoner at all). Both experience and reason depend upon impressions, and first impressions thus become our first steps into full human life. To overstress this may become a matter suitable for burlesque, but as a general proposition it is not inherently so.

To add to this proposition the reminder that first impressions, indeed all impressions, may need subsequent revision is only to say that full human life is a complex affair, and Jane Austen makes us well aware of this complexity. From the problematical irony of the opening assertion—'It is a truth universally acknowledged'—there are constant reminders of the shiftingness of what people take to be 'truth'; for what is 'universally acknowledged' can change not only from society to society but from person to person, and indeed within the same person over a period of time. There is in the book a whole vocabulary connected with the process of decisions, opinion, conviction, stressing or suggesting how various and unstable are people's ideas, judgements, accounts and versions of situations and people. After one evening of seeing Darcy 'His character was decided. He was the proudest, most disagreeable man in the world'; Elizabeth asks Wickham about Lady Catherine and 'allowed that he had given a very rational account'; she also believes his account of his treatment by Darcy and it is left to Jane to suggest that 'interested people have perhaps misrepresented each to the other'. Jane, however, has her own myopia, for, in her desire to think well of the whole world, she sees Miss Bingley's treatment of her as agreeable while Elizabeth more accurately discerns it as supercilious. However, Elizabeth is too confident, as when she asserts to her more tentative sister, 'I beg your pardon; one knows exactly what to think.' She is 'resolved' against Darcy and for a while takes pleasure in Wickham, who is, temporarily, 'universally liked'. She questions Darcy whether he has never allowed himself 'to be blinded by prejudice', without thinking that she may at that very moment be guilty of prejudging, with its resulting screening of vision. Opinions are constantly changing as people's behaviour appears in a different light. Elizabeth 'represents' a person or a situation in one way, while Jane adheres to her own 'idea' of things. It is Jane who, when Darcy is condemned by everybody else as 'the worst of men', 'pleaded for allowances and urged the possibility of mistakes'. Of course it is not long before opinion shifts against Wickham. 'Everybody declared that he was the wickedest young man in the world', just as everybody's opinion quickly reverses itself towards the Bennet family. 'The Bennets were *speedily pronounced* to be the luckiest family in the world, though only a few weeks before, when Lydia had first run away, they had been *generally proved* to be marked out for misfortune' (emphasis added). The fallibility of our 'proofs' and the prematurity of all too many of our 'pronouncements' are amply demonstrated in this novel. The 'anxious interpretation' which is made necessary on social occasions is examined, and the 'interest' which lies behind this or that reading of things is alluded to. When Mrs Gardiner '*recollected having heard* Mr Fitzwilliam Darcy *formerly spoken of* as a very proud, ill-natured boy' she takes it, temporarily, as knowledge (emphasis added).

It is of course Elizabeth who most importantly comes to 'wish that her former opinions had been more reasonable, her expressions more moderate'. As opposed to Jane, whom she calls 'honestly blind', Elizabeth has more 'quickness of observation'. But in Darcy's case her observation proves to be too quick. Not that we can or wish to count her wrong in her 'first impressions' of Darcy, for his manner is proud, patronising and, in his famous proposal, insulting and unworthy of a gentleman—as Elizabeth very properly points out to our great delight. But she had formed a fixed 'idea' of the whole Darcy on insufficient data, and in believing Wickham's account of the man—a purely verbal fabrication—she is putting too much confidence in unverified and, as it turns out, completely false, evidence.

However, it is important to note that her *éclaircissement* first comes through language as well—in the form of Darcy's letter. The passages describing her changing reaction to that letter are among the most important in the book. In effect she is having to choose between two opposed and mutually exclusive versions—Wickham's and Darcy's. 'On both sides it was only assertion.' She had at first been taken in by Wickham's plausible physical manner, but she gradually comes to put more trust in Darcy's authoritative writing-manner—she is discriminating between styles at this point. (Note that she immediately judges that Mr Collins is not a sensible man from the pompous style of his letter-writing—in this case, first impressions are validated.) She realises that 'the affair ... was capable of a turn which must make him [Darcy] entirely blameless throughout the whole'. *The affair was capable of a turn*—there in essence is the whole problem which for ever confronts the interpreting human consciousness, which can turn things now this way, now that way, as it plays, seriously or sportively, with the varying versions of reality which it is capable of proliferating: one concrete world—many partial mental pictures of it. But if it is the problem of consciousness, it can also be its salvation, for it enables a person to change his version or interpretation of things. Just how tenacious a man can be of a fixed version, and how disastrous that tenacity can be when it is a wrong version, is indeed the very subject of *King Lear*. Elizabeth thinks for a time that her wrong version has cost her a perfect mate and a great house, crucial things for a young lady in that society:

> She began now to comprehend that he was exactly the man who, in disposition and talents, would most suit her.... It was an union that must have been to the advantage of both.... But no such happy marriage could now teach the admiring multitude what connubial felicity really was.

But of course she does not have to undergo Lear's tribulations. By an intelligent and just reading of Darcy's letter she not only changes her mind about him: she comes to a moment of intense realisation about herself.

> How differently did everything now appear in which he was concerned! ... She grew absolutely ashamed of herself. Of neither Darcy nor Wickham could she think without feeling that she had been blind, partial, prejudiced, absurd. 'How despicably have I acted!' she cried; 'I, who have prided myself on my discernment! ... Till this moment I never knew myself.'

This may seem somewhat excessive—it is part of Darcy's improvement that he comes to acknowledge the justness of much of what she has said about his behaviour and manner. The important thing is that in perceiving her own pride and prejudice—notice she uses both words of herself—Elizabeth can now begin to be free of them. There can be few more important moments in the evolution of a human consciousness than such an act of recognition. There is much in our literature as well as our experience to suggest that the person who never comes to the point of saying, 'I never knew myself', will indeed remain for ever cut off from any self-knowledge—what possible effect there is on his or her vision and conduct need not here be spelt out. If we don't know ourselves, we don't know our world.

It is not surprising that after wandering alone for two hours 'giving way to every variety of thought—re-considering events, determining probabilities', as Elizabeth does after receiving Darcy's letter, she experiences 'fatigue'. For she has indeed been through an ordeal and engaged in a critical effort of rearranging her mental furniture. As F. Scott Fitzgerald once wrote, 'I was impelled to think. God, was it difficult! The moving about of great secret trunks.' That there are internal expenditures of energy quite as exhausting as any bout of external action is a truth which Jane Austen, with her restricted position in a fairly immobile society, was peculiarly able to appreciate. Elizabeth's particular ordeal is indeed a very ancient one, for she has been confronting for the first time the problematical discrepancies between appearances and reality, and the unsuspected limits of cognition. It is a theme as old as *Oedipus Rex*, and, even if all that is involved is recognising a rake and a gentleman respectively for what they really are, in Elizabeth's society, no less than in ancient Greece, such acts of recognition are decisive in the procuring of happiness or misery.

The constant need to be alert to the difference between appearance and reality is made clear from the start. Compared with Bingley and Darcy, Mr

Hurst 'merely looked the gentleman'. Since Mr Hurst alternates between playing cards and sleeping, he is hardly a problematical character. Wickham of course is more so. 'His appearance was greatly in his favour' and he has a 'very pleasing address'. He is 'beyond' all the officers of his regiment 'in person, countenance, air, and walk'. Elizabeth does not have it 'in her nature to question the veracity of a young man of such amiable appearance as Wickham'. He 'must always be her model of the amiable and the pleasing'. It is only after reading Darcy's letter that she has to start changing that model. As the above-quoted words make clear (none of them has pronounced ethical connotations), Elizabeth has hitherto responded to Wickham's manner, or that part of the self which is visible on social occasions. After the letter she thinks back:

> As to his real character had information been in her power, she had never felt a wish of inquiring. His countenance, voice, and manner had established him at once in the possession of every virtue. She tried to recollect some instance of goodness, some distinguished trait of integrity or benevolence ... but she could remember no more substantial good than the general approbation of the neighbourhood.

She has now started to think about 'substance' as being distinct from 'appearance', and from this point on Darcy's character will continue to rise in her estimation as Wickham's falls, until she can complain to Jane, 'There certainly was some great mismanagement in the education of these two young men. One has got all the goodness, and the other all the appearance of it.' Poor Jane, so reluctant to believe in the existence of human duplicity and evil scheming, would like to believe in the goodness of both men, but Elizabeth, with her more rigorous mind, points out that there is 'but such a quantity of merit between them; just enough to make one good sort of man; and of late it has been shifting about pretty much. For my part, I am inclined to believe it all Mr Darcy's.' Even here, as we can see, Elizabeth's sense of humour has not deserted her; and it enables her to disconcert Wickham with a nice irony. On her return from Rosings, Wickham asks if Darcy's 'ordinary style' has improved, adding, 'For I dare not hope that he is improved in essentials.' Elizabeth, by now convinced of the essential goodness of Darcy, can thus reply meaningfully, 'Oh, no! ... In essentials, I believe, he is very much what he ever was.' Wickham makes a rather agitated retreat, adding with weak insolence, 'I must rejoice that he is wise enough to assume even the *appearance* of what is right.' The emphasis is Jane Austen's and the word occurs again later in the chapter, again italicised, as if to stress that Elizabeth is now fully awakened to the possible disparities between appearance and substance.

Just what constitutes a persons 'real character' is one of the concerns of the book: the phrase occurs more than once, usually with the added idea that it is something that can be 'exposed' (and thus, by the same token, concealed). In particular, Darcy in his letter writes that, whatever Elizabeth may feel about Wickham, it 'shall not prevent me from unfolding his real character', just as later in the letter he narrates Wickham's attempt to seduce Georgiana, 'a circumstance ... which no obligation less than the present should induce me to unfold to any human being'. Cordelia's last words before being banished are

> Time shall unfold what plighted cunning hides
> Who covers faults, at last shame them derides.

'Unfolding' a hidden reality is of course replacing mere appearance with substance. The fact that reality can get folded up and hidden away—because we are so built that we are forced to work from first impressions which can be cynically manipulated—means that it is very important to be careful about what we regard as convincing evidence. It is the mistake of both Lear and Othello that they ask for the wrong kind of evidence, thus making themselves vulnerable to those who are willing to fabricate a set of false appearances. But in Shakespearean tragedy, as also in *Pride and Prejudice*, the 'real character' of both the good and the bad—of Cordelia and Iago, of Darcy and Wickham— is 'unfolded'. The cost and process of the unfolding are of course very different in each case. But the perennial theme is common to both.

At this point we may ask if Elizabeth has any more than calligraphic evidence for her new belief as to the relative merits of Darcy and Wickham. Obviously something more is required to give 'substance' to what could be mere 'assertion'. There is of course the magnanimous part he plays in the crisis precipitated by the elopement of Lydia and Wickham, but Elizabeth's improved vision has already by then 'learned to detect' the boring affectation in Wickham's manner, and appreciate the solid merit of Darcy. The education of her vision, if we may call it so, starts with Darcy's letter, but it is not complete until she has penetrated his house and confronted his portrait. This occurs on her visit to Derbyshire when the Gardiners persuade her to join them in looking round Pemberley, Darcy's fine house, and its beautiful grounds. This physical penetration of the interior of Pemberley, which is both an analogue and an aid for her perceptual penetration of the interior quality of its owner, occurs at the beginning of Book III, and after the proposal-letter episode I regard it as the most important scene in the book and wish to consider it in some detail.

The word 'picture' occurs frequently in the novel, often in the sense of people 'picturing' something—a ball, a married couple, a desired situation—to themselves. One important example of this is the following: 'Had Elizabeth's opinion been all drawn from her own family, she could not have formed a very pleasing picture of conjugal felicity or domestic comfort.' These pictures, then, are mental images, either derived from impressions or conjured up by imagination. (It is of course a particular quality of Elizabeth's that she is able to think outside the reality picture offered to her by her own family.) There are also more literal references to pictures—as when Miss Bingley suggests to Darcy, by way of a spiteful joke, that he should hang portraits of some of Elizabeth's socially inferior (to Darcy) relatives at Pemberley, adding, 'As for your Elizabeth's picture, you must not attempt to have it taken, for what painter could do justice to those beautiful eyes?' The relation between actual portraits and mental pictures is suggested when Darcy is dancing with Elizabeth. She has teased him with a witty description of their common characteristics. '"This is not a very striking resemblance of your own character, I am sure," said he. "How near it may be to *mine*, I cannot pretend to say. *You* think it a faithful portrait undoubtedly."' Later in the same dance he says, 'I could wish, Miss Bennet, that you were not to sketch my character at the present moment, as there is reason to fear that the performance would reflect no credit on either.' Her answer is, 'But if I do not take your likeness now, I may never have another opportunity.' This is more than mere banter because, since we cannot literally internalise another person, it is at all times extremely important what particular picture or portrait of that person we carry with us. The portrait metaphor allows one to suggest that the picture should be done with some care in order that the gallery of the mind should not be hung with a series of unjust unlikenesses.

We know that Jane Austen herself went to art galleries when she could. Thus in a letter to Cassandra in 1811: 'May and I, after disposing of her Father and Mother, went to the Liverpool Museum, & the British Gallery, & I had some amusement at each, tho' my preference for Men & Women, always inclines me to attend more to the company than the sight.' And in 1813 it is clear that when she went to a portrait gallery she had her own fictional portraits in mind. Again the letter is to Cassandra:

> Henry and I went to the Exhibition in Spring Gardens. It is not
> thought a good collection, but I was very well pleased—

particularly (pray tell Fanny) with a small portrait of Mrs Bingley, excessively like her. I went in hopes of finding one of her Sister, but there was no Mrs Darcy;—perhaps, however, I may find her in the Great Exhibition which we shall go to, if we have time;—I have no chance of her in the collection of Sir Joshua Reynolds Paintings which is now shewing in Pall Mall & which we are also to visit.—Mrs Bingley's is exactly herself, size, shaped face, features and sweetness; there never was a greater likeness. She is dressed in a white gown, with green ornaments, which convinces me of what I had always supposed, that green was a favourite colour with her. I dare say Mrs D. will be in Yellow.

Later in the letter she adds,

We have been both to the Exhibition & Sir J. Reynolds',—and I am disappointed, for there was nothing likes Mrs D at either. I can only imagine that Mr D. prizes any Picture of her too much to like it should be exposed to the public eye.—I can imagine he wd have that sort of feeling—that mixture of Love, Pride & Delicacy.—Setting aside this disappointment, I had great amusement among the Pictures....

It is worth noting that she does not expect to find a recognizable portrait of Elizabeth in Sir Joshua Reynolds's collection. For Reynolds, the artist, including the portraitist, 'acquires a just idea of beautiful forms; he corrects nature by her self, her imperfect state by her more perfect'. In his *Discourses* Reynolds laid typical neoclassical stress on 'central forms', and generalised figures which are not 'the representation of an individual, but of a class'. This neoclassic approach tended to minimise the individuating qualities of a person or thing in favour of more generic attributes or in deference to classical models. But for Jane Austen, the novelist and admirer of Richardson, it was precisely the individuating qualities, which sharply differentiated even the sisters in the same family, which held most interest. Elizabeth is not a type; indeed she has that kind of independent energy which is most calculated to disturb a typological attitude to people. She wants recognising for what she is and not what she might represent (Mr Collins's regard for her, as for Charlotte, is, she knows, wholly 'imaginary'—he sees her only as a suitable wife figure, and is dismissed according to his deserts). She is fortunate in attracting the discerning eye of Darcy—he is always staring at her, as if trying to read her fully, or capture the most complete likeness for his memory—for he alone of the men in the book is equipped to do justice to all her real qualities. It is thus only right that she should be brought to a full recognition of his real qualities. And this finally happens at Pemberley.

As they drive through the grounds Elizabeth admires the unobtrusive good taste in evidence—'neither formal nor falsely adorned'—and 'at that moment she felt that to be mistress of Pemberley might be something!' Then they are led through the house, where again the elegance and genuine taste—'neither gaudy nor uselessly fine'—awakens her admiration, and she again reverts to what she regards as her lost opportunity: '"And of this place," thought she, "I might have been mistress!"' Showing them round the house is Mrs Reynolds, a sort of cicerone who may be guilty of 'family prejudice' but whose testimony concerning the youthful qualities of Darcy and Wickham has authority for Elizabeth. She is a voice from within the house and thus acquainted with Darcy from his origins, and is not, as Elizabeth necessarily is, a purely social acquaintance. She shows them some miniatures, including one of Darcy ('the best landlord, and the best master') and invites Elizabeth to go and look at a larger portrait of Darcy upstairs in the picture gallery. Elizabeth walks among the portraits

> in quest of the only face whose features would be known to her. At last it arrested her—and she beheld a striking resemblance of Mr Darcy, with such a smile over the face as she remembered to have sometimes seen when he looked at her. She stood several minutes before the picture, in earnest contemplation.... There was certainly at this moment, in Elizabeth's mind, a more gentle sensation towards the original than she had ever felt in the height of their acquaintance.... Every idea that had been brought forward by the housekeeper was favourable to his character, and as she stood before the canvas on which he was represented, she fixed his eyes upon herself, she thought of his regard with a deeper sentiment of gratitude than it had ever raised before; she remembered its warmth, and softened its impropriety of expression.

One can almost detect the unformulated thought: 'and of this man I might have been the wife'. It is a thought which explicitly occurs to her in due course.

Standing in the middle of the house, contemplating the qualities in the face in the portrait (qualities imparted and corroborated to some extent by the housekeeper), Elizabeth completes the act of recognition which started with the reading of Darcy's letter. Notice the fact that the truest portrait is the large one in the more private part of the house upstairs; downstairs Darcy is only visible in 'miniature'. We can imagine that, the further a man goes from the house in which he is truly known, the more liable he is both to misrepresentation and to non-recognition. Standing before the large and true image of the real Darcy, Elizabeth has in effect completed her journey. When she next meets the original, outside in the grounds, she is no longer in any doubt as to his true worth. The rest of the book is, indeed, for the most part concerned with externalities—the mere melodrama of Wickham's elopement with Lydia, which gives Darcy a chance to reveal his qualities in action. But all this is only delay, not advance, in terms of the novel. For the most important action is complete when Elizabeth has finished the contemplation of the portrait. In answer to Jane's questions concerning when Elizabeth first realised she was in love with Darcy, Elizabeth replies, 'I believe it must date from my first seeing his beautiful grounds at Pemberley.' This is not wholly a joke, nor should it be taken to indicate that at heart Elizabeth is just another materialist in what is shown to be a distinctly materialistic society. In this case the grounds, the house, the portrait all bespeak the real man—they represent a visible extension of his inner qualities, his true style. And, if Pemberley represents an ordering of natural, social and domestic space which is everything that the Bennet household is not, who shall blame Elizabeth for recognising that she would be more truly at home there? However, it is true that such a remark could only be made in the context of a society which shared certain basic agreements about the importance and significance of objects, domiciles and possessions. One can well imagine Charlotte Brontë's response to a remark of this kind. But these are matters to which we shall return.

Having mentioned the central importance of Darcy's letter, which contains an 'account of my actions and their motives' for Elizabeth to peruse and re-peruse in private, we might at this point consider the overall importance of letters in this novel. So much of the main information in the novel is conveyed by letter—whether it be Mr Collins's vapid but acquisitive pomposity, or Miss Bingley's competitive coldness, or Mr Gardiner's account of Darcy's role in securing the marriage of Lydia and Wickham—that there has been some speculation that the novel was initially conceived in epistolary form. Thus Brian Southam:

> In *Sense and Sensibility*, twenty-one letters are mentioned, quoted, or given verbatim, and in *Pride and Prejudice* no fewer than forty-

four, including references to a 'regular and frequent' correspondence between Elizabeth and Charlotte Lucas, and the further regular communications of Elizabeth and Jane with Mrs Gardiner, a very credible system of letters to carry much of the story in epistolary form. If this reconstruction is feasible it supports my theory that, like *Sense and Sensibility*, *Pride and Prejudice* was originally a novel-in-letters.

On the other hand critics have been drawn to note the brilliance of much of the dialogue and have suggested that the novel has close affinities with the drama. In an excellent essay entitled 'Light and Bright and Sparkling' Reuben Brower writes, 'In analysing the ironies and the assumptions, we shall see how intensely dramatic the dialogue is, dramatic in the sense of defining characters through the way they speak and are spoken about', and he proceeds to show just how much, and how subtly, is revealed in various passages of dialogue. Walton Litz in his book on Jane Austen says that the tripartite structure of the novel is similar to the structure of a three-act play, and adds that in many of the passages 'we are reminded of the novel's affinities with the best in eighteenth-century drama'. But he also notes that the early part of the novel is more dramatic than the latter.

Howard S. Babb has shown how Jane Austen plays on the word 'performance' in the early dialogues, bringing all the implications of the word together in the great scene at Rosings, where Elizabeth's actual performance at the piano becomes the centre of a dramatic confrontation. 'But after the scene at Rosings, when Darcy's letter begins Elizabeth's movement toward self-recognition, the term "performance" quietly disappears from the novel. The first half of *Pride and Prejudice* has indeed been a dramatic performance, but in the second half a mixture of narrative, summary, and scene carries the plot towards the conclusion.' As he rightly says, this reveals that Jane Austen felt able to take advantage both of scenic representation and of authorial omniscience using third-person narrative, but I think there is another interesting aspect of the combination of the dramatic and the epistolary-particularly bearing in mind that, as Babb has noted, the word 'performance' fades after Elizabeth receives Darcy's letter.

In essence a letter is written and read in retirement from the social scene; this is certainly true of Darcy's major epistolary clarification. The letter enables him to formulate things and convey information in a way which would not be possible on a social occasion, where public modes of utterance necessarily restrict the more private ones. A letter is also a transforming of action into words, which may then be reflected on in a way which is impossible while one is actually involved in the action. 'Introspection is retrospection', said Sartre, and so is letter-writing, even if the letter seems to be written in the midst of some anxious situation. By combining the dramatic and the epistolary modes, Jane Austen has deftly set before us a basic truth—that we are both performing selves and reflective selves. It is in social performance that Elizabeth reveals all her vitality, vivacity and wit, as well as her actual physical magnetism; it is in private reflection ('reflection must be reserved for solitary hours') that she matures in judgement, reconsiders first impressions, and is able to make substantial changes to her mental reality picture. How suitable, then, that after giving us some of the most brilliant 'performances' in English fiction, Jane Austen should allow her novel to move away from performance towards reflection after Darcy's letter. She thus subtly offers an analogue of how—in her view—the individual should develop. For, if the human being is to be fully human, then to the energy of performance must be added the wisdom of reflection.

The idea of the self as a performer has taken hold of much recent thought, and most people recognise that society is effectively held together by a series of tacitly acknowledged rituals in which we all play a number of different parts. Jane Austen certainly believed in the value of the social rituals of her time—be they only balls, dinners, evening entertainments—and would have seen them, at their best, as ceremonies and celebrations of the values of the community. What she was also clearly aware of was how the failings of some of the performers—insensitivity, malice, arrogance, foolishness and so on—could spoil the ritual, and transform a ceremony to be enjoyed into a nightmare to be endured, as Elizabeth has so often to endure her mother's agonising ceremonial violations. But, although we are all role-players for much of the time we spend with other people, there will obviously be a difference between those people who are unaware of the fact—who disappear into their roles, as it were—and those who are at all times quite aware that the particular role they are performing in any one particular situation is not to be identified as their self, that they have facets and dimensions of character which cannot always be revealed on every occasion. The former type of person may sometimes appear to be something of an automaton, incapable of reflection and detachment, while the latter type of person may often wish to make a gesture of disengagement from the roles he is called on to play, to indicate that he has not become mindlessly imprisoned in those roles. Such gestures are expressive of what Erving Goffman calls 'role distance'.

Considering the characters in Jane Austen's novel in this light, we can see that Mr Bennet has become completely cynical about the social roles he is called on to play. He extracts a somewhat bitter pleasure from making gestures of disengagement from these roles, to compensate for the familial miseries brought about by his having married a sexually attractive but unintelligent woman (another example of the dangers of unreflective action based on first impressions—Lydia is her father's daughter as well as her mother's). It is Lydia's precipitous elopement, in addition to the more remote but not dissimilar marriage of her father, that provokes Jane Austen to her most direct attack on first impressions. She is justifying Elizabeth's change of mind about Darcy.

> If gratitude and esteem are good foundations of affection, Elizabeth's change of sentiment will be neither improbable nor faulty. But if otherwise—if the regard springing from such sources is unreasonable or unnatural, in comparison of what is so often described as arising on a first interview with its object, and even before two words have been exchanged—nothing can be said in her defense, except that she had given somewhat of a trial of the latter method in her partiality for Wickham, and that its ill success might, perhaps, authorize her to seek the other less interesting mode of attachment.

It is fairly clear here that Jane Austen is showing her particular suspicion of the pre-verbal immediacy of sexual attraction. In this area in particular, she obviously thought that to act on first impressions could only be disastrous.

Mr Bennet effectively abdicates from the one role it is most incumbent on him to perform: that is, the role of father. He has taken refuge in mockery just as he takes refuge in his library—both are gestures of disengagement from the necessary rituals of family and society. Mrs Bennet, incapable of reflection, loses herself in her performance. Unfortunately she has a very limited view of the requirements of that performance; lacking any introspective tendencies she is incapable of appreciating the feelings of others and is *only* aware of material objects—hats, dresses, uniforms—and marriage, not as a meeting of true minds but as a disposing of redundant daughters. On another level Lady Catherine de Bourgh has none of what Jane Austen elsewhere approvingly calls 'the Dignity of Rank' but only the mindlessness of rank. She thinks her position entitles her to dictate to other people and impose her 'schemes' on them (a recurrent word in the book). She has never thought out, or thought round, the full implications of her performance. Being incapable of reflection she makes people suffer. At the other extreme Mary Bennet sees herself as a sage reflector before she has had any experience; when reflection portentously precedes performance in this way it is shown to be comical and useless. Darcy of course *has* thought about all the implications of his role in society, at least by the end of the book. His hauteur makes him go in for a certain amount of 'role distance', as at the first ball, when he slights Elizabeth to show his contemptuous detachment from the social ritual of the moment; but, unlike Wickham, he is not cynical about role-playing, and by the end his performing self is shown to be in harmony with his reflecting self.

Jane Bennet is incapable of role distance, but she has such a generous and high-minded conception of the roles she has to perform—daughter, sister, lover, wife—that she strikes us at all times as being both sensitive and sincere. Much the same could be said of Bingley, whose rather spineless plasticity in the hands of Darcy's more decisive will indicates nevertheless that his basic good nature extends to a willingness to perform roles which are thrust upon him—obviously a potential source of vulnerability. Elizabeth is of course special. She can indeed perform all the roles that her familial and social situations require of her; moreover, she performs many of them with an *esprit* or an irony which reveal, as it were, a potential overspill of personality, as if there is more of her than can ever be expressed in any one role. She is also capable of role distance, not in her father's spirit of cynicism but in her own spirit of determined independence. She will put truth to self above truth to role. Thus in two of the scenes which give us the most pleasure to read we see her refusing to take on the roles which people in socially superior positions attempt to impose on her. To Darcy's first, lordly proposal she refuses to respond in the role of passive grateful female, as he obviously expects she will; while in the face of Lady Catherine's imperious insistence that she promise not to marry Darcy she refuses to act the compliant social inferior to which role Lady Catherine is relegating her. The assertion of the free-choosing self and its resistance to the would-be tyranny of roles imposed on it from socially superior powers is a spectacle which delights us now quite as much as it can have done Jane Austen's contemporaries.

All that has been said makes it clear that there are at least two different kinds of characters in the book: those who are fully defined by their roles, even lost in them, and those who can see round their roles and do not lose awareness of what they are doing. D. W. Harding uses the terms character and caricature to point to this difference, and, commenting that 'in painting it must be rather rare for caricature and full portraiture to be brought together in one group', he goes on to show what Jane Austen achieves by her carefully handled interaction of character and caricature, and what she is implying about a society in which such interactions are possible. (Examples are the meetings between Elizabeth and Mr Collins, and Elizabeth and Lady Catherine. See 'Character and Caricature in Jane Austen' in *Critical Essays on Jane Austen*, ed. B. C. Southam.) There is an important conversation in which Elizabeth announces that she comprehends Bingley's character completely. He replies that it is pitiful to be so transparent. 'That is as it happens. It does not necessarily follow that a deep, intricate character is more or less estimable than such a one as yours.' Bingley replies that he did not know she was a 'studier of character'.

> 'It must be an amusing study.'
> 'Yes, but intricate characters are the most amusing. They have at least that advantage.'
> 'The country', said Darcy, 'can in general supply but few subjects for such a study. In a country neighbourhood you move in a very confined and unvarying society.'
> 'But people themselves alter so much, that there is something new to be observed in them forever.'

Elizabeth's last remark is not wholly borne out by the book, for the Collinses and the Mrs Bennets and Lady Catherines of this world do not change. But 'intricate' characters are capable of change, as both she and Darcy change. Marvin Mudrick has examined this separation of Jane Austen's characters into the simple and the intricate, and shown how central it is to *Pride and Prejudice*, and there is no point in recapitulating his admirable observations here. Very generally we can say that obviously it is always likely to be in some ways oppressive for an intricate person to find himself or herself forced to live among simple people. Elizabeth has a dimension of complexity, a questing awareness, a mental range and depth which almost make her an isolated figure trapped in a constricting web of a small number of simple people. Darcy is posited as intricate to make her a match, but in truth he appears more to be honourable and reserved. He is not Benedick to Elizabeth's Beatrice. He is, however, capable of appreciating the intricacy of Elizabeth, so that in effect he can rescue her from the incipient claustrophobia of her life among simple people, and offer her more social and psychological space to move around in. (The good simple people, Jane and Bingley, join them in Derbyshire—the rest are left behind.)

This matter of social space is an important one, but another word may be said about what we may refer to as mental space or range, and its effect on language. We can recognise at bast two very different ways in which people use language in this book. Some people employ it unreflectively as an almost

automatic extension of their other behaviour; they are unable to speak, as
they are unable to think, outside their particular social situation. (Consider,
for example, the extremely limited range of Mrs Bennet's conversation, its
obsessive repetitions, its predictable progressions.) Others, by contrast, are
capable of using language reflectively and not just as an almost conditioned
response to a social situation. Such people seem to have more freedom of
manoeuvre within language, more conceptual space to move around in, and
as a result they can say unpredictable things that surprise both us and the
other characters in the book, and they seem capable of arriving at
independent and thought-out conclusions of their own. Obviously such
people are capable of thinking outside their particular social context—thus
Elizabeth's mind and conversation are not limited to what she has seen and
heard within her own family. (Compare Basil Bernstein's work in socio-
linguistics, in which he differentiates between a restricted speech code and an
elaborated speech code, the former determined by a person's particular
position in the social structure, while the latter is not thus restricted.) It is not
surprising that a person who has achieved a certain amount of mental
independence will wish to exercise as much free personal control over his or
her own life as is possible. He, or she, will not readily submit to the situations
and alliances which society seems to be urging them into—hence Elizabeth's
incredulity when Charlotte unhesitatingly accepts the role of Mr Collins's
wife, to Elizabeth an inconceivable capitulation to the solicitations of social
convenience. By contrast she will strive for a maximum of personal control
(in defiance of real economic and family pressures), as is consistent with her
having the quickest and furthest-ranging mind, and the most richly
developed linguistic capacities.

Because the same space is occupied by people using language both
reflectively and unreflectively, the claustrophobia for someone highly
sensitive to speech can become very great, as witness the agonies of
embarrassment which Elizabeth goes through while her mother rattles
unreflectively on. This can obviously lead to a desire to escape, and, although
Jane Austen does not seem to envisage how someone might renounce society
altogether, she does show the relief with which an intricate person seeks out
some solitude away from the miseries which can be caused by the constant
company of more limited minds. Thus in the fragment *The Watsons*, which
Jane Austen wrote some time between *First Impressions* and *Pride and
Prejudice*, the isolated, because more complex, consciousness of the heroine,
Emma, is glad to seek out the refuge of her father's quiet sick-room away
from the family downstairs:

> In *his* chamber, Emma was at peace from the dreadful
> mortifications of unequal Society, & family Discord—from the
> immediate endurance of Hard-hearted prosperity, low-minded
> Conceit, & wrong-headed folly, engrafted on an ontoward
> Disposition. She still suffered from them in the Contemplation of
> their existence; in memory & in prospect, but for the moment,
> she ceased to be tortured by their effects.

(Compare Elizabeth, who 'sick of this folly, took refuge in her own room, that she might think with freedom'.) Elizabeth is fortunate to make a more permanent escape through marriage to Darcy; 'she looked forward with delight to the time when they should be removed from society so little pleasing to either, to all the comfort and elegance of their family party at Pemberley'. Pemberley is an all but impossible dream of a space—both social and psychic—large enough to permit a maximum of reflecting speech and personal control.

There is another aspect to the problems which can be posed by lack of social space. In a clearly stratified class society, such as Jane Austen depicts, there are invisible restrictions, boundaries and chasms, which the properly deferential person will not dare to traverse. There are quite a number of malicious remarks about people in trade made by some of the members of the landed aristocracy; one of the things Darcy has to do is to learn to appreciate the merits of people such as the Gardiners. The absurd and cringing servility of Mr Collins is an extreme example of the kind of mind, or rather mindlessness, which such a society can exact as a condition of belonging. It is a point, indeed, whether Elizabeth can be contained within such a society. One of the trials which Darcy has to pass is to confront the fact that he will become related not only to Mrs Bennet, but also to Wickham, if he marries Elizabeth. Elizabeth is sure that there is 'a gulf impassable between them' after the marriage of Lydia and Wickham. 'From such a connection she could not wonder that he should shrink.' Lady Catherine insists to her that 'connection with you must disgrace him in the eyes of everybody'. In this society, as in any highly structured society, it is a matter of some moment just who may be 'connected' to whom. Darcy has already dissuaded Bingley from a defiling connection with the Bennets, and the connection—from an external point of view—had indeed become more disgraceful by the end. The question is, can Darcy cross the social space which, in the eyes of society (and in his own up to a certain stage) exists between himself and Elizabeth?

There is a curious little scene between Elizabeth and Darcy shortly before he proposes to her for the first time. They are discussing, of all apparently trivial things, whether it could be said that Charlotte Lucas is living near to her family, or far from them, now that she has moved fifty miles and become Mrs Collins. Darcy says it is near, Elizabeth that it is far; it is possible that he is wondering whether he will be able to move Elizabeth a sufficient distance away from the rest of her socially undesirable family. Elizabeth makes the politic remark, 'The far and the near must be relative, and depend on varying circumstances.' At this point Darcy 'drew his chair a little towards her', then a little later in the conversation he 'experienced some change of feeling; he drew back his chair, took a newspaper from the table', and coldly changes the drift of the conversation. In that small advance and retreat of his chair, Darcy is miming out, albeit unconsciously, his uncertainty as to whether he can bring himself to cross the great social space which, as he sees it (he is still proud), separates Elizabeth from himself. They live in a society which all but dictates certain 'connections' and works strongly to prevent others. Part of the drama is in seeing whether two people can resist the connections which society seems to be prescribing for them (as Lady Catherine has the 'rational scheme' of marrying her daughter to Darcy,[1] and Mrs Bennet wishes to thrust Elizabeth at Mr Collins), and make a new connection of their own, one which is not made in response to society's controlling power but freely made according to the dictates of their judgement, their reason and their emotions. One of the gratifications of the book is that Elizabeth and Darcy seem to demonstrate that it is still possible for individuals to make new connections in defiance of society. That there is perhaps a fairy-tale touch to their total felicity at the conclusion in the dream world of Pemberley should not discourage us from recognising the importance of holding on to this possibility as one which is essential to a healthy society. That is to say, a society in which the individual can experience freedom as well as commitment.

At this point it is perhaps worth considering in a little more detail just what kind of society Jane Austen does portray in this novel. It is a society which stresses social control over individual ecstasy, formality over informality, sartorial neatness over bodily abandon, and alert consciousness over the more Romantic states of reverie and trance. The schemes and structures of the group—family, community, society—tend to coerce and even predetermine the volition and aspirations of the self. No novelist could have valued consciousness more than Jane Austen, and some of the dialogue between Elizabeth (in particular) and Darcy requires a very high degree of alertness of consciousness. Indeed, this is just the point, that in this society linguistic experience is stressed almost to the exclusion of bodily experience. True, the men hunt, the women go for walks, and the sexes may come together at a ball. But all the important transactions (and most of the unimportant or vexatious ones) take place through language. When Darcy makes his second, and now welcome, proposal, we read of Elizabeth, 'though she could not look, she could listen, and he told of feelings which ... made his affection every moment more valuable'. At this crucial moment 'love' has been transformed into a completely linguistic experience. This is quite appropriate in a society setting a high value on consciousness.

Intimate physical contacts and experiences, while not denied, are minimised. Hands may meet, though it is more likely to be the eyes which come together across a distinct social space. Faces may be turned towards, or away from, other faces, and Elizabeth is prone to a good deal of blushing (allowing that the body has its own language, it is perhaps not entirely irrelevant to note that Norman O. Brown, following Freud, suggests that blushing is a sort of mild erection of the head). In general we are more likely to be shown dresses than bodies, public greetings than private embraces. It is interesting to compare, for instance, Jane Austen's description of an important ball with Tolstoy's. In Jane Austen the dancing (which from her letters we know she thoroughly enjoyed) is almost exclusively an occasion for conversation; indeed, it is a social ritual which permits something approaching private conversation in public, and there are some important exchanges between Darcy and Elizabeth while dancing. There is movement, there is grouping; there are *longueurs* and excitements. (In *The Watsons*, interestingly, Jane Austen describes what it is like for a young girl to enter a ball—the sweeping of dresses on the floor, the cold and empty room in which conversation is stiffly started, the noise of approaching carriages, and so on— a rather unusual excursion into private sensations which is not, however, taken very far.) What we do not get is the *physicality* of a ball. The following passage from *Anna Karenina* is inconceivable in Jane Austen. Kitty is watching Anna and Vronsky at the moment when they are falling in love with each other:

> She saw that they felt as if they were alone in the crowded ballroom. And she was struck by the bewildered look of submission on Vronsky's face, usually so firm and self-possessed—an expression like that of an intelligent dog conscious of having done wrong.
>
> If Anna smiled, he smiled in reply. If she grew thoughtful, he looked serious. Some supernatural force drew Kitty's eyes to

Anna's face. She was charming in her simple black gown, her rounded arms were charming with their bracelets, charming the firm neck with the string of pearls, charming the unruly curls, charming the graceful, easy movements of her little hands and feet, charming the lovely, animated face: but in that charm there was something terrible and cruel.

Kitty is 'sure that the blow had fallen'. At this decisive moment when the blow falls which will determine the rest of their lives, there is no language. It is Anna's body which is speaking to Vronsky, and speaking a language which Kitty can also read. Rational consciousness is drowned in an intensity of purely physical, sensory awareness and response. We have moved a long way from the sparkling dialogue maintained by Elizabeth with her partners, and are indeed approaching something like a state of trance, each dancer almost drugged just by the presence and proximity of the other. This is not intended as any indictment of Jane Austen's novel, for who would wish it other than it is? It is pointing to something characteristic of the society she wrote out of and in turn portrays: namely, the minimising of a whole range of physical experiences which can often change lives more forcibly than rational reflection.

As we have mentioned, Jane Austen is particularly suspicious of the immediacy of sexual attraction. It is worth asking, then, what is 'love' as it emerges from the book? And we should notice first that, if Jane Austen's society minimises the bodily dimension, so it does the possibility of a transcendental one. Her concern is with conduct, almost never with religious experience. (Gilbert Ryle points out in his interesting essay 'Jane Austen and the Moralists' (which appears in *Critical Essays on Jane Austen*, ed. B. C. Southam) in which he argues that Shaftesbury's ideas influenced Jane Austen's ethics—aesthetics, that, while she often uses the word 'Mind', she almost never uses the word 'soul'.) Her society is secular and materialistic, and the terms need not be pejorative. It was a society which valued objects and the actual edifices which made up its structure; it was quite capable of sustaining a fairly nominal or unexamined piety towards the Unknown, but at its best it concentrated on how man and woman may best live in harmony with each other. (What may happen in such a society when it is not at its best, Jane Austen unsparingly reveals.) All of this obviously influenced the notion of 'love' and its relationship to marriage. Mrs Gardiner complains to Elizabeth that 'that expression of "violently in love" is so hackneyed, so doubtful, so indefinite, that it gives me very little idea', and Elizabeth duly rephrases her reading of Bingley's attitude towards Jane as a 'promising inclination'. Early in the book Charlotte and Elizabeth discuss the conscious strategies that a woman must deploy to secure the attachment of a man, and Charlotte of course demonstrates the complete triumph of conscious calculation over spontaneous emotion by her decision to marry Mr Collins. She admits that she is 'not romantic' and asks only for 'a comfortable home'. Of course Mr Collins's company is 'irksome', but in her eyes the state of marriage, as a 'preservative from want', is much more important than the actual man who makes up the marriage. As Elizabeth realises when she sees them married, Charlotte will survive by having recourse to selective inattention, deriving satisfaction from the house and screening out as far as possible the man who provided it. Elizabeth's spontaneous reaction when told of their coming marriage is, 'Impossible', but her remark is not only indecorous: it is excessive. In such a society, the need for an 'establishment' is a very real one, and in putting prudence before passion Charlotte is only doing what the economic realities of her society—as Jane Austen makes abundantly clear—all but force her to do.

Indeed passion, as such, is hardly differentiated from folly in the terms of the book. Lydia's elopement is seen as thoughtless and foolish and selfish, rather than a *grande passion*; while Mr Bennet's premature captivation by Mrs Bennet's youth and beauty is 'imprudence'. This is a key word. Mrs Gardiner warns Elizabeth against becoming involved with the impoverished Wickham, yet when it seems he will marry a Miss King for her money she describes him as 'mercenary'. As Elizabeth asks, 'what is the difference in matrimonial affairs, between the mercenary motive and the prudent motive?' Elizabeth will simply not accept Charlotte's solution as a model of true 'prudence', nor will we. There must be something between that kind of prudence and her father's imprudence. And one of the things the book sets out to do is to define a rationally based 'mode of attachment'—something between the exclusively sexual and the entirely mercenary. Thus words such as 'gratitude' and 'esteem' are used to describe Elizabeth's growing feeling for Darcy. She comes to feel that their union would have been 'to the advantage of both: by her ease and liveliness, his mind might have softened, his manners improved; and from his judgement, information, and knowledge of the world, she must have received benefit of greater importance'. A word to note there is 'advantage': consciousness has penetrated so far into emotions that love follows calculations and reflections. What differentiates Elizabeth's choice from Charlotte's is not its greater impetuosity—indeed, it is Charlotte who is the more precipitate. It is the fact that it is a free choice which is not dictated by economic pressure (though Pemberley is a great attraction, as she readily admits); and it is a choice which is based on more awareness, knowledge, and intelligence than Charlotte brings to her cool but instant capitulation. Elizabeth loves for the best reasons, and there are always reasons for loving in Jane Austen's world. Consider this sentence from Tolstoy's *Resurrection*: 'Nekhludov's offer of marriage was based on generosity and knowledge of what had happened in the past, but Simonson loved her as he found her; *he loved her simply because he loved her*' (emphasis added). Tolstoy takes in a far wider world than Jane Austen, both socially and emotionally. He knew that there are feelings of such intensity, directness and tenacity that they reduce language to tautology when it attempts to evoke them. The kind of emotion pointed to in the remarkable clause I have emphasised—not to be confused with lust, for this is far from being a purely sexual attraction—is a kind of emotion which is not conceived of, or taken into account, in Jane Austen's world. This is not to censure Jane Austen for blinkered vision. It is, rather, to point out that in her books, and thus in the society they reflect, emotion is either rational—capable of being both conceptualised and verbalised—or it is folly.

And yet we sense that there is a capacity for depths and animations of feeling in Elizabeth which is not allowed for in the above description of the 'rationally founded' emotions preferred by Jane Austen. It is that extra something which dances through her words conveying an emotional as well as a semantic energy; it is what glows from her eyes and brings the blood to her cheeks so often; it is what sends her running across the fields and jumping over stiles when she hears that Jane is ill at Netherfield. After this last piece of anxious exertion she is said to look 'almost wild', and there in fact we have the beginning of a problem. The word 'wild' is applied to Elizabeth—and to Lydia, and to Wickham. In the case of the last two named, 'wildness' obviously has nothing to recommend it and is seen as totally and reprehensibly anti-social. Elizabeth's special quality is more often referred to as 'liveliness'; this is what Darcy is said to lack (his understanding—i.e. rational consciousness—is apparently impeccable), and it is the main quality that Elizabeth will bring to the marriage. It is a fine point, and not perhaps a fixed one, at which liveliness becomes wildness, yet the latter is a menace to society, while without the former society is merely dull. Elizabeth is also often described as laughing (she differentiates her state from Jane's by saying, 'she only smiles, I laugh') and laughter is also potentially anarchic, as it can act as a negation of the principles and presuppositions, the rules and rituals, which sustain society. (Her famous declaration, 'I hope I never ridicule what is wise and good. Follies and nonsense, whims and inconsistences, *do* divert me, I own, and I laugh at them whenever I can', puts her in the line of eighteenth-century satirists who worked to uphold certain values and principles by drawing comic attention to deviations from them. But Elizabeth's love of laughter goes beyond the satisfactions of a satirical wit, and she admits to a love of 'absurdities'. A sense of the absurd in life can be very undermining of a belief in society's self-estimation.)

With her liveliness and laughter it is not at first clear that Elizabeth will consent to be contained within the highly structured social space available to her. There is a suggestive episode when Mrs Hurst leaves Elizabeth and joins Darcy and Miss Bingley on a walk. The path only allows three to walk abreast and Darcy is aware of the rudeness of leaving Elizabeth out in this way. He suggests they go to a wider avenue, but Elizabeth 'laughingly answered—"No, no; stay where you are.—You are charmingly group'd, and appear to uncommon advantage. The picturesque would be spoilt by admitting a fourth. Good-bye." She then ran gaily off, rejoicing as she rambled about....' Social rules, like aesthetic prescriptions, tend to fix people in groups. Elizabeth is happy to leave the group, laughing, rambling, rejoicing. It is only a passing incident, but it aptly suggests an independence and liveliness of temperament which will not readily submit to any grouping found to be unacceptably restricting. Marriage is part of the social grouping and is also a restriction. The dream aspect of Pemberley is that it presumably offers an amplitude which, while still social, is large enough to offer a maximum field for expansion of both liveliness and understanding in which they can complement rather than constrain each other, and in which liveliness need never seek to express itself as anti-social wildness.

At one point Elizabeth is said to pass beyond the 'bounds of decorum' and it is part of her attraction that her energy and vitality seem to keep her right on that boundary where the constrained threatens to give way to something less willingly controlled. It is, indeed, just this that attracts Darcy to her, for, while the cold 'critical eye' which he casts on society immediately detects failures of 'perfect symmetry in her form', he is 'caught' by the 'easy playfulness' of her manners, and he stays caught by it. Where there is what Darcy calls 'real superiority of mind' he maintains that 'pride will always be under good regulation', and throughout his behaviour is a model of regulation. But 'good regulation' is not sufficient for a good society; it is what we expect from an efficient machine, and the danger in the sort of society portrayed by Jane Austen is a tendency away from the organic towards the mechanical. (Thus Elizabeth finds out that the 'civilities' of Sir William Lucas are 'worn out, like his information'. With his empty repetitions Sir William is a dim adumbration of some of Dickens's more memorable automata.) In a society that is still alive there will always be some awareness of, and pull towards, those qualities which that society has had to exclude in order to maintain itself. Ralph Ellison puts the idea in its sharpest form when the narrator of *The Invisible Man* asserts that 'the mind that has conceived a plan of living must never lose sight of the chaos against which that pattern was conceived'. It would be foolish indeed to pronounce Elizabeth as a spirit of chaos with Darcy as the incarnation of pattern. (Indeed, in many ways Elizabeth is the best citizen, for she brings real life to the values and principles to which too many of the others only pay lip service, or which they mechanically observe in a spirit of torpid conformity.) But in their gradual coming together and Darcy's persistent desire for Elizabeth we do witness the perennial yearning of perfect symmetry for the asymmetrical, the appeal which 'playfulness' has for 'regulation', the irresistible attraction of the freely rambling individual for the rigidified upholder of the group. Indeed, it could be said that it is on the tension between playfulness and regulation that society depends, and it is the fact that Elizabeth and Darcy are so happily 'united' by the end of the book which generates the satisfaction produced by the match. 'Uniting them' are the last two words of the book, and we do, I suggest, witness apparently mutually exclusive qualities coming into unity during the course of the book. Elizabeth at one point, in the presence of the insupportable Mr Collins, is said to try to 'unite truth and civility in a few short sentences'. The casual phrase is a passing reminder that civility is so often a matter of considerate lying, and another part of Elizabeth's appeal is her determination to hold on to what she refers to as 'the meaning of principle and integrity'. As Jane Austen shows, it is not always possible to unite civility and truth in this society, and the fact that there is often a dichotomy between the two produces that mixture of outward conformity and inner anguish experienced by her more sensitive characters. Pemberley is, once again, that dream place where such unities are possible. Given the importance of Elizabeth's 'playfulness'—for Darcy, for society, for the book—there is perhaps something too abject in her self-accusing retraction and apology to Darcy near the end. Although Darcy concedes to Elizabeth that 'By you I was properly humbled', we may feel that she is somewhat too willing to abandon her 'playfulness'. (For example, she redefines her 'liveliness' of mind as 'impertinence'.) There is the famous moment near the end when Elizabeth is about to make an ironical remark at Darcy's expense, 'but she checked herself. She remembered that he had yet to learn to be laughed at, and it was rather too early to begin.' One might be prompted to speculate whether Darcy will learn to laugh at himself (as the sentence half promises) or whether this is just the first of many and more serious checks and repressions which Elizabeth will be obliged to impose on herself as she takes her place in the social group.

But this is a happy book and we are not shown the wilting of playfulness under the force of regulation, but rather a felicitous 'uniting' of both. In 1813 Jane Austen wrote to Cassandra about *Pride and Prejudice*,

> I had had some fits of disgust.... The work is rather too light, and bright, and sparkling; it wants shade, it wants to be stretched out here and there with a long chapter of sense, if it could be had; if not, of solemn specious nonsense, about something unconnected with the story; an essay on writing, a critique on Walter Scott, or the history of Buonaparte or anything that would form a contrast, and bring the reader with increased delight to the playfulness and epigrammatism of the general style. I doubt your quite agreeing with me here. I know your starched notions.

Some critics have taken this as indicating Jane Austen's repudiation of her own light, bright, sparkling qualities; and it is true that, in going on to write about Fanny Price in *Mansfield Park*, Jane Austen turned to a heroine not only in a different plight, but of a very different disposition, while giving all the 'playfulness' to the socially unreliable and ultimately undesirable Mary Crawford. And there is no doubt that there is a diminishing of playfulness, a growing suspicion of unsocialised energy, in Jane Austen's subsequent work. Nevertheless I do not think this letter should be taken too seriously as an omen of repression to come. It is in fact ironical at the expense of books stuffed with the sort of sententiousness which Mary Bennet delights to quote, or the meandering digressions which could be found in many of the less well-formed works of the day. Jane Austen's disparagement of playfulness is here, surely mock-disparagement. She is herself still being 'sparkling', and if her later works grow more sombre in tone we may yet be glad that she gave us this one novel in which the brightness and the sparkle of the heroine's individuality are not sacrificed to the exacting decorums or the manipulative persuasions of the social group. Elizabeth Bennet says she is 'checked', but we shall always remember her as laughing.

As it can be seen, we are in the proximity of a major problem here: namely, that of the relationship and adjustment between individual energy and social forms. If one were to make a single binary reduction about literature, one could say that there are works which stress the existence of, and need for, boundaries; and works which concentrate on everything within the individual—from the sexual to the imaginative and the religious—which conspires to negate or transcend boundaries. Looking back at the terms of Charlotte Brontë's criticisms of *Pride and Prejudice* quoted at the start of this chapter, we notice a preponderant vocabulary of boundaries—'accurate', 'carefully fenced, highly cultivated gardens', 'neat borders', 'elegant but confined houses'. Her own impulse is towards the 'open country' and the boundless 'air', as the whole progress of her aptly named Jane Eyre reveals. In the eighteenth century, however, the stress was on the need for, or inevitability of, boundaries. Thus Locke in the first chapter of his *Essay Concerning Human Understanding*:

> I suspected we began at the wrong end, and in vain sought for satisfaction in a quiet and sure possession of truths that most concerned us, while we let loose our thoughts into the vast ocean of Being; as if all that boundless extent were the natural and undoubted possession of our understandings, wherein there was nothing exempt from its decisions, or that escaped its comprehension.... Whereas, were the capacities of our understandings well considered, the extent of our knowledge once discovered, and the horizon found which sets the bounds between the enlightened and dark parts of things—between what is and what is not comprehensible by us—men would perhaps with less scruple acquiesce in the avowed ignorance of the one, and employ their thoughts and discourse with more advantage and satisfaction in the other.

And thus Hume:

> Nothing, at first view, may seem more unbounded than the thought of man, which not only escapes all human power and authority, but is not even restrained within the limits of nature and reality.... And while the body is confined to one planet, along which it creeps with pain and difficulty; the thought can in an instant transport us into the most distant regions of the universe; or even beyond the universe, into the unbounded chaos, where nature is supposed to lie in total confusion.... But though our thought seems to possess this unbounded liberty, we shall find, upon a nearer examination, that it is really confined within very narrow limits, and that all this creative power of the mind amounts to no more than the faculty of compounding, transposing, augmenting, or diminishing the materials afforded us by the senses and experience.

By turning the negative words in these passages into positive ones, and vice versa, one could begin to establish a basic vocabulary to describe the very different kind of epistemology posited by the whole movement we know as Romantic. 'The vast ocean of Being', 'the most distant regions of the universe', even 'the unbounded chaos, where nature is supposed to lie in total confusion'—these were the very realms the Romantic imagination set out to explore; for it *did* claim for itself 'unbounded liberty' and refused to accept the notion that man and his mind are 'really confined within very narrow limits'. Locke invites us, in the interests of sanity, to recognise and accept the 'horizon' which 'sets the bounds between the enlightened and dark parts of things'. Blake took the word 'horizon', transformed it into 'Urizen' and made that figure the evil symbol of all that restricted and restrained man. He thus stood the Enlightenment on its head, and, if it was at the cost of his sanity, then, like other Romantics, he preferred to enjoy the visionary intensities of his 'madness' rather than subscribe to the accepted notions of mental health. Other Romantics too have preferred to cross that horizon and boundary and explore 'the dark parts of things', and often they have found this sphere to be full of dazzling illuminations.

This is not the place to embark on a summary of the Romantic movement. The point is that Jane Austen was brought up on eighteenth-century thought and was fundamentally loyal to the respect for limits, definition and clear ideas which it inculcated. Yet among writers who published work the same year as *Pride and Prejudice* were Byron, Coleridge, Scott and Shelley; the *Lyrical Ballads* were already over a decade old, and Keats would publish four years later. Jane Austen was writing at a time when a major shift of sensibility was taking place, as indeed major social changes were taking place or were imminent, and to some extent she was certainly aware of this. She had depicted at least one incipient Romantic in the figure of Marianne Dashwood in *Sense and Sensibility*, and her treatment is a rather ambiguous mixture of sympathy and satire. In the figure of Elizabeth Bennet she shows us energy attempting to find a valid mode of existence within society. One more quotation from Blake will enable me to conclude the point I am trying to make. In the *Marriage of Heaven and Hell* Blake writes, 'Energy is the only life, and is from the Body; and Reason is the bound or outward circumference of Energy. Energy is eternal Delight.' As I have said, I think that Jane Austen's suspicion of energy increased in her later work. But in *Pride and Prejudice* she shows us energy and reason coming together, not so much as a reconciliation of opposites, but as a marriage of complementaries. She makes it seem as if it is possible for playfulness and regulation—energy and boundaries—to be united in fruitful harmony, without the one being sacrificed to the other. Since to stress one at the expense of the other can either way mean loss, both to the self and to society, the picture of achieved congruence between them offered in *Pride and Prejudice* is of unfading relevance. It is perhaps no wonder that it has also proved capable of giving eternal delight.

NOTE

1. 'It was the favourite wish of his mother, as well as of hers. While in their cradles, we planned the union: and now, at the moment when the wishes of both sisters would be accomplished in their marriage, to be prevented by a young woman of inferior birth, of no importance in the world, and wholly unallied to the family!'

The spectacle of Elizabeth holding out against the wishes, plans, schemes of society—positional control—is one which helps to sustain our belief in the possibility of some degree of individual autonomy. (It is tolerably savage comment on this society's power to enforce connections based on respectability that it is felt to be a blessing by the Bennets when it is announced that Wickham is to marry Lydia after the elopement. 'And they must marry! Yet he is such a man! ... How strange this is! And for this we are to be thankful.' Elizabeth's characteristically penetrating sense of the ironies in her society sees at once the strangeness of a marriage which is at once undesirable, in view of the character of the bridegroom, and absolutely essential in view of society's rigid rules. Public propriety entirely pre-empts private felicity. The fact of the connection has become more important than the individuals who will compose it.)

JOHN BAYLEY

Characterization
in Jane Austen

T olstoy always maintained that a novelist must write about the things
most important to him, which should also—and for that reason—be the
things most important to everyone else. Birth, death, love, marriage, faith
and belief, how a man should live: it was as natural for him to be as absorbed
by such matters in his art as in his living and thinking. And Tolstoy is only a
particularly emphatic example of what the nineteenth century, its great
classic period, came to take for granted where the novel was concerned.

There is a natural logic about this, because the novel, an art form that
had not previously been taken seriously, came in the course of the century to
seem the natural vehicle for discussion and ventilation of what most mattered
in life. For Dickens such seriousness was everything, and yet Dickens was
writing for a wide popular audience that had to be kept interested in
installments from week to week. Seriousness, in his sense, was quite
compatible both with popularity and with sensationalism. But for Jane
Austen things were rather different. Seriousness for her was a matter of
literary propriety, of grafting the received morality of eighteenth-century
literature—sermons, poems, and essays—onto the novel form. Her
originality as a novelist had nothing to do with this kind of seriousness.

And this seems to be the key to the way in which she creates her
characters. However much alive they may be or become, she is not deeply

From *The Jane Austen Companion*, edited by J. David Grey, A. Walton Litz, and Brian Southam.
©1986 by Macmillan Publishing Company.

and seriously involved with them in the sense in which Tolstoy or George Eliot were; in the way that even Dickens was when he absorbed himself in the fortunes of Little Nell or Oliver Twist, Pip or David Copperfield. It is often said or implied not only by thoughtful readers such as Richard Simpson in the latter part of the nineteenth century but by such critics as Mary Lascelles and C. S. Lewis in our own time that Jane Austen is earnest in revealing the development of her heroines, as if, like Dickens's Pip, they were intimate studies in the growth of self-knowledge.

Henry James has often been cited for his unexpected obtuseness in referring to her lack of pondered idea, leaving us no more conscious of her process than of "the brown thrush who sings his song." In fact, this image of spontaneity is by no means infelicitous, suggesting it does the high spirits with which Jane Austen sees her characters, understanding them by not inquiring too closely and not making a show of establishing the grounds of inquiry. However "deeply studied and elaborately justified," George Eliot's characters are not, for Henry James, "seen in the irresponsible plastic way." James touches here on the crux of the matter. Jane Austen does not study her characters but enjoys them. And she enjoys them in two ways.

In the first place, they are people who excite humor. It is surely essential, even now, to state that she values her characters above all for their humorous potential. Humor in her case, of course, means a great deal more than being funny, displaying comic characters who make us smile. Although she scarcely could have been aware of it consciously herself, humor for Jane Austen and her art is the ground of existence. By being ludicrous, we survive and endure: the virtuous possibilities of human existence are for her all involved in the sense of absurdity. Since her work has been so widely admired and her stature as a novelist so fully accepted, we have had eloquent essays about her moral vision and weighty analyses of her perception of social and personal values. These can be very illuminating, particularly when done by such thoughtful critics as Lionel Trilling or Denis Donoghue, for much matter for the intelligence and the intellect follows from her peculiar genius for the absurd. Yet such studies have the grave drawback of assuming that Jane Austen was herself intellectually original, incisive, even profound. This she was not, and never attempted to be.

It is true that she plays into the hands of the modern critic by taking what might be called an "interest in ideas" and assuming, with an innate modesty, that the novel should be a vehicle for moral and social demonstration and improvement. That was a tradition she took for granted. She leaned most heavily here, perhaps, on Samuel Richardson, her great progenitor. But just as Richardson himself had concealed, however unconsciously, the true impetus and the real fascination of his writings—their grasp of sex and power and of the reader's avid response to these matters—and concealed them in the proper conventions of literary and moral culture, so Jane Austen, with an equal lack of hypocrisy or intention, enlisted under the same moral and literary tradition.

She worked its method conscientiously, for her genius was quite compatible with it, though also quite separate. And of course she was serious, in her own way. She took her art very seriously indeed, labored at it, sought eagerly for others' opinions about it. But this kind of seriousness is very different from that attributed to her by her modern critics. She was not a morally imaginative explorer; she went along with what other people thought. Her seriousness as a novelist is intimately connected with her own secret, life-giving pleasure in the absurdity of human existence.

Naturally, "absurdity" does not have here its modern existentialist sense. The comic is for Jane Austen the saving grace of life, the comfort of it, the irradiation of the sympathetic and the human. "I am comical, therefore I exist" might be the Cartesian formula underlying her sense of her personages and of her own self, too, her self as artist. This basic perception of her being seems to me so obvious as to be something taken for granted; and yet it is, surprisingly, ignored or even denied by many of Jane Austen's most important and most intelligent critics. They talk of her wit, her irony, the sharpness of her eye and ear, and the keen edge of her pen, but they are apt to pass over the fact that not only is she humorous, but also her successful characters embody that humor and achieve their reality by means of it.

The liveliest are both comic themselves and keenly aware of comedy, although this awareness is never conscious or superior. Indeed, one of the secrets of Jane Austen's art is to deprive humor of the superiority of those who are continually aware of it. As with Falstaff, her sense of humor is the reason why the same sense is in others. It makes her modest rather than exclusive. We would not value her art so highly or find her characters so attractive if she deliberately set out to substitute her own style of comic vision for the traditional modes of the novel. It is because she is so obedient to the idea of precept and moral demonstration that her art reveals its real independence of them.

This point was intuited by Thomas H. Lister in his anonymous review of Harriet Martineau's novel *Deerbrook* (*Edinburgh Review*, 1839) in which he compared the two artists. "Miss Austin [sic] is like one who plays by ear, while Miss Martineau understands the science. Miss Austin has the air of being led to right conclusions by an intuitive tact—Miss Martineau unfolds her knowledge of the principles on which her correct judgment is founded"

(Southam, p. 121). There could hardly be a deadlier though more inadvertent disclosure of the difference between a major artist and a very minor one. Miss Martineau does indeed "unfold her principles"; she sets them, and herself, busily before us on every page. Jane Austen conceals herself and her interests and convictions behind the perfect conventionality of principles and morals that lend her novels their appropriate weight but none of the creative magic.

A clear example is her first wholly successful heroine, Catherine Morland in *Northanger Abbey*. Her two earliest heroines, Elinor and Marianne in *Sense and Sensibility*, are constructed from principles that invade their speech and behavior to such an extent that the second never achieves the true status of a Jane Austen character, and the first only precariously. The story enlivens them in its onward movement, and so do their mother and the John Dashwoods, but they remain derivative of Jane Austen's models and lack that potential for and of the absurd that is the clue to the success of her main characters, heroines included. Catherine Morland is the prototype of all her heroines, and she probably arrived almost by accident, however much she may owe to Fanny Burney's *Evelina* and other ingenues of the eighteenth century. The vitality of Catherine derives from her combination of instinctive sense, taste, and humanity in all detailed social contexts—Emma Watson of the fragment *The Watsons* has the same kind of spontaneity—and her extreme and engaging silliness in relation to art and life in general. The imagination that informs the novel seems unawares to have seen and developed the link between silliness and goodness. Catherine's illusions form a natural incongruity with her equally unreflecting goodness. Jane Austen has hit upon the way to portray a virtuous heroine without the slightest symptom of priggishness and without any of the lack of naturalness caused by adherence to "principle." Marianne and even Elinor Dashwood are cardboard figures beside Catherine Morland.

Indeed, so potentially successful is Catherine that Elizabeth Bennet develops from her, and Emma brings her promise to full and perfect fruition. The most interesting thing about Emma as a character is the way in which Jane Austen sets her vitality against the almost overpowering commonplaceness of her daily living, in the past and in the future. This is Jane Austen at her most "natural," that is to say, the point at which her art is most effectively in harmony with what she knew and experienced in life. The consciousness of her heroines dominates the fools (who are never allowed to get out of hand) because it knows and accepts how much it depends itself on triviality. The difference between Emma and Elizabeth, on the one hand, and Mr. Collins, Lady Catherine de Bourgh, the Eltons, and Mr. Woodhouse, on the other, is that whereas the latter are entirely absorbed in the trivial, which they exemplify, Elizabeth and Emma transcend it by their very awareness of its life-giving essentiality.

The use Jane Austen makes of the process can be seen in its first schematic form in some of the rather laborious conversations in *Sense and Sensibility* between Elinor and her brother John Dashwood. His anxiety to appear poor in order not to have to help his sisters is set forth in Jane Austen's most artfully ludicrous vein; but Elinor becomes the stock figure in a satiric exercise, the figure whose sense and discernment act as the gauge and scale of folly. This stereotyping is the more marked because Jane Austen's ear for absurdity is already unerring, and she knows just how to exaggerate it to the right pitch, as when Dashwood deplores the fact that his father left his household linen and china to his mother and sisters: "Far be it from me to repine at his doing so; he had an undoubted right to dispose of his own property as he chose" (p. 225).

The insipid orotundity of those phrases places John Dashwood fairly in the tradition of English comic satire. "Far be it from me" is a locution perfect in its character and context, but so it would be, too, for a Dickens character like Mr. Chadband. The tendency is for the figure of comic satire to become the main, indeed the true, center of animation in the novel, leaving little interest to the rational characters who act as a foil to him and a gauge of his absurdity. This is so usual a result of comic method, as it is handed down from Smollett to Dickens and beyond, that it becomes almost an acceptable and expected tradition, allying the novel to the stage of comedy. It was instinctive for Jane Austen to use it at first, but it was another and surer instinct of her genius to transform it, as she did, into a wholly different method of uniting the characters and discourse of a fiction into a harmony that discards the oppositional method of satire and with it the open demonstration of moral principles. In her mature fiction Jane Austen has discarded both the cipher figure who stands for principle and the figure of folly or vacuity who engrosses the vitality of the story by displaying these satirized characteristics.

We can catch the contexts of transition now and again in *Sense and Sensibility*, the novel that, by being the first she worked on, reveals most about the nature of things to come. Elinor Dashwood's sister Marianne, the "sensibility" figure of the novel, can only be convinced of the way things are by "better knowledge of mankind" (p. 261). This is bald enough, but it is emphasized by Jane Austen's inability to detach Marianne from her function as the representative of sensibility other than by manipulating her arbitrarily into such "knowledge" and by demonstrating in Dr. Johnson's vein how she acquires it. She and Elinor converse like two exemplary ladies in a *Rambler* essay, and in these conversations Elinor herself, as representative of "sense," becomes as wholly formal and artificial in her function as her sister. But when Elinor is faced with one of the absurd figures of the fiction, she begins to come alive, and Jane Austen achieves this by relating her, in a subtle way, to the world of comic triviality. Instead of acting as the rational foil to Robert Ferrars's tales of how he persuaded his grand friends to follow his advice, she capitulates to his world of absurdity with a compliance that is in itself quietly comic. "Elinor agreed to it all, for she did not think he deserved the compliment of rational opposition" (p. 252).

At once Elinor herself becomes human, with a full humanity lacking in the caricatures like Robert but present in her because of her reaction to him. The notion of rationality itself becomes comic because of Elinor's drolly resigned inability to exercise it. The moment looks forward to Emma's exchanges with her father in which the spirit of comic truth and comic redemption descends equally on both of them by virtue of the fact that they belong together without the need for argument or comprehension. After an exchange about marriage, and the respect due to brides, Mr. Woodhouse becomes a little agitated and says to his daughter, "My dear, you do not understand me." What follows has the logic of real comedy. "Emma had done. Her father was growing nervous, and could not understand *her*" (p. 280).

In terms of Jane Austen's art of characterization, the exchange is a crucial one. Not only do the "caricatures" not understand the "characters," but the incomprehension is now admitted to be mutual. No longer do reader, author, and primary character unite in forming the scale of reason against which the John Dashwoods, Mr. Collinses, and Miss Bateses perform their amusing and predictable antics. The world is no longer divided, along the lines of conventional comedy, into those who provide the mockery and those who have the superiority of enjoying it.

This, perhaps, is the real significance of the famous episode with Miss Bates on Box Hill, where Emma treats her openly with the kind of mockery that author, reader, and heroine have always been apt implicitly to share. The result is the diminution of Emma's own high spirits; she feels wretchedly dull and depressed, and book and reader suffer with her. It is a signal instance of the way in which the withdrawal of the comic spirit, which is the inspiration and animation of her characters, reveals the vulnerability of those who assume they direct it. They must be mockable themselves if they are the cause of mockery's being enjoyed in relation to others.

The mature heroines are therefore, like the dyer's hand in Shakespeare's sonnet, subdued to what they have to work in and with, the trivialities and diversions and preoccupations that make up the world in which they can exist as creatures of Jane Austen's art. Sometimes these conditions almost parody themselves as part of the humor extracted by that art from the small repetitive business of living. There is a whole perspective of comedy in the remark that Emma makes to Harriet Smith about the way of life she may expect to be enjoying if she still remains a spinster at fifty. "Woman's usual occupations of eye and hand and mind will be open to me then, as they are now.... If I draw less, I shall read more; if I give up music, I shall take to carpet work" (p. 85).

There is a comic contrast (the word ironic, too often used in Jane Austen's context, is seldom suited to it) between this vision and the actual pleasure we are obtaining in the society of Emma. "Woman's usual occupations of eye and hand and mind" are transformed by the text and then abruptly brought into contact with the world outside it. Emma's merry presentation of herself as a spinster at fifty not only reveals the actual anxieties and hopes she must be entertaining about herself in relation to a woman's possible destinies but also brings before the reader a kind of continuous Emma, outside time, untroubled by what its necessities may bring to a woman but which the text itself cannot share.

The reading and the "carpet work" imply a cheerful acceptance of life as it has to be lived in this world. The riches of the novel are themselves gently mocked by reference to the repetitive monotonies that lie behind them. Most implicit in the comedy, however, is the feeling that this Emma at fifty would be still our Emma, still able to take part in a novel that the author could produce and she as heroine play in. Such a novel would be, it slyly assures us, the literary equivalent of carpet work and the like, an occupation for eye and mind with which we are thoroughly familiar, comfortable, and at home. If Emma, on the other hand, were to marry like Elizabeth Bennet, the novel would have nothing to say about her; her status as heroine would have gone irretrievably, together with the eye and mind that have been creating themselves for us in the novel's world.

All this and more lies behind Emma's playful words, words that reveal with the most realistic clarity Jane Austen's outlook and methods as a mature artist. It could be said that her problem is to bring the "carpet work" of her comedy—with all its truth of small daily events and absurdities—as close as possible to the larger events that lie outside it: work and business, birth, death, and marriage. Our sense of these things must not contrast with the comedy and be revealed as the mere artificial mechanism of plot and story but must be enhanced by the comedy and acquire from it its own background reality. This would be another way of saying that in Jane Austen's mature art there is no distinction between character and caricature but that the fools who are laughed at, and the persons of sense and sensibility who laugh at them with us, are united—as we ourselves are—in a common absorption in the banalities of existence.

In *Emma* the process is seen at its most artful, an art that wholly dissolves the distinction that D.W. Harding made in his essay "Character and Caricature in Jane Austen." No novel gets more enjoyment out of the submission of all parties to the long littleness of life; and we may remember that Emma's contemplation of her future in carpet work at the age of fifty recalls the chief pastime of the widowed Mrs. Jennings in *Sense and Sensibility*. No doubt the Bateses, too, mother and daughter, are redoubtable practitioners of the craft. Jane Austen's finest achievement is to make us in love in art with what might appear most wearisome, tedious, and petty in living, with what we have to do every day and prefer to forget.

The key to her characters, therefore, is their immersion for art's sake in the tedium of existence. Where most novelists have to heighten the feeling of living in the interests of their art, Jane Austen deliberately lowers it and, by doing so, gives its quotidian dullness an unexampled vitality. Her lively sense of the ridiculous makes all kinds of tedium amusing, and we smile at the thought of the conversation at Cleveland (*SS*) "which a long morning of the same continued rain had reduced very low" (p. 304). Not the extravagances but the deprivations of being are the deepest spring of her comedy, and she realized this in the ways an artist does. When she remarked to her sister that *Pride and Prejudice* wanted light and shade, had too much brilliancy about it, she professed the intention of writing on more serious topics, questions of "ordination" and of "principles" (*Letters*, January 29, 1813). What actually takes place is the installation of dullness in the place of honor, the foreground of the next novel. From this solid posture it makes everything else in *Mansfield Park* as real and solid. The humdrum comfort of the sofa encompasses both Fanny Price and Lady Bertram, and when Fanny goes to her mother in Portsmouth, the humdrum takes a more virulently comic form, which helps to give a touching kind of truth and vitality to Fanny herself. Mansfield Park, that abode of insipid and sleepy decorum, seems to her a romantic paradise compared to the sordid facts of life in a Portsmouth tenement. Such touches thoroughly humanize Fanny, and in just the same way that the forlorn situation of Anne, in *Persuasion*, rests upon a comic rather than a tragic basis. The heart of Anne's situation is to be compelled to share a small sofa with the large Mrs. Musgrove and listen to her lamentations. Her deprived and isolated state appears all the more poignantly in the background from the fact that it is foregrounded in comic tedium.

In *Mansfield Park* there are penalties to be paid for the inspired move into monotony as a comic principle. Its funniest manifestation in the novel is the appearance of Sir Thomas Bertram, blandly uncomprehending, in the drawing room at Mansfield where all the excitement of the theatricals is going forward. Victorian connoisseurs of Jane Austen used to deplore the fact that those rehearsals, with all their possibilities of a comic *scène à faire*, were so abruptly cut off. Modern critics, less robust and more anxious to demonstrate Jane Austen's fine moral discriminations, are eloquent on the significance of her disapproval of the acting and performing ego. The real reason is surely that anticlimax is for her much more full of comic potential than any number of big scenes. She brings the theater business to a hilarious close by confronting it with all the natural dullness of restored Mansfield routine.

The penalty, however, is that the characters who represent rebellion against that routine cannot share in its life-giving powers, the reality conferred by the comic principle of humdrum monotony. Leaving aside the hopeless case of Willoughby in *Sense and Sensibility*, even the much more subtle and comprehensive picture of the Crawfords in *Mansfield Park* suffers from the inability of her art to draw them inside its charmed circle of comic boredom. Jane Austen's eye for the ridiculous is happy with them in the theatrical connection, but her mature vision can find no compromise between enjoying the Crawfords as adding to the gaiety of life and dismissing them to the fate of caricatures for their bad principles and shocking want of decency. By being as interesting as they are, the Crawfords show how genuine, and in a sense how honest, are Jane Austen's limitations where character is concerned. She will not "explore" a character, and if she suggests ambivalence—as in the case of the Crawfords—she is quick to sacrifice them to plot and to fall back on simplistic commentary. "Let other pens than mine dwell on guilt and misery ..." (p. 461). It is not just a formula for winding up the fiction, however; it is entirely true to Jane Austen's own wishes and preferences. Other pens than hers must equally dwell on passion and consummation. She dismisses her heroines equally along with her wrongdoers, without a peep into their future or a suggestion that they possess one. Comedy abandons them, but the leave-taking is itself part of the comic mode.

In *Sense and Sensibility*, in fact, it is only at the end that comedy comes into its own. As she prepares to take leave and is no longer weighed down by the responsibilities of demonstrating the behavior of the sensible and the sensitive girl, the author's eyes begin to sparkle. Elinor, along with her mother, has by now been fully humanized by the intimacy of humor, but we can see the precise moment at which she, too, is abandoned to humor of a different sort, the objective and no longer intimate flourish of high spirits. Elinor's meeting with Edward Ferrars produces "a most promising state of embarrassment" (p. 288), and when the plot has arranged matters and he can declare his feelings, embarrassment is still the best indication of the author's kindness, the understanding of them that writing her novel has produced. "When Elinor had ceased to rejoice in the dryness of the season, a very awful pause took place" (p. 359).

This is the same kindness with which Jane Austen regards Catherine Morland, after Henry Tilney has come to propose, but it is the kindness of leave-taking. The marriages of Elinor and Marianne take second place, in the winding up of the novel, to comedy's pleasure in the vigor and cunning with which Lucy Steele, now Mrs. Robert Ferrars, gets herself back into the good graces of her mother-in-law and establishes herself as indispensable in that sphere of watchful imbecility and competitive conceit of which she is the type and paramount.

There is no need for Jane Austen to have to pass judgment on Lucy, as she has to do on the Crawfords, and the ending of *Sense and Sensibility*, in its spontaneous high spirits, is more natural to her art than the adjustments that have to be made at the end of *Mansfield Park*. So misleading is D. W. Harding's concept of "regulated hatred" as informing the comedy of her work that it would be truer to see her natural high spirits, so abundant at the end of *Sense and Sensibility* and *Northanger Abbey*, having to be regulated by the more sober conceptions she undertook in *Mansfield Park* and *Persuasion* and being freely indulged again, at the end of her writing life, in the composition of *Sanditon*.

Emma, the heroine "whom nobody but myself will like" (*Memoir*, p. 157), of course fits most harmoniously the play of these high spirits and their natural pleasure in limitation. Significantly, it is the only novel in which Jane Austen can remain with her heroine, rejoicing in the swaddled humor of her situation, with her invalid father, the husband who will be a second sort of father, the house and village from which she will never move. Here is limitation enough to satisfy even Jane Austen's art and enough implicit absurdity to feed it forever. For its intelligence and high spirits require their opposites to work on, and Emma in her situation is the symbol and social paradigm of that work in progress. By opposing Emma's high spirit and intelligence to the utter banality of her life, Jane Austen reveals the heart of her own formula and the way in which humor is for her characterization not only the medium of the moral life but of the romantic life, as well. Without it, neither affection nor "principles" can be made convincing in fictional terms.

Reality itself depends on it. When he deplores Jane Austen's refusal to draw more upon the other kinds of life she knew, to introduce her heroines into more varied and worldly social scenes and more extended opportunities, Angus Wilson takes for granted that fiction has always the duty and the need to bring everything in, to expand to the limits of observation. Jane Austen no doubt knew, felt, and saw more than she wrote about, but this gives a special compression and quality to what she *did* write about. Into banality itself she can put a kick like the strongest drink: she never coyly compounds, as Mrs. Gaskell and other women writers were to do, for insipidity and coziness of manner by implying that cozy and homely subjects required them. There is nothing in the least homely about any of her characters.

Her plots, of which the leading characters form a part, give them an extraordinary sense of *potential*. It matters not that nothing but the most ordinary married state awaits them; for the duration of the novel they enjoy as much vividness and variety of consciousness as if they were taking part in a Shakespeare play. Potentiality is closely tied to limitation; nor would it be misleading to claim that for Jane Austen both are aspects of the romantic life, the life that relates to reverie, speculation, and daydream. The principal fascination of all her heroines is the gap between the play of their consciousness and the conditions under which they live. In *Jane Austen: A Study of Her Artistic Development*, A. Walton Litz quotes from the eighteenth-century philosopher Shaftesbury an extremely significant sentence, on which Jane Austen's eye may have rested more than once. "The natural free spirits of ingenious men, if imprisoned and controlled, will find out other ways of motion to relieve themselves in their constraint." Her characters exemplify the link between such an observation and the romantic sensibilities of her own time. She made her own kind of use of them, and a unique one.

Philip Larkin has noted a similar quality—the quality of "innocent irony"—in the work of a novelist whose unpretentious but altogether outstanding art has contrived to make the best possible use of Jane Austen's—Barbara Pym. In her novels, too, the heroines live in a world of comic limitation and potential wonder, whereas other fictional heroines of our time appear to have drained all experience—sensory and intellectual, sexual or marital—to the dregs before the novels in which they figure are well under way.

Works Cited

Donoghue, Denis. "A View of *Mansfield Park*," in B.C. Southam, ed., *Critical Essays on Jane Austen* (London, 1968), 39–59.

Harding, D.W. "Regulated Hatred: An Aspect of the Work of Jane Austen," *Scrutiny*; 8 (1939–40), 346–62.

———— "Character and Caricature in Jane Austen," in B.C. Southam, ed., *Critical Essays on Jane Austen* (London, 1968), 83–105.

James, Henry. "The Lesson of Balzac" (1905), in Leon Edel, ed., *The House of Fiction* (London, 1957), 60–85.

Lascelles, Mary. *Jane Austen and Her Art* (London, 1939).

Lewis, C.S. "A Note on Jane Austen," *Essays in Criticism*, 4 (1954), 359–71.

Lister, Thomas H. Review of Harriet Martineau's *Deerbrook* (1839), excerpted in B.C. Southam, ed., *Jane Austen: The Critical Heritage* (London and New York, 1968), 121.

Litz, A. Walton. *Jane Austen: A Study of Her Artistic Development* (London and New York, 1965).

Simpson, Richard. Review of the *Memoir*, reprinted in B. C. Southam, ed., *Jane Austen: The Critical Heritage* (London and New York, 1968), 241–65.

Trilling, Lionel. "In Mansfield Park," in his *The Opposing Self* (London and New York, 1955), 206–30.

————. "*Emma* and the Legend of Jane Austen," in his *Beyond Culture* (London and New York, 1965), 31–55.

ROGER GARD

Emma's Choices

The ease afforded by Jane Austen to her readers is nowhere so evident as in contemplating the formidable intellectual structure that underpins the bright and lucid comedy of *Emma*. The novel is a structure of the utmost complexity and delicacy. Everything in it depends on everything else and on its context within the fiction. Since this texture is so dense it is easy to represent by brief analyses of suggestive examples. So—as a beginning to this chapter—I shall take two of these: the opening, and a passage near the end. Then, having, I hope, built up an impression of the compressed economy immanent in the work, I shall go on to look once again at some of the characteristics of Jane Austen's unique kind of realism—which should illuminate both characteristics and this novel, interactively. Finally, I shall offer some reflections on the significance of the heroine's trajectory through the book and into the future.

I

The opening of *Mansfield Park* is one of the great bravura expositions in fiction. It is a massively improved and enhanced rewriting of the first chapter of *Sense and Sensibility*, in that it summarises, though with a wonderful characterising dramatic touch, the *past* of a situation:

From *Jane Austen's Novels: The Art of Clarity*. © 1992 by Yale University.

> About thirty years ago, Miss Maria Ward, of Huntingdon, with
> only seven thousand pounds, had the good luck to captivate Sir
> Thomas Bertram ...

The whole moral *ambience* into which the heroine is to be cast becomes
present, and succeeding pages, chapters, sustain the impetus. The opening of
Emma matches and even surpasses this, but with a focus on the immediate
subject, Emma, (almost *in medias res*) and brilliantly entertaining from the
first paragraph:

> Emma Woodhouse, handsome, clever, and rich, with a
> comfortable home and happy disposition, seemed to unite some
> of the best blessings of existence; and had lived nearly twenty-one
> years in the world with very little to distress or vex her. (5)

This, of course, is so famous as almost to blind the reader with familiarity.
But consider it. It invites quick and easy reading partly because it is a single
sentence. It promises a happy and attractive theme. Nobody could take it for
the opening of a tragedy. There is no tedious indirection or scene-setting to
allow the mind to wander, or to wonder when the real story is going to start.
It is not self-conscious, or learned or allusive—and so on. Yet all this happy
plainness is qualified by the first verb—at first unobtrusively charged—which
is to be crucial to the action: "seemed".[1] Emma's advantages only potentially
confer the best blessings of existence—as is obvious if we think about the
question.

    The second paragraph extends the effect. It is similarly crisp,
informative and subtle. In the major key, as it were, we learn of Emma's
"affectionate" father, her being mistress of the house so young, and of her
excellent and loving governess. In the minor, that her father is over-
"indulgent", her mother, long dead, and her governess, however admirable,
"short" of a mother.

    These subtle qualifications extend into the third paragraph. Miss
Taylor's love and kindness had resulted in her having only a nominal
authority; she has been able to impose hardly any restraint, and Emma does
what she likes. It comes as no surprise, therefore, when the fourth paragraph
starts by taking up the "seemed" with: "The real evils indeed of Emma's
situation were the power of having rather too much her own way, and a
disposition to think a little too well of herself". Real evils? Are we then,
contrary to the expectations excited by the light and happy opening, to be
faced with a story solemnly moralising about how dangerous it is to be

handsome, clever and rich? Fortunately not, for the subtle qualifications have now gone over to the other side: "rather too much", "a little too well". Happiness begins to reassert itself.

In very few words Jane Austen has not only stated her subject, but also alerted us as to how to read about it. In the rest of the first chapter the idea of an only apparent happiness remains subdued, but is in fact crucial. Emma lives in a desperately dull society: and it is in this context that we are asked to see her impetuous and high-handed actions. "Highbury ... afforded her no equals" (7): this states a satisfying social eminence, but it also suggests the possibility of a demoralising tedium. (We later learn that although Emma has been to London she has never seen the sea—a poetically suggestive limitation, which also differentiates her further from the heroines just before and after.) The very first *action*, accordingly, in this powerful blend of retrospect, dialogue and action, is of Mr. Woodhouse composing himself for his "sleep after dinner, as usual" (6)—a prelude to the first of their apparently endless long evenings together. The attitude of both daughter and narrator to Mr. Woodhouse repays examination. They have a similarly unsentimental view of him. The narrator informs us succinctly that he had "been a valetudinarian all his life, without activity of mind or body ... and though everywhere beloved for the friendliness of his heart and his amiable temper, his talents could not have recommended him at any time" (he is unsatisfactory, as are most of the Jane Austen parents). Emma faces the same problem. For the moment, since Emma's skilful companion for her. He could not meet her in conversation, rational or playful (7), but, most remarkably, her love is not simply felt as a duty, but is an active principle which rules this headstrong and critical girl throughout the novel.

Typically, Jane Austen immediately develops this situation in multiple relation to its most likely possible solvent: marriage. Equally typically, the description is focussed and proved by the dramatisation afforded by dialogue. The conversation beginning "Poor Miss Taylor!—I wish she were here again. What a pity it is that Mr. Weston ever thought of her!" (8) is, of course, comic—which is just as well, for with a different tone Mr. Woodhouse's ludicrous worries about James and the "poor horses" would seem a biting demonstration of silly egotism. He can see no reason for a newly married woman to have a "house of her own"—a hint superbly taken up over 400 pages later when Emma faces the same problem. For the moment, since Emma's skilful "exertions" merely steer him round towards a happier end to the evening, we are left with the question as to whether or not to admire her for being so indulgent. As if to determine this, "Mr. Knightley, a sensible man of about seven or eight- and thirty", steps in with the dramatic appropriateness and realistic credibility that we have learned to expect. He quickly earns the right to be called sensible—both feeling and rational—by the cordial tact with which he handles Mr. Woodhouse's hypochondriacal worries and by his pleasant settling of the issue of Mrs. Weston: "... but when it comes to the question of dependence or independence! ..." (10). By now, five pages into the novel, the action is fully set and launched, and the first short chapter not even over yet.

Now consider one of the final episodes. Frank Churchill's intrigue is sustained through a series of hints, half revelations and misunderstandings which interweave with other motifs through the main action and are only fully articulated in his rueful, though still rather chirpy, explanations to Emma in chapter eighteen of volume three. "But is it possible that you had no suspicion?" he says, "I was once very near—and I wish I had" (477)—and we know from his letter to Mrs. Weston that what he wishes is that he had come clean about Jane Fairfax on first leaving Highbury in February, half the book ago. Here the first-time reader may fully understand, for the first time, that his nervous velleities on that farewell visit (which was preceded by a visit to the Bateses): "In short ... perhaps, Miss Woodhouse—I think you can hardly be without suspicion" (2, xii, 260)—were a prelude to his failure to confess something she certainly did not begin to guess, as opposed to a prelude to a failure to propose marriage to her. The control of this strand with so many others—it surfaces also in the crowded texture of the ball at the Crown (3, ii)—is in itself of remarkable fineness and would grace any tale of cross currents in love. But what makes it especially rich—especially Jane Austen's and no one else's—is that it is the *same* scene at the end which confirms in us the feeling that Emma has really had about Frank from the start—and which Mr. Knightley has too firmly articulated. The happy, open lover is, of course, a gentleman: but he will not quite do. He is merely *aimable*.[2] His attitude to Jane, whose superior mind and spirit we have come to admire, is that of the proud possessor of an excellent piece of livestock. His apologies to Emma are interlarded with regular, too regular, exclamations of pleasure:—"Did you ever see such a skin?—such smoothness! such delicacy!" (478); "Look at her. Is she not an angel in every gesture? Observe the turn of her throat. Observe her eyes ..." (479); "I see it in her cheek, her smile, her vain attempt to frown. Look at her" (480). In this appreciation there is a certain glutinous quality which, in its way, harks back to the courtship language of Mr. Elton; and Emma, who could have been bored and affronted, rightly and happily feels that "she had never been more sensible of Mr. Knightley's high superiority of character" (480). All this complexity is immediately apprehensible, and only the formal analysis of it is difficult.

Therefore, I want now to examine and explain a little of the richness by reverting to the problem of what Jane Austen typically selected out of experience to serve her larger enterprise; and to a point made earlier (about *Sense and Sensibility* and by Henry on *Pride and Prejudice*, in chapter five, above) concerning her *creative* use of those artistically conventional ludicrous types whose ludicrousness consists largely in the dependability of their reactions.

The commonplace, indeed the natural, account of the action of *Emma* runs like this: the over-confident heroine, in purposeful contrast to the heroine of *Mansfield Park*, rightly considers herself superior to most of the people around her—to the rather boring and *borné* Highbury, a place "almost amounting to a town" and more really dispiriting than Lionel Trilling's description of it as a "pastoral" location would suggest. Therefore she must find relief for her mind. Therefore she makes the series of wonderful imaginative mistakes of which the book largely consists—and of which no reader needs to be reminded. Later I shall consider the happy exceptions to this pattern, and the nature of her hungry imagination. But first let us reexamine dull Highbury. Apparently it differs from the other dull locales in Jane Austen (nostalgically so very attractive to the twentieth-century reader) mainly in the narrowness with which it confines the protagonists—though there is nothing in it so nakedly unpleasant as there is in parts of *Sense and Sensibility*. Even Box Hill—that genuinely beautiful but not exotic spot—is a considerable outing, and so on. But, of course, as well as being a very credible picture of Regency *moeurs de province*, Highbury is an artistic construct.

According to Flaubert later, everything becomes interesting if you look at it long enough. The truth of this depends on the kind of look we are able to give. Clearly the look of art is magical. Highbury is the very devil of boredom for an intelligent person with nothing much to do. Mr. Knightley, obviously a progressive and improving farmer with his drains and fences and planned cropping and new drills and philanthropy, is a busy man; but Emma has only, in the serious external business of life, the care of her father and the occasional care of the poor:

> They were now approaching the cottage, and all idle topics were
> superseded. Emma was very compassionate; and the distresses of
> the poor were as sure of relief from her personal attention and
> kindness, her council and her patience, as from her purse. She
> understood their ways, could allow for their temptations, had no

romantic expectations of extraordinary virtue from those, for
whom education had done so little; entered into their troubles
with ready sympathy, and always gave her assistance with as much
intelligence as good-will. In the present instance, it was sickness
and poverty together which she came to visit ... (1, x, 86)

This warming and precise passage comes in the middle of an episode where
Emma is being particularly complacent and even a little odious in her bossing
about of Harriet, and so redresses a balance. But what is further remarkable
about it is, that though such intelligent charity was certainly a part of good
Christian living for a wealthy woman in England then, this is the only
reference to it in *Emma*—one of the few in Jane Austen generally. And it is only
a reference; the poor are not dramatically present in all their ugliness and
brutality, defiance and gratitude, as they would be in mature Dickens or in
George Eliot and Mrs. Gaskell—or even in Charlotte Smith. The "idle topics"
quickly reassert themselves in the drama of Mr. Elton and the bootlace, for
they are the real business of the book. So our reacquired admiration for Emma
also reminds us of how much the intent gaze of this author habitually omits, as
I suggested in chapter one, in the interests of a sharp vision.

What is it to represent nature in a novel? If I want to evoke something
I may want to exclude what is next to it in phenomenal circumstance, but
irrelevant. I need to include only enough for verisimilitude—and even what
I thus include (if I am Jane Austen at any rate) will only rarely be there solely
as dressing. Even when we take the weight of Philippa Tristram's interesting
observation that, since servants were becoming less and less obtrusive in
well-run households of the period, their relative absence in Jane Austen (as
opposed to Richardson) is quite natural—an observation crowned by the
astonishing anecdote that a little later in the century any lower servant in the
Duke of Portland's who was seen by the Duke was automatically
dismissed[3]—the lack of accompanying bustle in Jane Austen clearly owes
more to art than to nature. As with the material details in *Mansfield Park*, in
Emma James the coachman will show what a fusspot his employer is; gruel,
what a valetudinarian; and the mending of spectacles will encompass a move
in an amorous game. This rigorous process, or creative flowering, is precisely
what Henry James described by the mild word "selection".

Part of what it achieves is a paradox usually accepted more or less
automatically by readers, but not often enough made explicit by critics: that
what is tedious and stifling for the protagonists is matter for delight and
interest for the audience. To observe this is to observe no more unfamiliar a
psychological fact than that we enjoy tragedies. We pursue edifying

representations of suffering, as Aristotle first said. Likewise we enjoy the depiction of boredom. It is not to my purpose to speculate again on the causes of this *datum*; but it is necessary to keep it in mind particularly firmly when reading Jane Austen's kind of novel, which so plausibly offers itself as an account of the real and the very everyday.

III

So, further: what is the relation of such disciplined selection to characterisation by the parade of expected responses? One of the reasons why *Emma* is really a, perhaps the, high point of Jane Austen's writing is that the integration, the seamless use, of comically predictable voices is at its densest. Consider the misunderstandings surrounding Mr. Elton and his ambitious marital design on Emma. By the time this is introduced the reader is already highly trained to develop a sympathetic wariness as to her estimate of things around her. Not only the narratorial direction with its subtle qualifications ("seemed to unite some of the best blessings of existence"), but the tiniest nuances from episode to episode accomplish this.

For example, and naturally relevant to Emma's limited environment— one of the reasons, from the point of view of the solicitious Mrs. Weston who is early reviewing the prospect of a visit from her new stepson Frank, why her recent marriage will not badly impair relations with Hartfield is the "very easy distance" between it and Randalls "so convenient for even solitary female walking". And equally obviously Emma is "no feeble character" with her "sense and energy and spirits" (1, ii, 18). So much for *imagined* inconveniences. But in the next chapter but one Emma herself is full of her brilliant new idea of bringing out Harriet from the extremely plain education offered at Mrs. Goddard's "real, honest, old-fashioned Boarding-school", and one of the reasons she is able to give herself for undertaking a little character formation *à la Rousseau* is that, since her father never goes beyond the shrubbery (and in this rich household there is no suitable female domestic), she needs a walking companion:

> ... since Mrs. Weston's marriage her exercise had been too much confined. She had ventured once alone to Randalls, but it was not pleasant; and a Harriet Smith, therefore, one whom she could summon at any time for a walk, would be a valuable addition to her privileges.... Harriet certainly was not clever, but she had a sweet, docile, grateful disposition ... (1, iii, 22)

So the choice is now between two great active rationalising powers: the characteristic Weston optimism and Emma's genius for having things her own way. If we add common sense, two to one says that Emma probably does not absolutely need a companion. And her thought could not be more lifelike. Sound, practical reasons for doing as one likes are rarely wanting with clever people.

But in either case we are enabled—by this amongst a hundred, or, as Harriet herself would express it "five hundred million" other things—to follow Mr. Elton's courtship with appropriate scepticism and to experience some strict ironies—i.e. we view the action from a different and superior position to that of any of the participants.[4] And what is striking about the climax of the sequence in 1, xiii–xv—especially to the reader of *Pride and Prejudice* and the connoisseur of comic proposals in general—is how like and yet unlike it is to the eruption of Mr. Collins into his book. Both men are vicars, and both masters of a comparable vocabulary of insincere excess. Both also careerists, who after their failure with the heroine go on to a marriage which is anatomised within their novel. Yet Elton has not the fame, the glory, of Collins. And one of the chief reasons for this is that his upsurge is more gradual, and more integrated with the rest of the action. His presence "spruce, black, and smiling" (1, xiii) is, especially in view of John Knightley's brotherly warning to Emma just previous, ominous enough. But he is far from being given a whole *set piece*, or the equivalent of a "new scene at Longbourn". Before dinner at Randalls "Mr. Elton's civilities were dreadfully ill-timed" to a heroine eager to hear about the Frank Churchill who "if she ever *were* to marry" would be the least unsuitable person; but she is rescued by the affable chatter of her host about this son. Elton then returns to his wooing with embarrassing over-familiar nonsense—beautifully observed of a would-be lover, and proleptic of the tone of his actual future wife—about Emma's supposed self-sacrifice over Harriet's cold: "Is this fair, Mrs. Weston?—Judge between us. Have not I some right to complain?" (1, xv, 125). No, none at all *knowingly* accorded by Emma—who perhaps chills him with a Miss Woodhouse look (she thinks he is a little drunk). But again his voice is temporarily submerged by the commotion caused by the new problem of how to get back to Hartfield in face of a few flakes of snow. Mr. Woodhouse is, of course, completely *bouleversé*—and everyone proceeds to act out their own rôle. John Knightley embraces the chance for a sarcastic vision of disaster; Mr. Weston enthusiastically grasps the opportunity for extending even more of his unwanted unpractical good-will and good wine; Isabella is heroically ready to brave the storm in order to get back to her children: and "What is to be done, my dear Emma?—what is to be done?"

Mr. Woodhouse exclaims, for, as always, "To her he looked for comfort". What is to be done is that Mr. Knightley goes out to look at the weather and talk to the coachmen, sees that it offers no inconvenience, let alone threat, and reports. The resolution is as precise as the consternation was diffuse:

> Mr. Knightley and Emma settled it in a few brief sentences: thus—
> "Your father will not be easy; why do not you go?"
> "I am ready, if the others are."
> "Shall I ring the bell?"
> "Yes, do."
> And the bell was rung, and the carriages spoken for. (128)

This clear-headed efficiency is a kind of moral pointer. Clear speech is always indicative in Jane Austen. But here it is the final piece of sense before Elton's final sticky onslaught in the enclosed carriage. Like his fellow cleric he finds it very difficult to take no for an answer in love. "Believe me, sir, I am far, very far, from being gratified in being the object of such professions", protests Emma still thinking of Harriet. But he replies—with some embarrassing justice—that "adoration of yourself" has been his object, and that "You cannot really, seriously, doubt it. No!—(in an accent meant to be insinuating)—I am sure you have seen and understood me." Even worse, and more Collins-like:

> "Charming Miss Woodhouse! allow me to interpret this interesting silence. It confesses that you have long understood me." (131)

There follows Emma's first long, important, day of self-accusation. This is a small, partial, *anagnorisis*, or recognition, including a small newly acknowledged sense of Mr. Knightley's wisdom. But it is swiftly recovered from and ignored in a new morning and with the alacrity of youthful spirits bolstered by her intuition of Elton's not really being in love.

Obviously a lot of the interest of the proposal has been in our enjoying the extended display of Emma's failure to see Elton properly—blinded typically not by Cupid but by the Harriet project; just as through most of the book she fails, often though not always, accurately to intuit what forms itself around her because, setting "up as I do for Understanding" (3, xiii, 427), she is the victim of her own marvellous ideas. More of this later. But what is most notable here is that the proposal does not spring unexpected and undeserved, as it were, out of the action—as does that to Elizabeth Bennet—but is part of a dense counterpoint of motifs around the heroine: or, continuing the metaphor from the previous chapter, a *leitmotif* or a line in a fugue rather than a Collins-type *aria*.

My point is that the predicted responses of dull Highbury are not just a comic background for the main protagonists' lives, not merely a frame. They are interactive with those lives, and each depends intimately on each. This example further indicates another important fact that commentary on Jane Austen's development of 'humourous' comedy tends to overlook, but which, again, is obvious to the simplest reading: that a predictable response is not necessarily a ludicrous one. Mr. Woodhouse's dependence on his daughter is funny, if funny, in a different way from Isabella's defiance of "possible accumulations of drifted snow" to cover the few hundred yards to Hartfield to see little Henry, little John, Bella, George and Emma before the morning. Modern readers may find in Mr. Woodhouse a subtle paternal exploiter as much as a deserving object of filial devotion; but here a mild pathos can also be felt. Further, Mr. Knightley's good sense and swift action is as predictable as anything in the book, but here it is reassuring amidst the dithering—and a trifle moving (it foreshadows, of course, his much larger intervention in favour of poor Harriet at the Crown, for he is made from the first for positive interventions, until his shyness nearly prevents him from proposing to Emma at last).

But whatever the emotional—the human—value and weight of a particular staple and expected response, I guess that the reader's pleasure derives much, and is much involved with, the *anticipation* of its application to a changing situation? When the response is duly exhibited the effect is of satisfaction—a satisfaction perhaps the greater the further the distance travelled by the character in order to adapt the situation to a reigning preoccupation or a ruling passion?

Consider the wonderful familial comedy on the evening of the John Knightleys' first visit (1, xii)—where Mr. Woodhouse and Isabella vie in wrenching everything round, and then back again, to the respective merits of their physicians, rival seaside towns and the healthiness of Hartfield *versus* Brunswick Square, whilst the Knightley brothers talk good farming business and Emma, aided finally by Mr. Knightley, brilliantly negotiates between possible collisions of obsession. Or *try* to consider the genuine relevance of Maple Grove, Selina etc. to almost anything Mrs. Elton says. We find comparable satisfactions in the encounter with circumstances by stock figures in a great deal of literature: in *Volpone*, say, or in much of Molière. In a more complex mode, the fascination and the terrible unease felt about

Shylock is not attributable wholly to his mixture of Jewish outsider and palpable man—something is due to the clash between his comic-rôle mannerisms as gulled miser and father ("My daughter! O my ducats! ... O my Christian ducats!") and the feeling that he has sustained a truly pernicious loss, like Brabantio in *Othello*.

However, literary and stylistic problems are rarely solved by the adduction of respectable parallels—though they may seem to be; nor by the argument that certain characteristics of a work of art are integrated into it in a lovely manner—they could remain rotten characteristics. The problem here, as I have suggested, is that Jane Austen's novels persist in seeming—in spite of the high economy of selection and elision artfully practised—to be fairly straight representations of everyday reality. How, to rephrase the question—how on earth—can this accord with the extensive creation and deployment of what is patently an artistic device?—and one that thrives, as it were, on being recognised as such, while at the same time giving the air of being the palpable observation of living things?

IV

With the hope of clarifying this issue I shall consider a challenge to *Emma's* kind of perfection—so influential on later novels—which is traditional in its terms and assumptions, but as a critique actually much more upsetting than anything likely to be produced by modern versions of scepticism. D.H. Lawrence was dismissive of Jane Austen (discussed in ch. 5); and part of his animus—which has everything to do, like much really telling literary criticism, with his own creative preoccupations—is likely to have derived from the conviction that:

> ... In the novel, the characters can do nothing but *live*. If they keep on being good, according to pattern, or bad, according to pattern, or even volatile according to pattern, they cease to live, and the novel falls dead. A character in a novel has got to live, or it is nothing.
>
> We, likewise, in life have got to live, or we are nothing.[5]

Now, exactly such patterns are what I have admired in Jane Austen's earlier novels—developed and seen as even more closely woven, and finer, in *Emma*. Yet Lawrence's "even volatile according to pattern" seems a near and even a particularly apt description. So what prevents these works—so evidently alive—from falling dead?

The question looks ineffable, looming with portentous difficulty and
the likelihood of mere assertions. Nevertheless, it is possible to avoid the
temptation to reply merely dogmatically with 'well, everyone finds them
alive, so there' by a further recourse to the specific. I shall consider in a
moment the scene structured round Jane Fairfax's significant visit to the
post-office in 2, xvi and the typical counterpoint of character this provokes.
But first note that Lawrence's challenge raises the whole question of
representation in art. Nobody who thinks, just once, on the matter thinks
that characters in a fiction are real. Even to formulate the question thus is to
destroy it; and it is reserved to contemporary commentators in pursuit of
their ideals to say unreflective things such as that "the author adds a less than
candid sketch of" Jane Fairfax's "past life"[6]—since there *is* no past life, this
is impossible. On the other hand, we can say, as I argued in chapter one, that
the ordinary and natural response to Jane Austen's creation of part of
England in the early 1800s (in spite of its exclusions) is also epistemologically
the most correct. 'So that was what it was like', we exclaim; and this is
legitimate since we learn, as I also argued, what and how the past thought
and *felt* most directly from documents of this kind—from works of art.
(Which is not, of course, to exclude all or any of the other more external and
factual records.) Imaginative writers are the most obviously powerful first-
hand authorities on the sensibilities of their own times, for the very obvious
reason that they *were* the sensibilities of their times. Of course, it is then up
to the reader to gauge whether what is written purports to be accurate—
realistic—in regard to everyday facts, or not. (That is a part of the present
enterprise.)

But the real challenge extending from Lawrence bears a different
emphasis: are these characters—these imaginative verbal constructs, these
figments—just individuals, just individual manifestations (one-offs), or are
they as well in some way representative or universal figures? Actually, they
need not be universal to be representative. They could dramatise or illustrate
a historically local condition like the 'alienation' 'under capital' of social
relations and the consequent 'externalisation and objectification' of these, as
is claimed by some neo-marxists (though I do not think they *do*), and still be
representative—indeed, they would have to be representative.[7] What
Lawrence seems to want is a kind of ideal individuality which denies any
typicality and any predictability. I do not think that such pure spontaneity is
common even in what Henry James called in this context "untidy life"—most
of us, as I have said, perceive through and act out our stereotypes most of the
time—and such unpredictable unreflectiveness is certainly not a
characteristic of most art. It is nearly a contradiction in fact: for art suggests

patterns; and in what is shaped and told we automatically look for a significance greater than the particular—even in the most trifling anecdote, let alone the grandest myth. Merely being alive involves a jumble of sensation; and literary or visual artefacts which only retail the actual (memoirs, photographs etc.) are very likely to meander into literal inconsequence because they are confined and bound in a dogged particular channel—they are just there, nothing follows, and the likely response is 'Oh'. Truth can be stranger than fiction, but also more boring. This is one of the points of Aristotle's observation, echoed down the ages by serious thinkers on art (e.g. Sir Philip Sidney) that:

> ... It is not the poet's function to describe what has actually happened, but the kinds of thing that might happen, that is, could happen because they are, in the circumstances, either probable or necessary. The difference between the historian and the poet is not that the one writes in prose and the other in verse ... [but that] one tells of what has happened, the other of the kinds of things that might happen. For this reason poetry is something more philosophical and more worthy of serious attention than history; for while poetry is concerned with universal truths, history treats of particular facts.[8]

Not, of course, that Lawrence, either in theory or practice, wanted pure unshaped experience. He is obviously reacting to the second rate or worse; to formula work in which everyone or thing has mechanically to represent a larger banality (an entity like 'capital', 'alienation', 'reification' etc. perhaps?). He may well have had *specifically* in mind the lumbering heirs of the great Victorian novelists, such as Galsworthy and Arnold Bennett and their lesser derivatives. But in Jane Austen the patterns, and thus the qualities they evoke, are fresh and subtle. In her work predictability is not mechanical, but full of life and interest (however often we read it).

To take the proposed post-office example: in a society that depends so much as Highbury does on external stimulations for its interests, even the fastidious have to honour the "irresistible form" taken by a new arrival. So in 2, xvi Emma gives an obligatory dinner for Mrs. Elton—of whom in any case the reader desires to hear more after her first eruptions. Here we may note that in order that we may concentrate the better on issues genuinely current, one element of the possible tension in the love story convention—which might have been kept randomly alive in a less assured writer—has been deliberately defused: Mr. Knightley's disavowal in the previous chapter of

anything but a friendly interest in Jane Fairfax allows us to take John
Knightley's picking her out for sociability—"an old acquaintance and a quiet
girl"—as merely pleasant, apparently as it would be in day to day experience,
and not boding any family strategy. They talk of the commonplace: he (in the
company, of course, of little Henry and little John) has seen her in the rain
coming from the post-office that morning and twits her with his slightly
barking humour:

> "The post-office has a great charm at one period of our lives.
> When you have lived to my age, you will begin to think letters are
> never worth going through the rain for." (293)

He must be all of thirty-five (but a most domestic man). He continues with
serious concern for her and her slight embarrassment until the interruption of
Mr. Woodhouse, the "kind-hearted, polite old man" (a small narratorial
dressing of the balance), widens the conversation to allow a typical display by all
present around this subject. Mrs. Weston is concerned with health care. Mrs.
Elton surges in with manifestations of importance and assumptions of intimacy:

> "My dear Jane, what is this I hear? ... You sad girl, how could you
> do such a thing?—It is a sign I was not there to take care of you."
> (295)

—(and so on until one begins to dread for those servants whose names she
ostentatiously claims to be unable to remember), and even the gentle Jane is
forced back on hard, quiet resistance. When the talk becomes general
conventional praise of the postal service and modern convenience, and
thence chat about handwriting, Emma's sprightliness involves her in the
most fearful dramatic irony—for the *averti* reader. She cannot know that by
dutifully resolving not to tease Jane about her Dixon fantasy, and bravely
raising Frank Churchill's name instead, she is, in fact, talking about that
same, very embarrassing, handwriting that we know (or suspect) Jane went to
the post-office to collect. But this, flexible and humorous as it is, is far from
all there is in these three or so pages. Mr. Knightley says nothing until John
Knightley appeals to him about the theory that handwriting runs in families
and that Isabella's and Emma's are similar. His apparently casual reply is
actually full of importance:

> "Yes," said his brother hesitatingly, "there is a likeness. I know
> what you mean—but Emma's hand is the strongest."

"Isabella and Emma both write beautifully," said Mr. Woodhouse; and always did. And so does poor Mrs. Weston"— (297)

I do not suppose it particularly significant that Mr. Knightley says— "strongest" where "stronger" would be normal; but a hesitation from *him* must give us pause. The preference for Emma is, one supposes, marginally not what his brother might wish to hear; more importantly it confirms our deep wish that he should love her, and thus forms part of a series of unconscious or semi-conscious developing revelations on both their parts which form another and different kind of pattern through the book. His irrational jealousy—which every critic notices—of Frank Churchill even before Frank appears (1, xviii) and afterwards; her wishing him a potential dancer rather than an older man among the "husbands, fathers, and whist-players" at the Crown (3, ii), his dancing with Harriet being "extremely good" after all, their subsequent dance and his wonderful "Brother and sister! no, indeed" which precedes this; her memory of where he was standing on a certain day while Harriet remembers only Mr. Elton's place (3, iv); their mutually intelligent look—"her feelings were at once caught and honoured"—after she has apologised to Miss Bates about Box Hill in 3, ix, and the instinctive meeting of hands and his near kiss of her's which follows—rendered in such nervous, exploratory prose:

> He took her hand;—whether she had not herself made the first motion, she could not say—she might, perhaps, have rather offered it—but he took her hand, pressed it, and certainly was on the point of carrying it to his lips—when, from some fancy or other, he suddenly let it go.—Why he should feel such a scruple, why he should change his mind when it was all but done, she could not perceive ... (386)

—all these constitute a purposeful main design in the novel.[9]

But what I am noticing here is the art by which this *minute* detail about the handwriting is introduced within a crowded scene of comic expected responses. That it could easily be passed over in reading is indicative both of the density of Jane Austen's prose and of the control with which she picks out her themes in seemingly neutral contexts. In fact, no context is allowed to be neutral. It is the zest and depth imparted by such a marvellously complex use of patterns—volatile or otherwise—that effectively rebut the kind of criticism most trenchantly put by Lawrence. Even in the realist novel—

perhaps, from a certain point of view, especially there—conventions of representation fruitfully obtain: verisimilitude is, after all, only a version of similitude.

V

Not that Jane Austen does not experiment with representation. The relatively crude stereotypes of Fanny Burney have, after *Sense and Sensibility* at any rate, vanished from her work. But, in addition, there is in *Emma* an experiment which I do not think has been recognised by commentators quite enough as such.

Miss Bates is a famous figure. With educated people at least, she leads, like Mr. Collins again, a quasi-proverbial existence outside the book comparable to that of Falstaff—though not so grand. She is paradigmatic to the novel in being known as the bore who entertains. She is also the person who believes in the perfect suitability of Highbury for human life, and is its laudatrix:

> "We may well say that 'our lot is cast in a goodly heritage'"... "I say, sir," turning to Mr. Woodhouse, "I think there are few places with such society as Highbury. I always say, we are quite blessed in our neighbours.—My dear sir, if there is one thing my mother loves better than another, it is pork—a roast loin of pork"— (2, iii, 174–5)

Her function within the novel has usually been explained, since Mary Lascelles wrote admirably, in 1939, of the "cobweb lightness and fineness" of Jane Austen's workmanship,[10] by saying that her inconsequencies are an essential means of revealing information and directing the reader's attitudes. Also, of course, she is wonderful as the humble thankful recipient of Mr. Knightley's squirely gifts of apples etc., and as the equally humble and forgiving sufferer from Emma's hot and exasperated effort at wit on Box Hill. But not only does she *not* exhibit—as some of the characters in the novel do—what-Or. Johnson was pleased to find in the Ministers of the Hebrides "... such politeness as so narrow a circle of converse could not have supplied, but to minds naturally disposed to elegance":[11] she is further interesting as seeming an unusually naturalistic speaker within Jane Austen's conventions.

It is a common and amiable mistake to think that we talk like people in books, or *vice versa*. The mistake is easily recognised when the book is composed of speeches in alexandrines, like, say, *Andromaque*. It is fairly easily recognised when the speeches are in blank verse—though it is surprising how many people talk a little like Hamlet when pressed. But, again, the novel is a peculiarly deceiving form if we persist in thinking it is *as* naturalistic as it commonly seems. Sometimes it does not really even seem so. It can, in Jane Austen's time as well as any other, be exceedingly mannered. Consider, for example, this effusion supplied by Fanny Burney for Delvile on finding a heroine still steady and sensible at Vauxhall at four in the morning—just after Harrel has shot himself:

> "Amiable Miss Beverley! what a dreadful scene have you witnessed! what a cruel task have you nobly performed! such spirit with such softness! so much presence of mind with such feeling!—But you are all excellence! human nature can rise no higher! I believe, indeed, that you are its most perfect ornament!"
> Praise such as this, so unexpected, and delivered with such energy, Cecilia heard not without pleasure... (*Cecilia*, 5, 7)[12]

This is highly conventionalised: like a stage speech, and as much a direction as to how we are to think about Cecilia as a pretence of surface verisimilitude. Jane Austen, as is often said, has a vastly: more natural touch. Nevertheless, surely Norman Page is right when in his very useful discussion of Jane Austen's dialogue he mildly says:

> ... there seems good reason to doubt whether Jane Austen's contemporaries really spoke with the sureness and economy of effect which characterise the speech even of her foolish and vulgar figures.[13]

The "Ers" and "Aahs", grunts and sighs of one's conversation as revealed by tape recorder of TAM would of course make tedious reading (though there persists a sad convention of transcribing some of this into fiction in the interests of a delusive authenticity). Part of the fuller articulacy usual in novels must be to substitute for, or supply, the expressiveness given in nature by glance and gesture, and pitch, *timbre* and volume. So Miss Bates's egregious lack of emotional and mental sureness and economy is indicated by a special appropriate signal in her diction. The signal is that she meaninglessly fails to complete sentences. Mr. Knightley (and others) are quite capable of expressive English *aposiopesis*—as in the phrase about independence alluded to above; and others break off, like Mr. Elton, under the influence of emotion; but Miss Bates is genuinely, consistently, inconsequent. Here is the opening of one of her long speeches in 2, ix (just after poor Emma has been so infuriated by Harriet's dithering over the destination for her purchases at Ford's): the dots are, of course, part of the text:

> "I declare I cannot recollect what I was talking of.—Oh! my mother's spectacles. So very obliging of Mr. Frank Churchill! 'Oh!' said he, 'I do think I can fasten the rivet; I like a job of this kind excessively.'—Which you know shewed him to be so very.... Indeed I must say that, much as I had heard of him before and much as I had expected, he very far exceeds any thing.... I do congratulate you, Mrs. Weston, most warmly. He seems every thing the fondest parent could.... 'Oh!' said he, 'I can fasten that kind of rivet. I like a job of that sort excessively.'" (237–8)

And on it goes—full of information, as Mary Lascelles says, including information about Frank's affected manner—but in marked contrast to the formed speech usual to the other characters. A few lines down there is a further "That, you know, was so very...." and a little later "He would be so very...." both left hanging. This *tic* does sound near to literal transcription—and is something substantially exploited in subsequent literature. Henry James is fond of its use; and it is, for example, part of the distinguished tautened naturalism of Simon Gray's plays (the best contemporary dramatic writing) that characters constantly tail off their speeches into the significant air ...

Later, at the Crown ball (3, ii, 323–3), Miss Bates is punctuated predominantly by a series of breathless dashes. Later still, the style may seem to find its height in the wonderful passage of associative chatter by Mrs. Elton in the strawberry beds at Donwell in 3, vi: but here a distinction must be made, for with Mrs. Elton there is a different convention about the kind of reporting (creation really, of course) assumed. The *entirety* of Miss Bates's incompletions can be assumed to be present, and nature closely rendered. At Donwell, as it might be in a speech of hers, the reader is exposed to the speaker's nature and told by implication of the progress, the enthusiasm turning to boredom and fatigue, of the whole hilarious downgrade pastoral. But Mrs. Elton, "in all her apparatus of happiness, her large bonnet and her basket" (probably such Marie-Antoinette *voulu* excursions were by then a little vulgar, as Mr. Knightley's calm insistence on eating indoors implies) is as it were overheard from a distance, in brilliant *extracts*:

"... Morning decidedly the best time—never tired—every sort good—hautboy infinitely superior—no comparison—the others hardly eatable—hautboys very scarce—Chili preferred—white wood finest flavour of all—price of strawberries in London— abundance about Bristol—Maple Grove—cultivation—beds when to be renewed—gardeners thinking exactly different—no general rule—gardeners never to be put out of their way— delicious fruit—only too rich to be eaten much of—inferior to cherries—currants more refreshing—only objection to gathering strawberries the stooping—glaring sun—tired to death—could bear it no longer—must go and sit in the shade." (358–9)

Here the prose aspires to the condition of the index. If it were taken as a full transcription it would move near to those outer limits of the realm of the naturalistic normally inhabited by Mr. Jingle in *Pickwick*:

"Heads, heads—take care of your heads!" cried the loquacious stranger, as they came out under the low archway, which in those days formed the entrance to the coach-yard. "Terrible place— dangerous work—other day—five children—mother tall lady, eating sandwiches—forgot the arch—crash—knock—children look round—mother's head off—sandwich in her hand—no mouth to put it in—head of a family off—shocking, shocking! Looking at Whitehall, Sir?—fine place..." (ch. 2)

But Miss Bates's diffuseness is un-eccentric. It seems the result of an experiment with direct, unsummarised representation, closer to a copy of nature than is the speech of the equally commonplace people who surround her—but who finish their sentences. This is an extension of artistic range, as opposed, I think, to the evidence Fay Weldon (who daringly says that the part "goes on too long") finds for an "observed" as opposed to an "invented" character—"a slightly spiteful portrait".[14] (Let her speak for herself as a novelist; to me hers seems a confused distinction—and anyway the whole drift of *Emma* after Box Hill runs against the latter notion.)

VI

Enough, for the moment, of Jane Austen's perfected yet still evolving methods. All these descriptions merely concern the medium that creates, and is inseparable from, the possibility of Emma herself. She is Jane Austen's most fully created out-going heroine (temperamentally opposed to Fanny Price and Anne Elliot, and even finer than Elizabeth Bennet), and a moral flower of the novels.

I wish to praise her character.

Not, of course in the banal way that treats her as a real person with whom one may, for example, fall in love; but precisely as the speaker of J.F. Burrows's 21,501 words in a work of art. For she embodies a deeply sympathetic, though obviously vulnerable, positive ethic.

Her great attraction, the exact reverse of "my Fanny", lies in her openness, her *activity*. Every reader is made an expert on her failures—in self-knowledge, in self-control, in discipline, in humility, even in the proper assessment of what she grandly dubs "the yeomanry". And if there were (by some curious freak of obtuseness) a danger that these flaws—which fuel most of the scintillating drama of the book and are often made explicit—might escape someone, somewhere, critics have made it their business to expound them. So we are at liberty to look instead at the virtue implicit in all her mistakes: at their real cause, in fact. Without it the novel would merely be a harder and better *Cranford*.

Like everyone, and especially every main protagonist in a work of art, Emma is faced with choices. It is a commonplace about the book (in relation especially to Jane Austen's other heroines) that she is exceptionally well placed to make them—"handsome, clever, and rich" of course. However dull Highbury is, Emma is its admitted queen—and part of the nearly distracted nature of Mrs. Elton's showing off is in a way a tribute to how unshakable her rival's position is *au fond*. (In fact, Emma would not admit that there *is* a rivalry—and most of the others in the book would have to agree with her.) Above all, she is so placed as to be able to take up in plausible worldly strength that stance towards a woman's lot which is spiritually present in Elizabeth Bennet but not in her circumstances, and for which Fanny Price is unqualified in every way.

This very deliberate elevation, with its attendant temptations, could well be a subject to develop into a tragedy. Emma's characteristically sharp apprehension—"it is poverty only which makes celibacy contemptible to a generous public!" (1, ix, 85)—serves to focus the attention on, to insist on, the areas where her very lucidity misleads her. It is a characteristic of the clever and articulate to seal themselves off from wisdom by the facility, plausibility and apparent comprehensiveness of their formulations. On their way to visit the poor Emma boasts:

"If I know myself, Harriet, mine is an active, busy mind, with a great many independent resources; and I do not perceive why I should be more in want of employment at forty or fifty than one-and-twenty. Woman's usual occupations of eye and hand and mind will be as open to me then, as they are now; or with no important variation. If I draw less, I shall read more; if I give up music, I shall take to carpet-work. And for objects for the affections, which is in truth the great point of inferiority, the want of which is really the great evil to be avoided in *not* marrying, I shall be very well off, with all the children of a sister I love so much, to care about. There will be enough of them, in all probability, to supply every sort of sensation that declining life can need. There will be enough for every hope and every fear; and though my attachment to none can equal that of a parent, it suits my ideas of comfort better than what is warmer and blinder. My nephews and nieces!—I shall often have a niece with me.

"Do you know Miss Bates's niece? That is, I know you must have seen her a hundred times—but are you acquainted?"

"Oh! yes; we are always forced to be acquainted..." (1, x, 85–6)

How poignant, and cunning, the reference to Jane Fairfax. The passage is often cited—and it is too easy to moralise at Emma's expense on its complacency, to point out how she is proved wrong etc., and how she confuses art with occupation, while the commentator forgets, probably in pleasure at the effect, how very like it is to the sentiments of most twenty- or twenty-one-year olds who are above the mediocre. (Imagine Harriet thinking in anything like this style.) But such blindness could be the prelude to deep suffering. It easily could be, since the world in this novel—like but even more so than the world of a society ruled by laxer social conventions— is diffused with a perpetual contingency. The opportunity for significant personal contact depends on the fall of events rather than the individual will—a fact that, coupled with the dignity, restraint and shyness on both sides, makes for the terrific tension always felt (even while we appreciate the artistically inevitable) as to whether Mr. Knightley will succeed in proposing or not. But although there is suffering in Emma's part—her freedom is also freedom to endure three major episodes filled with self reproach—this, too, is a product of what is admirable in her, and thus accords with no tragedy but a serious comic resolution. For the quality that determines the choices and mistakes she makes is what gives particular piquancy to the speech, and it conduces eventually to happiness rather than grief. She is quite right about the nature of her mind, and absolutely wrong about being satisfied with the tranquil exploitation of "resources". But she has to do *something* with her resources. And it is quite true and partly proper that she is an "imaginist". In dull Highbury, with its lack of life-compelling stimulus save the overrated periodic visits of familiar or unfamiliar outsiders—who are naturally dubious assets when they do arrive—the life in the mind, if you have one, and nothing much else to do, is everything.

Emma's quality—and her tremendous, admirable charm—is that she always chooses what seems to her the *most exciting* option or interpretation available. That this is her implicit criterion—rather than the exercise of her potential good sense and her natural taste—is what makes her so attractive to the reader and, of course, perfect for Mr. Knightley. From it derive all the famous mistakes and occasions for moralising: she must make matches; she must be an itchy reader and never perfect her music;[15] she must cultivate the noble bastard Harriet and rule out Robert Martin; Mr. Elton must marry Harriet; she must fall temporarily in love in a not-too-emotional kind of way with Frank Churchill and he with her; Frank must marry Harriet; Jane Fairfax must be open as well as irritatingly elegant; Jane must be adulterously in love with Mr. Dixon—such a tangle is, as I say, the possession of every reader. But its root is something we should very much approve. For: what could be the alternatives for an intelligent person?

A tone suggested in Mary Brunton represents one kind of alternative. Laura Montreville is resisting the attentions and protection of her predatory adorer Hargrave:

> "Let me not hear you—let me not look upon you," said Laura;— "leave me to think, if it be possible,"—and she poured a silent prayer to Heaven for help in this her sorest trial. The effort composed her, and the majesty of virtue gave dignity to her form, and firmness to her voice, while she said,— ... "I dare not trust to principles such as yours the guardianship of this the infancy of my being. I dare not incur certain guilt to escape contingent evil. I cannot make you the companion of this uncertain life, while your conduct is such, as to make our eternal separation the object of my dreadful hope." (*Self-Control*, 1810/11, ch. 5.[16])

It is precisely the point about Emma that she is never in a position to have to protest in this way. In any case she is not pompous (though it should in justice be noted that Laura is capable of more lively tones). But also the strict negative virtue implied—even without its melodramatic trapping—is contrary to Emma's whole conception (whereas it would not be to that of Fanny Price, given the difference in quality of language).

Could she then, as a more plausible alternative, more promptly and thoroughly heed the irritant corrective quality of the other superior person in Highbury, Mr. Knightley, and subside into a dull supremacy that would satisfy neither of them? The question is rhetorical, and perhaps a stupid tribute to the vigour of Jane Austen's creation. Really, there are no alternatives, as the subtle insistent detail of the dramatisation of the generous restlessness of Emma's mental process demonstrates. To take a few examples of this: very early on the narrator insinuates that a part of Emma's gratitude to Miss Taylor has been because of the latter's complacency towards her "active, busy" mind. She has been "peculiarly interested in herself, in every pleasure, every scheme of her's;—one to whom she could speak every thought as it arose, and who had such an affection for her as could never find fault" (1, i, 6). Nurture for speedy disaster, one might think. But fortunately Emma is a good person, and one is inclined to see her as Lady Granville saw Lady Osborne at about the same time:

> Lady Francis [Osborne] puzzles me to death. I am tempted to pencher to the admiring side. Granville (who likes her extremely) has been arguing the point of her superiority of character. He says (and I three quarters agree with him), that her conduct is regulated by an uncontrollable determination to follow all her own inclinations. That she is born with good ones is no *merit* of hers.[17]

This is no place to engage in a debate about Nature *versus* Nurture— otherwise the question would arise as to how the debile Mr. Woodhouse could be as it were genetically responsible for his vivid daughter. But the carrying through the novel of the implications of "every pleasure, every scheme" is to the point. Emma is always sharp: so sharp on occasion as even to be able to draw attention to the novelist's own delicate effects. When, for instance, the scheme over Harriet's portrait is in train the characters react to it in succession, in character; and Mr. Knightley, with typical accuracy, says, "You have made her too tall, Emma", but Mr. Elton replies:

> "Oh, no! certainly not too tall; not in the least too tall. Consider, she is sitting down—which naturally presents a different—which in short gives exactly the idea—and the proportions must be preserved, you know. Proportions, foreshortening.—Oh, no! it

gives one exactly the idea of such a height as Miss Smith's. Exactly
so indeed!" (1, vi, 48)

This literate/nonsensical essay in Miss Bates—style appreciation might be
passed over as part of the Elton gush. But Emma, in the midst of her delusion
as to the object of that gush, picks on it (to herself) with a clarity and exact
good sense worthy of Dr. Johnson:

> "This man is almost too gallant to be in love.... He is an
> excellent young man, and will suit Harriet exactly; it will be an
> 'Exactly so,' as he says himself..." (49)

It is a comparable mental alacrity in the midst of blindness that, in
sensitive retrospective analysis, recognises after the *débâcle* in the carriage
from Randalls that "The first error and the worst lay at her door" (1, xvi,
136), but, beautifully, "It was rather too late in the day to set about being
simple-minded and ignorant" (1, xvii, 142)—and this is at the same period
that detaching Harriet from Robert Martin is still a subject for self
congratulation.

Emma wants things to be exciting, to choose, to initiate. She forms
part, one might say, of a very familiar tradition of witty young women in
fiction (Anna Howe in *Clarissa*, Lady Honoria in *Cecilia*, Miss Milner in *A
Simple Story* and Lady Delacour in *Belinda* spring to mind in high-quality
work—though the type seems to have been common—and they are followed
immediately by the notable Lady Juliana in Susan Ferrier's *Marriage* [1818]
and by Lady Cecilia in *Helen* [1834]). But—to generalise—these creations,
though usually 'good', are also usually structurally subordinate in that their
imperfections and their freedom *contrast* with the real heroine. Emma, with
Elizabeth Bennet, is moved to the centre, is the real heroine, and therefore
revivifies the rôle. Together they are heroines for the future. (How far the
future followed them up is another, and complex, matter.) And, as I have said,
she is obviously marked off from Elizabeth by her money and status. She is
therefore able to act on events, rather than merely to react, however strongly.
She is pivotal in combining internal freedom with external independence and
being therefore in a position to realise her freedom without threat (and
without discipline): she can refuse Elton and merely dally with Frank
Churchill; it is, famously, a prompting from within herself that directs her to
Mr. Knightley—and she scarcely adopts a passive stance toward him. She is
a kind of amatory protestant. And the bustling inward activity of her spirit is
constantly brilliant. Consider some more details of her play of mind

immediately Frank Churchill arrives:

> Emma wondered whether the same suspicion of what might be
> expected from their knowing each other which had taken strong
> possession of her mind had ever crossed his.... She had no doubt
> of what Mr. Weston was often thinking about. His quick eye she
> detected again and again glancing ... (2, v, 192–3)

A little later she looks forward to the chance of:

> ... judging of his general manners, and by inference, of the
> meaning of his manners towards herself; of guessing how soon it
> might be necessary for her to throw coldness into her air; and of
> fancying what the observations of all those might be, who were
> now seeing them together for the first time. (2, viii, 212)

As the last phrase indicates, Emma assumes that every one is as acute as she
thinks herself. Her mind is almost absurdly generous as well as patronising.
And she enthusiastically gives to some of the people around her a glamour
and vividness which make them worthy to inhabit her own drama. But she is
mistaken about this too, and it is of her, gazing idly—no, actively—at the
mundane Highbury scene that the narrator brilliantly, and with unusual
philosophical overtones, says:

> A mind lively and at ease, can do with seeing nothing, and can see
> nothing that does not answer. (2, ix, 233)

Such a mind must of course, in one of the broader comic passages of the
novel, turn Harriet's undangerous encounter with a few gypsies (children and
women) into a drama that might have come out of the more childish parts of
Richardson or Fanny Burney, and with Frank, though not on horseback, in
the tenor rôle:—

> Could a linguist, could a grammarian, could even a
> mathematician have seen what she did, have witnessed their
> appearance together.... How much more must an imaginist, like
> herself, be on fire with speculation and foresight!—especially
> with such a groundwork of anticipation as her mind had already
> made. (3, iii, 335)

—and thereby miss the actual exciting clue in the incident which is Frank's visit to the Bates's, lamely explained as the return of a "pair of scissars".[18]

In remarking these things I merely pick out strands from a texture the strength of which every reader will have felt. But the principle behind them—that Emma is in lively pursuit of any excitement offered by her limited environment and some which are not offered—naturally informs the most talked of and most impressive parts of the novel as well. It is not malice or ill nature that insults Miss Bates on Box Hill, but restlessness and boredom coupled with an habitual *esprit*—so that we can see the episode sympathetically as well as through Mr. Knightley's justified dismay. It is the fresh and spring-like activity of Emma's approach to her fusty and *gêneant* world which constitutes her value and explains her charm. The mistakes recede. Unlike the would-be grander choices made through the imaginative powers of a Victorian fictional descendant (with whom I have declined to compare Catherine Morland)—Isabel Archer confronting her destiny in *The Portrait of a Lady*—Emma's choices are all in favour of enhancement. What she desires she receives—of course, from the most familiar and the least expected quarter.

VII

Nevertheless, it would be misleading to conclude this discussion of *Emma* with Emma alone. For in this lively comic achievement there is still something of a parallel and inheritance from the grim outer world of *Sense and Sensibility*.

It is obvious to all that the didactic intent—a truly respectable thing which every writer has—is never rammed home or insisted upon in Jane Austen's work, as it can be in that of most of her predecessors and, indeed, most of her successors. The moral definitions of her novels are not *obscure*—they are definitely felt; but at their most important they reside in the interplay of embodiments of value—frequently negative embodiments—and usually at the centre, as in *Emma*, imperfect ones—and not in the remarks of a directive narrator. Nor is any one character proposed as a 'mouthpiece'—Mr. Knightley is perhaps the nearest to this, and he is seen often with a very amused eye.[19] Most of this is received wisdom, and it is one of the reasons why Jane Austen seems so temporally unlocal, so unformidable, and so unreservedly entertaining. Nevertheless, an intent is there, and it can be illuminated in this case by considering why it is that the heroine's own love drama is happily concluded in its essentials a good fifty pages before the end of the book? A good deal of the story needs working out, of course: Frank and Jane; Harriet; the practicalities of having to adjust Mr. Woodhouse's system to the shocking news; a poultry raid—and so on. Nor does the interest flag. None the less, Mr. Knightley's proposal could easily, and more traditionally, have come after most of it had been done—or most of it could have been sidelined.

The deep reason for this structure must surely be that the romantic climax is being, literally, 'placed' in a not very romantic world. In spite of the novel's having (to use a word beloved of theatre reviewers) an eponymous heroine, her actions are inextricably linked to her context—a feature that I have tried to echo in this chapter. James Thompson sharply observes that Jane Austen lived at the beginning of a period which was beginning to idealise marriage as an individual "compact of love and affection" as opposed to a contractual and dynastic (or, I suppose, merely useful) business, and that we live at the end of this period.[20] The reader of *Emma*—or of any of Jane Austen—should not really need this observation with its shaky historical ground and its dubious present. As we constantly realise, everything is within the fiction. But although the novel offers the central couple a temporary support, as it were, from the other new couples, this is assumed rather than dramatised; and the Churchills will not be in Highbury and the Martins (embarrassingly enough) not in the same social sphere. So the satisfaction of the ending must be a little muted. Or, rather, "the perfect happiness of the union" among "the small band of true friends" (3, xix, 484) *is* there and felt; but it is equi-present, so to speak, and simultaneous with, the dull and unredeemed environment. Elizabeth Darcy can remove to Pemberley, and Fanny Bertram reform Mansfield—but Emma's privileged position in this deeply original conception scarcely allows of external change—a fact amusingly enforced by her not even changing houses. How definite the novel is being on this point is illustrated by two manifestations of those Highbury leading lights, the Eltons. One might expect Mrs. Elton to fade in bafflement when faced with the betrothals of the two dignified couples in the book. On the contrary, her indelicate coy boasting is even more irrepressible—to their faces: about Jane, who dislikes and resents her, to Emma who adds scorn (now with equanimity) to these feelings: "Do not you think, Miss Woodhouse, our saucy little friend here is charmingly recovered?" (454)—and on, and, excruciatingly, on. And surely it is a fairly acid piece of anti-Donatism to have everybody married by her husband in his official capacity but with no murmur at all? Sandra Gilbert and Susan Gubar hazard in their usual lively way of novels in this period that "a girl without a benevolent narrator would never find her way out of either her mortifications or her parent's house".[21] But here all is natural, and the narration not a bit over managed. Emma finds herself at last freely and spontaneously choosing to prefer Mr. Knightley's vision of "the beauty of truth and sincerity"—though with a blush for Harriet (3, xi, 404–5)—to her own hectic, wonderful, inner life; and we are deeply moved and believe it. Perhaps this is because unglamorous Highbury remains with us, and there can be no danger, there, of having a sentimental dream. It remains for *Persuasion* to move a heroine right out of this world.

NOTES

1. There is a comparable buried charge in "seemed" as used by Maria Edgeworth in *The Dun* (1802) where the bawd Mrs. Carver seems to be "touched with compassion" for the innocent sixteen-year-old Anne, and sustains five pages of excellent charitable behaviour until she reveals what she is—yet we are not surprised.

2. In *The Idea of the Gentleman in the Victorian Novel*, London, 1981, Robin Gilmour gives an interesting, acute and un-nostalgic account of this key idea and ideal.

As to *aimable versus* amiable: Maria Edgeworth has her (French, of course) Marmontel prefer the English sense in the near contemporary *Ormond*, 1817—so the topic seems to have been current. Norman Page remarks in *The Language of Jane Austen*, that it was a habit of that age to be alert to, and discuss, the meanings of such concepts and their appropriate definition. A sympathetic example of this can be found from life, as it were, in the letters of (the extremely *grande dame*) Harriet Granville, a large selection of which is available in *A Second Self* (1810–45), ed. Virginia Surtees, Salisbury, 1990. With Mr. Knightley's:—

> "He [Frank] may be very 'aimable,' have very good manners, and be very agreeable; but he can have no English delicacy towards the feelings of other people: nothing really amiable about him." (1, xviii, 149).

— we may set her judgement on Mme. de Lieven:

> It is every thing that makes a person amiable which is wanting in her— gentleness, sweetness, cheerfulness, kindness, abnegation de soi. There is a great deal of decorum and propriety ... (89)

And note the French here.

3. *Living Space in Fact and Fiction*, London, 1989, 38 ff.; 59.

4. The common meaning of 'irony' or 'ironic' nowadays is either odd/amusing or sarcastic. But it scarcely needs noting again how very fond critics of Jane Austen are of the term.

5. 'Why the Novel Matters', published posthumously in *Phoenix*, London, 1936, 537.

6. Janet Todd, *Women's Friendship in Literature*, New York, 1980, 290.

7. See Thompson, *Between Self and World*, 13 ff. Mary Poovey, *The Proper Lady*, is on much the same trail when she argues that "romantic" love flatters "bourgeois" society because it disguises the system of "economic and political domination" by "foregrounding" personal relations which actually do not "materially affect society". Particularly it disguises the exploitation of women (237–9). This is very neat and grand; but like so much of this materialist stuff it seems out of touch with the real as experienced in Jane Austen's novels; *or* the real real. To feel *paranoia* on behalf of (some of) the past is a poor way of understanding it. To do Mary Poovey justice, she admits that her "ideological bias" is ahistorical and recognises that such "hindsight" may impair her "sensitivity" (245).

Perhaps English readers feel less remote from Jane Austen on these matters than some Americans apparently do?

8. *Poetics*, ch. 9; trans. T.S. Dorsch, Harmonsdworth, 1965.

9. For a more systematic and fuller account of these sequences see my *'Emma' and 'Persuasion'*, Harmondsworth, 1985.

For a convincing analysis of various technical modes involved see Hough, 'Narrative and Dialogue in Jane Austen', 201–29.

10. *Jane Austen and her Art*, 177. It is an academic vulgarism to think that the more recent critical work is the better it is.

11. *A Journey to the Western Islands of Scotland*, 1775, ed. R.W. Chapman, Oxford, 1930, 95.

12. *Cecilia* was published in 1782. Of course, more naturalistic speech than this occurs in many novels before it—including more naturalistic polite speech—as well as the obvious uses of dialect from at least Defoe onwards, and the use of genteel vulgarisms, of which the dialects of the Steele sisters in *Sense and Sensibility* are the important expressive example in mature Jane Austen (see above, ch. 4).

13. *The Language of Jane Austen*, 117.

14. *Letters to Alice on First Reading Jane Austen*, London, 1984, 72.

15. She too fitfully, and amusingly, knows this fault: "She did most heartily grieve over the idleness of her childhood—and sat down and practised vigorously an hour and a half." (2, vii, 208).

16. Page 37 in the Pandora edition, London, 1986.

17. Surtees, *A Second Self*, 183.

18. Though it is confusing for critics to speculate about the relations between the life and works of a writer, it is hard to forego the description of Emma as a creative person, though shockingly lacking in the necessary discipline. (Her idea of an interesting consequence of the death of Mrs. Churchill is the revelation of "Half a dozen natural children, perhaps—and poor Frank cut off!"—3, vi, 357).

In which case we *could* say that, unlike Tolstoy and Joyce (for instance), Jane Austen did not start with autobiography and then move into a wider and more distanced, more 'objective' creation, but, very remarkably, the other way round.

A speculation of comparable intellectual dubiety which, none the less, gives some enjoyment to Jane Austen fans is the classification of her heroines into headstrong (H) and obedient (O), and the evenness, or symmetry, of the resulting pattern, or graph. Taking the works in order of probable completion we get: H (*Lady Susan*); O (*Northanger Abbey*); H & O (*Sense and Sensibility*); H (*Pride and Prejudice*); O (*Mansfield Park*); H (*Emma*); O (*Persuasion*). H O H/O H O H O.

19. J.F. Burrows convincingly questions the sage-like character often given to Mr. Knightley in his expanded analysis, *Jane Austen's 'Emma'*, Sydney, 1968.

20. *Between Self and World*, 18.

21. *The Madwoman in the Attic*, 169.

STUART M. TAVE

What are men to rocks and mountains?
Pride and Prejudice

A young lover in *A Midsummer Night's Dream* or in *Man and Superman* who finds the course of true love becoming too difficult to negotiate has the option of escaping to a country where he, or she, imagines this matter can be better ordered. But time and place are not so magically disposable in *Pride and Prejudice*. The story here is familiar: we are presented with two sets of young lovers who have problems which must be worked out, and here too are those who try to direct their lives for them, and varied clowns doing their own foolish acts, before the lovers can attain the deserved happiness we expect for them; but here their solutions cannot be sought in another world among the powers of more than mortal spirits.

As in *Man and Superman* the lovers are not interchangeable pairs, as Elizabeth points out to her kind and less perceptive sister. When Jane and Bingley have finally come together in their felicity Jane wants everybody to be as happy as she: "If I could but see you as happy!" she says to Elizabeth. "If there *were* but such another man for you!" It does not seem possible to her that there could be a second Bingley in the universe, but for Elizabeth that limitation is just as well. "If you were to give me forty such men, I could never be so happy as you. Till I have your disposition ... I never can have your happiness." She'll have to shift for herself and perhaps with very good luck she may meet with another Mr. Collins in time (III, xiii, 350). Elizabeth's

From *Lovers, Clowns, and Fairies: An Essay on Comedies*. © 1993 by The University of Chicago.

time has not been and will not be so empty and desperate as that, but certainly as she has not her sister's disposition a duplicate of her sister's fortune cannot fulfill her desires. Her sister's difficulties in the course of true love have been rather simple as she and Bingley fell in love very quickly, to say the least, and were kept apart only by the interference of others; or if there is a defect in Bingley which made him vulnerable to such interference in the happiness of himself and the woman he loves it is because, as Elizabeth says gently now, "He made a little mistake to be sure; but it is to the credit of his modesty" (350). She has had, for herself, a different opinion of Bingley's weakness and he would never be the man for her. There is certainly no sign that he has learned anything or will ever be any different. Like him Jane is not one to profit much by experience: she does not ever comprehend why the false Miss Bingley wished to be intimate with her, "but if the same circumstances were to happen again, I am sure I should be deceived again" (II, iii, 148). She and Bingley are well matched, they being two of a kind, so easy, Mr. Bennet says, every servant will cheat there (III, xiii, 348). Two of a kind is not Elizabeth's style. And if there are external problems in the matching of Elizabeth they are not what delays her happiness. Unlike the story of Jane the story of Elizabeth takes time because it takes time for Elizabeth to learn and to change, and the story is complicated further because it takes time for Darcy to learn and to change and because those processes are continually affected by one another.

We have here too, as in our previous tales, interfering elders who are busy breakers and makers of matches; and, as before, these are ineffective clownish figures with none of the power of their pretensions to arrange the fates of others. Mrs. Bennet is one of the best ever in this role, a legend for all time—that mother whose main business in life is match-making, with five daughters and slender means, but so eager and silly that she is marvellously incompetent at her business, simply by being herself. She is a grand hazard in the course of the true loves of Jane and Elizabeth; she also pushes Elizabeth as hard as she can to take that clown Mr. Collins (commending him for speaking so sensibly to Mr. Darcy and for being a remarkably clever young man, I, xviii, 101); she pushes her favorite Lydia into a danger where Lydia, the likest to her mother, succumbs, thereby immediately prostrating her mother and then quickly throwing her into ecstasy. But then in a year Mrs. Bennet has surprisingly married off three of five, a commendable, statistically remarkable, record. "Three daughters married! ... Oh, Lord! What will become of me. I shall go distracted" (III, xvii, 378): one of those great fools who succeed so well in spite of herself. Then there is that other clown, Lady Catherine—Mr. Darcy has already been forced to see that he too has relatives to blush for, "ashamed of his aunt's ill breeding" (II, viii, 173)—that other match-making mother. This one has arranged the marriage for her own daughter and nephew when they were children, and she has not been in the habit of brooking disappointment: "depend upon it I will carry my point" (III, xiv, 358). Her superb effort to break the engagement of Darcy and Elizabeth, which in fact doesn't yet exist, helps bring that match to its happy conclusion. "Lady Catherine has been of infinite use," Elizabeth says, "which ought to make her happy, for she loves to be of use" (III, xviii, 381).

But then Elizabeth and Darcy, the young lovers very like Jack Tanner in this respect, also think of themselves as superior spirits with strong confidence in their own abilities to oversee the lives of others. They know how to read minds and characters and thereby to predict conduct and to determine proper matches for their friends. What they know least is the proper marriage for themselves, knowing least their own minds and characters. Like Shaw, Jane Austen has a special delight in such interesting people, handsome and clever, and sometimes rich, the most attractive people we have ever met: those who are so bright they think they are Puck, and who must discover that they are really mortals in love, much in need of the time and place of the eye-opening experience.

Emma might have been a better example for this chapter. She has charm, the charming Miss Woodhouse, and though that is a commonplace compliment, and though there is a false charm, as it is offered in Augusta Hawkins, there is a reality in Emma's which is validated by that contrast. It is made convincing not only by what we can see for ourselves but by the denial of Mr. Knightley, early in the novel: "But I ... who have had no such charm thrown over my senses, must still see, hear, and remember" (I, v, 37). He, unlike Miss Taylor (as was) and most of those within Emma's circle, has kept his senses clear, which is not always gratifying to Emma. But it is borne in on us at the start how effective she thinks she is. If Mr. Knightley, hearing her abuse the reason she has, in breaking the match between Harriet Smith and Robert Martin, thinks it would be better to be without reason than misapply it as she does, Emma has a higher certainty of her knowledge of love and of the minds of men: men fall in love with girls like Harriet (or what Emma thinks Harriet is) and Emma confers on her the power of choosing from among many. And, playful with Mr. Knightley, as we have seen her from the start (I, i, 10), she informs him of how bewitchment works on men. "'To be sure!' she cried playfully. 'I know that is the feeling of you all.'" She knows that such a girl as Harriet is exactly what every man delights in, what at once "bewitches his senses" and satisfies his judgment. We know Mr. Knightley's senses are neither charmed nor bewitched, but Emma is certain that "Were you, yourself, ever to marry, she is the very woman for you" (I, viii, 63–64), a delightful promise. And so it is not surprising that a few pages later Emma then begins to create a play and assures Harriet that Mr. Elton's sweet verses of courtship are certainly for her: "It is a sort of prologue to the play ... and will soon be followed by matter-of-fact prose," as indeed it will be. Harriet, with a better sense of uncertainty, but now overridden, is more like the open Hippolyta—"The strangest things to take place!" To Emma it is nothing strange or out of the common course but so evidently, so palpably, desirable; what courts her pre-arrangement immediately shapes itself into the proper form. Her Hartfield, under her rule, seems to have a magic quality, seems to have "a something in the air," she says, "which gives love exactly the right direction, and sends it into the very channel where it ought to flow." She has the right text—

The course of true love never did run smooth—

and she is the right editor. "A Hartfield edition of Shakespeare would have a long note on that passage." She has her map of misreading, because under her direction, she expects, all will run smooth, and she will be distressed later to find that the text of her own play will run closer to Shakespeare's. There may be some without common sense who will not find agreeable Harriet's match with Mr. Elton, she says, but "we are not to be addressing our conduct to fools" (I, ix, 74–75). She is, like Puck, above that mortal condition. The charade of courtship found on the table was, she tells her father, "dropt, we suppose, by a fairy"; but it is so pretty, her father says, that he can easily guess "what fairy brought it." Nobody could have written so prettily but Emma, a pretty confusion that helps to define her status among the fairies. Emma only nodded and smiled (78). She can indeed laugh: Harriet may so wonder that Miss Woodhouse should not marry, "so charming as you are!" but "Emma laughed and replied, 'My being charming, Harriet, is not quite enough to induce me to marry; I must find other people charming—one other person at least.'" And, free from the charms of others, in maiden meditation fancy free, as we may offer our own quotation for the Hartfield edition, she has very little intention of ever marrying at all. "I must see somebody very superior to any one I have seen yet, to be tempted," and she would rather not be tempted. The fact is "I cannot really change for the better." If she were to fall in love that would be a different thing, but "I have never been in love; it is not my way, or my nature; and I do not think I ever shall." So she would be a fool to change such a situation as hers (I, x, 84).

We may be certain that such exemption from the human condition is not a role a young lady or man can play for long on this earth. By the end of Volume I Emma has learned that she has been in error, that she did not see into Mr. Elton's mind, though the misread signs were fairly obvious even to her unimaginative brother-in-law, that she has been foolish, wrong in taking so active a part in bringing any two people together, adventuring too far, assuming too much, making light of what ought to be serious, and, not being tricky Puck, "making a trick of what ought to be simple." She is ashamed and resolved to do such things no more (I, xvi, 137). But of course she is not done; she is still "acting a part" on a succeeding matter (I, xviii, 145); or she is rebuking Mrs. Weston for trying Emma's specialty—"My dear Mrs. Weston, do not take to match-making. You do it very ill," without seeing why Mrs. Weston's suggestion of Mr. Knightley and Jane Fairfax is so irritating to her—and then running off into ridicule of the possibility by expertly imitating Miss Bates as Mr. Knightley's prospective relative. "For shame, Emma! Do not mimic her. You divert me against my conscience" (II, viii, 225). She has some real talents in this Puckish line of acting and of mimicry and of seeing into others and directing them, but that is part of her problem since she enjoys the power and cultivates it until her limits close in on her painfully. By the late stages of her third volume the faith of Miss Smith, her most malleable creation, who is still certain that Miss Woodhouse "can see into everybody's heart" is no longer gratifying (III, xi, 404).

Emma has been a disinterested fairy, exerting her talents to be helpful, enjoying the fun of match-making. "It is the greatest amusement in the world!" But Mr. Knightley knows she is not good at it and is more likely to do harm to herself than good to others (I, i, 11–13). He is better in foretelling things than she, as she is forced to see at several times and, most painfully, when it appears that she has unwittingly brought together Harriet and Mr. Knightley. The discovery of her blindness is mortifying. She had believed herself "in the secret of everybody's feelings," had "proposed to arrange everybody's destiny," and proved to be universally mistaken: and, incompetent fairy that she was, "she had not quite done nothing—for she had done mischief" (III, xi, 411–13). Happily she is still mistaken in foretelling the results of these evils, for Harriet, that clown, will always bounce, and Mr. Knightley, that superior spirit administering the counter-charm, with no charm thrown over his senses, had doted on her, faults and all (III, xvii, 462).

But for our purposes we will stay with *Pride and Prejudice*. It's a story that enables us to follow more readily the pattern we've been working with, both in the symmetrical contrasting of the two main sets of young lovers, and in the way in which the primary couple play off one another to bring about their eye-opening changes. Elizabeth, of course, is the central and most active character, and it is the mind and fortunes of her spirit we follow in its wit and its wanderings. We pick up the bright and attractive quality of Elizabeth from the beginning, her first encounter with Darcy when, catching her eye, he makes the mistake of underestimating her powers of temptation and leaves her with no very cordial feelings towards him: she tells the story "with great spirit" among her friends; "for she had a lively, playful disposition, which delighted in any thing ridiculous" (I, iii, 12). With all the right equipment, the liveliness, playfulness, the delight in all that is ridiculous, the imagination, this young lady is a spirit who will change his vision and tell his story in another way. The result is confirmed in the final chapter when Georgiana Darcy listens with astonishment bordering on alarm at Elizabeth's "lively, sportive, manner" of talking to him, now the object of open pleasantry; by Elizabeth's instruction Georgiana's mind receives knowledge which has never before fallen in her way, how a woman may take liberties with her husband (III, xix, 388). We, not as naive as the young sister and with more opportunities for observation, have seen this spirit in its liberty, the "easy playfulness" of manner by which Darcy is caught (I, vi, 23), the continual "liveliness," "lively imagination," "lively talents" and the "spirits soon rising to playfulness" and "liveliness of your mind" Darcy learns to admire (III, xviii, 380). Others do not notice the effect of the first meeting of Darcy and Wickham, but characteristically Elizabeth sees and is astonished. "What could be the meaning of it?—It was impossible to imagine; it was impossible not to long to know" (I, xv, 73). When she arrives at Hunsford to visit Charlotte and Mr. Collins she anticipates quickly how her visit will pass, for "A lively imagination soon settled it all" (II, v, 158). If she cannot find out a secret in an honorable manner she is quite capable of "tricks and stratagems" to find it out (III, ix, 320). To the uncomprehending, like Mrs. Hurst and Mrs. Bennet, her look and manner may seem even "wild" (I, viii, 35; ix, 42), a shocking free spirit.

    She has more than the manner, or the art to please by her easy playing and singing, or the lightness to run across the fields when she has an important mission, for she has the superior power of the mind reader. We see that early, just after the great spirit of her response to Darcy, as Jane, who has had better dancing, expresses her admiration for Bingley. "He is just what a young man ought to be," with sense and good humor, Jane says, "and I never saw such happy manners!—so much ease, with such perfect good breeding!" Elizabeth sees quickly what Jane is really thinking of, besides these proper social qualities. "He is also handsome," she replies, "which a young man ought likewise to be, if he possibly can. His character is thereby complete."

And she gives her approval: "Well, he certainly is very agreeable, and I give you leave to like him. You have liked many a stupider person." Jane is easy to read, though no one appreciates her goodness and its weaknesses better than Elizabeth: "Oh! you are a great deal too apt you know, to like people in general. You never see a fault in any body." (Jane is the sort of girl who, in another time, might become a school-teacher because, as the happy saying goes, she likes people.) "With *your* good sense, to be so honestly blind to the follies and nonsense of others!" (I, iv, 14). When she sees Jane's smile of sweet complacency and glow of happy expression in Bingley's company, "Elizabeth instantly read her feelings." Loving sister that Elizabeth is, her own concerns of the moment give way to Jane's happiness (I, xviii, 95). But that lively mind stays sharp in its understanding of the minds of even those she loves. Jane's honest blindness to the faults of others leads her to faulty assumptions—that Bingley's sisters can only wish his happiness and if he is attached to her she cannot believe they would influence him against her, the only woman who can secure his happiness. Elizabeth knows a defective syllogism when she sees one: "Your first position is false. They may wish many things besides his happiness ..." (II, i, 136).

Elizabeth ranges more widely than her family out into the neighborhood, has rather a vocation for seeing into thoughts and characters, is therefore capable of predicting action. If Bingley says that whatever he does he does in a hurry, that he may depart Netherfield in five minutes, "That is exactly what I should have supposed of you," Elizabeth replies. "You begin to comprehend me, do you?" "Oh! yes—I understand you perfectly." He would like to take that for a compliment, "but to be so easily seen through," he is afraid, is pitiful. She can make better distinctions than that: it does not necessarily follow that "a deep, intricate character" is more or less estimable, she tells him, "than such a one as yours." She doesn't give a name to such a one as his, though shallow and simple do seem to be implied. Bingley continues immediately, "I did not know before ... that you were a studier of character. It must be an amusing study." She is a connoisseur: "Yes; but intricate characters are the most amusing. They have at least that advantage." Even in a country neighborhood, where there are few subjects, a confined society, people themselves alter so much there is something new to be observed forever (I ix, 42–43): she has a delighted sense of the effects of time on character.

It is amusing and she dearly loves a laugh. There, is a sisterly resemblance to Lydia, but Lydia is louder and more violent ("Lord! how I laughed! ... I thought I should have died.... any body might have heard us ten miles off!"), whether her enjoyment is a silly joke or a good journey to an unthinking immoral end (II, xvi, 221–22; III, v, 291). Elizabeth has a discriminating appreciation of levels and occasions. Her enjoyment is often private, as she sees into how others are making fools of themselves: she turns away "to hide a smile," from Darcy's assurance of his "real superiority of mind" (I, xi, 57); "nor could she think, without a smile," what Lady Catherine's indignation would have been if Elizabeth had been presented to her ladyship as the future niece (II, xiv, 210); "and she could hardly suppress a smile" when Darcy later seeks the acquaintance of some of her relatives, perhaps thinking them people of fashion (III, i, 254). Mr. Collins's proposal brings her closer to an open expression, when the idea of Mr. Collins, "with all his solemn composure, being run away with by his feelings," makes her "so near laughing" that for the moment she can't stop him (I, xix, 105). Some of these opportunities, as with Collins, or Sir William Lucas, are rather too easy, as she knows. "Elizabeth loved absurdities, but she had known Sir William's too long" (II, iv, 152). It is more impressive to hear that the sensible Mrs. Gardiner, who knows her nieces well, can say to her of Jane's disappointment in love that "It had better have happened to *you*, Lizzy; you would have laughed yourself out of it sooner" (II, ii, 141). Elizabeth is admirable, for she has that awareness of herself too as object. If observant Mrs. Gardiner then points out that it would be better if Elizabeth did not *remind* her mother to invite Wickham, she understands immediately: "'As I did the other day,' said Elizabeth, with a conscious smile" (II, iii, 145). If Darcy says, with some truth, that she finds great enjoyment in occasionally professing opinions which are not in fact her own, "Elizabeth laughed heartily at this picture of herself" (II, viii, 174).

But she is herself best able to draw for him the picture of Elizabeth as the witty laugher. Miss Bingley is incapable of punishing what is, in her trivial language, a shocking speech of Darcy's, but for Elizabeth "Nothing so easy, if you have but the inclination." She knows we can all punish one another: "Teaze him—laugh at him.—Intimate as you are, you must know how it is to be done." Witless Miss Bingley does not know that, even her intimacy has not yet taught her; his temper may defy teasing, "And as to laughter, we will not expose ourselves, if you please, by attempting to laugh without a subject. Mr. Darcy may hug himself." That absurdity will not pass with Elizabeth, who knows that all mortals are subjects. "'Mr. Darcy is not to be laughed at!' cried Elizabeth. 'That is an uncommon advantage, and uncommon I hope it will continue, for it would be a great loss to *me* to have many such acquaintance. I dearly love a laugh.'" Darcy is not prepared to hug himself, for he knows the general principle that "The wisest and the best of men, nay, the wisest and the best of their actions, may be rendered ridiculous by a person whose first object in life is a joke." But Elizabeth is as well read in eighteenth-century comic theory as he. Certainly; she replies, there are such people, "but I hope I am not one of *them*. I hope I never ridicule what is wise or good. Follies and nonsense, whims and inconsistencies *do* divert me, I own, and I laugh at them whenever I can.— But these, I suppose, are precisely what you are without." And from there she draws him out until she must turn away to hide the smile (I, xi, 57). Her diversions are impeccable in principle and skillful in execution. As with the family resemblance and distinction in the laughter of Lydia, her sport in exposing follies and nonsense has her father's talent but is essentially different. For one thing, he lacks depth and his range is limited to hitting easy marks. He does well with Mr. Collins, who is deserving of the ironic contempt which we enjoy, but Mr. Collins is such an obvious fool that he walks with happy cooperation into the wit-traps Mr. Bennet sets for him. Mrs. Bennet, who, in her way, appreciates her husband's ability to give what she calls "one of your set downs" (I, iii, 13), is herself the continual victim of his traps, but she, and her younger daughters too, are hardly worth the effort. Worse yet, there is a cynical disappointment in this treatment of his wife, whom he chose for foolish reasons and without accepting responsibility thereafter for the consequences of his choice. The effect is not amusing and creates a family with unhappy defects, "hopeless of remedy." He is "contented with laughing at them," and never exerts himself (II, xiv, 213). He sees into others, this man who is "a mixture of quick parts, sarcastic humour, reserve, and caprice" (I, 1, 5), but not into himself (except for one moment in his life which he knows will pass soon enough, III, vi, 299).

Elizabeth sees with a better eye. The eyes are the first thing that catch Darcy, make her an object of some interest in his eyes who had at first scarcely allowed her to be pretty and looked at her only to criticize: he no sooner made it clear to himself and his friends that she had hardly a good feature in her face "than he began to find that it was rendered uncommonly intelligent by the beautiful expression of her dark eyes." What he is beginning to see of course is a superior mind and his own "critical eye" is forced to a better discrimination (I, vi, 23). It is the first indication the obtuse Miss Bingley receives of his admiration. She thinks, watching him exchange a few words with Elizabeth, that she can read his mind, that "I can guess the subject of your reverie." Darcy knows her better: "I should imagine not." Miss Bingley assumes they think alike, that she is quite of his opinion in contempt of present company, but her conjecture, as he tells her, is totally wrong: "I have been meditating on the very great pleasure which a pair of fine eyes in the face of a pretty woman can bestow." She immediately fixes her eyes on his face and desires to know who is the lady inspiring such reflections and when he replies, with great intrepidity, that it is Miss Elizabeth Bennet she is astonished. "How long has she been such a favourite?—and pray when am I to wish you joy?" Darcy is the one who can read the mind: "That is exactly the question which I expected you to ask." This is a bit unfair to Miss Bingley, because after all it is he who had misled her and has now changed his own mind, but we don't mind anything unfair to Miss Bingley. What is of more interest to us is, first, that she is an easy read, and he is making his read by an easy generalization about what he calls "A lady's imagination," so he doesn't get much credit for that; and, second, that he is still quite ignorant of who Elizabeth is and what will be the effect, how much greater and different the pleasure and how unsuspected the pain, which she will have on him. But for us it is a pleasure to see this sign of a better vision in him (I, vi, 27). Miss Bingley continues to act blindly when Elizabeth turns up at Netherfield after the active cross-country walk—hair untidy, blowsy, petticoat six inches deep in mud as the ladies see her—and Miss Bingley whispers to Darcy that this adventure must have rather affected his admiration of her fine eyes. "Not at all," he replies; "they were brightened by the exercise" (I, viii, 36). Poor Miss Bingley cannot let it alone and is at it again in the next chapter, forcing even more precise detailed observations from Darcy. "As for your Elizabeth's picture, you must not attempt to have it taken, for what painter could do justice to those beautiful eyes?" No, Darcy agrees, "It would not be easy, indeed, to catch their expression, but their colour and shape, and the eyelashes, so remarkably fine, might be copied." It is lovely to see Elizabeth, who of course hasn't heard this, conclude the chapter by laughing at them all and refusing to spoil their picturesque grouping. "Good bye," and she runs gaily off (I, x, 53).

But the fact is those fine eyes, bright and beautifully expressive of an uncommon intelligence, and they are all of that, with their quick sight into the minds of others, are not always properly observant or accurate. They do not see Darcy and his thoughts very well, even, or especially, when she is his object. "Occupied in observing Mr. Bingley's attentions to her sister, Elizabeth was far from suspecting that she was herself becoming an object of some interest in the eyes of his friend." She notices that Darcy is attending to her conversation with others. What does he mean by listening? she asks Charlotte. Charlotte, who is an accurate observer, pretends to no more than she sees: "That is a question which Mr. Darcy only can answer." Elizabeth is more sharp: "… if he does it any more I shall certainly let him know that I see what he is about. He has a very satirical eye," and if she doesn't begin to become impertinent herself she will soon grow afraid of him (I, vi, 23–24).

But she does not see what he is about and his eye is not now satirical, and she does grow mistakenly impertinent in self-defense. Darcy deserves it all, and at the moment he doesn't himself know what he is about, but our concern is for her and her overconfidence in her sight and for the insufficient self-defense to which it leads.

Darcy is not the only young lover who gives her difficulties in understanding, because even Mr. Collins, so much simpler to see through and to escape, in some ways rather an enjoyable object, even he in his strange way does puzzle her. Mr. Collins is a wonderful clown, a gentleman and a stranger who announces himself before he arrives, in the language of his letter, with its formal pretensions to the higher literacy, its ideas of healing the breach and offering the olive branch, its ponderous sentences. He has no noun without its adjective, "valuable rectory ... earnest endeavour ... grateful respect," no word where two will do, "bounty and beneficence ... rites and ceremonies ... promote and establish," and he has the loftier diction, "subsisting," and "demean myself," with the happy ambiguity of that last. As he says, "I flatter myself...." "He must be an oddity, I think," Elizabeth says. "I cannot make him out.—There is something very pompous in his stile ... Can he be a sensible man, sir?" "No, my dear; I think not," says Mr. Bennet, "I have great hopes of finding him quite the reverse. There is a mixture of servility and self-importance in his letter, which promises well. I am impatient to see him." This polite young man's appearance fulfills the promise of his language, heavy looking, air grave and stately, manners very formal (I, xiii, 62–64). Mr. Bennet cultivates him and brings him out. When he solemnly discloses his feelings for Elizabeth she is near laughing, to be sure, but when the critical moment comes—"And now nothing remains for me but to assure you in the most animated language of the violence of my affection"—she has a problem, because he is so fixed in his form that she cannot make him understand her language. He is so confident of his understanding of the minds and motions of ladies that, "with a formal wave of the hand," he dismisses her own words of declination: "it is usual with young ladies to reject the address of the man whom they secretly mean to accept, when he first applies for their favour ..." "Upon my word, Sir," she says, she is perfectly serious in her refusal. She considers the matter finally settled and, rising as she speaks, she wants to quit the room; but no, her word cannot mean, he will speak to her again, not accuse her of cruelty at present, "because I know it to be the established custom of your sex to reject a man on the first application ..." "Really, Mr. Collins ... you puzzle me exceedingly ... I know not how to express my refusal in such a way as may convince you of its being one." But, once more, in words we have heard before in his letter (and once more earlier in the present dialogue), "You must give me leave to flatter myself, my dear cousin, that your refusal of my addresses is merely words of course." He must conclude that she wishes to increase his love by suspense, "according to the usual practice of elegant females." What can she say? "Can I speak plainer?" she asks, "... as a rational creature speaking the truth from her heart." "You are uniformly charming!" cries he. And to such perseverance in willful self-deception she can only immediately and in silence withdraw (I, xix, 106–09). Mr. Collins is the fool who sees himself as the master of language and reading of minds and as the irresistible lover. And he does play the lover with success. If he is told that his first possible choice, Jane, is already spoken for, he can turn to Elizabeth, and when he finds that she really is unwilling, he could turn readily to the third sister, who might have been prevailed on to accept him. Mary had appreciated, judiciously, the composition of his letter (I, xiii, 64), the solidity of his reflections often struck her, and though he was by no means so clever as herself she thought he could improve himself by such an example as hers (I, xxii, 124). But clever Mr. Collins surprises them all by his proposal to Charlotte when even Charlotte had little dared to hope that so much love and eloquence awaited her so quickly. "In as short a time as Mr. Collins's long speeches would allow" she accepted him, to the satisfaction of both (121–22). He runs his course in three days, not quite as fast as Puck in one night switches lovers around, but a creditable performance for a mortal playing both roles. (And really in not much more time than the whole of *A Midsummer Night's Dream*).

For Mr. Collins, that unchangeable clown, time can have no meaning—and he has done remarkably well for himself. He appears very fortunate in his choice of a wife, Darcy says. Yes indeed, Elizabeth can confirm; "his friends may well rejoice in his having met with one of the very few sensible women who would have accepted him, or have made him happy if they had" (II, ix, 178). Fortunate Mr. Collins has found a sensible woman for whom time has no meaning; to the bright-eyed Elizabeth's astonishment it is her intimate friend, a character she discovers she has never understood. Charlotte had never deceived her. Charlotte had been quite clear in advice about Jane's slowness with Bingley: "if she were married to him tomorrow, I should think she had as good a chance of happiness, as if she were to be studying his character for a twelve-month." Charlotte needs no time, no affection, no movement in feeling or knowledge; knowing does not advance felicity in the least and "it is better to know as little as possible of the defects of the person with whom you are to pass your life." Elizabeth, we know already, delights in anything ridiculous: "You make me laugh, Charlotte; but it is not sound. You know it is not sound, and that you would never act in this way yourself" (I, vi, 23). Charlotte knows quite well how she would act and does not lose the opportunity of "fixing" her man (21). "You are uniformly charming," Mr. Collins had declared to Elizabeth, and we can assume that he used the same uniformity with Charlotte, but Charlotte's own eye cannot be and has no need to be charmed. If Mr. Collins entreats her to name the day that is to make him the happiest of men, the lady feels no need to trifle with his happiness. "The stupidity with which he was favoured by nature, must guard his courtship from any charm that could make a woman wish for its continuance; and Miss Lucas, who accepted him solely from the pure and disinterested desire of an establishment, cared not how soon that establishment were gained" (I, xxii, 122). It is a long time before Elizabeth becomes at all reconciled to the idea of so unsuitable a match; she had always felt Charlotte's opinion of matrimony was not exactly like her own, "but she could not have supposed it possible that when called into action, she would have sacrificed every better feeling to worldly advantage." It is a most humiliating picture. And to this is added the distressing conviction that it is impossible for her friend to be tolerably happy in that lot she had chosen (125).

When she visits Mr. and Mrs. Collins at Hunsford she "looked with wonder" at her friend who can have so cheerful an air with such a companion. Charlotte knows how to manage that air, by wisely not hearing or seeing her husband. It costs only a faint blush, because it is certainly "not unseldom" when such wisdom is not possible, and Elizabeth, seeing her composure in bearing with her husband, has "to acknowledge that it was all done very well" (II, v, 156–57). By the time the visit ends Elizabeth sees Charlotte more clearly, in that friend's acceptance of a permanent diminishment of life. "Poor Charlotte!—it was melancholy to leave her to such society!—But she had chosen it with her eyes open." Charlotte does not seem to ask for compassion. She keeps busy: her home and housekeeping, parish and poultry and all their dependent concerns "had not yet lost their charms" (II, xv, 216). Charlotte is no blind lover, makes her choice with her eyes open, takes the consequences and does as well as can be done with them. The charm that needs no time was not in love but in the home, the parish and the poultry; and yet they too, it seems, like all charms, may be not fixed but subject to time.

Elizabeth is never liable to the charm that needs no time as it appears in the grave and stately air of clownish Mr. Collins, but there is another stranger who has an air and to whom she is blind. It takes little or no time, she later realizes, "a first interview ... and even before two words have been exchanged" (III, iv, 279). Wickham charms her. Her first sight of him comes when she is walking in Meryton with her sisters, so that her vision is merged for that moment with Kitty's and Lydia's. "All were struck with the stranger's air, all wondered who he could be ..." Kitty and Lydia, determined to find out, lead the way across the street and it is found that Mr. Wickham has accepted a commission in the corps: "This was exactly as it should be; for the young man wanted only regimentals to make him completely charming." The thought and the words sound not like Elizabeth's but her silly sisters', but this time she is with them. His gentlemanlike appearance, the fine countenance, good figure and very pleasing address, is followed by a happy readiness of conversation—a readiness at the same time perfectly correct— "and the whole party" are still talking together very agreeably when Darcy comes by (I, xv, 72). At that point the more perceptive Elizabeth does notice a difference, but it will be a while before she can understand what that means. At their next meeting when Wickham talks "she is very willing to hear him," and her curiosity is unexpectedly relieved by the conversation of this man who is more than ready to tell her about Darcy. She has a quick ear for the pompous style of Mr. Collins, but what does she hear in the words of Wickham?

> His father, Miss Bennet, the late Mr. Darcy, was one of the best men that ever breathed, and the truest friend I ever had; and I can never be in company with this Mr. Darcy without being grieved to the soul by a thousand tender recollections.

When a girl like Elizabeth Bennet hears that sort of language she should be trying to hide a smile, be near laughing. But this agreeable handsome man is saying what she wants to hear. She honors his feelings, "thought him handsomer than ever as he expressed them." "She could have added," this observant studier of character, "'A young man too, like *you*, whose very countenance may vouch for your being amiable.'" He speaks well, does all gracefully (I, xvi, 78, 80–81). The man was completely charming upon his entry into her life and the next time she thinks of that is at the moment when she reads the letter with the mortifying truth about him and remembers: "She could see him instantly before her, in every charm of air and address," but could remember no substantial good; she is now struck with the impropriety of what he communicated to a stranger "and wondered it had escaped her before" (II, xiii, 206–07). The last time she hears of his charm is in Lydia's language—"and what do you think of my husband? Is not he a charming man? I am sure my sisters must all envy me" (III, ix, 317), which completes the circle of the first meeting with him. As for Wickham and his several roles, he begins by playing the charming deceiver, proves to be unsuccessful as lover, and ends by marrying a fool in, to that degree, an appropriate match.

That discerning eye which gives Elizabeth such amusing power to see through character has difficulties with strangers. She may laugh at her dear Jane who is at first so uncertain in deciding the truth about Wickham and Darcy; but Jane, for her own weak reasons, does say rightly that they can't conjecture the causes or circumstances, and she will not give in: "Laugh as much as you chuse, but you will not laugh me out of my opinion." Bright Elizabeth has no difficulty seeing the truth, can't believe that Wickham should invent such a history—names, facts, everything mentioned without ceremony—her hard evidence. "Besides, there was truth in his looks." To simple Jane it is not so simple. "It is difficult indeed—it is distressing—One does not know what to think." "I beg your pardon;—one knows exactly what to think" (I, xvii, 85–86). More difficult and distressing, however, is Charlotte, her intimate friend who turns out to be strange. "The strangeness of Mr. Collins's making two offers of marriage within three days, was nothing in comparison of his being now accepted" (I, xxii, 125). "It is unaccountable! in every view it is unaccountable!" If Jane, in her ineffective way, tries to defend Charlotte, Elizabeth will have none of it. "You shall not defend her, though it is Charlotte Lucas. You shall not, for the sake of one individual, change the meaning of principle and integrity, nor endeavour to persuade yourself or me, that selfishness is prudence, and insensibility of danger, security for happiness" (II, i, 135–36). That is clear enough, but when Wickham's attentions are over and he becomes the admirer of someone else—the sudden acquisition of ten thousand pounds is "the most remarkable charm" of this young lady-Elizabeth, "less clear-sighted perhaps in his case than in Charlotte's," does not quarrel with him for his wish of independence. "Nothing, on the contrary, could be more natural ..." (II, iii, 149–50).

That stranger who gives most trouble is Darcy, another confidently superior spirit whose eye has its own problems in seeing what lies beyond his assured vision. His first remark, when he looks at her, catches her eye, withdraws his own, and speaks coldly of her, is reason enough for her to remain with no very cordial feelings towards him (I, iii, 11–12). At the point when she can't help observing how frequently his eyes are fixed on her she hardly knows how to suppose she can be an object of admiration to so great a man, but that he should look at her because he dislikes her is "still more strange." What she cannot see is that her eye has now caught his "and Darcy had never been so bewitched by any woman as he was by her." If she does not understand him it is in part because he does not understand his own mind;

he really believes that but for the inferiority of her family connections he should be in some danger (I, x, 51–52). Her dislike makes her the ready dupe of Wickham's invented history: "'How strange!' cried Elizabeth. 'How abominable!'" (I, xvi, 81). Wickham's tale of injustice makes her wonder that the very pride of Darcy has not made him just, if from no better motive than that he would be too proud to be dishonest—a sharp insight of Elizabeth at her best, now lost in strangeness. Neither she nor Darcy performs very well in this area. "I should like to know how he behaves among strangers," Colonel Fitzwilliam says to her, and Elizabeth can tell him how dreadful Darcy is in his unwillingness to dance with, or even seek an introduction to, young ladies outside his own party. Darcy is by now prepared to admit he might be more forthcoming, "but I am ill qualified to recommend myself to strangers." Shall we ask him, she says to Colonel Fitzwilliam, why an intelligent and experienced man is ill qualified to recommend himself to strangers? Because he will not give himself the trouble, Fitzwilliam answers for him. Darcy's answer is that he has not the talent some possess, of conversing easily with those he has never seen before. Elizabeth, at the pianoforte, says she cannot perform as well as many women she has seen, but she has always supposed it to be her own fault, because she would not take the trouble of practicing. Darcy turns that to a compliment: "We neither of us perform to strangers" (II, viii, 174–76). They do have that in common; and what they both must find, and each will show the other, is that it takes trouble and practice to learn the art.

What is strange, as we have seen before and will see in later chapters, is in simplest terms what is outside the limits of one's ability to understand, for lack of experience or of vision. But in different tales those limits and the response to them have different meanings, and in this story they present a moral test: to stop with that deficiency of comprehension, not move to extend one's ability, is the mark of a mind either uncommonly weak or uncommonly clever. Mrs. Bennet, who sees nothing that is not beyond her, is the best example of the one and Elizabeth, who sees everything clearly, of the other. The family resemblance here is that, in their unlike ways, they both sit down with their grievances, very discontented with the ways in which other people have insisted on acting beyond their powers of comprehension, acting badly of course. Elizabeth has got to move from this and with the right moves, as the response to the perception of the strange will be a reduction or an increase of life.

She does not like Darcy's unwillingness to move in the dance, and rightly so, but she does not do very well at that liveliness herself. If he refuses her as partner she then refuses him, as she had said she would, and both of them deserve that moment. But when, at the Netherfield ball, he takes her so much by surprise in his next application for her hand, "without knowing what she did, she accepted him." She is left to fret over her own want of presence of mind with this man she says she is determined to hate. When she takes her place in the set, "They stood for some time without speaking a word." Her first dances of the evening had brought distress, with awkward and solemn Mr. Collins who is "often moving wrong without being aware of it"; but now neither she nor Mr. Darcy is capable of making the right move. The dance, as we have seen in *A Midsummer Night's Dream*, is not simply the celebration at the end when the lovers in the action fall into the right places, but it is part of the process by which they change positions in coming to find the right partners for themselves. In the present tale, where young lovers cannot easily find a way of running off to the wood, the dance is properly the best opportunity they have for private conversation, for coming to understand one another. These two must learn the language in which to talk to one another and, as the most articulate speakers and speakers of the best language in their society, at this point neither is good at this dance. Neither will break the silence, till Elizabeth, in an unpromising countermove, fancies that it would be the greater punishment to her partner to oblige him to talk. She puts him through a mock-rehearsal of the trite commonplaces of dance-conversation, which again he deserves. "Do you talk by rule then, while you are dancing?" he asks. "Sometimes. One must speak a little, you know," though for some, conversation ought to be arranged that they may have the trouble of saying as little as possible. The pace is picking up, moving from talk by rule to talk of persons present. Is she talking of her own feelings, he asks, or what she imagines to be his? Both, says she, making things more interesting by bringing them together: she has always seen a great similarity in the turn of their minds, that they are each unsocial, taciturn, unwilling to speak unless they expect to say something that will amaze the whole room. It is a deft cut, under cover of a proffered identity. He understands that it is not meant for herself (part of the irony is that she's rather closer to the whole truth than she intends); and he won't accept it for himself either, though "You think it a faithful portrait undoubtedly." "I must not decide on my own performance."

No, she should not, because this small success is going to tempt her to more dangerous performance. After another silence Darcy refers to their recent meeting in Meryton and, "unable to resist the temptation," she takes that as her opening to make him talk about Wickham. She sees that the hit goes home, "but he said not a word, and Elizabeth, though blaming herself for her own weakness, could not go on" (she is not seeing her right weakness). She has stopped the conversation and when at length he speaks of Wickham it is in constraint. She pushes the emphasis, to how Wickham is likely to suffer all his life from Darcy's treatment. "Darcy made no answer ..." They are given a short interlude, and a proper punishment, by an interruption from the foolishly well-spoken Sir William Lucas—who compliments Darcy on his very superior dancing, not often seen, except in the first circles, and adds, in a courteous after-thought, that his fair partner does not disgrace him. Sir William, with equal adroitness, offers them congratulations on what he assumes is their common pleasure in the forthcoming marriage of Jane and Bingley; and that does strike Darcy forcibly. But he will not interrupt, Sir William says, for he will not be thanked for detaining Darcy from "the bewitching converse" of that young lady, whose "bright eyes" are also upbraiding him. Such talk of bewitching converse and bright eyes could not be less to the moment. The interruption has made him forget what they were talking of, Darcy says, less than candidly. "I do not think we were speaking at all," Elizabeth replies; "Sir William could not have interrupted any two people in the room who had less to say for themselves ... and what we are to talk of next I cannot imagine." Books? he tries again. No, she's sure they have nothing in common there. Besides, she can't talk of books in a ballroom; "my head is always full of something else." It certainly is, and she is now talking "without knowing what she said, for her thoughts had wandered from the subject," as then appears by her "suddenly exclaiming." Her head is stuffed full with Wickham, which does not improve her ability to see, and her exclamation is directed at Darcy's blindness. You "never allow yourself to be blinded by prejudice?" "I hope not." She continues the cross-examination, to make out his character, but she does not get on at all, she says, is puzzled exceedingly— which should give her pause if she means it, and give them both more time, but it was only a few pages ago that she had already known exactly what to think. He asks her not to sketch his character at present, as he has reason to fear that "the performance would reflect no credit on either," and it would not, because neither is performing creditably at present (I, xviii, 9–94). They will have to converse more of performance.

They will have to make better use of their time, the time needed to move with more credit in this dance. There is no magic here which will produce instantaneous effects, no other realm in which time and space will be suspended, for here they are marked with a careful precision. The chronology of this tale was worked out by its author and can be followed with an almanac (Chapman's Appendix, 400–07), because time is a measure of change, month by month and day by day, and Elizabeth Bennet, not yet one-

and-twenty, must be changing in this daily world if she is to become a woman, capable of love and worthy of being loved, which here means capable of understanding that world and herself. She is not a clown and there is no chance that she will not change, no choice of standing still. She has the lively mind and the eyes that see and only someone so bright could go so far astray, could use that power so mistakenly; this wit must move either for the better or the worse, and if she does not move in the right direction she will corrupt, will be amusing and destructive, her father's daughter. She has come to a stopping point, when all those other people whom she has understood so well have unexpectedly refused to act as they should and disappointed her so: when Charlotte has accepted Mr. Collins; when Bingley has gone from Jane; when "The more I see of the world, the more am I dissatisfied with it" (II, i, 135). And now Wickham too has defected, to a young lady whose "most remarkable charm" was the sudden acquisition of ten thousand pounds. Of course she does know that she wasn't distractedly in love with Wickham because she doesn't feel the accepted symptoms of the deserted romantic heroine, and Kitty and Lydia take his loss more to heart than she does: "They are young in the ways of the world, and not yet open to the mortifying conviction that handsome young men must have something to live on, as well as the plain" (II, iii, 149–50). That is the witty Elizabeth we like to hear, turning the wit on herself as she has before, but there's now also something of the self-protective role of the worldly-wise disillusioned lady, which doesn't become her. She hasn't known yet what it is to love, as she sees, but then she doesn't know yet the ways of the world either, or what it is to be mortified.

She seems to be standing still, as the almanac moves on and for the first time we hear almost nothing of the days because Elizabeth is going nowhere. The next sentence and chapter begins: "With no greater events than these in the Longbourn family, and otherwise diversified by little beyond the walks to Meryton, sometimes dirty and sometimes cold, did January and February pass away." Elizabeth is looking forward to March, when she will visit Charlotte and Mr. Collins, for though she had not at first thought seriously of going there it now seems to be a greater pleasure; there will be a novelty in it, and with Jane away in London, and home as it is, "a little change was not unwelcome for its own sake" (II, iv, 151). The first stage to Hunsford is a journey of only twenty-four miles, to see Jane and the Gardiners in London, and there, as we see under the questioning of the sensible Mrs. Gardiner, the previous little note of a disillusion is sounding more like a cynicism. Mrs. Gardiner wants to hear about Wickham and his new affair, where Wickham seems to have been indelicate and the lady deficient in sense or feeling. Elizabeth keeps turning away from Mrs. Gardiner's careful distinctions, trying to blur the moral lines between money and affection-which had been so certain when she looked at Charlotte's pursuit of Mr. Collins's establishment, but are of little meaning now that she looks at Wickham's pursuit of the willing girl with ten thousand pounds. Well, have it as you choose, she says in unfair exasperation with her persistent aunt, "*He* shall be mercenary, and *she* shall be foolish." Elizabeth has had enough of men. "I am sick of them all. Thank Heaven! I am going tomorrow where I shall find a man who has not one agreeable quality, who has neither manner nor sense to recommend him. Stupid men are the only ones worth knowing, after all." Mrs. Gardiner loves her niece and will not let go. "Take care, Lizzy; that speech savours strongly of disappointment" (153–54). It does and the word is a strong one, as Elizabeth understands, the balked desire which can become spleen, a sour moroseness. Lizzy is not standing still but slipping back. She will need more than a short journey and it will have to be a journey to a better end.

She has the unexpected happiness of an invitation to join her aunt and uncle on a tour of pleasure in the summer: "We have not quite determined how far it shall carry us," says Mrs. Gardiner, "but perhaps to the Lakes." We will be interested in finding how far north this will carry Elizabeth and her need to be carried is loud in her response. "My dear, dear aunt," she rapturously cries, "what delight! what felicity! You give me fresh life and vigour. Adieu to disappointment and spleen. What are men to rocks and mountains?" So Elizabeth, unable to solve her problems at home, sees happiness in the opportunity to run off to another place, where she can leave behind all those frustrating people and find felicity, be given new life, not with men, not even Mr. Collins, but with rocks and mountains. "Oh! what hours of transport we shall spend!" We do hope not and hope that she will make better use of her hours on the journey; and we can have faith in Elizabeth from what we have seen of her and from her present insistence on what she wants it to be when she returns from the journey. "And when we *do* return, it shall not be like other travellers, without being able to give one accurate idea of any thing. We *will* know where we have gone—we *will* recollect what we have seen." It shall not be jumbled together in their imaginations and they will agree when they describe what they have seen (II, iv, 154). For Elizabeth this will not be a dream and she wants to get it all clear and get it all together, unlike other travelers. But like other runaways who want to escape into that better place she will find her journey more strange than anything she could have imagined.

At this moment of excitement she is only at the first stop in her first journey, and she is still expecting to see at the next stage a stupid man, the only kind worth knowing. Off she goes and "Every object in the next day's journey was new and interesting to Elizabeth," her spirits in a state for enjoyment and "the prospect of her northern tour ... a constant source of delight" (II, v, 155). Her time at Hunsford is both instructive and amusing as she sees and understands better the life of Charlotte at the Parsonage and is introduced to Lady Catherine and the honors of Rosings. But she also sees, and it was not an expected part of her journey, much more of Mr. Darcy. In going from Hertfordshire to Kent she is more on his ground, at the home of his aunt, with his cousin Colonel Fitzwilliam, with more and better opportunities to talk and to learn about him. Charlotte, who has a better eye for this sort of thing, watches Darcy as he looks at Elizabeth a great deal, and once or twice she suggests to Elizabeth the possibility of his being partial to her; "but Elizabeth always laughed at the idea" (II, ix, 181). She dearly loves a laugh, as she had told him, but now with his love he will astonish her beyond expression (II, xi), and from this point in her story Elizabeth's moments of laughter will be not amusing but painful; there will be more tears, and those begin by the end of this chapter. Her response to his declaration is resentment and anger, which he well deserves because he too still has a long way to go. His response to her rejection is his own anger and astonishment.

Elizabeth has been quick to read the blindness in others, in the Jane she loves for Jane's too generous feelings, in the Darcy she thinks so ill of for his ungenerous feelings (pp. 204, 216, above), and when she receives Darcy's letter she will have her moment to define her own blindness. "Her feelings as she read were scarcely to be defined." She read in a way "which hardly left her power of comprehension" to a point "when she read with somewhat clearer attention," and her feelings become "yet more acutely painful and more difficult of definition" and the oppression of emotion makes her put the thing away hastily, protesting that "she would never look in it again." She walks on, but it will not do and "in half a minute" the letter is unfolded again "and collecting herself as well as she could, she again began the mortifying perusal ... and commanded herself so far as to examine the meaning of every sentence." It takes time and she is now down to the critical half-minutes. She does not want to see and (like Mr. Collins) "for a few moments, she flattered herself" that her wishes did not err; but she reads and re-reads line by line and every line proves more clearly what she has not been able to see before (II, xiii, 204–05).

> She grew absolutely ashamed of herself—Of neither Darcy nor Wickham could she think, without feeling that she had been

blind, partial, prejudiced, absurd.... "I, who have prided myself on
my discernment! ... How humiliating is this discovery!—Yet, how
just a humiliation!—Had I been in love, I could not have been
more wretchedly blind.... Till this moment, I never knew myself."
(208)

It is the familiar moment when the young lover moves from blindness to self-
knowledge (and for her the time is still not fulfilled). As we have seen it
before it requires the administration of an eye-opening agency, Dian's bud in
the hand of Puck or the Life Force in Nature. Jane Austen's word for that is
"mortification," the just humiliation Elizabeth feels and repeats in this
speech, and, as she reads on, "the terms of such mortifying yet merited
reproach" which bring their sense of severe shame. But in her day-to-day
world there is no designated superior power to drop the juice into the eye;
Elizabeth must do it for herself, a difficult and a painful task. Happily, she has
one other to help her, the man who writes the letter she must learn to read,
as indeed she has been teaching him, both of them unknowingly. Both of
them have been proud powers of superior discernment into the minds of, and
the proper matches for, the mortals they see, but there will be none to help
open their eyes except as they may be able to do it for each other. It is a
process of mutual mortification.

We have seen mortification before and we will see it again, in both its
trivial and its painful forms. The Devil of *Man and Superman* is mortified
when Don Juan speaks a truth (p.45, ch. 2) but in the life of the Devil it is
only a brief embarrassment, without effect because the Devil is a clown
incapable of profiting from the truth about himself. To Hermia the law of
Athens brings a literal threat of mortification if she does not depart from her
love and change to another; but it is a foolish law, with the worse alternative
that she may wither on the virgin thorn, and we are happy to see her simply
escape from death and emerge with a better life and love. The more
interesting mortification which must be faced by the lovers of *Pride and
Prejudice* can be understood profitably only by characters who are capable of
feeling the justice of a wound to their pride and self-esteem. It is not easy and
it is part of a movement that takes time. It is here a necessary condition for
the satisfactory coming together of the lovers, forcing a self-recognition that
requires giving up a part of the character for which each has felt self-esteem
and taking on a changed character, the end of the old and blinded self and
the beginning of the renewed and more liberal life. The inception, the
turning-point, and the resolution of the changing relations of Elizabeth and
Darcy are marked by mortifications: the first rousing effect each has on the

other; the proposal and letter; and the elopement of Lydia, the event that brings the conclusive proofs of affection. The series begins at their first encounter as Darcy sees her and withdraws his eye because she is not handsome enough to tempt him to the dance; Elizabeth could easily have forgiven *his* pride, she says, "if he had not mortified *mine*" (I, v, 20). A few pages on she becomes an object of some interest in his eyes when he finds the intelligence and beauty in hers: "To this discovery succeeded some others equally mortifying," as he is now forced to acknowledge that his critical eye has been mistaken and is now caught by her form and her manner (I, vi, 23). But neither has yet been able to benefit from this; the effect has not been strong enough, in good part because neither is in a moral position to make the other feel the effect. The occasions multiply upon Elizabeth, especially in that ball at Netherfield, in "the dances of mortification" she has, with badly timed liveliness, prepared for herself with Mr. Collins (I, xviii, 90), in the several ways in which the members of her family make her blush with shame and vexation, as though they had made an agreement to expose themselves as much as they could; and, more importantly, in the confident ways in which she has made her own unknowing contributions to this carnival of fools by her style of dancing with Mr. Darcy. All this does not come home to her until, at the eye-opening moment she reads Darcy's letter and the memory it brings of the "mortifying" family conduct at the Netherfield ball (II, xiii, 209). The proposal and letter bring, as at the start of their course, a moment of reciprocal wounded pride, but now to better effect. She has been quite right to reject him; he would not be a good husband. He has not, even in proposing, she tells him, behaved in a "gentleman-like manner" and he is startled to be told that truth, and more than startled. "You could not have made me the offer of your hand in any possible way that would have tempted me to accept it": this he must hear from the woman whose pride he mortified by saying she was not handsome enough to tempt *him*. He is astonished and he looks at her with "mingled incredulity and mortification" (I, xi, 192–93). Her accusations of his treatment of Wickham are ill founded, but, as he later says, his behavior to her merited the severest reproach. It takes time to work, as the incredulity goes but not the mortification. The recollection of what he said, his conduct, his manner, his expression, is for many months inexpressibly painful to him. Her reproof, that he had not behaved in a gentleman-like manner—the words remain with him—had been a torture, and it was some time before he was reasonable enough to allow their justice. Realizing the pride and selfishness of a lifetime is a hard lesson and he owes much to her who taught him. "By you, I was properly humbled" (III, xvi, 367–69).

His letter produces more immediately a change in her life. That fresh life and vigor she had desired so ardently from her journey will follow his effect. One of the first things she hears on her return home is Lydia's happy news that the wretched Wickham is not going to marry the young lady with the ten thousand pounds; evidently the lady has been sent safely away by worried relatives, but Lydia is certain he never cared three straws about her: "Who *could* about such a nasty little freckled thing?" "Elizabeth was shocked to think that, however incapable of such coarseness of *expression* herself, the coarseness of the *sentiment* was little other than her own breast had formerly harboured and fancied liberal!" (II, xvi, 220). It is a new moment for her, that recognition of sisterly similarity under the apparent superiority of language. That wit which dearly loved a laugh, amused at Mr. Darcy's uncommon advantage of immunity, looks different to her now. She had meant to be uncommonly clever in taking such a decided dislike to him, without any reason, she tells Jane, for it is such a spur to one's genius, "such an opening for wit ..." One may abuse a man without saying anything just, "but one cannot always be laughing at a man without now and then stumbling upon something witty" (II, xvii, 225–26). We will be seeing the effects of mortification, of different kinds, in some of the succeeding works; and we will see it again in the course of Elizabeth's life, because she has not yet come to the end of her journey. She has yet to reach Pemberley, where, in one reward of improvement she can eventually leave the mortifying society of her family (III, xviii, 384).

On her second journey, with its promised rapture of the hours of transport in the rocks and mountains of a north without men, she does not get quite as far as she had hoped, that longed-for place. It is a stranger journey than she had expected and another vision. When she sees Darcy's home ground it is she who is now the stranger. "Every disposition of the ground was good" and the home itself she sees, with admiration of his taste, as she compares it with the Rosings where she saw him in her first journey, has less of splendor, and more real elegance. "'And of this place,' thought she, 'I might have been mistress! With these rooms I might now have been familiarly acquainted! Instead of viewing them as a stranger ...'" She sees family portraits, "but they could have little to fix the attention of a stranger" and she walks on in quest of the only face whose features are known to her until at last it arrested her: "she beheld a striking resemblance of Mr. Darcy, with such a smile over the face, as she remembered to have sometimes seen, when he looked at her. She stood several minutes before the picture in earnest contemplation ..." Now, with a gentler sensation towards the original than she had ever felt, she walks out, and—this is an earned sight—

"suddenly" she sees the original. "… so abrupt was his appearance that it was impossible to avoid his sight. Their eyes instantly met …" It is for him too a startling moment and each has cause for the deepest blush. But she is overpowered again by shame and vexation, because it may seem as if she has purposely thrown herself in his way again. "How strange must it appear to him! In what a disgraceful light might it not strike so vain a man!" (III, i, 246, 250–52). He is stranger than she yet knows.

She is astonished at such a change as she sees in him, that he not merely once loved her but that he loves her still well enough to forgive all her manner and the unjust accusations in her rejection (III, ii, 265–66). But this is not enough and the promising indications that the course of true love is about to reach its desired end are suddenly stopped, by Lydia's elopement. Elizabeth and Darcy have come far in their mutual mortifications but they have further to go, to bear the effects of their past, the old self, and respond with the liberal conquest of the new. To Elizabeth the elopement is "humiliation" and misery. It justifies Darcy in the two chief offenses she had laid to his charge—his offenses against Wickham and against her family— and it brings those two things together in such a way as to sink Elizabeth's power over him. She believes that he has now made a self-conquest, is no longer subject to his feelings for her, and the belief is exactly calculated to make her understand her own wishes, that she could have loved him (III, iv, 278). After Lydia's marriage is assured, Elizabeth is heartily sorry that she had not concealed from him her initial fears for Lydia: there was no one whose knowledge of her sister's frailty could have "mortified her so much" (III, viii, 311). What she does not know is that Darcy has been stronger, in a more difficult self-conquest, than she could have known. Lydia, who is incapable of understanding the meaning of her affair with Wickham, can't understand why Elizabeth doesn't share her delight and isn't curious to hear all the details of the marriage. "La! you are so strange!" But it is stranger than that. Irrepressible Lydia must tell her how it went off and, in her way, reveals to the utterly amazed Elizabeth that Mr. Darcy was at the wedding. It was exactly a scene, and exactly among people, where, as Elizabeth sees it, he had apparently least to do or temptation to go: how could a man unconnected with any of her family, comparatively speaking "a stranger to our family," be amongst them at such a time? (III, ix, 318–20). But he has seen the connection (III, x, 321–22), takes responsibility for Wickham's act. Elizabeth had thought such an exertion of goodness "too great to be probable," and painful to her in the obligation, but it is proved "beyond … greatest extent to be true!" He has "taken on himself all the trouble and mortification" of searching out and supplicating and bribing those he had most reason to

abominate, despise, avoid (326). When she finally has the opportunity she
thanks him for the compassion that enabled him to "bear so many
mortifications" (III, xvi, 366) and he has done it in his affection. They have
both learned how to perform to strangers.

It has not been an easy course for her. When Mr. Bennet receives the
last of his diverting letters from Mr. Collins, this one with the idle report,
and the warning, that Elizabeth may marry Darcy, he shares the surprise with
his daughter. Mr. Darcy, who never looks at any woman but to see a blemish,
he says, "and who probably never looked at you in his life! It is admirable!"
Elizabeth tries to join in her father's pleasantry, "but could only force one
most reluctant smile. Never had his wit been directed in a manner so little
agreeable to her." He won't let go of the sport. "Are you not diverted?" "Oh!
yes, Pray read on." He, as always, lives "but to make sport for our
neighbours, and laugh at them in our turn," and knows his favorite daughter
ought share his amusement. "'Oh!' cried Elizabeth, 'I am excessively
diverted. But it is so strange!'" "Yes—*that* is what makes it amusing." If it is
not that for her it is because at that point she is not certain that she really
understands the relations of strange and true. "It was necessary to laugh,
when she would rather have cried. Her father had most cruelly mortified
her," for what he has said of Darcy's indifference may be true (III, xv,
363–64).

It is only after that last deserved stroke that Elizabeth is allowed her
return to laughter. The Mr. Darcy who was not to be laughed at is to be
educated, by a wife who now understands better how to laugh. As they
compare notes at the end he explains how he arranged Bingley's love, first
interfering in the match and then assuring happiness. "Elizabeth could not
help smiling at his easy manner of directing his friend." He certainly has
been the superior director of the loves of foolish mortals who, in that
tradition, has made a small mistake and now repairs it easily. Did he speak
from his own observation, Elizabeth asks, or merely from her information
about Jane? (sounding a bit like Mr. Bennet drawing out Mr. Collins). "I had
narrowly observed her," he reports. And that assurance, Elizabeth supposes,
carried immediate conviction to Bingley? Elizabeth sees how well Darcy still
plays that role of instant power and she longs to observe that Mr. Bingley had
been a most delightful friend, so easily guided, but she checks herself. "She
remembered that he had yet to learn to be laught at, and it was rather too
early to begin" (III, xvi, 371). Darcy, it would seem, in his aristocratic line,
has been taught, like Lord Chesterfield's son perhaps, that the vulgar laugh,
whereas well-bred people smile but seldom or never laugh; but we can be
confident he will have a better tutor now, one who has herself earned the

right. "I am happier even than Jane," Elizabeth confides to Mrs. Gardiner; "she only smiles, I laugh" (III, xviii, 383).

NOTE

The text for *Pride and Prejudice* is Vol. II of *The Novels of Jane Austen*, ed. R. W. Chapman, 3rd ed. (Oxford 1932), and for *Emma* Vol. IV of the same edition (1933). References are to volume, chapter and page numbers; where successive quotations in the same paragraph are from the same chapter the volume and chapter numbers are not repeated. (In reprints which number the chapters continuously Vol. II of *Pride and Prejudice* is chaps. 24–42, Vol. III is 43–61; Vol. II of *Emma* is chaps. 19–36, Vol. III is 37–55.) The chapter has drawn much upon my own book, listed below, the parts on *Emma* and *Pride and Prejudice*.

WORKS CITED

Babb, Howard S., *Jane Austen's Novels: The Fabric of Dialogue* (Columbus, 1962).

Brower, Reuben Arthur, *The Fields of Light: An Experiment in Critical Reading* (New York, 1951).

Butler, Marilyn, *Jane Austen and the War of Ideas* (Oxford, 1975).

Chandler, Alice, "'A Pair of Fine Eyes': Jane Austen's Treatment of Sex," *Studies in the Novel*, VII (1975), 88–103.

Duckworth, Alistair M., *The Improvement of the Estate: A Study of Jane Austen's Novels* (Baltimore, 1971).

Dussinger, John A., *In the Pride of the Moment: Encounters in Jane Austen's World* (Columbus, 1990).

Fergus, Jan, *Jane Austen and the Didactic Novel* (Totowa, N.J., 1983).

Hardy, Barbara, *A Reading of Jane Austen* (London, 1975).

Harris, Jocelyn, *Jane Austen's Art of Memory* (Cambridge, 1989).

Krieger, Murray, *The Classic Vision* (Baltimore, 1971).

Lascelles, Mary, *Jane Austen and Her Art* (Oxford, 1939).

Mansell, Darrel, *The Novels of Jane Austen: An Interpretation* (London, 1973).

Moler, Kenneth L., *Pride and Prejudice: A Study in Artistic Economy* (Boston, 1989).

Monaghan, David, *Jane Austen: Structure and Social Vision* (London, 1980).

Morgan, Susan, *In the Meantime: Character and Perception in Jane Austen's Fiction* (Chicago, 1980).

Mudrick, Marvin, *Jane Austen: Irony as Defense and Discovery* (Princeton, 1952).

Page, Norman, *The Language of Jane Austen* (Oxford, 1972).

Polhemus, Robert M., "Jane Austen's Comedy," in *The Jane Austen Companion*, ed. J. David Grey, A. Wilton Litz and Brian Southam (New York, 1986).

Sacks, Sheldon, "Golden Birds and Dying Generations," *Comparative Literature Studies*, VI (1969), 274–91.

Spacks, Patricia Meyer, "Austen's Laughter," *Women's Studies*, XV (1988), 71–85.

Tanner, Tony, *Jane Austen* (Cambridge, Mass., 1986).

Tave, Stuart M., *Some Words of Jane Austen* (Chicago, 1973).

Trickett, Rachel, "Jane Austen's Comedy and the Nineteenth Century," in *Critical Essays on Jane Austen*, ed. B. C. Southam (London, 1968).

Wright, Andrew H., *Jane Austen's Novels: A Study in Structure* (New ed., London, 1961).

JO ALYSON PARKER

Mansfield Park:
Dismantling Pemberley

The heroine's friendship to be sought after by a young Woman in the same Neighbourhood, of Talents & Shrewdness, with light eyes & a fair skin, but having a considerable degree of Wit, Heroine shall shrink from the acquaintance.

—Jane Austen, "Plan of a Novel" (MW 429)

The woman who has only been taught to please will soon find that her charms are oblique sunbeams, and that they cannot have much effect on her husband's heart when they are seen every day, when the summer is passed and gone. Will she then have sufficient native energy to look into herself for comfort, and cultivate her dormant faculties? or is it not more rational to expect that she will try to please other men, and, in the emotions raised by the experience of new conquests, endeavour to forget the mortifications her love or pride has received?

—Mary Wollstonecraft, Vindication of the Rights of Woman

If, indeed, women were mere outside form and face only, and if mind made up no part of her composition, it would follow that a ballroom was quite as appropriate a place for choosing a wife, as an exhibition room for choosing a picture....

—Hannah More, Stricture on the Modern System of Female Education

In *The Opposing Self*, Lionel Trilling points out that "Fielding's *Amelia* ... may be said to bear the same relation to *Tom Jones* that *Mansfield Park* bears

From *The Author's Inheritance: Henry Fielding, Jane Austen, and the Establishment of the Novel.* ©1998 by Northern Illinois University Press.

to *Pride and Prejudice*."[1] Trilling's statement anticipates the intra-canonic, trans-gendered, trans-generational connections that I have been making throughout. I would add that *Mansfield Park* not only serves as the dark counterpoint to *Pride and Prejudice* but also revises many of the themes and motifs of *Amelia*. It explores the implications of the conduct-book heroine ideal that Fielding's final novel helped promulgate, addresses the issue of adultery from a woman's perspective, and problematizes the issue of moral and literary authority in a patriarchal society.

Tom Jones and *Amelia*, its contrapuntal sequel, test various ways of reviving a moribund social structure, each with varying degrees of success. Seemingly subversive in both content and presentation, *Tom Jones* comes to argue for the recuperability of traditional forms through the incorporation of something new—the bastard Tom or the novel form. With its exemplary heroine and its didactic tone, *Amelia* ostensibly puts forth a conservative agenda, but this conservatism is straining at the seams.

Pride and Prejudice and *Mansfield Park* have a similar obverse relationship. Like *Tom Jones*, *Pride and Prejudice* attempts to solve the problem of societal decline through seemingly subversive means—the insertion of a woman into the patriarchal plot of the reconstitution of the estate. But, as with Fielding's novel, Austen's also falls back on the old verities; traditional forms may require the introduction of a new element but they are intrinsically good. To a certain extent, just as *Amelia* appears at first as a sort of sequel to *Tom Jones*, the opening setup in *Mansfield Park* speaks back to the conclusion of *Pride and Prejudice*. Claudia Johnson notes that "The Bertrams end where Darcy begins—with the family circle which Austen's more attractive patricians learn to outgrow."[2] But we might also say that the Bertrams begin where Darcy ends—with the marriage of a proud and wealthy gentleman to a woman of inferior social standing. Lady Bertram may not be an older avatar of Elizabeth Bennet; but Sir Thomas Bertram, like Darcy, is the quintessential patriarch—sober, authoritative, responsible—and Mansfield Park, like Pemberley, is the repository of traditional values. The manor, in fact, provides the model for proper social behavior, as Fanny Price's wistful assessment makes clear: "At Mansfield, no sounds of contention, no raised voices, no abrupt bursts, no tread of violence was ever heard; all proceeded in a regular course of cheerful orderliness; every body had their due importance; every body's feelings were consulted" (*MP* 391–92). The "cheerful orderliness," the "due importance" of everyone, the consultation of everyone's feelings—such a description suggests that this is a well-regulated world, its hierarchical structure balanced with an almost democratic consideration of the wishes of all its members. But Fanny deludes herself, seemingly forgetting the miserable experiences she has so recently undergone there. As we see, the inhabitants of Mansfield Park often pervert or ignore such values. Whereas *Pride and Prejudice* holds forth hope for a renewal—an improvement—of the estate, Mansfield Park implicitly qualifies such hope, calling such values into question even as it attempts to assert their soundness.

The predominant features of *Mansfield Park* explicitly support traditional values. Fanny Price is an exemplary heroine, faithful to a hero who is momentarily deflected from her steadfast love but finally cognizant of her perfections. The resolution of the plot—wherein the constant Fanny gets her man and the instigators of change are banished from Mansfield— validates the argument for supporting the status quo.

However, the surface polemic of Austen's novel is disturbed by an underlying countercurrent of skepticism. Austen may explicitly sanction Fanny's good behavior, but as Fanny's story shows, female exemplarity is an insidious notion. The attributes of the exemplary woman—obedience to authority, self-effacement, and silence—actually disable her from fulfilling her function of providing proper moral guidance. The plot may resolve itself in a conventionally happy ending, but such happiness is built upon an underlying foundation of misery. The very things that promise social reformation highlight the fissures in society, fissures that have an implicit connection with the overarching values of Austen's time. Like *Amelia*, *Mansfield Park* reworks, recontextualizes, and refutes the easy solutions of an earlier text.[3]

Yet *Mansfield Park* also calls into question several of the assumptions underlying *Amelia*. Drawing on the motif of the beleaguered heroine, each text attempts to revise the status quo and testifies to the difficulty of so doing. Yet although *Amelia* demonstrates Fielding's increasing doubt that society can return to traditional values, it never questions the appropriateness of such a return. By reworking Fielding's material Austen calls such values into question, however. She shows us the underside of Amelia-like exemplarity and faults the overarching patriarchal structure that implicitly encourages behavior leading to social breakdown.

EXCELLENT WOMAN

From the outset, nobody has known what to make of Fanny Price. Austen's earliest readers were divided on the subject; one of her nieces, for example, was "delighted with Fanny" while another "could not bear" her ("Opinions of *Mansfield Park*," *MW* 431, 432). Our own assessments of *Mansfield Park* are, in fact, integrally related to our assessments of Fanny.

Her perverse integrity and her unprepossessing virtues prompt the ambivalence and dissatisfaction we feel in regard to the text as a whole. Nina Auerbach subtitles an essay on *Mansfield Park* "Feeling as One Ought about Fanny Price"—a title suggestive of the quandary in which we find ourselves when confronted with Austen's least engaging heroine.[4] Fanny's sickliness, her voicelessness, her rectitude put us off, especially in that she is wedged between Austen's two most lively heroines, Elizabeth Bennet and Emma Woodhouse. Although Tony Tanner notes that "nobody falls in love with Fanny Price," he joins with Lionel Trilling in defending her, arguing that she is a typical Christian heroine, thus subject to unwarranted antipathy on the part of the more secular modern-day reader.[5] Auerbach, on the other hand, seems to regard Fanny's connection with otherworldly realms as tending toward the demonic rather than the angelic: Fanny is "a blighter of ceremonies and a divider of families," a vampire figure who "feasts secretly upon human vitality in the dark."[6] Yet the problem lies not so much with Fanny's conduct-book character, off-putting as that may sometimes be. Rather, it lies with the fact that Fanny's story shows us how little is to be gained by maintaining such a character.

Although the conduct-book heroine had thrived in the half-century since Richardson and Fielding put forward their paragons, Jane Austen generally mocked it. Austen's most memorable protagonists are not of the conduct-book type but instead are lively, somewhat wrong-headed characters capable of change and growth. They consistently transgress, or at least stretch, the bounds of what is considered proper behavior for women. The texts we have tended to favor, such as *Pride and Prejudice*, follow a bildungsroman structure; the protagonist errs, faces up to her faults (generally at the instigation of the male mentor), and undergoes a certain amount of development. Violations of what is strictly proper lead in part to chastisement and self-recognition, certainly, but such violations also bring about positive outcomes—for example, Elizabeth's sassing of Lady Catherine makes Darcy aware of her love for him. Furthermore, although each heroine may renounce a propensity toward imaginative flights, none evidences a newfound desire to become a model woman.[7] Elizabeth Bennet persists in "her lively, sportive manner" of talking to Darcy (*PP* 387–88); and Mr. Knightly marries Emma in part, we are to assume, because she is "faultless in spite of her faults" (*Em* 433), that is, because her very faults make her attractive in his eyes.

Fanny may not be Austen's only conduct-book protagonist, but she is the most insistently so. With her strict adherence to duty Elinor Dashwood has affinities to the model, but she also has an acerbic, domineering quality that keeps her out of the ranks of exemplary womanhood; her sister, Marianne, has gotten all the allotment of tenderness that is essential for ideality. Anne Eliot, although she has often been regarded as an older version of Fanny, explicitly questions the implications and consequences of her own dutifulness, which thus enables Austen to engage in a deliberate self-conscious assessment of conduct-book behavior.

Fanny, however, is consistently exemplary, the text validating her as the epitome of womanhood. She just about fulfills Edmund Bertram's prescription for "the perfect model of a woman" (*MP* 347)—and he only holds back his full praise because he lacks the insight that has been granted his gentle cousin. Henry Crawford describes her in terms that elevate her above the common run of womankind: "She is exactly the woman to do away every prejudice of such a man as the Admiral, for she is exactly such a woman as he thinks does not exist in the world. She is the very impossibility he would describe" (293). Such panegyrics come not only from Edmund and Henry but also from the Austen narrator, the narrative voice thus lending authority to a definition of womanhood that, because of our prior acquaintance with Austen, we might otherwise suspect. The narrator continually sings Fanny's praises; she has "heroism of principle" (265) and a "delicacy of taste, of mind, of feeling" (81) that we are told Mary Crawford lacks. Despite Mary's attractiveness to readers, in the contest between her and Fanny the narrator always weighs in on Fanny's side, encouraging us to champion her, as is evidenced by the epithet "my Fanny" (461), the phrase marking a brief, uncharacteristic return to the overtly authorial stance. Constant in her affections and her principles, combining a melting tenderness with an adherence to what is right, Fanny is represented as the most gendered of her gender according to contemporary notions of femininity.

Fanny comes from a long line of model heroines, and by comparing her with some of these we can begin to see how Austen attenuates the tradition. Fanny's forebears include not only Fielding's happy homemaker Amelia, but also the angelic martyr Clarissa and the noble-minded name-dropper Cecilia. Like them Fanny is gentle and pious; she is the only one of Austen's heroines for whom a place of worship clearly means more than a gathering place for village society, although Anne Eliot's concern for her cousin's traveling on Sunday might indicate that she is equally pious. It is likely that when we picture Fanny, we think of her in her virginal white dress—"A woman can never be too fine while she is all in white," says Edmund (*MP* 222)—and her amber cross, as if she were a little nun.

With regard to the piety of conduct-book heroines, we might reverse the old cliché and say that behind every great woman is a great man. Often, the exemplary heroine owes her moral authority to a male mentor who is a man of the cloth. Amelia has her Dr. Harrison, Clarissa has her Dr. Lewen, Cecilia her Dean, and Matilda (the heroine of the second half of Elizabeth Inchbald's *A Simple Story*) her priest Sandford. This configuration of church-sanctioned female exemplarity is suggestive of what Jacques Donzelot calls the "ancient complicity" operating "between the system of matrimonial exchanges—the key to the old familial order—and the religious apparatus."[8] In effect, by having the female exemplar authorized/authored by the clergy, the novels can provide a transcendental imperative for her behavior and thus mask how well it serves secular interests. And Fanny is no exception. As with her sister heroines, her mind has been "formed" by a clergyman (in this case, an aspiring one): Edmund "recommended the books which charmed her leisure hours, he encouraged her taste, and corrected her judgment; he made reading useful by talking to her of what she had read, and heightened its attraction by judicious praise" (*MP* 22). Fanny indeed outdoes her mentor, standing firm against Henry Crawford while Edmund succumbs to the temptation of Crawford's sister.[9] Overall, Austen locates the source of Fanny's moral authority firmly in a patriarchal structure.

To a certain extent, Fanny outdoes her sister heroines in exemplarity. Lionel Trilling points out that, in creating her frail heroine, Austen was following "the tradition which affirmed the peculiar sanctity of the sick, the weak, and the dying."[10] Fanny must be on her way to sainthood—we hear a litany of her ills, from headache to exhaustion to excessive sensitivity to noise. Clarissa, after all, is fairly robust up until the time of the rape, and Amelia seems to bounce back from her fainting fits with renewed vigor. We should bear in mind that, as Mary Wollstonecraft had pointed out fifteen years earlier, conduct books advise a woman to hide the fact that "she can take more exercise than another" and that "she has a sound constitution."[11] Fanny's illness thus goes hand in hand with ultra-femininity. Whereas Amelia and Cecilia properly disdain putting themselves forward, Fanny effaces herself to the point of disappearing altogether. She is not just quiet-spoken ("an excellent thing in woman"), she is practically voiceless—the sentence "Fanny coloured, and said nothing" (*MP* 225) epitomizes her behavior. When Sir Thomas attempts to gauge Fanny's feelings toward Henry Crawford, he realizes that she is a cipher to him: "She was always so gentle and retiring, that her emotions were beyond his discrimination" (366). Pamela, Clarissa, Amelia, and Cecilia make a few missteps, Clarissa indeed stepping fatally outside her father's walls and into the arms of her ravisher. But Fanny makes no false moves. She understands the pernicious nature of the theatricals, she correctly assesses the true character of the Crawfords, and so forth. Overall, she is hyper-exemplary.

Yet, as the text demonstrates, pushed to its logical conclusion the notion of the exemplary woman will show signs of strain, on the levels of both symbol and plot. Clarissa's physical disintegration after the rape symbolizes her gradual transcendence to a higher plane where she will leave earthly woes behind and, presumably, take her place among the angels. Fanny's illness, on the other hand, tends toward no heavenly elevation; it leaves us instead with an idea of chronic enervation, suggestive of the enervation of exemplars. If Fanny represents enduring values, such values are sickened.

The implicit connection between Fanny and Lady Bertram bears out this notion. I would not go so far as Gilbert and Gubar, who argue that Fanny is "destined to become the next Lady Bertram, following the example of Sir Thomas's corpselike wife."[12] But there certainly are similarities between the two. Fanny prefers Lady Bertram for female companionship: "She talked to her, listened to her, read to her; and the tranquillity of such evenings, her perfect security in such a *tête-à-tête* from any sounds of unkindness, was unspeakably welcome to a mind which had seldom known a pause in its alarms or embarrassments" (*MP* 35). Both Fanny and Lady Bertram depend on others to articulate for them, although Fanny (unlike her indolent aunt) actually has a thought or two to articulate. Both are fixed— Lady Bertram on her couch, Fanny in her opinions. Fanny, of course, has a core of moral fiber that Lady Bertram lacks, but the outward appearance is the same. Rather than considering Fanny as the replacement for Lady Bertram, we might consider Lady Bertram as the replacement for Fanny, a bloodless doppelgänger with the form—though not substance—of the proper lady. This connection is suggestive of the fact that hyper-exemplarity and hyper-insipidity can be easily confused.

Fanny's gentleness points to another area of strain in the notion of exemplary womanhood. She cannot make herself understood. Henry Crawford persists in his suit in part because Fanny is too ladylike in her refusals: "Her manner was incurably gentle, and she was not aware of how much it concealed the sternness of her purpose. Her diffidence, gratitude, and softness, made every expression of indifference seem almost an effort of self-denial; seem at least, to be giving nearly as much pain to herself as to him" (*MP* 327). The very sweetness "which makes so essential a part of every woman's worth in the judgment of man" (294) renders her own judgment incapable of being considered.

We have one anomalous instance of Fanny's voicing opposition to the match between herself and Crawford. In *Pride and Prejudice* Elizabeth's rejection of Mr. Collins's proposal provided Austen with an opportunity to expose the plight of women forced to hear out the addresses of men they do not like. Yet Austen leaves it to the generally taciturn Fanny rather than the loquacious Elizabeth to articulate most fervently this plight. Fanny's speech to Edmund to this effect is, in fact, her longest speech in the text. Herein she protests against the assumption that a woman must find a man acceptable because he has found her so: "Let him have all the perfections in the world, I think it ought not to he set down as certain, that a man must be acceptable to every woman he may happen to like himself" (*MP* 353). She questions a code of sexual conduct that both prohibits a woman from having feelings for a man until he has made clear he has feelings for her and then requires that the woman reciprocate in kind: "How then was I to be—to be in love with him the moment he said he was with me?" (353). Fanny may generally conform to conduct-book behavior, but she herein voices a sharp critique of the behavioral absurdities to which women are expected to accede, a critique Austen seems to agree with.[13] It is significant that Edmund just does not get it: "My dear, dear Fanny," he tells her, "now I have the truth.... the very circumstance of the novelty of Crawford's addresses was against him" (353–54). He lays claim to "the truth"—but by seizing on the notion of novelty he ignores Fanny's truth, that she does not and cannot love Henry. Fanny's statement that "we think very different of the nature of women" points to a rift between female and male assessments of woman's nature that even the seemingly enlightened Edmund cannot bridge and that the text brings to the fore with its portrait of the conflicted Fanny.

Generally, however, Fanny "properly" lacks assertion and rhetorical force, and as a consequence she is unacknowledged. When paragons undergo trials, they usually have the dubious satisfaction of having their perfections recognized. As Anna Howe writes Clarissa, in the first letter of the novel, "Every eye, in short, is upon you with the expectation of an example."[14] Cecilia's excellencies are known far and wide, prompting the male paragon Delvile to seek her out. Even the rivalrous Miss Mathews acknowledges that Amelia is "a much better Woman" than herself, and Amelia's husband, Booth, talks of "the general Admiration which ... pursued her, the Respect paid her by Persons of the highest Rank" (*Am* 38, 66). Few sing Fanny's praises, however. Edmund and (later) Henry Crawford recognize her virtues, certainly, and by the end of the novel her importance to the Mansfield residents has been acknowledged. But no one says of her, as Anna Howe says of Clarissa, "She was a wonderful creature from her infancy."[15] People are much more likely to point out, as Mrs. Norris does, that her behavior "is very stupid indeed, and shows a great want of genius and emulation" (*MP* 19). And although Edmund discovers her virtues early on, not until he has undergone disappointment and heartbreak does he "learn to prefer soft light eyes to sparkling dark ones" (470). Sir Thomas eventually realizes that she is "the daughter that he wanted" (472), but it is only his actual daughters' transgressions that throw his niece's virtues into relief. Henry's love is an odd one, spurred perhaps as much by his desire for the unattainable as his recognition of Fanny's excellencies. Neither Mrs. Norris nor the Bertram daughters nor Fanny's parents ever recognize that they have a little paragon in their midst, and in the concluding pages Lady Bertram, after some initial resistance, soon comes to substitute Susan for Fanny, even coming to find her "the most beloved of the two" (472-73). So much for Fanny's importance to Lady Bertram!

Readers themselves may have a hard time recognizing Fanny's importance. Like Amelia, Fanny is somewhat of a hidden heroine. Granted, we are in her mind pretty much from the outset of the novel. But, as the other characters are active rather than passive, they take over the action and thus the interest of the story. They often take over the narrative focus as well. In each of her novels Austen shifts the focalization at times from her main character to various subsidiary ones. In no other, however, does she so consistently explore the motives and feelings of the other characters or give us so much access to the minds of her villains. We receive vivid, emotionally charged accounts of Mary Crawford's fondness for Edmund and her disappointed hopes, of Julia's jealousy of her sister, of Maria's humiliation at Henry's defection. We end up feeling that the other stories have potential. Mary certainly threatens to supplant Fanny in the readers' affections just as she supplants her in Edmund's. As has often been noted, she has the liveliness that makes Elizabeth Bennet so endearing; "with her lively dark eye, clear brown complexion, and general prettiness" (*MP* 44), Mary bears more than a passing resemblance to Elizabeth, whose "fine eyes" first attract Darcy and whose tanned complexion later prompts his defense of her to Caroline Bingley. Fanny's closest analogues in Austen's novels (besides Anne Eliot, who is a deepened, matured, more self-aware version) are the shadowy secondary characters that occur in the texts written before and after *Mansfield Park*—the two Janes, Bennet and Fairfax. Both are sweet girls, forced to bear in silence a lover's apparent defection. With Fanny it is as if Austen tries to bring forward the kind of character she is generally content to leave in the background—and then runs up against the problem that a Rosencrantz can never have the impact of a Hamlet.

Ignored and unrecognized for what she is, Fanny virtually has no impact. Richardson's Pamela almost single-handedly reforms a corrupt squirarchy; Clarissa is highly influential in life and death; Cecilia's noble example prompts noble action on the part of others. Although Amelia cannot single-handedly reform the corrupt society that surrounds her (Fielding also acknowledging the fading power of exemplars, though for different purposes), she does manage to provide important instruction to her children and, ultimately, to inspire Booth and a small circle of friends. Moreover, throughout the text that bears her name, Amelia functions consistently as the emblem for good to which Booth must aspire. But Fanny is granted little or no capacity for influence. She is unable to stop Maria Bertram from slipping around the iron gate with Mr. Crawford, to bring order to the Portsmouth house, or to dissuade Edmund from participating in the play and falling in love with the improper Mary. The only significant influence she has is over her sister, Susan, and rather than attempting to reform the Portsmouth residents the two sisters retreat up the stairs to avoid "a great deal of the disturbance of the house" (*MP* 398), just as the Mansfield residents retreat from the rest of society at the end of the novel.

Fanny's most significant failure is with Henry Crawford. Austen clearly sets up a story that is meant to remind us of the "rake reformed" theme of *Pamela*. Henry sets out a net for Fanny, but he is caught in it himself. He seems to be on the road to reformation—he recognizes her superiority to other women, and he takes on the squirarchical duties he had previously neglected. But, as Frank Bradbrook suggests, there is more than a little of a Laclos influence in *Mansfield Park*, and Henry may be more of a Valmont than a Mr. B., mouthing a reformation that has only partially taken hold.[16] If Fanny is indeed "the woman whom he had rationally, as well as passionately loved" (*MP* 469), we must wonder at a passion that can be deflected by seeming whim, and all the narrator's explanations as to the faultiness of Henry's education do little to satisfy us. To a certain extent Henry's love for Fanny seems to have less to do with his growing appreciation of her virtues than with her indifference to his suit: "it was a love which ... made her affection appear of greater consequence because it was withheld, and determined him to have the glory, as well as the felicity, of forcing her to love him" (326). Henry thus regards Fanny not so much as a person to be valued than as an object to be conquered, and he pursues a course similar to that of the Noble Lord in *Amelia*, who abandons a woman once he has seduced her. It is significant that Henry turns his attention to the less-than-exemplary Maria when she seems to offer greater resistance: "He must exert himself to subdue so proud a display of resentment" (468). By thwarting our expectations that Fanny will reform Henry and become his bride, Austen drives home the inadequacy of the exemplary woman/reformed rake paradigm.

She seems here to have borrowed a leaf from Hannah More's book. Fifteen years prior More had scoffed at "that fatal and most indelicate, nay gross maxim, that a reformed rake makes the best husband," arguing that it goes on the "preposterous supposition ... that habitual vice creates rectitude of character, and that sin produces happiness."[17] In undermining the maxim herself, Austen reinforces our sense of Fanny's negligible capacity for influence.

Indeed, whatever reformation occurs in *Mansfield Park* results not from Fanny's influence but from the bad experiences the characters undergo. Fanny essentially wins Edmund's affections by default, Mary's weaknesses rather than Fanny's virtues leading him to transfer his affections to his gentle cousin. Sir Thomas recognizes his folly only after Maria's elopement. And it takes a brush with death to make Tom Bertram a better man.

Not only is Fanny incapable of influencing the characters within the text, but the representation of her is probably incapable of influencing those who read the text. As Nancy Armstrong argues in *Desire and Domestic Fiction*, the rising novel enabled a social agenda whereby "the female relinquishes political control to the male in order to acquire exclusive authority over domestic life, emotions, taste, and morality."[18] In effect, the versions of female exemplarity that novels put forth were intended to provide a model for feminine authority and to carve out its particular realm of influence—the inculcation of values within the domestic sphere. Samuel Richardson, for instance, made no bones about his didactic purposes. After listing Pamela's manifold virtues at the conclusion of the novel, he points out that they "Are all so many signal instances of the excellency of her mind, which may make her character worthy of the *imitation* of her sex" (*Pam* 509, emphasis mine). More grandly, in his postscript to *Clarissa*, he explains that he intended the novel to "inculcate upon the human mind, under the guise of an amusement, the great lessons of Christianity," specifically through making the reader desire to emulate his saintly-heroine: "And who that are in earnest in their profession of Christianity but will rather envy than regret the triumphant death of CLARISSA, whose piety from her early childhood, whose diffusive charity; whose steady virtue; whose Christian humility; whose forgiving spirit; whose meekness, whose resignation, HEAVEN only could reward?"[19] Fielding's and Burney's heroines are also put forth as worthy of emulation. How worthwhile can it be to emulate Fanny, however, if such emulation leads to naught? Imitating Fanny would not give one the capacity to lead others to virtue, or so *Mansfield Park* implies.

Moreover, imitating Fanny would mean resigning oneself to a painful existence. Stories such as those of Pamela, Clarissa, Amelia, Miss Sidney

Biddulph, and Cecilia show us that the lot of the model woman is to suffer. After all, if the protagonist's exemplary character is fixed, the novel's action cannot depend upon self-revelation and internal growth but must instead depend upon the external events that beset the heroine—preferably, events that enable her exemplarity to shine forth. Fanny ostensibly goes through no more than her sisters in ideality.

Or does she? Her sister heroines at least can pride themselves on their consciousness of their own virtue, but Fanny has no such salve. Pamela and Clarissa, for example, know that they are right to resist the importunities of their would-be seducers. Cecilia, in renouncing a secret marriage with Delvile, takes consolation in her own virtue, as the following passage indicates:

> notwithstanding the sorrow she felt in apparently injuring the man whom, in the whole world, she most wished to oblige, she yet found a satisfaction in the sacrifice she had made, that recompensed her for much of her sufferings and soothed her into something like tranquillity; the true power of virtue she had scarce experienced before, for she found it a resource against the cruelest dejection, and a supporter in the bitterest disappointment.[20]

Compare the above with Austen's description of Fanny's feelings after she has told Sir Thomas she cannot marry Henry Crawford:

> Her mind was all disorder. The past, present, future, every thing was terrible. But her uncle's anger gave her the severest pain of all. Selfish and ungrateful! to have appeared so to him! She was miserable for ever. She had no one to take her part, to counsel, or speak for her. Her only friend was absent. He might have softened his father; but all, perhaps all, would think her selfish and ungrateful. She might have to endure the reproach again and again; she might hear it, or see it, or know it to exist for ever in every connection about her. She could not but feel some resentment against Mr. Crawford; yet, if he really loved her, and were unhappy too!—it was all wretchedness together. (*MP* 321)

Fanny is damned if she does and damned if she does not. She cannot act without violating some prescription of proper feminine behavior. She may see more clearly than Sir Thomas, but she may not derive consolation from this fact.

The changes Austen rings on the term "duty" underscore the double bind in which the model woman finds herself. For Fanny, duty consists of sticking to her principles, as she acknowledges resignedly after that dreadful interview with Sir Thomas: "she believed she had no right to wonder at the line of conduct he pursued. He who had married a daughter to Mr. Rushworth. Romantic delicacy was certainly not to be expected from him. She must do her duty, and trust that time might make her duty easier than it now was" (*MP* 331). But only a few pages later Lady Bertram puts forward a different definition of duty with her reiteration of Sir Thomas's view that Fanny has an obligation to accept Henry: "And you must be aware, Fanny, that it is every young woman's duty to accept such a very unexceptionable offer" (333). We have, of course, encountered a similar notion of female duty in an earlier passage—and we might recall what fatal results attend it:

> Being now in her twenty-first year, Maria Bertram was beginning to think matrimony a duty; and as a marriage with Mr. Rushworth would give her the enjoyment of a larger income than her father's, as well as ensure her the house in town, which was now a prime object, it became, by the same rile of moral obligation, her evident duty to marry Mr. Rushworth if she could. (38–39)

The contested meanings of "duty" underscore Austen's point that the model woman often must attempt to align what may be mutually exclusive aims— the preservation of moral integrity and the attainment of wealth and standing. Here we have no happy resolution as in *Pride and Prejudice*, wherein Elizabeth manages to preserve her integrity and marry a man with ten thousand pounds a year. (Charlotte Lucas's situation, of course, hints at the dilemma faced by Fanny.) Fanny's conception of her "moral obligation" is directly at odds with the Bertrams'.

By the end of the text the Bertrams will come to redefine duty, teaming that Fanny's conception of it really serves the family's interests after all, but in the meantime we are made privy to Fanny's suffering as she struggles with impossible demands. Indeed, she is unable to find a Cecilia-like tranquillity until the end of the volume. Overall, few moments of pleasure relieve the long scenes of torture that Fanny undergoes. Even her pleasures are riddled with painful sensations: as she prepares for the ball given in her honor she worries about whether to wear Mary's or Edmund's necklace and sighs over Edmund's profession of love for Mary; the welcome news of William's promotion is followed by Henry's unwelcome proposal. Austen makes clear the connection between Fanny's feelings of oppression and her conduct-book behavior. After refusing Henry's proposal, Fanny dreads an encounter with Mary, rightly fearing that Mary will bring up distressing issues. But Mary need only appeal to Fanny's notion of proper behavior:

> She was determined to see Fanny alone, and therefore said to her tolerably soon, in a low voice, "I must speak to you for a few minutes somewhere;" words that Fanny felt all over her, in all her pulses, and all her nerves. Denial was impossible. Her habits of ready submission, on the contrary, made her almost instantly rise and lead the way out of the room. She did it with wretched feelings, but it was inevitable. (*MP* 357)

The intensity of Fanny's emotions is played off against her almost automaton-like behavior. As in the scene after her interview with Sir Thomas, Fanny's sense of propriety renders her miserable. No wonder that the text gives us such oxymorons as "painful gratitude" (322); to be an exemplary woman means to he beset with contradictory impulses.

Austen's final disposition of her conduct-book protagonist is ambivalent. Fanny does get the requisite happy ending that would seem to validate her "womanly" behavior: she is married to Edmund; William is on his way to naval glory; and Susan has supplanted her as Lady Bertram's companion, thus freeing Fanny of the guilt she might feel at not being able to make all of the people happy all of the time. But we might bear in mind that Austen rewards all her protagonists with a happy ending, and she gives us no indication that Elizabeth will stop teasing Darcy or that the imperious Emma will be satisfied with any but "the best treatment." Austen's improper ladies may briefly pay penance for their sins. The scene wherein Emma reproaches herself after insulting Miss Bates, for example, may be one of the most emotionally charged in the Austen canon. The proper Fanny, however, continually pays penance for sins she does not commit, essentially serving as a scapegoat for society's failures to regulate itself correctly. At one time, she evokes a Griselda-figure, willing to humble herself for the sins of others: "Sir Thomas's look implied, 'On your judgment, Edmund, I depended; what have you been about?'—She knelt in spirit to her uncle, and her bosom swelled to utter, 'Oh! not to him. Look so to all the others, but not to him'" (*MP* 185). We must assume that only Fanny's habitual self-effacement keeps her from kneeling in actuality. And, despite the uncharacteristic emphasis on religion, Austen offers us no more suggestion that a heavenly reward awaits Fanny than she does in regard to her other protagonists.

When Mrs. Norris—that mouthpiece for all that is awry in the social structure—tells Fanny that she "must be the lowest and the last" (*MP* 221), she may indeed be voicing the implicit agenda of a society that depends on female submission. For the behavior that it prescribes for rendering women "womanly" is that which calls for their obedience, their dependence, their sense of their own inferiority. We might consider Fanny as exemplary to the second power—as the exemplary case of the exemplary woman, allowing us to see the consequences of the concept. The character of Fanny may stem from Austen's internalizations of society's "should-be's," but the plot in which she is inscribed may stem from Austen's concurrent resistance to the plot of feminizing women.

THE FALL OF THE HOUSE OF MANSFIELD

As in *Amelia*, the resolution of the plot overtly champions conservative values but simultaneously problematizes them by the evidence put forward in their support. Maria's adulterous liaison with Henry flies in the face of such values, but it also is the inevitable offshoot of an extreme version of them. The reestablishment of spiritual principles in Mansfield, represented by Fanny's new role there, serves as an ostensible solution to the problems besetting the estate, but Austen implicitly demonstrates that the solution works on only a limited scale.[21]

Soon after the Crawfords arrive in the Mansfield neighborhood, Mrs. Grant optimistically predicts that "Mansfield shall cure you both—and without any taking in. Stay with us and we will cure you" (*MP* 47). In a world wherein Mansfield had maintained its emblematic significance as a center of moral authority, such an outcome might be possible. Henry would marry Fanny, renouncing his libertine ways and taking his squirarchical duties seriously. Mary would marry Edmund, learning like Elizabeth Bennet to use her wit as a corrective rather than destructive force. Maria Bertram would console herself with high society. Aunt Norris, after her initial resentment had passed, would take credit for Fanny's match, becoming as obnoxious in her attentions to Fanny as she had been in her snubs. Henry himself offers a view of an ideal community that might, in other circumstances, have served Austen as a final line for the novel: "'Mansfield, Sotherton, Thornton Lacey,' he continued, 'what a society will be comprised in those houses! And at Michaelmas, perhaps, a fourth may be added, some small hunting-box in the vicinity of every thing so dear'" (405). Such an outcome does not occur, of course, and the contrast between Henry's vision and the actual conclusion throws into relief the fissures running through the seemingly solid edifice of Mansfield Park.

Rather than finding a cure at Mansfield, the Crawfords infect—or at least lower—the Bertrams' resistance to disease. Although the taint of city living may give the Crawfords a certain outsider status, essentially they are insiders, members of the same class as the Bertrams and certainly more acceptable socially than the child of a lieutenant of Marines. Henry is, after all, a landowner, responsible for the well-being of his tenants. In effect, the threat to the gentry comes from within the gentry.

Such a threat has all the more force in that it cannot be easily discerned. Despite Henry's fears of being "taken in," it is the Bertrams who are taken in, blinded to the Crawfords' moral bankruptcy by their attractiveness. Sir Thomas regards both Crawfords as suitable matches for his own children; the connection he envisions ends up, ironically, an illicit one. We might expect Edmund—the only one of Austen's clergymen with an actual vocation (with the possible exception of Edward Ferrars)—to have the surest sense of the threat posed by the Crawfords, but he becomes the particular friend of both. Only Fanny, the silent observer, can assess the true implications of their apparently innocent high-spirited behavior, and she has no voice with which to alert the others.

The characterization of the Crawfords also blinds us—or at least destabilizes our expectations. In *Amelia* Fielding eschews his usual practice of succinctly summing up the characters when he introduces them, thus often leaving us uncertain as to characters' motives and dependent on further revelations. Austen similarly keeps us off-balance. The Crawfords are initially attractive to us as well as to the characters within the novel, and for the most part Austen forgoes the sort of commentary that might give us clear indications as to how we are to read them.[22] If, as Q. D. Leavis has argued, *Mansfield Park* is a revised version of Austen's epistolary "Lady Susan," it subtilizes the blatant character revelations of the earlier work, in which Lady Susan's letters to Mrs. Johnson provide a clear illustration of her character, and Mrs. Vernon's suspicions of her seem fairly disinterested.[23] In *Mansfield Park*, however, our main clues come from the Crawfords' speech and actions and Fanny's unvoiced assessments. But we may be inclined to read the Crawfords' speech and actions as evidence of a proper lack of control rather than of villainy, and we may consider Fanny's assessments, when unseconded by the narrator's validation, as somewhat skewed, especially in light of her evident jealousy of Mary. Furthermore, the Crawfords' genuinely kind acts mitigate their improprieties. Mary pays marked attention to Fanny after one of Mrs. Norris's particularly virulent barbs, and Henry envisions that in making Fanny his wife he can elevate her from her "dependent, helpless, friendless, neglected, forgotten" condition (*MP* 297). Granted, their behavior (particularly Henry's) often verges on the improper, but the Crawfords appear redeemable.

After giving us an instance of misbehavior on the Crawfords' part, Austen generally juxtaposes an instance of kindness. It is only in the very last chapters of the novel that the scales tip irrevocably toward the bad. Mary's mercenary desire for Tom Bertram's death, expressed in a self-serving letter to Fanny, reveals a cold-bloodedness that is inexcusable according to Austen's worldview. Henry's elopement with Maria Bertram is an egregious social transgression, indicative of his overweening selfishness and heartless lack of concern for consequences. But it may be that up until these particular occurrences, we expect—perhaps even hope—that Austen will allow each Crawford an epiphanic moment of self-revelation and a subsequent reformation. Unlike Austen's other novels, wherein we can predict the eventual partners if not what will bring them together, *Mansfield Park* offers several possible plot paths, and the hypothetical resolution envisioned by Henry does not seem to be completely out of the question.

The elopement of Henry and Maria marks the point at which characters in the novel and readers of the novel must have done with the Crawfords. The man who "so requited hospitality, so injured family peace" (*MP* 469) no longer has a place in the Mansfield world. Despite Edmund's high-mindedness, we might expect (as Fanny does) that his feelings for Mary would win out over his elevated sense of propriety and that she at least would not have the gates of Mansfield forever barred to her. But her plan to persuade Henry to marry Maria implicates her in Henry's crime, at least in Edmund's eyes, as he makes clear to Fanny:

> but the manner in which she spoke of the crime itself, giving it every reproach but the right, considering its ill consequences only as they were to be braved or overborne by a deficiency of decency and impudence in wrong; and, last of all, and above all, recommending to us a compliance, a compromise, an acquiescence, in the continuance of a sin, on the chance of a marriage which, thinking as I now thought of her brother, should rather be prevented than sought—all this together most grievously convinced me that I had never understood her before. (458)

Mary's attempt to unite the two transgressors in marriage might seem to have a certain affinity to Darcy's engineering of the wedding of Lydia and

Wickham. But an adulterous liaison is not recuperable, and there is no grateful Elizabeth Bennet to thank Mary for her pains. Instead, Edmund regards the suggestion as evidence of Mary's duplicity: "How have I been deceived! Equally in brother and sister deceived!" (495). To Edmund the woman who can speak lightly of adultery is as culpable as the adulterer. Clearly, a proper lady must condemn adultery, and Fanny's "shudderings of horror" (41) mark the correct response.

The Henry-and-Maria elopement marks both the point beyond which the Crawfords can no longer be part of the Mansfield world and the point beyond which the Mansfield family unit cannot survive as a whole. In *Pride and Prejudice* Mr. Bennet receives the unrepentant Lydia Wickham back into the family circle. Sir Thomas, however, refuses to receive the abandoned Maria, offering the following justification: "Maria had destroyed her own character, and he would not by a vain attempt to restore what never could be restored, be affording his sanction to vice, or in seeking to lessen its disgrace, be anywise accessary to introducing such misery in another man's family, as he had known himself" (*MP* 465). No one, except the silly Mr. Collins, frets that Lydia's bad example may cause others to emulate her. Maria's dissimilar fate enables Austen to demonstrate that adultery signals an unassimilable infraction of the social code.

Although almost all of Austen's novels touch on some sort of illicit sexuality, none of these situations has the disruptive force—both within the story and as a symbolic element—of the Henry-and-Maria elopement. Maria's marriage to Rushworth links the grand estate of Mansfield with "one of the largest estates and finest places in the country" (*MP* 38); it is "a connection exactly of the right sort; in the same country, and the same interest" (40). If it does not have the symbolic resonance of, say, Tom Jones's marriage to Sophia Western, the Bertram–Rushworth marriage nonetheless signifies a consolidation of squirarchical power, property, and wealth, and it reaffirms the continuation of the status quo through propagation. Maria and Henry's transgression flies directly in the face of such values, for it essentially disregards Rushworth's rights to his own "property." The potential threat of bastardy lies at the margins of the text, symbolically reinforced by the fact that Maria plays an unwed mother in *Lover's Vows*. As in *Amelia* adultery undermines the values that preserve the status quo, and adulterers cannot be reabsorbed into the society that they threaten.[24]

By drawing on the adultery motif Austen introduces an undermining element not only into Mansfield Park but into *Mansfield Park*. Once adultery has entered the world of the text, there can be no return to prior assumptions about the appropriateness of the status quo, despite the text's effort to establish this very point. As Tony Tanner suggests in *Adultery in the Novel*, adultery is a disruptive force for the novel genre itself: "In confronting the problems of marriage and adultery, the bourgeois novel finally has to confront not only the provisionality of social laws and rules and structures but the provisionality of its own procedures and assumptions."[25] This text's focus on adultery is much more limited than that of the bourgeois novels Tanner discusses or even that of *Amelia*, wherein adultery serves as the central problem addressed. After all, the Henry-and-Maria elopement takes place only within the last three chapters. Yet it is the crucial action of the novel, effecting the final disposition of all the major characters. Too, as with the bourgeois novels Tanner studies, the adultery motif in Mansfield implicitly undermines the surety of the values the text expresses.

As in *Amelia* adultery serves as both cause and effect of social breakdown, a positive feedback loop dismantling traditional values. Sir Thomas is the archetypal patriarch, perhaps the most formidable authority figure in the Austen canon. In a novel ostensibly pushing traditional values, we might expect that he would be their most staunch supporter. After all, despite his overabundance of pride, Darcy fulfills his patriarchal duties: he saves both Georgiana and Lydia from ruin, essentially preserving two households. Sir Thomas, however, enables or encourages the tendencies that lead to the destruction of the household. Sir Thomas errs throughout in valuing appearance over essence. Because his daughters have been educated in the surface accomplishments he is satisfied: "the Miss Bertrams continued to exercise their memories, practise their duets, and grow tall and womanly; and their father saw them becoming in person, manner, and accomplishments, every thing that could satisfy his anxiety" (*MP* 20). However, as Sir Thomas discovers too late, "with all the cost and care of an anxious and expensive education, he had brought up his daughters, without their understanding their first duties, or his being acquainted with their character and temper" (464–65). Making no attempt to delve below appearance, Sir Thomas is willing to accept Maria's feigned professions of respect for Rushworth. Prizing a blind obedience to the dictates of authority over a considered attempt to formulate right values, he browbeats Fanny in order to make her accept Henry Crawford. His manner authoritarian rather than authoritative, he prompts both Maria and Julia to flee from the restrictions he imposes.[26]

Granted, by the final chapter, Sir Thomas realizes his errors, and we must assume that he will be a better baronet in the future. But what is significant is that, unlike Darcy, the highest representative of social order in the novel facilitates, rather than quells, disorder. Nor do we have a sense that his children can do much better. Sir Thomas's heir has become, by the close of the novel, "useful to his father, steady and quiet" (*MP* 462), but we are given no instances of model behavior on Tom Bertram's part. Edmund, the guardian of Mansfield's spiritual values, gets no opportunity actively to enforce them. We have here no Darcy or Knightley to reassure us that, though flawed, the patriarch will ultimately put things to rights.

The critique of patriarchal values in *Mansfield Park* at times echoes Mary Wollstonecraft's radical *Vindication*. In the following passage, Wollstonecraft might as well be discussing Sir Thomas's confusion of external accomplishments with internal virtues, epitomized in the education he provides his daughters: "Manners and morals are so nearly allied that they have often been confounded; but, although the former should only be the natural reflection of the latter, yet when various causes have produced factitious and corrupt manners, which are very early caught, morality becomes an empty name."[27] When Wollstonecraft describes how woman's lack of real power "gives birth to cunning," we may recall how the Bertram daughters learn "to repress their spirits in [Sir Thomas's] presence" (*MP* 463), their powerlessness before their authoritarian father occasioning duplicity.[28] Even Fanny, exemplary in her powerlessness as well as in her virtue, may possess some share of this quality; we can certainly see in her some evidence of the contemporary manifestation of cunning—passive aggressive behavior. When things are not going as she would like, she tends to fall ill or assume a martyr role, as in the following passage wherein Fanny sulks at Edmund's absence: "she thought it a very bad ex-change, and if Edmund were not there to mix the wine and water for her, would rather go without it than not" (66). Finally, as the epigraph at the outset of this chapter indicates, Wollstonecraft suggests that adultery itself results from a system of female education that teaches women their only object is to render themselves pleasing to men. Once trained in the art of attracting men, women will continue to do so even after they are married, a hypothesis confirmed by Maria's actions. In *Mansfield Park* Austen gives concrete representation to some of the arguments that Wollstonecraft makes in *Vindication*.

But Austen is not here subjecting patriarchal values to a radical critique à la Wollstonecraft. Some of the same sorts of concerns that Wollstonecraft addresses are addressed by Hannah More in her Strictures on female education. She too deals with the matrimonial difficulties of a woman who has been taught only to attract and please: she will "escape to the exhibition room" and put herself on display once more; she will be "exposed to the two-fold temptation of being at once neglected by her husband, and exhibited as an object of attraction to other men."[29] Thus, although Austen's text has affinities to Wollstonecraft's, it has affinities to More's as well, and although it is tempting to regard Austen as putting forward a feminist agenda, we can just as likely regard her as putting forward a *feminine* one—one wherein women's improvement is put in service of patriarchal values. The elevation of morals over manners would sustain, rather than undermine, the authority of the Sir Thomas Bertrams of the land. Overall, Austen advocates not that traditional values be overthrown but that they be strengthened or revived— thus seemingly taking the same sort of conservative stance that we saw Fielding take in *Amelia*.

For all its conservatism, however, *Mansfield Park* unlike *Amelia* implicitly links societal breakdown to an overarching patriarchal structure. Through the fates meted out to its female characters, the text exposes the underside of a system that constrains and undermines women. Fielding gives us the exemplary Amelia, cheerful and supportive in the face of her husband's adultery, unfounded accusations, and improvidence. He also gives us transgressive female characters, such as Miss Mathews and Mrs. Atkinson, who are subject to ridicule and shown as deserving the fates they get. Austen, on the other hand, shows us that the fate of the exemplary woman is to suffer silently as she experiences the defection of the man she loves and faces conflicting demands. Even Austen's transgressive women are presented sympathetically. We are made aware that, however misguided they are, Mary Crawford, Maria Bertram, and Julia Bertram have feelings that may be wounded and manipulated. Mary does indeed care for Edmund, and when all intercourse has come to an end between them she finds herself "in need of the true kindness of her sister's heart" (*MP* 469). Maria succumbs to Henry's "animated perseverance" (468) of her, and although his pursuit of her is prompted by mere vanity, she is in love with him, hoping that he will marry her. Maria's act of adultery irrevocably destroys her reputation, necessitating her banishment from England, but Henry's will be forgiven, as Austen dryly acknowledges: "That punishment, the public punishment of disgrace, should in a just measure attend his share of the offence, is, we know, not one of the barriers, which society gives to virtue" (468). The text demonstrates the psychic toll that a patriarchal structure takes on women even as it overtly argues in favor of its soundness.

In order for traditional values to be revived and sustained, Austen—like Fielding in *Amelia*—emphasizes the important role played by religion. We might recall that one of the first acts performed by the reformed Mr. B. in *Pamela* is the reconsecration of the family chapel—a reconsecration symbolic of Pamela's accession to spiritual authority in Mr. B.'s household. Austen, too, gives symbolic resonance to the motif of the family chapel, making an implicit connection between the degeneration of the Rushworth family and the unused chapel at Sotherton. Fanny considers the custom of family prayers a vital part of the regulation of a great estate: "It was a valuable part of former times. There is something in a chapel and chaplain so much in character with a great house, with one's ideas of what such a household should be!" (*MP* 85). We are left with the sense that the continuance of such a custom may have made Rushworth less foolish and his mother less vain. We are told too that paying attention to religion might have saved the Bertram daughters from disgrace: "they had never been properly taught to govern their inclinations and tempers by that sense of duty which alone can suffice. They had been instructed theoretically in their religion, but never required to bring it into daily practice" (463). Religion it seems might provide the missing element that would keep society on track.

As the clergyman son of a noble family Edmund would appear to provide a hope for the future. Attempting to justify his choice of profession to Mary Crawford he prescribes the proper function of a clergyman, a prescription to which he will no doubt adhere:

> And with regard to their influencing public manners, Miss Crawford must not misunderstand me, or suppose I mean to call them the arbiters of good breeding, the regulators of refinement and courtesy, the masters of the ceremonies of life. The manners I speak of might rather be called conduct, perhaps, the result of good principles; the effect, in short, of those doctrines which it is their duty to teach and recommend; and it will, I believe, be every where found, that as the clergy are, or are not what they ought to be, so are the rest of the nation. (*MP* 93)

The proper clergyman as Edmund defines him could supply what is wanting in the Bertram daughters, in the Crawfords, in the household at Sotherton, in society at large.

Although the text gives us an optimistic glimpse of what that revitalized society might be, it concurrently undermines the likelihood of such a society occurring. In the world of Mansfield, Mary's succinct comment that "A clergyman is nothing" (*MP* 92) seems more apt. During the discussion of the Sotherton chapel, Mary offers an astute—if tactless—rejoinder to Fanny's notion about the importance and efficacy of family prayers: "It must do the heads of the family a great deal of good to force all the poor housemaids and footmen to leave business and pleasure, and say their prayers here twice a day, while they are inventing excuses themselves for staying away" (86–87). Fanny and Edmund take umbrage at Mary's remarks, Austen nudging us to identify with their values. Yet the dialogic interchange undermines our surety that religion ever did or could have the sort of regulatory power with which Edmund and Fanny invest it. Mary's high-spirited comment that "The young Mrs. Eleanors and Mrs. Bridgers" had their "heads full of something very different-especially if the poor chaplain were not worth looking at" compels us to consider that reinstituting family prayers may simply lead to false piety (87).

Rather than influencing others to do well, Edmund tends to be influenced by others to go against his principles. Granted, when he gives in to the others over the play, he is not yet ordained, but he clearly knows it is his duty to dissuade, not succumb. Although by the close of the novel Edmund has presumably become a proper shepherd to his flock, the only instance we have of his pastoral influence is the guidance he gives Fanny during her youth—and by the time of the actual story, teacher and pupil seem to have changed places. The only other clergyman in the novel is Dr. Grant, who, as Mary indecorously but accurately says, is "an indolent selfish bon vivant, who must have his palate consulted in every thing, who will not stir a finger for the convenience of any one, and who, moreover, if the cook makes a blunder, is out of humour with his excellent wife" (*MP* 111). With Dr. Grant, Austen gives us a picture of a bad clergyman in the tradition of Mr. Collins and Mr. Elton, and we are compelled to wonder whether this picture is not more apt than the one she gives us of Edmund Bertram. In any case, Austen does not reassure us as to the corrective influence of the clergy.

Because Austen gives neither Crawford an internal moment of self-revelation, we are left with the feeling that they will continue their thoughtless ways. Certainly, we are told that they regret their past actions. Mary, after all, is "long in finding" someone who can "put Edmund Bertram sufficiently out of her head" (*MP* 469). But she nonetheless is "perfectly resolved against ever attaching herself to a younger brother again"—a sign that she has not renounced the mercenary interests that made her wish for Tom Bertram's death. Henry, we are told, ends up with "no small portion of vexation and regret" (468). But as we get this information only in summary, we are divorced from any emotional involvement; we do not get a sense of the potency of Henry's pain as we get, for example, from Willoughby's anguished confession to Elinor in *Sense and Sensibility*. In forgiving Henry, society will enable if not encourage him to follow the course he has always followed.

Mansfield Park ends on an apparently happy note, like *Amelia*, but this conclusion—similar to that of Fielding's text—offers us little hope of societal reformation. In the final pages we are told that Tom Bertram has become "useful" and "steady"; Lady Bertram has found Susan to be an indispensable companion; Sir Thomas has discovered "the daughter he wanted"; and most important, Fanny and Edmund have been united in marriage. Tanner regards this marriage as a positive outcome: "a marriage it is, and a celebratory one, symbolising or suggesting more far-reaching reconciliations and restorations; a paradigmatic marriage for society in a larger sense, which transcends personal gratifications."[30] But the conclusion of *Mansfield Park* is suggestive of alienation and exclusion rather than of celebration and reconciliation. The effects of adultery, like those of a stone thrown in a pond, spread beyond the original incident, leaving havoc in their wake. Henry and Maria must be expelled from the world of Mansfield because their action threatens social breakdown. Despite their expulsion, however, social breakdown nevertheless occurs. The adultery divides Edmund from Mary, the Grants and the Rushworths from the Bertrams, and the Bertrams from one another. Whereas the ending of *Pride and Prejudice* allows all to join in the final celebration, this is not the case with *Mansfield Park*. Even Lady Catherine, with all her arrogance and bossiness, can finally be readmitted to Pemberley; Aunt Norris, on the other hand, must die in exile.

Too, although clearly put forward as a happy event, the marriage of Edmund and Fanny is nevertheless suggestive of social regression. Several recent discussions of *Mansfield Park* have dealt with the troubling "incest" motif in the novel, and I think that we cannot ignore its symbolic import.[31] Cousin marriage, though legally sanctioned, still manages to invoke the old incest taboo. By continually referring to the consanguineous connection between Fanny and Edmund, Austen ensures that we keep this thought before us. At the end of the novel Fanny and Edmund are not "the married couple" but "the married cousins" (*MP* 473), their kinship relationship seemingly more important than their marital one. In his study of the connection between the incest taboo and social structure, Talcott Parsons suggests that the taboo enables the proper functioning of society: "it is essential that persons should be capable of assuming roles which contribute to functions which no nuclear family is able to perform, which involve the assumption of non-familial roles. Only if such non-familial roles can be adequately staffed can a society function." Without the incest taboo there can be no "formation and maintenance of supra-familial bonds on which major economic, political and religious functions of the society are dependent."[32] The happy ending for Fanny and Edmund is paradigmatic of the ending of social intercourse. Mansfield may have its emblematic function restored, but this function will not extend beyond its grounds. We might playfully extend Austen's story and envision a marriage between Susan—"the stationary niece"—and the other Bertram son.[33]

What happens with the triangular romantic configurations in the novel reinforces the motif of *Mansfield Park* closing in on itself. In Volume I (wherein Fanny is not "out") we have Mary Crawford and the two Bertram brothers and Henry Crawford and the two Bertram sisters. Once Fanny has entered the game the configurations shift, and their elements are reduced; the triangles now consist of Mary–Edmund–Fanny and Edmund–Fanny–Henry. By the novel's conclusion only the two elements both triangles have in common—the cousins Fanny and Edmund—remain.

The final centering of Edmund and Fanny within the household does indeed make clear that moral values have been restored to Mansfield Park. As Tony Tanner points out, Fanny is "the true inheritor of Mansfield Park."[34] Although Tom Bertram is the actual heir, Fanny and Edmund—installed in the living on the estate—presumably inherit Sir Thomas's moral authority and hold out the promise that Mansfield Park may attain the ideal that Fanny envisioned while exiled to Portsmouth.[35] As a good conduct-book heroine, of course, Fanny will work behind the scenes in her domestic realm, leaving to clergyman Edmund the active enforcement and modeling of morality.

But such moral revitalization is achieved at what cost? The first line of the final chapter has often been marked as signaling Austen's desire to hurry through the process of tying things up. What has not often been marked is the statement's irony. When Austen proclaims, "Let other pens dwell on guilt and misery" (*MP* 461), we expect that she intends to have done with such subjects. But rather than abandoning them she revels in them. The happy ending is offset by language hammering us with reminders of the unhappy events that have taken place, as the following somber litany, culled from the final chapter, demonstrates:

> guilt misery odious melancholy suffering disappointment regret sorry sorrow misery self-reproach anguish evil grievous bitterly wretchedly disappointment wretchedness hatred punishment misery despised disappointments punishment punishment guilt mortified unhappy reproach melancholy destroyed misery punishment evil bitter danger evil irritation tormenting hurtful disappointment bitterness dread horrors selfish guilt folly ruined cold-blooded coldness repulsive mortified anger regretting

> punishment punishment vexation regret vexation self-reproach
> regret wretchedness wound alienate distressing regret
> disappointment apoplexy death regretting anxious doubting sick
> poor hardship struggle death painful alarm.

No wonder we have trouble with Austen's claim that "the happiness of the married cousins must appear as secure as earthly happiness can be" (473). Such a positive statement lays but a thin veneer over the negative terms embedded within the chapter. In order "to complete the picture of good" (the accession of Fanny and Edmund to the Mansfield living), "the death of Dr. Grant" must occur, the happiness of the principles thus dependent upon the misfortune of others (473).

This is not to say that we can ignore the strong argument in favor of traditional values that is presented in the novel. The happy ending that rewards Fanny and Edmund ratifies the values they espouse. Although the Mansfield community ends up reorganized in part, it nevertheless revolves around most of its original members, the return to the status quo confirming the soundness of things as they are. Moreover, the argument of *Mansfield* is quite in keeping with views Austen expresses in a letter, which appeared soon after the publication of the text, in which she gives her niece Fanny Knight advice about a suitor:

> And as to there being any objection from his *Goodness*, from the danger of his becoming even Evangelical, I cannot admit that. I am by no means convinced that we ought not all to be Evangelicals, & am at least persuaded that they who are so from Reason and Feeling, must be happiest & safest.—Do not be frightened from the connection by your Brothers having most wit. Wisdom is better than Wit, & in the long run will certainly have the laugh on her side; & don't be frightened by the idea of his acting more strictly up to the precepts of the New Testament than others. (Letter 103, *LSC* 410)

Wisdom does indeed seem to have the laugh on her side as Austen banishes the Crawfords from the sacrosanct grounds of Mansfield and installs Fanny and Edmund as guardians of the Old World order.

We, on the other hand, do not laugh. Not (as sometimes has been argued) because we are uncomfortable with an Austen who validates the status quo. After all, she does pretty much the same thing in the beloved *Pride and Prejudice* when she lets super-patriarch Darcy save the day. We are uncomfortable with an Austen who puts forward an argument in favor of tradition but who presents evidence that makes another case entirely.

Mansfield Park (as does *Amelia*) poses a problem to its readers in that the ideological conflicts are never satisfactorily resolved. Austen here embraces the traditional conduct-book heroine, a figure she had earlier ridiculed; in doing so she ostensibly embraces the conduct-book novel. There is not, as in the first inheritance plot in *Pride and Prejudice*, a direct confrontation with the patriarchal system of estate settlement, not is there any sense that the nontraditional woman may revitalize the estate. Whatever revitalization Mansfield Park undergoes occurs because Fanny adheres to tradition, seeing more clearly than the patriarch how she can best serve him. If we regard *Mansfield Park* simply as an exemplary conduct-book novel, then we can say that Austen puts her authorial vocation in the service of a patriarchal literary tradition, creating a model version of feminine behavior.

Like *Amelia*, however, *Mansfield Park* works against its own ostensible aims. Austen speaks with a double voice, as she does in *Pride and Prejudice*, and she subtly interweaves her championing of traditional values with her critique of patriarchal institutions that define and deny women. Like Fanny, Austen generally is eminently ladylike and proper in expressing her sentiments here. Yet, also like Fanny, she draws our attention to the vexed position in which the exemplary woman finds herself. When Fanny, discussing Henry's proposal with Edmund, attempts to articulate the truth of a woman's experience she mirrors her creator, turning a perceptive eye to the ambiguities of lived experience for women in her society. Austen may try her hand at the conduct-book novel of her predecessors, but she problematizes its didactic tendencies and reveals, perhaps unwittingly, that this particular literary lineage has come to an end.

NOTES

1. Lionel Trilling, *The Opposing Self: New Essays in Criticism*, 214.

2. Johnson, *Women, Politics, and the Novel*, 119.

3. Austen's "problem novel" has, not surprisingly, received a good deal of critical attention over the last few decades—perhaps because it mitigates against any facile assumption of a coherent political stance on Austen's part. *Mansfield Park* has divided the critics as to whether it espouses conservative or subversive values. Duckworth has argued for its status as the paradigm text in the Austen canon—a Burkean affirmation of "improvement" over "innovation" (*Improvement of the Estate*). His chapter on *Mansfield Park* is the first chapter in a study that is otherwise ordered chronologically. Butler, in *War of Ideas*, similarly argues for Austen's essential conservatism, regarding

Sense and Sensibility and *Mansfield Park* as exemplary. Said makes a case for the text's complicity in "imperialist expansion," arguing that it is "the most explicit in its ideological and moral affirmations of Austen's novels" (*Culture and Imperialism*, 84). Johnson in *Women, Politics, and the Novel* makes her case for a subversive Austen, arguing that *Mansfield Park* parodies conservative fiction and puts forth a consistent argument about the hollowness of the gentry's moral pretensions. I might point out that to an earlier generation of Austen readers the conservatism of Mansfield Park was taken as a given (and regarded as off-putting). One of the most recent debates over the novel occurs in Whit Stillman's witty film *Metropolitan*, wherein the Fanny-like heroine defends the novel to the hero, who, citing Lionel Trilling, calls it "notoriously bad" (Whit Stillman, writer and director, Westerly Films, 1991).

4. Nina Auerbach, *Romantic Imprisonment: Women and Other Glorified Outcasts*, 22–37.

5. Tanner, *Jane Austen*, 143, 156. See Trilling's comments on Fanny as a Christian heroine (*The Opposing Self*, 129). Andrew Wright defends Fanny on similar grounds in *Jane Austen's Novels: A Study in Structure* (New York: Oxford University Press, 1961), 124.

6. Auerbach, *Romantic Imprisonment*, 25, 27.

7. Gilbert and Gubar in *Madwoman in the Attic* argue that Austen's heroines are punished for their flights of imagination. None, however, end up adhering to a standard of proper female behavior that the notion of punishment implies.

8. See Jacques Donzelot, *The Policing of Families*, 171.

9. In his biography of Austen, Park Honan implies that the private theatricals the Austen family enjoyed in 1787—wherein they were joined by their glamorous cousin Eliza de Feuillide—may have provided a real-life instance of morally upright young men succumbing to the charms of a worldly young woman: "it is probably true that before the rehearsals of *The Wonder* were over, both James and Henry were in love with [Eliza].... [Henry's] feeling for Eliza might have been predictable, but his behavior was as unusual as James's neglect of clerical decorum. Jane Austen's attitude to theatricals was not that of Fanny Price in *Mansfield Park*, but she did have a chance to see how rehearsals mix with seduction" (*Her Life*, 50).

10. Trilling, *The Opposing Self*, 129.

11. Wollstonecraft, *Vindication*, 111–12.

12. Gilbert and Gubar, *Madwoman in the Attic*, 165.

13. This situation may be akin to the one Austen faced when Harris Wither proposed—a proposal she initially accepted but then turned down. Honan suggests that Austen probably had no idea she was the object of Wither's affections until he actually proposed: "nothing obviously had induced her to view him as a lover before he spoke. Initial attraction, flirtation and a deep, particular concern develop within a social world subject to intense social scrutiny, but neither she nor Cassandra nor anyone else could have seen that happening in her relations with poor Harris" (*Her Life*, 194).

14. Richardson, *Clarissa*, 40.

15. Ibid., 1466.

16. Bradbrook, *Jane Austen and Her Predecessors*, 123.

17. More, *Strictures*, 2:119. Spencer argues that "Jane Austen is deliberately undercutting the complacent belief in the power of love to reform" (*Rise of the Woman Novelist*, 174). Samuel Richardson himself turned the rake-reformed model on its head with Lovelace in *Clarissa*, but his purpose was not to show the receding power of the exemplary woman but the extraordinary fortitude with which she was possessed.

18. Armstrong, *Desire and Domestic Fiction*, 41.

19. Richardson, *Clarissa*, 1495, 1498.

20. Frances Burney, *Cecilia, or Memoirs of an Heiress*, 585.

21. David Spring argues that "the theme of landed decay and crisis has been taken to extremes" in interpretations of *Mansfield Park*: "It needs therefore to be said again that the world of the rural elite was neither going bankrupt in the early nineteenth century nor disintegrating spiritually and socially." Although he acknowledges that Austen might have "read the nature of her society differently from the way we might," he does not give that notion much credit ("Interpreters of Jane Austen's Social World," 66–67). I would, however, argue that even if there were no actual crisis, Austen perceived one, as the novels indicate.

22. In a letter to Cassandra, Austen noted that their brother Henry, who was then reading *Mansfield Park*, "admires H. Crawford: I mean properly as a clever, pleasant man" (Letter 92, *LSC* 377–78).

23. See Q.D. Leavis, "Jane Austen," *A Selection from "Scrutiny,"* 2:1–80.

24. For Copeland it is not adultery but runaway consumption that poses the greatest threat to the values of *Mansfield Park* (*Women Writing about Money*, 102–6). Copeland notes, however, the connection between runaway consumption and sexual transgression: "Consumer desire fuels the moral action of *Mansfield Park*, and sexual desire is inextricably intertwined in the struggle" (102).

25. Tanner, *Adultery in the Novel*, 15.

26. Johnson provides a thorough account of the failures of Sir Thomas: "He quiets but he does not quell lawlessness; his children tremble at the detection, rather than the commission of wrongs" (*Women, Politics, and the Novel*, 97). Unlike Johnson, however, I do not find in Austen an overall rejection of the values for which Sir Thomas stands.

27. Wollstonecraft, *Vindication*, 86. For an extended argument about Wollstonecraft's influence on Austen, see Kirkham, *Feminism and Fiction*. Although I think Kirkham exaggerates Austen's feminist tendencies, the connections she makes are provocative. For a discussion of Austen's and Wollstonecraft's methods of dealing with constructions of femininity, see Poovey, *The Proper Lady*.

28. Wollstonecraft, *Vindication*, 83.

29. More, *Strictures*, 2:163. Guest discusses the affinities between the conservative More and the radical Wollstonecraft in "The Dream of a Common

Language." As Guest implies, women who were politically opposed could find a common ground as they considered means for female improvement. Yet, as I suggest, although the means may be the same, the ends are different.

30. Tanner, *Jane Austen*, 173.

31. Johnson regards the incest motif as reinforcing Austen's critique of patriarchy. See also Johanna M. Smith's argument that the motif "demonstrate[s] the constrictions of sister–brother love," in "'My Only Sister Now': Incest in *Mansfield Park*" (13). For an argument on the positive nature of the incestuous marriage see Glenda A. Hudson, "Incestuous Relationships: *Mansfield Park* Revisited."

32. Talcott Parsons, "The Incest Taboo in Relation to Social Structure," 21, 19.

33. Marilyn Sachs notes that Mrs. Francis Brown's 1930 *Susan Price, or Resolution*, a sequel to *Mansfield Park*, features such a cousin marriage. See her essay "The Sequels to Jane Austen's Novels," 375.

34. Tanner, *Jane Austen*, 157. Tanner discusses the main characters in *Mansfield Park* in terms of "guardians," "inheritors," and "interlopers" (142–75).

35. Greene argues that in *Mansfield Park*, "Jane Austen comes as close as she ever does to a thoroughgoing presentation of a Tory democracy" ("Jane Austen and the Peerage," 163). It is a Tory democracy that Fanny envisions.

JOHN WILTSHIRE

"The Hartfield Edition":
Jane Austen and Shakespeare

Critics have consistently linked Jane Austen's name with Shakespeare's. One of Jane Austen's first promoters, Richard Whately, remarked that she conducts conversations with "a regard to character hardly exceeded even by Shakespeare himself" (Southam 98). Lord Macaulay wrote in 1843 that "among the writers who have approached nearest to the manner of the great master, we have no hesitation in placing Jane Austen, a woman of whom England is justly proud" (603). George Lewes, who declared that Macaulay had referred to Austen as a "prose Shakespeare," thought her, with Fielding, the greatest novelist in English, and praised her as one who, in contrast to Scott, possessed "Shakespearean" qualities of "tenderness and passion," and "marvellous dramatic power" (Southam 125). Tennyson also spoke of Jane Austen as "next to Shakespeare" in her "realism and the life-likeness of her characters." (24). This nineteenth-century tradition was summarized by A. C. Bradley in 1911. He wrote of Jane Austen's "surpassing excellence within that comparatively narrow sphere whose limits she never tried to overpass ... which ... gives her in that sphere the position held by Shakespeare in his" (32).

Austen's most important nineteenth-century critic, Richard Simpson, a Shakespearean scholar, writing in 1870, also remarked on her dramatic quality. In addition, Simpson introduced the new idea that her relation to

From *Persuasions* no. 21 (1999). © 1999 by John Wiltshire.

Shakespeare was not one of resemblance merely, but of indebtedness or influence. Giving a particular illustration of earlier critics' claims, he describes Miss Bates's talk as being made up of "the same concourse of details" as that which makes up Mistress Quickly's in *Henry IV part II* (Southam 262). Moreover, "Anne Elliot is Shakespeare's Viola translated into an English girl of the nineteenth century." "Miss Austen," he declares more explicitly, "must surely have had Shakespeare's *Twelfth Night* in her mind while she was writing this novel" (*Persuasion*). He argued that the novelist remembered the dialogue between Orsino and the disguised Viola when she wrote the exchanges between Captain Harville and Anne Elliot in which Anne speaks of women's constancy, and indirectly of her own.

Contemporary writers take up this link between Shakespeare and Austen. Claire Tomalin compares *Mansfield Park* with *The Merchant of Venice* to suggest how "Shakespeare's play and Austen's novel are both so alive and flexible as works of art that they can be interpreted now one way, now another" (229). Closer relationships have often been claimed. "Like *Mansfield Park*, Shakespearean drama characteristically pivots upon the performance of a play within a play," claims Nina Auerbach, who compares Fanny Price's reluctance to act with Hamlet's (55–6). More persuasively, Roger Gard compares the "lethal rationality" of the conversation in Chapter 2 of *Sense and Sensibility* between Fanny and John Dashwood with the dialogue in which Lear's daughters progressively strip their father of all his comforts (77–8). More wholesale recapitulations of Shakespeare have been suggested: Isobel Armstrong has seen many affinities between Shakespeare's *As You Like It* and *Henry VIII* and *Mansfield Park*. Jocelyn Harris has argued that *Emma* is a reimagining of *A Midsummer Night's Dream*.[1]

What are the grounds for this assumption that Jane Austen was so familiar with Shakespeare that she was continually echoing and reworking his plays? One might turn to the discussion of Shakespeare in *Mansfield Park*. Responding to Edmund Bertram's congratulations on his reading of *Henry VIII*, Henry Crawford remarks: "'I once saw Henry the 8th acted.—Or I have heard of it from somebody who did—I am not certain which. But Shakespeare one gets acquainted with without knowing how. It is part of an Englishman's constitution ... one is intimate with him by instinct.'" Edmund Bertram's response is less indolent and more intelligent: "'His celebrated passages are quoted by every body; they are in half the books we open,'" he says, "'we all talk Shakespeare, use his similes, and describe with his descriptions'" (*MP* 338).

All but Miss Austen, that is. Unlike Fanny Burney, for example, Austen rarely uses those Shakespearean expressions that have passed into the language—the milk of human kindness, my almost blunted purpose, the finger of scorn, from top to toe. She does not use his similes and describe with his descriptions. Scott (and Dickens, too) show far more obvious signs of indebtedness to Shakespeare than Austen does. Moreover, Austen often mocks Shakespeare, as near the opening of the "History of England," by "a partial, prejudiced and ignorant historian": "[T]he Prince of Wales came and took away the crown, whereupon the King made a long speech, for which I must refer the Reader to Shakespeare's Plays, & the Prince made a still longer. Things being thus settled between them the King died ..." (139).

Catherine Morland, "in training for a heroine," acquires a store of "those quotations which are so serviceable and so soothing in the vicissitudes of their eventful lives" (*NA* 15). Among them are three from "Shakspeare," made to sound extremely silly as items in a keepsake book, including the lines from *Measure for Measure* about the beetle that we tread upon feeling a pang as great as when a giant dies, and those lines from *Twelfth Night* that Simpson suggested were her source in *Persuasion*, which declare, as Austen disingenuously claims, "that a young woman in love always looks" like Patience on a monument. When Emma declares that a "Hartfield edition" of Shakespeare would need a long note on the line from *A Midsummer Night's Dream*, "the course of true love never did run smooth," she too is less than reverential towards the writer whom the eighteenth century treated with "bardolatry." Can this skittish attitude towards Shakespeare be reconciled with any deep dept or affinity?

I propose that Shakespeare's impact on Jane Austen is not to be discovered on the surface, but is structural. A hint at what this might mean is in K. C. Philips's study of Jane Austen's language. Commenting that "Jane Austen shows great freedom, and even daring, in her conversion and use of almost any part of speech as any other part of speech," he remarks that "Shakespeare was the precursor to whom she might look in this.... At least two of her conversions emanate from *Hamlet*." He instances "[e]ver since her being turned into a Churchill she has out-Churchill'd them all in high and mighty claims" (*E* 310), which "echoes" Hamlet's famous "out-Herods Herod" (200). His point is that Austen does not imitate the semantic content but instead replicates the grammatical structure made possible by Shakespeare.

This may at least suggest the level of Jane Austen's relation to Shakespeare. More importantly, one can question the very notion of influence itself. The term influence originally meant the action of the stars on human affairs—a direct, unmediated, magical transmission. This is the way influence is often conceived—especially by the Romantics: it literally flows in upon someone from an outside source. It is certainly an ancient way of conceiving the relation of one writer to another. But there is an alternative mode of thought. In Seneca, Horace, and others we come across the idea of the later writer being like a bee, gathering honey from his original. More elaborately, we have the idea that the later writer gathers food from the source, and digests it, making it part of his own body. This tradition is put memorably by Ben Jonson in his collection of thoughts *Timber, or Discoveries*:

> The third requisite in our poet or maker is imitation, *imitatio*, to be able to convert the substance or riches of another poet to his own use.... Not as a creature that swallows what it takes in, crude, raw, or undigested; but that feeds with an appetite, and hath a stomach to concoct, divide, and turn all to nourishment. Not to imitate servilely, as Horace saith, and catch at vices for virtue, but to draw forth out of the best and choicest flowers, with the bee, and turn all into honey, work it into one relish and savour; make our imitation sweet. (119)

There is an interesting convergence between this way of seeing relatedness between authors and a much more modern way of seeing relatedness between people and the others who have been important to them—psychoanalysis. Psychoanalytic thought speaks of our "identification" with others, but also of our incorporating others into our psychic life. This is because psychoanalysis is theoretically committed to the view that all psychic processes are extrapolations, or sophistications, of very early experiences of the infant. These are of necessity primarily physical. Psychoanalysis therefore proposes that the infant's earliest experience of consuming the mother, actually taking her in—taking in her milk—becomes elaborated in our later "incorporation" of others. Others are taken into the self as "internal objects," by which is meant a strong impression or memory that becomes a formative part of the self. An important component of the notion of incorporation is processing. The self takes in the other, but also, as when we eat, breaks it down, making it, in the process of incorporation, something else, part of the "new" self's own substance.

This model offers a more complex analogy for thinking about the relation between authors than does the idea of influence. Influence is like milk, taken in and absorbed, unproblematically. Alternatively, one can think of the other writer as solid food, offering much more resistance to incorporation, requiring much more psychological and creative labor to incorporate. "These are obviously no more than ideas, suggestions about a difficult to define process that has many levels and may differ greatly from author to author. But this is the analogy I propose to keep in mind with Jane Austen.

The very fact that Shakespeare wrote plays and Austen novels provides a barrier to the notion of direct or unmediated influence. Obviously, the act of conversion of a play into a novel must always be a complex one: the transposition of forms of dramatic action into the other techniques required by the novel seems to prevent the application of an unproblematic notion of literary imitation. A sculpture can't imitate a painting, or an opera a play, without immense recreative labor, and in the course of this the artist must substitute his or her own purpose and design for the original, even whilst he or she may be aiming for the "same" or an equivalent effect. This is as obviously true of the film "adaptations" of Austen's novels (as of Shakespeare's plays). When they are successful, they move away from the attempt to be faithful to, or capitalize on, the novels, and instead recreate something obtained from the novels by employing radically different means.

The term "recreation" in fact is a helpful one. This is partly because of its punning quality. It includes the idea of "recreation" as play, as well as the idea of remaking. The idea of play suggests that the later artist has attained a state of freedom from the earlier, no longer constrained by, or working in deference to, his or her authority. Sometimes this state of freedom manifests itself in the desire to "make over" or destroy the original. But any account of the relationship between two artists that emphasizes the aggressive motif that is certainly implicit in the notion of incorporation is bound to be partial and incomplete.[2] Poets and novelists have no biological ties to their predecessors: they *choose* their artistic parents. We must therefore have a theory of creative love before we have a coherent theory of creative rivalry.

I should pause for a moment and give an idea of what I mean by recreation. One of the very earliest reviewers of *Pride and Prejudice* remarked that Elizabeth Bennet is "the Beatrice of the piece" and thus saw immediately that the dialogues between Elizabeth and Darcy resemble the contests of wit between the heroine of *Much Ado About Nothing* and Benedict. As an example: in company with Darcy and Bingley, Mrs Bennet is boasting that Jane was so pretty at fifteen that "a gentleman" wrote "some verses on her." "'And so ended his affection,'" said Elizabeth impatiently. "'There has been many a one, I fancy, overcome in the same way. I wonder who first discovered the efficacy of poetry in driving away love!'" Darcy replies quickly, "'I have been used to consider poetry as the *food* of love.'" Elizabeth returns: "'Of a fine stout healthy love it may be, but I am convinced that one good sonnet will starve it entirely away'" (44).

If the contest between these two figures does remind us of Beatrice and Benedick, the material of their exchange alludes to another Shakespeare comedy, *Twelfth Night*, or rather to its famous opening lines. The dialogue is used to suggest that the participants have more in common with each other than they know. When Elizabeth says "'I wonder who first discovered ...?'" she is putting lightly a historical or cultural question and it is this hint that Darcy is able to respond to with his play on Shakespeare's line. He in fact *feeds* her this line so that she can go on to cap her earlier comment. But it's also notable that Elizabeth's remark expresses a refreshing scepticism about the relation of true feeling to literary expression. So whilst the exchange is "feeding off" Shakespeare, it is simultaneously questioning whether repeating the language of another can ever express true feeling. We tend to find some such mark of independence, of recreation as play, whenever we detect Austen "using" or alluding to Shakespeare.

One might well conclude that the impact on her work of Austen's reading of Shakespeare is impossible to prove. Nevertheless, as the discussion in *Mansfield Park* suggests, Shakespeare probably was important to Jane Austen. In the second part of this paper I shall briefly outline two main areas in which one might plausibly discern his presence. To begin with Macaulay's suggestive equation: as Fanny Burney is to Ben Jonson, Jane Austen is to Shakespeare. In Burney's novels, he wrote, we find "striking groups of eccentric characters, each governed by his own peculiar whim, each talking his own peculiar jargon, and each bringing out by opposition the oddities of all the rest." In Shakespeare's characters, by contrast, he thought, "no single feature is extravagantly overcharged" (605, 604). He implies that the effect of individuality in Austen is achieved by some form of parallelism or affinity rather than "opposition," but Macaulay does not explore this consequence of his terms. I suggest that it is the multiplication of lines of connection between figures which gives the sense of an integrated "world" in Shakespeare's plays and Austen's novels, whilst simultaneously generating the sense of depth and moral drama. This successfully gives the effect of verisimilitude, whilst at the same time brings the pleasures of a tightly organized psychological or moral argument.

Shakespearean criticism has often recognized that characteristic feature of his work that Hazlitt in 1817 called "the use he makes of the principle of analogy"[3] and A. P. Rossiter in 1961 called "beautifully complicated parallelisms" (52). More recently G. K. Hunter has described the characteristic: "creation of meaning by antithetical structuring" (392) in the romantic comedies, and Graham Bradshaw has similarly spoken of "dramatic 'rhyming'" (63–8). As Bradshaw points out, "it is by now a critical commonplace to observe that *Hamlet* presents the differing responses of three sons and a daughter to the loss of their fathers, so that our reactions to Fortinbras, Laertes, or Ophelia figure in our thinking about Hamlet." Bradshaw goes on to demonstrate that it is often the case that the resemblance, the "rhyming," is "'off' in some dramatically pointed or provoking way; there is enough of a resemblance to set us thinking about differences, which may be far more important" (64).

It is clear enough that the employment of allusions and cross references between characters, rather than sharp contrasts, becomes a crucial part of the three novels written at Chawton. Consider how Fanny Price as virtual orphan and ward is rhymed by Mary and Henry Crawford as orphans and wards, how the influence of one adopted uncle is paralleled with the influence of another, how the notion of fraternal love is worked through the Crawfords, through Fanny and William and through Fanny and Edmund. Or reflect how Emma's dependence on the whims of her hypochondriac father is echoed or duplicated by Frank Churchill's dependence on the whims of his hypochondriac adoptive mother, and how Frank's inventive mischief—serving an erotic purpose—throws light on Emma's mischief, where the underlying impulses are less obvious. If *Hamlet* presents a range of different reactions to loss, consider the varieties of mourning that are represented and "rhymed" throughout *Persuasion*.

The other point of comparison relates to the representation of inner life. Jane Austen's later novels employ "free indirect discourse" as a mode of representing the private thoughts and feelings of her characters. Consciousness is narrated as a sequence of unspoken sentences, often overlayed or colored with irony. The form of free indirect discourse allows the narrator to move in and out of a character's thoughts, here giving there directly, there summarizing and commenting, all in a seamless continuum. Emma often talks to herself, but it is a deeper level of inner life that free indirect discourse is able to represent. The heroines of the two other Chawton novels, Fanny Price and Anne Elliot, are more withdrawn, more introspective, and Austen more consistently uses free indirect discourse with them to suggest aspects of the self that are less easy to access, that are less directly available, than the "secrets" about which Emma laughs to herself. She uses it to imply motives or feelings that emerge into light only when they have been elicited or disentangled from other motives and thoughts that harbor them.

In her presentation of such inner life, Jane Austen, I believe, must have absorbed the soliloquies of Shakespeare's characters. These are of different kinds, and perform many different functions, some of them merely giving the audience information, but there would be general agreement that the most remarkable of them (the most "Shakespearean") have two main characteristics. They express feelings or intentions that sharply contrast with the demeanor of the character in society (Hamlet's ironic wit at court, followed by "O that this too, too solid flesh would melt") and they vividly express psychological conflict. It is these two aspects of the soliloquy that Jane Austen adopts and adapts in her representation of the inner life of Fanny and Anne.

In this paper I shall comment only on Fanny Price. There are many resemblances between Fanny's situation and that of Helena in Shakespeare's *All's Well That Ends Well*, not the least of them being that both heroines are secretly, passionately and tenaciously in love with young men named Bertram.[4] Helena's feelings about her Bertram are revealed in two soliloquies after the family has left the stage. Her imagination is full of him, yet she knows she cannot marry Bertram, the difference in their social positions is too great. She feels that he is so far above her in status that she might as well love "a bright particular star / And think to wed it." She struggles to overcome her feelings, though not very determinedly, and seems to resign herself to an unfulfilled, hapless love.

Just as Helena's thoughts are divulged in a soliloquy after a departure, Fanny Price's feelings about Edmund are divulged in a passage of free indirect discourse after he leaves her with the words that she is "one of his two dearest." "[T]hough it told her no more than what she had long perceived, it was a stab;—for it told of his own convictions and views.... It was a stab, in spite of every long-standing expectation; and she was obliged to repeat again and again that she was one of his two dearest, before the words gave her any sensation" (*MP* 264). Fanny Price too, feels that Edmund is too far above her for her ever to marry him. Like Helena, she feels her desires are transgressive. "To think of him as Miss Crawford might be justified in thinking, would in her be insanity. To her, he could be nothing under any circumstances—nothing dearer than a friend. Why did such an idea occur to her even enough to be reprobated and forbidden? It ought not to have touched on the confines of her imagination" (264–65).

More importantly, Jane Austen's representation of Fanny's inner thoughts derives not from Helena's soliloquies but from the way Shakespeare represents private psychological lite in most of his later plays. Jane Austen has taken from the dramatist what Hazlitt, the critical contemporary of Jane Austen, referred to as "Shakespear's peculiar manner of conveying the painful struggle of different thoughts and feelings, labouring for utterance and almost strangled in the birth" (Bate 175–6). This Shakespearean sense of emotional complexity, and particularly of the emergence of one feeling out of another, as if one feeling were hiding behind or within another, is not something that requires intense study of the plays—it will strike anyone who reads or sees an effective performance of *Hamlet* or *Macbeth*. This is what we find when Fanny's love for Edmund emerges out of her attempts to repress it, or when Anne's desire for Wentworth bursts through her struggles for rational self-control. "Now, how were his sentiments to be read? Was this like wishing to avoid her? And the next moment she was hating herself for the folly which asked the question" (*P* 60).

Perhaps the comparison can be made sharper. Is it too much to imagine that the exclamations and repetitions that convey emotional strain and conflict within the thoughts of Austen's heroines derive from her assimilation of Shakespeare's plays? "Could she believe Miss Crawford to deserve him, it would be—Oh! how different would it be—how far more tolerable!" Fanny thinks to herself (264). These are dramatic moments, but the way they puncture and punctuate the run of thoughts makes there quite different from the overblown gestures and language that are so consistently the substance of dramatic speech in Burney or Elizabeth Inchbald.

I would argue then that Jane Austen did learn a great deal from Shakespeare, but that she did not imitate him. One might say rather that she had forgotten Shakespeare than that she remembered him. She learned how to organize a dramatic presentation so that it would simultaneously express a moral or psychological problem, and she learned how to present the complex inner life of characters, through a mode that none of her predecessors in the novel, not Burney, not Richardson, could readily have taught her. If, however, we call the novels "re-readings" of Shakespeare's plays, I believe we are indulging our own fancies and merely molding the novelist into a replica of the critic.

To conclude, then. When Emma imagines "the Hartfield Edition" of Shakespeare she is full of "enchanting hubris" (Harris 169), imaginatively rivaling her great predecessor. Later in the novel she quotes Shakespeare again, but in a very different style. "The world is not their friend, nor the world's law": the line from *Romeo and Juliet* she calls up to express her feeling about the concessions that might be granted to a person in Jane Fairfax's situation reflects too her own now chastened mood. Jane Austen may he alluding to a letter in Johnson's *Rambler* (107) as much as she is to Shakespeare.[5] If so, not just one male cultural icon is being called up but two. "My dear Dr. Johnson," Samuel Johnson, the most famous editor of Shakespeare, is as important a presence in Jane Austen's novels as was Shakespeare himself—and a very different one. But that's another story.

NOTES

1. *Jane Austen's Art of Memory*, CUP, 1989; Jocelyn Harris, "Jane Austen and the Burden of the (Male) Past: The Case Reexamined" in Devoney Looser, ed. *Jane Austen and Discourses of Feminism*, New Pork: St Martin's Press, 1995, pp. 87–100. Harris claims that "*Emma* draws all its main elements from *Midsummer Night's Dream*" (93). Claire Tomalin, on the other hand, finds that the parallels between *Mansfield Park* and *A Midsummer Night's Dream* are "obvious" (329).

2. Harold Bloom's fatuous polemic *The Anxiety of Influence* (1973) proposes a relation between poet and successor poet that is almost entirely one of conflict and antagonism: Oedipus and Laius fighting each other at the crossroads.

3. "The striking and powerful contrasts in which Shakespeare abounds could not escape observation; but the use he makes of the principle of analogy to reconcile the greatest diversities of character and to maintain a continuity of feeling throughout, have not been sufficiently attended to" (William Hazlitt, *Characters of Shakespear's Plays, Complete Works*, ed. P. P. Howe, 21 Vols. IV, 183, quoted by Jonathan Bate, *Shakespearean Constitutions*, 151).

4. These parallels have never (to my knowledge) been noticed, perhaps because *All's Well* is one of the least read, and least frequently produced, of Shakespeare's plays.

5. Emma actually says "'the world is not their's nor the world's law,'" which is how Shakespeare's line is cited in *The Rambler*. See Mary Lascelles's note in Chapman's edition, p. 493. This letter is not actually by Johnson, but Jane Austen wouldn't know that.

WORKS CITED

Armstrong, Isobel. *Mansfield Park*. Harmondsworth: Penguin Critical Studies, 1988.

Auerbach, Nina. "Jane Austen's Dangerous Charm," in *Mansfield Park and Persuasion*, ed. Judy Simons. London: Macmillan, 1697.

Austen, Jane. *The Novels of Jane Austen*. Ed. R. W. Chapman, 3rd ed. Oxford: OUP, 1969.

Bate, Jonathan. *Shakespearean Constitutions, Politics, Theatre, Criticism 1730–1832*. Oxford: Clarendon Press, 1989.

Bradley, A.C., *A Miscellany*. London: Macmillan, 1929.

Bradshaw, Graham. *Misrepresentations: Shakespeare and the Materialists*. Ithaca and London: Cornell UP, 1993.

Gard, Roger. *Jane Austen's Novels: The Art of Clarity*. New Haven and London: Yale Up, 1992.

Harris, Jocelyn. Jane Austen's Art of Memory. Cambridge: CUP, 1989.

Hunter, G.K. *English Drama 1586–1642: The Age of Shakespeare*. Oxford: Clarendon Press, 1997.

Jonson, Ben. *Timber, or Discoveries, being observations on men and manners* [1641]. London: Dent and Co., 1898.

Macaulay, Thomas Babington. "Madame d'Arblay," in *Critical and Historical Essays*, arranged by A. J. Grieve. London: Dent [1903] 1967. 563–612.

Philips, K.C. *Jane Austen's English*. London: Andre Deutsch, 1970.

Rossiter, A.P. *Angel with Horns, and other Shakespearean Lectures*. Ed. Graham Storey. London: Longmans, 1961.

Southam, Brian. *Jane Austen: The Critical Heritage*. London: Routledge, 1975.

Tomalin, Claire. *Jane Austen: A Life*. London: Viking, 1997.

LAURA DABUNDO

Jane Austen's Opacities

Like Wordsworth and the other great poets of her times, Jane Austen balances her art between silence and speech and knows the limits beyond which speech cannot proceed.[1] One of the principal insights of the Romantic movement in England is this very privileging of silence. The Grecian urn, the ruined cottage, Mont Blanc, and midnight frost are all exemplary of this poetic attempt to capture the ineffable, to point to something that cannot be spoken but yet for which the gesture is the poem, the message, and the meaning. Yet whereas Wordsworth, for instance, deploys many characters in his poetry who are rudely educated, roughly hewn, lower-class partisans for whom speech is indeed difficult and their purchase upon it too inadequate for the dimensions of their experience, Austen's characters are fully comfortable in their idiom. If they do not speak or if their words are less than equal to their emotion or their truth, it is their decision, or, even more significantly, that of their author. In both, the poetry and novel of the early nineteenth century, however, instances occur in which the words are defeated; the blankness, embraced.

I believe that Austen is like the contemporary poets, not perhaps in the form of art she deploys, but certainly in the attitudes and customs with which she animates it. Therefore, one might posit that one of the achievements of early nineteenth-century literature, foreshadowing the deconstructionists

---

From *Jane Austen and Mary Shelley and Their Sisters.* © 2000 by University Press of America.

perhaps, concerns the spaces and silences between the words, the gaps and pauses that punctuate speech but yet have meaning. (Obviously, much else concerns English Romanticism, but for purposes of this essay my focus on these writers is restricted to what they don't write).

This interest in a fiction writer raises, of course, the broader issue of her sympathetic convergence in general with the leading male poets of the day, whose aesthetic would increasingly come to represent the age. Four particular instances of overlap come to mind, including two that seem to engage specific canonical Romantic poems.

In *Sense and Sensibility* (published 1811, but first written more than a decade before), a tantalizing interlude anticipates and corrects Percy Shelley. Following the over-heated transports of emotional, passionate Marianne, the outwardly practical but inwardly long-suffering Elinor remonstrates: "'It is not every one who has your passion for dead leaves'" (76). Even if the Dashwood sisters are at least one and possibly two decades in advance of Shelley's magisterial tribute to the West Wind (Reiman and Powers 221 n.1), still few would deny, I imagine, that Marianne in time would swoon over Shelley's verse, which would probably prove to be a trifle too vaporous for her elder sister's taste, a reasonably acceptable contiguity that nevertheless reinforces the implication that this poetry and these people inhabited the same time and space. That is to say, the sentiment accords even if the dates do not.

Second, *Persuasion*, the last novel (published posthumously in 1818), also participates in the Romantic milieu by looking forward to another Romantic poetic staple associated with dying leaves. Anne Elliot finds delight in strolling out-of-doors on a lovely fall day, amid "the tawny leaves and withered hedges," meanwhile

> repeating to herself some few of the thousand poetical descriptions extant of autumn, that season of peculiar and inexhaustible influence on the mind of taste and tenderness, that season which has drawn from every poet, worthy of being read, some attempt at description, or some lines of feeling. (82)

This passage harmonizes Anne with the Romantic sensibility that finds Keats's "season of mists and mellow fruitfulness" both "peculiar and inexhaustible," even as it links Austen with Keats, offering in advance a bouquet for the poet's exquisite verse, inspired by his own walk through fields and hedgerows (written in 1818, published in 1819; Perkins 1204).

Third, a somewhat more satisfying connection with the Romantic period's Lake Poets is established for Austen by *Pride and Prejudice* (begun probably in the 1790s but published in 1813) when Elizabeth Bennet expresses her exhilaration, similar to Marianne Dashwood's raptures, at the prospect of her excursion to Lakeland: "'What delight! What felicity! You give me fresh life and vigour. Adieu to disappointment and spleen. What are men to rocks and mountains? Oh! what hours of transport we shall spend!'" (138). Her euphoria is dashed when the quotidian demands of her uncle's business shear the trip of its original Cumberland destination, grim reality cropping airy dreaming (although, since Elizabeth gets Pemberley rather than the Lakes, the exchange is in fact romance for Romanticism, true passion for an imagined one). Additionally, the failure to reach the Lake District is in keeping with a Romantic aesthetic both in terms of Romanticism's recognition of the inevitability and the potency of loss, as well as, thereby, securing the Lakes into the novel, not actually but only—and thus always superiorly—imaginatively. That the Lakes do provide the vehicle for this affinity with Romantic poetry is evident by the easy familiarity with which Byron bandies the term "Lakes" to castigate Southey, Wordsworth, and Coleridge in his dedication to *Don Juan* (1818), though critics have found the association as early as 1807 in a review of Wordsworth by Francis Jeffrey (Aubrey 314).

Finally, and yet more to the point of Austen's convergence with the English Romantic poets is the place in her oeuvre when this modern poetry is actually discussed. In yet another poetic correspondence in *Persuasion*, Anne Elliot discusses Byron and Scott with the stricken, grieving Captain Benwick who has turned to them for solace and reaffirmation. However, he is more fully delivered by the vital and immediate company of the literally fallen, and therefore subdued, Louisa Musgrove, a restoration simply reported but not demonstrated to the readers. Thus in miniature is shown that to which art aspires but that to which in the face of larger realities it must pale and subside. Now to the direct dealings of the novels on this subject of the silences and spaces within and around the artistic language.

Two of the most famous and, to twentieth-century critics, vexing examples of Jane Austen's acknowledgment of aesthetic boundaries to what language can convey are found in her later masterpieces *Mansfield Park* (1814) and in *Emma* (1815)[2], although Austen first raises the issue of silence in two earlier works.

Both *Sense and Sensibility* and *Northanger Abbey* (published 1818, probably written in the 1790s) contain unexpected authorial intrusions. Here Austen disrupts her narrative to interpose herself via her commentary, thereby shattering the fictional illusion and privileging the fictional artifice.

In *Northanger Abbey*, the interruption is her famed defense of novels; in *Sense and Sensibility*, the narrator suddenly interjects the first person to comment upon a comparatively minor event in the life of a decidedly minor character. The effect in both cases is to spotlight the inadequacy of the otherwise prevailing narrative strategies and fictional language, ironically in *Northanger Abbey* inasmuch as the point is to champion that very mode of discourse, and awkwardly in the other novel, since nothing is made of the interruption and it nowhere repeats or echoes. But perhaps nothing, or no humanly created thing, is the idea. Austen's biographer Park Honan attributes the authorial irruption in *Northanger Abbey* to a twofold purpose: first, she is responding to the domestic dismissal leveled by her Tory elder brothers toward the Whiggish propensities of prose fiction; second, she is developing and refining the narrative voice later to be unmistakable, certain, and serene (144–45). These are compelling arguments, which implicitly indicate that Austen is looking elsewhere, over the shoulders of her readers and not so much focused here on the novel at hand and what the interrupted, silenced narrative at hand portends.

More explicit on the subject are the two later written books, in which the confident narrator exercises her discipline and concentrates her focus. Here they appear to offer a more concerted, polished, and unified project. *Mansfield Park* moves toward closure with the disgrace of Maria Bertram at the hands of Henry Crawford and Mary Crawford's failure to condemn her brother. Thus the villainy and immorality of the Crawfords are finally and irremediably revealed. Edmund can no longer deny seeing what Mary, in particular, is and what she is not—that is, acceptable and appropriate as a wife of a Bertram and of a priest of the Church.

However, Edmund's disillusionment with Mary is only half the way toward marriage with Fanny Price; although he has always felt kindly disposed toward Fanny, his affection has seemed almost avuncular, certainly tutorial and fraternal. Therefore, even though the movement and pace of this carefully proportioned tripartite book are now toward resolution, an important component of the essential comedic nuptials of the conclusion is lacking. Edmund does not yet love Fanny correctly, that is, sexually. But in the last pages of the final chapter, in the concluding exposition, Austen writes:

> I purposely abstain from dates on this occasion, that every one may be at liberty to fix their own, aware that the cure of unconquerable passions, and the transfer of unchanging attachments, must vary much as to time in different people—I

only intreat every body to believe that exactly at the time when it was quite natural that it should be so, and not a week earlier, Edmund did cease to care about Miss Crawford, and became as anxious to marry Fanny, as Fanny herself could desire. (429)

Thus at what for many readers would be the acme of the love story, the culmination of the stress, the reward for travail, the point at which the hero and heroine mutually declare their passion and arrange to spend the remainder of their lives together in wedded bliss, Austen chooses to fall silent.

And likewise in *Emma*, the pertinent ellipsis occurs following Mr. Knightley's proposal, when Emma, having finally realized that it is he whom she loves, has just been told that he loves her and not Jane Fairfax or Harriet Smith or any other worthy damsel:

Her way was clear, though not quite smooth.—She spoke then, on being so entreated.—What did she say?—Just what she ought, of course. A lady always does. (391)

Why does Austen tease her readers so? Why does she not give them what they want? Obviously she might have elaborated. In *Persuasion*, in *Northanger Abbey*, in *Pride and Prejudice*, her characters come much closer to revealing their affection in front of and to the readers.

The answer, it seems, lies in just the same epitaphic direction that Wordsworth's verse takes. In both novels, the interest of the reader, as choreographed and designed by the author, is not toward the revelation of love, but toward the arrangement of characters so that they are in position toward one another and their circumstances that will enable them to accept and recognize that emotion and in their personal development so that they can properly house and maintain that affection. In other words, the crucial issue in *Mansfield Park* is the obstacle that worldly, cultivated Mary Crawford represents to decorous, clerically intended Edmund Bertram. When she is removed, when Edmund sees the error of his ways, then all conflict evaporates. Telling the reader what happens between him and Fanny Price would be belaboring the obvious, gilding the lily.

And the same is true in *Emma*. Once Emma grasps, first, that she loves Mr. Knightley and, second, that she need not remain single, in fact that she could happily, successfully, and prosperously marry, all that remains is for her to learn of his affection for her. Anything more would be superfluous. Roger Gard, in his recent commentary, offers a similar analysis when he observes,

"... the reason for this inspired brevity ... is that this is the climax and clearing of a long, intense, and elegant sequence of erotically charged moments, and that we need no more than this to be appropriately moved. More reference or description—let alone the direct presentation of, for example, a kiss—would negate the whole piercing effect" (20). More would certainly be less.

Therefore, what Austen writes about is what is fairly, accurately, and interestingly within the purview of language. What she omits is that for which, compared with which, her language, however masterly, succinct, and eloquent it might be, would be inadequate or trifling, if not hostile and maleficent. Austen is acknowledging, thereby, the truth to which Wordsworth and the other Romantic poets come, that there is a point where language fails, where experience overwhelms, where reality supervenes. Austen, that is to say, deals in the deployment of character and situation toward particular ends; when those ends are achieved, she withdraws.

The larger reality of what she has prepared her characters for or what she has presented them with is theirs, finally. She is aware of terrain into which language cannot travel, bounds of human emotion and experience that need not, indeed, cannot be idly recreated. By drawing the curtain as she has done, she is acknowledging a larger reality than what exists on the page in her words. She is acknowledging a reality, as in *Mansfield Park*, which is simultaneously "natural" and variably timely "in different people" while also open to imaginative interpretation, and also "always," as in *Emma*, true to what a generic "lady does" and yet recognizably individual both to the experience of the character and to that of socially adept readers. Thus, Austen draws the curtain on what is outside her reach in an imaginative, natural, true, and eternal world. That is not the range or scope of her fiction. As the testimony of her letters and her relatives makes clear[3], she, like Wordsworth and the other Romantic poets, becomes epitaphic and sibylline when her message approaches the close and becomes final, serious, and universal. She recognizes the opacities of language, that its abilities are limited, that its extent is not transcendent.

WORKS CITED

Aubrey, Bryan. "The Lake School." *Encyclopedia of Romanticism*. Ed. Laura Dabundo. New York: Garland, 1992, 314–15.

Austen, Jane. *Emma*. Ed. James Kinsley. rpt. New York: Oxford University Press, 1990.

———. *Mansfield Park*. Ed. James Kinsley. rpt. New York: Oxford University Press, 1990.

———. *Northanger Abbey*. Ed. John Davie. rpt. New York: Oxford University Press, 1990.

———. *Persuasion*. Ed. John Davie. rpt. New York: Oxford University Press, 1990.

———. *Pride and Prejudice*. Ed. James Kinsley. rpt. New York: Oxford University Press, 1990.

———. *Selected Letters, 1796–1817*. Ed. R.W. Chapman. New York: Oxford University Press, 1985.

———. *Sense and Sensibility*. Ed. James Kinsley. rpt. New York: Oxford University Press, 1990.

Bloom, Harold, ed. *Modern Critical Views: Jane Austen's Emma*. New Haven: Chelsea House, 1987.

———, ed. *Modern Critical Views: Jane Austen's Mansfield Park*. New Haven: Chelsea House, 1986.

Brown, Julia Prewitt. *Jane Austen's Novels: Social Change and Literary Form*. Cambridge: Harvard University Press, 1979.

Butler, Marilyn. *Jane Austen and the War of Ideas*. Oxford: Clarendon Press, 1975.

Duckworth, Alistair. *The Improvement of the Estate: A Study of Jane Austen's Novels*. Baltimore: Johns Hopkins University Press, 1971.

Gard, Roger. *Jane Austen's Novels: The Art of Clarity*. New Haven: Yale University Press, 1992.

Handley, Graham. *Jane Austen: Criticism in Focus*. New York: St. Martin's, 1992.

Honan, Park *Jane Austen: Her Life*. New York: Fawcett Columbine, 1987.

Lodge, David, ed. *Jane Austen. Emma: A Casebook*. London: Macmillan, 1968.

MacDonagh, Oliver. *Jane Austen: Real and Imagined Worlds*. New Haven: Yale University Press, 1991.

Morgan, Susan. *In the Meantime: Character and Perception in Jane Austen's Fiction*. Chicago: University of Chicago Press, 1980.

Perkins, David, ed. *English Romantic Writers*. New York: Harcourt, 1967.

Reiman, Donald H. and Sharon B. Powers, eds. *Shelley's Poetry and Prose*. New York: Norton, 1977.

Tanner, Tony. *Jane Austen*. London: Macmillan, 1986.

Toker, Leona. *Eloquent Reticence: Withholding Information in Fictional Narrative*. Lexington: University of Kentucky Press, 1993.

NOTES

1. A recent and most illuminating study of Jane Austen's narrative technique in *Emma* is contained in Leona Toker's *Eloquent Reticence*, which considers seven novels that, as her subtitle denotes, "withhold information," deliberately and effectively throughout their entirety. That to which Toker ascribes reticence is Austen's almost murder-mystery style of circumspect plotting; my approach, in contrast, is much smaller and more focused—I am concerned only with a particular point of the plot.

2. For relevant additional critical discourse, see Bloom, *Emma*; Bloom, *Mansfield Park*; Julia Brown; Butler, Duckworth, Gard, MacDonagh, Morgan, and Tanner.

3. This is evident both from her letters (see, for instance, Austen, *Selected Letters*, and her definitive biography.) (Honan)

Chronology

1775	Jane Austen is born on December 16 in the village of Steventon, Hampshire, to George Austen, parish clergyman, and Cassandra Leigh Austen. She is the seventh of eight children. She and her sister Cassandra are educated at Oxford and Southampton by the widow of a Principal of Brasenose College, and then attend the Abbey School at Reading. Jane's formal education ends when she is nine years old.
1787–93	Austen writes various pieces for the amusement of her family (collected in the three volumes of Juvenilia), the most famous of which is *Love and Friendship*. She and her family also perform various plays and farces, some of which are written by Jane, in the family barn.
1793–97	Austen writes her first novel, the epistolary *Lady Susan*, and begins the epistolary *Elinor and Marianne*, which will become *Sense and Sensibility*.
1796–97	Austen completes *First Impressions*, an early version of *Pride and Prejudice*. Her father tries to get it published without success. Austen begins *Sense and Sensibility* and *Northanger Abbey*.
1798	Austen finishes a version of *Northanger Abbey*.
1801–2	George Austen retires to Bath with his family. Jane probably suffers from an unhappy love affair (the man in question is believed to have died suddenly), and also

probably becomes engaged for a day to Harris Bigg-Wither.

1803   Austen sells a two-volume manuscript entitled *Susan* to a publisher for £10. It is advertised, but never printed. This is a version of *Northanger Abbey*, probably later revised.

1803–5   Austen writes ten chapters of *The Watsons*.

1805–6   George Austen dies. Jane abandons work on *The Watsons*. She, her mother, and her sister live in various lodgings in Bath.

1806–9   The three Austen women move to Southampton, living near one of Jane's brothers.

1809   Jane, her sister, and her mother move to Chawton Cottage, in Hampshire, which is part of the estate of Jane's brother Edward Austen (later Knight), who has been adopted by Thomas Knight, a relative. Edward has just lost his wife, who died giving birth to her tenth child, and the household has been taken over by Jane's favorite niece, Fanny.

1811   Austen decides to publish *Sense and Sensibility* at her own expense, and anonymously. It appears in November in a three-volume edition.

1811–12   Austen is probably revising *First Impressions* extensively and beginning *Mansfield Park*.

1813   *Pride and Prejudice: A Novel. In Three Volumes. By the Author of "Sense and Sensibility"* is published in January. A second edition of it, as well as a second edition of *Sense and Sensibility*, come out in November.

1814   *Mansfield Park* is published anonymously and in three volumes. It sells out by November. Austen begins *Emma*.

1815   Austen completes *Emma* and begins *Persuasion*. *Emma* is published in December, anonymously, in three volumes, by a new publisher.

1816   A second edition of *Mansfield Park* is published.

1817   A third edition of *Pride and Prejudice* is published. Austen begins *Sanditon*. She moves to Winchester, where she dies, after a year-long illness, on July 18. She is buried in Winchester Cathedral. After her death, her family destroys much of her correspondance in order to protect her reputation.

1818   *Persuasion* and *Northanger Abbey* are published posthumously together, their authorship still officially anonymous.

Contributors

HAROLD BLOOM is Sterling Professor of the Humanities at Yale University and Henry W. and Albert A. Berg Professor of English at the New York University Graduate School. He is the author of over 20 books, including *Shelley's Mythmaking* (1959), *The Visionary Company* (1961), *Blake's Apocalypse* (1963), *Yeats* (1970), *A Map of Misreading* (1975), *Kabbalah and Criticism* (1975), *Agon: Toward a Theory of Revisionism* (1982), *The American Religion* (1992), *The Western Canon* (1994), and *Omens of Millennium: The Gnosis of Angels, Dreams, and Resurrection* (1996). *The Anxiety of Influence* (1973) sets forth Professor Bloom's provocative theory of the literary relationships between the great writers and their predecessors. His most recent books include *Shakespeare: The Invention of the Human* (1998), a 1998 National Book Award finalist, *How to Read and Why* (2000), *Genius: A Mosaic of One Hundred Exemplary Creative Minds* (2002), and *Hamlet: Poem Unlimited* (2003). In 1999, Professor Bloom received the prestigious American Academy of Arts and Letters Gold Medal for Criticism, and in 2002 he received the Catalonia International Prize.

RUTH APROBERTS, Professor Emeritus of English at the University of California, Riverside, is the author of *The Biblical Web* as well as books on Anthony Trollope and Matthew Arnold.

MARTIN PRICE is Sterling Professor Emeritus of English at Yale University. He is the author of *Forms of Life: Character and Moral Imagination in the Novel* and the editor of *Restoration and the Eighteenth Century, Volume 3* and a book by Jonathan Swift.

SANDRA M. GILBERT teaches at the University of California at Davis. She is the author, editor, co-author, or co-editor of numerous books. Those she has written with SUSAN GUBAR, a Distinguished Professor of English and Women's Studies at Indiana University, include *No Man's Land—The Place of the Woman Writer in the Twentieth Century*. The two women also are the editors of *The Norton Anthology of Literature by Women*. Susan Gubar has also written on race and feminism.

IAN WATT, now deceased, was Professor Emeritus of English at Stanford University. He wrote *The Rise of the Novel*, *Conrad in the Nineteenth Century*, and other titles. Also, he was the editor of *Jane Austen: A Collection of Critical Essays* and a book of Joseph Conrad's.

ANN MOLAN has taught at Australian National University.

TONY TANNER, now deceased, taught at King's College, Cambridge. He published or edited several books, among them *The American Mystery: Essays on American Literature from Emerson to DeLillo* and books on Henry James and Thomas Pynchon.

JOHN BAYLEY was the Thomas Warton Chair of English Literature at Oxford from 1974 to 1992. The author of a book on Tolstoy, he also has edited works of Tolstoy, Hardy, and Henry James.

ROGER GARD has written books on Jane Austen and Henry James and also has edited a book by Henry James.

STUART M. TAVE, now retired, was William Rainey Harper Professor in the College, and Professor in the Department of English, at the University of Chicago. He has published *Some Words of Jane Austen* as well as other titles.

JO ALYSON PARKER teaches English at St. Joseph's University and has published *The Author's Inheritance*.

JOHN WILTSHIRE has been Reader and Associate Professor at La Trobe University, Melbourne. He has published two books on Jane Austen, as well as one on Samuel Johnson.

LAURA DABUNDO is Professor and Chair of the English Department at Kennesaw State University. She is the editor of the *Encyclopedia of Romanticism: Culture in Britain, 1780s to 1830s*.

Bibliography

Auerbach, Emily. "'A Barkeeper Entering the Kingdom of Heaven': Did Mark Twain Really Hate Jane Austen?" *Virginia Quarterly Review* 75, no. 1 (Winter 1999): pp. 109–20.

Bander, Elaine. "The Other Play in *Mansfield Park*: Shakespeare's *Henry VIII*," *Persuasions* 17 (December 1995): pp. 111–20.

———. "*Sanditon, Northanger Abbey*, and *Camilla*: Back to the Future?" *Persuasions* 19 (December 1997): pp. 195–204.

Beer, Patricia. "Elizabeth Bennet's Fine Eyes." In Enright, D. J., ed. *Fair of Speech: The Uses of Euphemism*. D. J. Oxford: Oxford University Press, 1985, pp. 108–121.

Benedict, Barbara M. "Jane Austen's *Sense and Sensibility*: The Politics of Point of View," *Philological Quarterly* 69, no., 4 (Fall 1990): pp. 453–70.

Benson, Robert. "Jane Goes to *Sanditon*: An Eighteenth Century Lady in a Nineteenth Century Landscape," *Persuasions* 19 (December 1997): pp. 211–18.

Bloom, Harold, ed. *Modern Critical Interpretations: Pride and Prejudice*. New York: Chelsea House Publishers, 1987.

———. Modern Critical Interpretations: *Emma*. New York: Chelsea House Publishers, 1987.

Breunig, Hans Werner. "Jane Austen: Romantic? British Empiricist?" In Bode, Christoph and Neuman, Fritz-Wilhelm, eds. *Re-Mapping Romanticism: Gender-Text-Context*. Studien zur Englischen Romantik. 14. Essen, Germany: Blaue, Eule, 2001, pp. 163–81.

Bristow, Catherine. "Unlocking the Rape: An Analysis of Austen's Use of Pope's Symbolism in *Sense and Sensibility*," *Persuasions* 20 (1998): pp. 31–37.

Brown, Lloyd W. *Bits of Ivory: Narrative Techniques in Jane Austen's Fiction*. Baton Rouge: Louisiana State Press, 1973.

Burdan, Judith. "*Mansfield Park* and the Question of Irony," *Persuasions* 23 (2001): pp. 118–29.

Castellanos, Gabriela. "Laughter, War and Feminism: Elements of Carnival in Three of Jane Austen's Novels." In *Writing About Women: Feminist Literary Studies*. New York: Peter Lang, 1994.

Clay, George R. "In Defense of Flat Characters: A Discussion of Their Value to Charles Dickens, Jane Austen and Leo Tolstoy," *Italia Francescana* 27, nos. 1–2 (2000): pp. 20–36.

Clifford-Amos, Terence. "Some Observations on the Language of *Pride and Prejudice*," *Language and Literature* 20 (1995): pp. 1–10.

Copeland, Edward. "Virgin Sacrifice: Elizabeth Bennet after Jane Austen." *Persuasions* 22 (2000): pp. 156–94.

Copeland, Edward and McMaster, Juliet. *The Cambridge Companion to Jane Austen*. Cambridge, England: Cambridge University Press, 1997.

Correa, Delia Da Sousa, ed. *The Nineteenth-Century Novel: Realisms*. London: Routledge for Open University, 2000.

Cowley, Malcolm and Hugo, Howard E. *The Lesson of the Masters: An Anthology of the Novel from Cervantes to Hemingway*. New York: C. Scribner's Sons, 1971, pp. 80–97.

Craig, G. Armour. "Jane Austen's *Emma*: The Truths and Disguises of Human Disclosure." In Brower, R. A. and Poirier, R., eds. *Defense of Reading: A Reader's Approach to Literary Criticism*. New York: E. P. Dutton & Co., 1962, pp. 235–55.

Curry, Mary Jane. "'Not a Day Went by Without a Solitary Walk': Elizabeth's Pastoral World," *Persuasions* 22 (2000): pp. 175–86.

Dabundo, Laura. "The Devil and Jane Austen: Elizabeth Bennet's Temptations in the Wilderness," *Persuasions* 21 (1999): 53–58.

DeForest, Mary. "Jane Austen: Closet Classicist," *Persuasions* 22 (2000): pp. 98–104.

Duckworth, William C. Jr. "Misreading Jane Austen: Henry James, Women Writers, and the Friendly Narrator," *Persuasions* 21 (1999): pp. 96–105.

Emsley, Sarah. "Practising the Virtues of Amiability and Civility in *Pride and Prejudice*." *Persuasions* 22 (2000): pp. 187–98.

Ferguson, Frances. "Jane Austen, *Emma*, and the Impact of Form," *Modern Language Quarterly* 61, no. 1 (March 2000): pp. 157–80.

Fischer, Doucet Devin. "Byron and Austen: Romance and Reality," *The Byron Journal* 21 (1993): pp. 71–79.

Fletcher, Loraine. "Emma: The Shadow Novelist," *Critical Survey* 4, no. 1 (1992): pp. 36–44.

Fraiman, Susan. *Unbecoming Women: British Women Writers and the Novel of Development*. New York: Columbia University Press, 1993.

———. "Jane Austen and Edward Said: Gender, Culture, and Imperialism," *Critical Inquiry* 21, no. 4 (Summer 1995): pp. 805–21.

Frye, Northrop. *The Secular Scripture: A Study of the Structure of Romance*. London: Harvard University Press, 1976.

Galperin, William. "Byron, Austen and the 'Revolution' of Irony," *Criticism: A Quarterly for Literature and the Arts* 32, no. 1 (Winter 1990): pp. 51–80.

———. "The Picturesque, the Real, and the Consumption of Jane Austen," *Wordsworth Circle* 28, no. 1 (Winter 1997): pp. 19–27.

———. "The Theatre at *Mansfield Park*: From Classic to Romantic Once More," *Eighteenth-Century Life* 16, no. 3 (November 1992): pp. 247–71.

Galperin, William, ed. *Re-Reading Box Hill: Reading the Practice of Reading Everyday Life*. College Park, MD: University of Maryland, 2000.

Giles, Paul. "The Gothic Dialogue in *Pride and Prejudice*." *Text and Context* 2, no. 1 (Spring 1988): pp. 68–75.

Gilman, Priscilla. "'Disarming Reproof': *Pride and Prejudice* and the Power of Criticism." *Persuasions* 22 (2000): pp. 218–29.

Goldstein, Philip. "Criticism and Institutions: The Conflicted Reception of Jane Austen's Fiction," *Studies in the Humanities* 18, no. 1 (June 1991): pp. 35–55.

Halperin, John. "Inside *Pride and Prejudice*," *Persuasions* 11 (December 16 1989): pp. 37–45.

Harmsel, Henrietta Ten. "The Villain-Hero in *Pamela* and *Pride and Prejudice*," *College English* XXIII (November 1961): pp. 104–108.

Havely, Cicely Palser. "*Emma*: Portrait of the Artist as a Young Woman,"

English: The Journal of the The English Association 42, no. 174 (Fall 1993):
pp. 221–37.

Hermansson, Casie. "Neither *Northanger Abbey*: The Reader Presupposes,"
Papers on Language and Literature 36, no. 4 (Fall 2000): pp. 337–56.

Heydt-Stevenson, Jill. "Liberty, Connection, and Tyranny: The Novels of
Jane Austen and the Aesthetic Movement of the Picturesque." In Pfau,
Thomas and Gleckner, Robert F., eds. *Lessons of Romanticism: A Critical
Companion*. Durham, NC: Duke University Press, 1998.

Hill, Reginald. "Jane Austen: A Voyage of Discovery," *Persuasions* 19
(December 1997): pp. 77–92.

Johnson, Gregory R. "The Great-Souled Woman: Jane Austen as Public
Moralist." In Edmondson, Henry T. III, ed. *The Moral of the Story:
Literature and Public Ethics*. Lanham, MD: Lexington, 2000, pp.
123–33.

Kaplan, Zoe C. "Emma and Her Influence on Future Self-Deceiving
Literary Heroines," *Persuasions* 22 (2000): pp. 87–97.

Katz, Richard A. "The Comic Perception of Jane Austen." In Cutler, Maxine
G., ed. *Voltaire, the Enlightenment and the Comic Mode: Essays in Honor of
Jean Sareil*. New York: Peter Lang, 1990, pp. 65–87.

Kearney, J.A. "Jane Austen and the Reason-Feeling Debate," *Theoria* 75
(May 1990): pp. 107–22.

Kliger, Samuel. "Jane Austen's *Pride and Prejudice* in the Eighteenth-Century
Mode," *University of Toronto Quarterly* 16 (July 1947): pp. 357–70.

Lambdin, Laura Cooner and Lambdin, Robert Thomas, eds. *A Companion to
Jane Austen Studies*. Westport, CT: Greenwood, 2000.

Lau, Beth. "Jane Austen, *Pride and Prejudice*." In Wu, Duncan, ed. *A
Companion to Romanticism*. Oxford, England: Blackwell, 1998, pp.
219–26.

Lawrence, Joseph P. "Poetry and Ethics: Their Unification in the Sublime,"
Southern Humanities Review 24, no. 1 (Winter 1990): pp. 1–14.

Lee, Judith. "'Without Hate, without Bitterness, without Fear, without
Protest, without Preaching': Virginia Woolf Reads Jane Austen,"
Persuasions 12 (December 16, 1990): pp. 111–116.

Lee, Miae. "What Makes Us Read Jane Austen? The Narrative
Development in Austen's Works," *Journal of English Language and
Literature* 46, no. 4 (Winter 2000): pp. 1197–1220.

Looser, Devoney, ed. *Jane Austen and Discourses of Feminism*. New York: St. Martin's, 1995.

Loveridge, Mark. "*Northanger Abbey*: Or, Nature and Probability," *Nineteenth-Century Literature* 56, no. 1 (June 1991): pp. 1–29.

Lucas, John. "Jane Austen and Romanticism," *Critical Survey* 4, no. 1 (1992).

Lynch, Deidre, ed. *Janeites: Austen's Disciples and Devotees*. Princeton: Princeton University Press, 2000.

Marsh, Nicholas. *Jane Austen: The Novels*. New York, NY: St. Martin's, 1998.

McMaster, Juliet. "Talking about Talk in *Pride and Prejudice*." In McMaster, Juliet, and Bruce Stovel, eds. *Jane Austen's Business: Her World and Her Profession*. Hampshire, England; NY: Macmillan, St. Martin's Press, 1996, pp. 81–94.

McMaster, Juliet and Stovel, Bruce, eds. *Jane Austen's Business: Her World and Her Profession*. New York: Macmillan, St. Martin's, 1996.

Mellor, Anne K. "Why Women Didn't Like Romanticism: The Views of Jane Austen and Mary Shelley." In Ruoff, Gene, ed. *The Romantics and Us: Essays on Literature and Culture*. New Brunswick: Rutgers University Press, 1990, pp. 274–87.

Millgate, Jane. "*Persuasion* and the Presence of Scott," *Persuasion* 15 (December 1993): pp. 184–95.

Morris, Pam. "Reading *Pride and Prejudice*." In Walder, Dennis, ed. *The Realist Novel*. London: Routledge in association with Open University, 1995, pp. 31–60.

Newman, Karen. "Can This Marriage Be Saved: Jane Austen Makes Sense of An Ending," *ELH* 50, no. 4 (1984): pp. 693–710.

Newton, Judith Lowder. *Women, Power and Subversion*. Athens: University of Georgia Press, 1985.

Nineteenth-Century Fiction. Jane Austen, 1775–1975. Vol. 30, no. 3 (December 1975).

Olsen, Stein Haugom. "Appreciating *Pride and Prejudice*." In Hawthorn, Jeremy, ed. *The Nineteenth-Century British Novel: Stratford-Upon-Avon Studies*. Baltimore; Arnold, 1986.

Ortells, Elena. "Bridging the Gap between Linguistics and Literary Criticism: The Role of the Narrator in the Presentation of Characters in Jane Austern's *Pride and Prejudice* and Henry James's *The American*," *SELL: Studies in English Language and Linguistics* 2 (2000): pp. 161–70.

Poovey, Mary. *The Proper Lady and the Woman Writer; Ideology as Style in the Works of Mary Wollstonecraft, Mary Shelley, and Jane Austen*. Chicago: University of Chicago Press, 1984.

Robertson, Leslie. "Changing Models of *Juvenilia*: Apprenticeship or Play?" *English Studies in Canada* 24, no. 3 (September 1998): pp. 291–98.

Rogers, Deborah D. *Two Gothic Classics by Women:* The Italian *by Ann Radcliffe and* Northanger Abbey *by Jane Austen*. New York: Signet, 1995.

Roth, Barry. "Jane Austen Bibliography for 2000," *Persuasions* 23 (2001): pp. 222–28.

Roulston, Christine. "Discourse, Gender, and Gossip: Some Reflections on Bakhtin and *Emma*." In Mezei, Kathy, ed. *Ambiguous Discourse: Feminist Narratology and British Women Writers*. Chapel Hill: University of North Carolina, 1996, pp. 40–65.

Rowen, Norma. "Reinscribing Cinderella: Jane Austen and the Fairy Tale." In Sanders, Joe, ed. *Functions of the Fantastic: Selected Essays from the Thirteenth International Conference on the Fantastic in the Arts*. Westport, CT: Greenwood, 1995, pp. 29–36.

Ruoff, Gene W. Jane Austen's *Sense and Sensibility*. New York: St. Martin's Press, 1992.

Sabor, Peter. "'Finished up to Nature': Walter Scott's Review of *Emma*," *Persusasion* 13 (December 16, 1991): pp. 88–99.

Shaffer, Julie A. "The Ideological Intervention of Ambiguites in the Marriage Plot: Who Fails Marianne in Austen's *Sense and Sensibility*?" In Hohne, Karen and Wussow, Helen, eds. *A Dialogue of Voices: Feminist Literary Theory and Bakhtin*. Minneapolis; University of Minnesota Press, 1994, pp. 128–51.

Shaw, Harry E. *Narrating Reality: Austen, Scott, Eliot*. Ithaca, NY: Cornell University Press, 1999.

Simons, Judy. Mansfield Park *and* Persuasion. New York: St. Martin's, 1997.

Spacks, Patricia Meyer. "Ideology and Form: Novels at Work." In Richter, David H., ed. *Ideology and Form in Eighteenth-Century Literature*. Lubbock, Texas: Texas Tech University Press, 1999, pp. 15–30.

Stovel, Bruce. "Jane Austen and the Pleasure Principle," *Persuasions* 23 (2001): pp. 63–77.

"Symposium: Jane Austen," *Philosophy and Literature* 23, no. 1 (April 1999): pp. 96–137.

Tave, Stuart Malcolm. *Some Words of Jane Austen*. Chicago and London: University of Chicago Press, 1973.

Tuite, Clara. *Romantic Austen: Sexual Politics and the Literary Canon*. Cambridge Studies in Romanticism 49. Cambridge, England: Cambridge University Press, 2002.

Waldron, Mary. *Jane Austen and the Fiction of Her Time*. Cambridge, England: Cambridge University Press, 1999.

Wallace, Tara Ghoshal. *Jane Austen and Narrative Authority*. New York; Hampshire, England: St. Martin's, Macmillan, 1995.

Wilkie, Brian. "Structural Layering in Jane Austen's Problem Novels," *Nineteenth-Century Literature* 46, no. 4 (March 1992): pp. 517–44.

Wiltshire, John. "Mrs. Bennet's Least Favorite Daughter." *Persuasions* 23 (2001): pp. 179–87.

Wisenforth, Joseph. "The Case of *Pride and Prejudice*." *Studies in the Novel* 16 (Fall 1984): pp. 261–73.

———. "The Revolution of Civility in *Pride and Prejudice*." *Persuasions* (December 1994): pp. 107–114.

Acknowledgments

A Section of the Introduction appeared in *The Western Canon* by Harold Bloom (New York: Harcourt Brace & Company, 1994): 252–263. © 1994 by Harold Bloom. Used by permission of the author.

"*Sense and Sensibility*, or Growing Up Dichotomous" by Ruth apRoberts. From *Nineteenth-Century Fiction* 30, no. 3 (December 1975): 351–365. © 1975 by the Regents of the University of California. Reprinted by permission.

"Manners, Morals, and Jane Austen" by Martin Price. From *Nineteenth-Century Fiction* 30, no. 3 (December 1975): 261–280. © 1975 by the Regents of the University of California. Reprinted by permission.

"Shut Up in Prose: Gender and Genre in Austen's Juvenilia" by Sandra M. Gilbert and Susan Gubar. From *The Madwoman in the Attic*: 107–145. © 1979 by Yale University Press. Reprinted by permission of Yale University Press.

"Jane Austen and the Traditions of Comic Aggression" by Ian Watt. From *Persuasions* no. 3 (December 16, 1981): 14–15, 24–28. © 1981 by Ian Watt. Reprinted by permission.

"Persuasion in *Persuasion*" by Ann Molan. From *The Critical Review* no. 24 (1982): 16–29. © 1982 by Ann Molan. Reprinted by permission.

"Knowledge and Opinion: *Pride and Prejudice*" by Tony Tanner. From *Jane Austen*: 103–141. ©1986 by Tony Tanner, reproduced with permission of Palgrave Macmillan.

"Characterization in Jane Austen" by John Bayley. From *The Jane Austen Companion*, edited by J. David Grey, A. Walton Litz and Brian Southam: 24–34. ©1986 by Macmillan Publishing Company. Reprinted by permission.

"Emma's Choices" by Roger Gard. From *Jane Austen's Novels: The Art of Clarity*: 155–181. © 1992 by Yale University. Reprinted by permission of Yale University Press.

"What Are Men to Rocks and Mountains? *Pride and Prejudice*" by Stuart M. Tave. From *Lovers, Clowns, and Fairies: An Essay on Comedies*: 58–89. © 1993 by The University of Chicago. Reprinted by permission.

"*Mansfield Park*: Dismantling Pemberley" by Jo Alyson Parker. From *The Author's Inheritance: Henry Fielding, Jane Austen, and the Establishment of the Novel*: 155–180. © 1998 by Northern Illinois University Press. Used by permission of the publisher.

"'The Hartfield Edition': Jane Austen and Shakespeare" by John Wiltshire. From *Persuasions* no. 21 (1999): 212–223. © 1999 by John Wiltshire. Reprinted by permission.

"Jane Austen's Opacities" by Laura Dabundo. From *Jane Austen and Mary Shelley and Their Sisters*: 53–60. © 2000 by University Press of America. Reprinted by permission.

Index